New Perspectives on U.S.-Japan Relations

The Japan Center for International Exchange wishes to thank

The Nippon Foundation

New Perspectives on
U.S.-JAPAN
Relations

edited by
Gerald L. Curtis

Tokyo • Japan Center for International Exchange • *New York*

The surnames of the authors and other persons mentioned in this book are
positioned according to country practice.

Copyediting by Pamela J. Noda.
Cover design by Anne Bergasse, abinitio Y.K.
Design and production by abinitio Y.K.
Cover photograph © Corbis Digital Stock © Photo Disc.

Printed in Japan
ISBN 4-88907-040-0

Distributed worldwide outside Japan by Brookings Institution Press,
1775 Massachusetts Avenue, N.W., Washington, D.C. 20036-2188

Japan Center for International Exchange
9-17 Minami Azabu 4-chome, Minato-ku, Tokyo 106-0047 Japan

URL: http://www.jcie.or.jp

Japan Center for International Exchange, Inc. (JCIE/USA)
1251 Avenue of the Americas, New York, N.Y. 10020 U.S.A.

Contents

Foreword

U.S.-JAPAN RELATIONS have been a central focus of the activities of the Japan Center for International Exchange (JCIE) since its establishment in 1970. As Mike Mansfield, American ambassador to Japan, repeatedly proclaimed, the United States and Japan have "the most important bilateral relationship in the world, bar none!" This volume attempts to critically review this important bilateral relationship from both sides of the partnership and, where possible, provide guidelines for improving relations.

How relevant today is an alliance that was forged between a powerful United States and a weak Japan in the context of a cold war struggle with the Soviet Union? In what ways have the changes in the relative power positions of the two countries and the structural changes in the world economy created new challenges to the U.S.-Japan relationship, and how are the two countries responding to those changes?

These are some of the important questions addressed by the four Japanese and four American authors of the chapters in this volume. The authors discuss a range of issues related to the U.S.-Japan alliance, namely, military relations, trade and financial management, shifting security perspectives, and the role of the mass media in the bilateral relationship. It was our good fortune to have Gerald Curtis—indisputably one of the most outstanding observers of the U.S.-Japan relationship—of Columbia University's East Asian Institute to lead and guide this bilateral team of the best-trained younger political scientists. The group met twice in the form of a workshop, once in April 1998 in Kisarazu, Japan, to discuss the division of labor among participants and again in July 1999 to discuss the drafts of each chapter.

This bilateral research project was undertaken by JCIE as a part of its Global

ThinkNet program, which is funded by various foundations and other philan-thropic institutions, most notably the Nippon Foundation. I would like to take this opportunity to express our deepest gratitude to these financial contributors. My thanks should also be directed to Gerald Curtis, who not only guided the team in their deliberations but also provided detailed comments on each draft chapter. Lastly, I would like to thank all the participants of the project; their truly bilingual interactions were an inspiration to all of us who were fortunate enough to observe the process.

Yamamoto Tadashi
President
Japan Center for International Exchange

New Perspectives on U.S.-Japan Relations

1

U.S. Policy toward Japan from Nixon to Clinton:
An Assessment

Gerald L. Curtis

THE CHAPTERS IN THIS VOLUME ANALYZE some of the most important issues in contemporary U.S.-Japan relations. Fully half the chapters, those by Robert Bullock, Jennifer Dwyer, Katō Junko, and Kojō Yoshiko, focus on economic matters, which is indicative of the central position occupied by issues related to government deregulation and fiscal and monetary policy in the research agendas of political scientists today, and in the policy agendas of those responsible for managing foreign policy. The chapters by Tadokoro Masayuki and Robert Uriu focus less on specific policies and more on the dominant ideas and assumptions of policymakers, and on the ways those ideas and assumptions are transmitted by the mass media and influence policymakers' choice of strategies. The chapters by Michael Green and Tanaka Akihiko discuss the security dimension of the U.S.-Japan relationship and the way security relations have been adapted to, and continue to be challenged by, momentous changes in the regional and global international system.

The purpose of this chapter is to provide an overview of U.S. policy toward Japan and a kind of backdrop for the following chapters. I do so by focusing my attention on two issues that have been matters of perennial concern in postwar U.S.-Japan relations, that have been sources of tension in the relationship across many administrations, that in many ways illustrate important general features of U.S. policy toward Japan, and that raise important questions about the future. The two issues are U.S.-Japan trade relations and the impact of China policy on the U.S.-Japan bilateral relationship.

In considering the implications of this history for the future of U.S.-Japan relations, I am cognizant of the dangers involved in making forecasts that are based upon projecting our knowledge of the past into the future. Few people in the years following the end of World War II, when the United States and Japan took the first steps to forge a new political, economic, and security relationship, imagined just how successful that effort would prove to be. Nor did American leaders in those days anticipate how quickly a prostrate Japan would rise from the ashes of defeat to resume at an accelerated pace its goal to catch up with the West economically. It is at least as difficult today to predict the impact on the United States and Japan, and on their bilateral relationship, of new forces unleashed by economic globalization and the information technology revolution or by the end of the cold war and China's emergence as a major power.

Nonetheless, looking back over the way the U.S. government has dealt with Japan over trade and China is useful for contemplating the future. An analysis of these issues draws our attention first of all to important continuities in postwar U.S. policy toward Japan. The assumptions with which American political leaders, Republican and Democrat, approach Japan have remained remarkably constant throughout the period under review. This fundamental continuity in policy toward Japan has threaded its way through changes in governments, in economic and social conditions, in public opinion, and in the international political system.

An analysis of U.S.-Japan trade relations and of the impact of China policy on relations between Washington and Tokyo also sets in sharp relief the profound changes that have occurred in the variables that constitute the context for U.S.-Japan relations. The end of the cold war and the emergence of a far more fluid and potentially unstable international situation in East Asia, the uncertainties about China's economic prospects and future foreign policy, and the United States' economic renaissance and Japan's economic troubles amidst a rapidly changing global economic and financial system raise important questions about whether long established continuities in U.S. policy toward Japan can be, or should be, sustained into the twenty-first century.

This chapter concludes on a note of cautious optimism about U.S. relations with Japan. The optimism is anchored in the reality, recognized by every postwar U.S. president, that a positive relationship with Japan serves American political, economic, and security interests. The caution is rooted in the equally important reality that many of the past assumptions that guided U.S. policy toward Japan are no longer operative. Continuity in U.S.-Japan relations should not be simply taken for granted. A changed context for U.S. relations with Japan means that U.S. policymakers have to pay greater attention to the way U.S. policies in East Asia will impact on Japanese foreign policy and how policy toward Japan can contribute to realizing U.S. goals in the region. The challenge is not to fundamentally change the U.S. relationship with Japan but to design a strategy to sustain that relationship in the changed world of the twenty-first century.

THE NEW BEGINNING

The story that I tell in these pages begins in the late 1960s when Richard Nixon became president. In many important ways, Nixon's election in 1968 marked the "end of the postwar" in U.S.-Japan relations and the beginning of a new era in the relationship, many features of which have characterized U.S. policy toward Japan ever since. The "textile wrangle" with Japan during the Nixon years was the first of countless bitter and highly politicized bilateral trade disputes. Nixon's "China shock" initiated a style of dealing with Japan over China that has continued to characterize subsequent administrations, including that of Bill Clinton. Suspension of the convertibility of the U.S. dollar into gold ended the postwar Bretton Woods system of fixed exchange rates. The return of Okinawa to Japanese control in 1972 set the basis for the development of an expanded security relationship.

President Nixon and his national security advisor, Henry Kissinger, established patterns of policy making toward Japan that marked a sharp departure from earlier practices and that would prove to have a profound influence on later administrations. Indeed, much of what we now think of as typical features of U.S. policy making concerning Japan had their genesis in the Nixon presidency.

One of these features has been the absence of consultation with Japan over policy toward China. This pattern of policy making got off to a dramatic start with Kissinger's secret visit to Beijing in 1971. President Jimmy Carter and his national security advisor, Zbigniew Brzezinski, followed the path laid down by Nixon and Kissinger, bypassing Japan on the way to China. This pattern of "going over the head" of Japan to pursue relations with China moderated somewhat under President Ronald Reagan and George Bush, as discussed below, but was very much in evidence once again in the Clinton administration.

The Nixon presidency also marked the beginning of a new and contentious period with respect to U.S.-Japan trade and economic relations. Ever since the Nixon-period textile dispute, U.S.-Japan trade relations have been marked by a pattern of recurring confrontations, intense Congressional pressure on the administration to get tough with Japan, and grudging minimal concessions by Japan in response to these pressures.

Every administration since Nixon's has been characterized by a kind of thrashing about for an effective approach to dealing with Japan over trade. This has led U.S. policy through import surcharges, antidumping sanctions, voluntary export restraints, "market oriented sector specific" negotiations (the MOSS talks), a Structural Impediments Initiative (the SII negotiations), and various efforts to secure guaranteed market share for American and other foreign businesses in Japan. The last effort culminated in the Clinton administration's spectacularly unsuccessful effort to establish a "results oriented" trade policy toward Japan.

If improvisation in terms of tactics in the face of Congressional pressure to do something about the trade problem has been a continuing feature of U.S. policy toward Japan since Nixon, so too has been the steadfast determination by every U.S. president to maintain a high fire wall to separate trade conflict from the two countries' security relations. No matter how heated trade and economic frictions have become, no president has sought to use the threat of withdrawal of the U.S. security commitment to Japan as a lever to extract trade concessions. Even the Clinton administration, which went further than any earlier administration in emphasizing the importance of economic factors in foreign policy, in the end kept the fire wall between the trade and security dimensions of the U.S.-Japan relationship high.

For Nixon and for his successors in the 1970s, Gerald Ford and Carter, this separation of economic and security issues in U.S.-Japan relations may have been partly a matter of luck. In those days, unlike our own now, trade and international economic relations were viewed as entirely distinct from national security concerns. Nixon, Ford, and Carter, and most especially their chief foreign affairs advisors, Kissinger and Brzezinski, were not particularly interested in or knowledgeable about trade and international economic matters. Their foreign-policy strategies were rooted in conceptions of geopolitics that gave scant room to trade and economic considerations. One reason there was no linkage of trade and defense relations was that the key foreign-policy makers did not tend to think in terms that crossed the security-economy divide.

Luck, however, could not have been more than a minor factor in accounting for this determination not to let trade disputes adversely affect the security relationship. Nixon must have been sorely tempted to hold back on Okinawan reversion in order to extract concessions from Japan on textiles, and he was furious when his expectations that Prime Minister Satō Eisaku would deliver important concessions were betrayed. Neither Nixon nor any subsequent president, however, was about to make the U.S.-Japan security relationship hostage to the satisfactory resolution of trade and economic differences. Every president since the end of World War II has recognized that maintaining a strong security alliance with Japan is in the vital national interest of the United States.

One might assume that the end of the cold war would cause U.S. leaders to reconsider that assessment of the importance of the Japan alliance. The evidence so far is that to the extent that a careful reassessment has been made, it has led to the conclusion that alliance with Japan remains just as important in the post–cold war world as it was when the cold war was raging. In April 1996, President Clinton and Prime Minister Hashimoto Ryūtarō issued a Joint Declaration on Security that emphasized the importance of the U.S.-Japan Security Treaty for maintaining peace and stability in the post–cold war Asia Pacific region, and they agreed to revise the Guidelines for U.S.-Japan Defense Cooperation that had been adopted in the late 1970s in order to strengthen military cooperation in the event of contingencies in the region. These developments suggest that both the United States and Japan are seeking ways to strengthen rather than loosen their security relationship.

Nixon's and Kissinger's style of foreign-policy making had an important effect in accelerating and reinforcing pressures that were already at work to shift control over political relations with Japan, and major foreign-policy decision making more generally, away from the Department of State and into the National Security Council. Nixon was secretive and confident of his own abilities when it came to foreign policy, and Kissinger was determined to wrest control over foreign policy away from the State Department and into his own hands. Together Nixon and Kissinger managed to shut out Secretary of State William Rogers from important decisions, the most dramatic example of course being the process by which Nixon and Kissinger engineered the administration's opening to China.

The decline of the State Department's control over Japan policy, however, was only partly due to Nixon's and Kissinger's determination to handle important foreign-policy issues themselves. By the early 1970s, the U.S.-Japan relationship, due in large part to Japan's rapid economic growth, had deepened and broadened considerably. This had the effect of changing the bureaucratic politics of Japan policy in Washington. The growing importance of trade and monetary issues created important stakes for the Departments of Commerce and the Treasury in relations with Japan and brought the Council of Economic Advisers, not just the National Security Council, into the Japan picture. It also made Congressional pressure a much more potent force in the formulation of Japan policy than ever before. Well into the 1960s, the assistant secretary of state for East Asia and the chief of the Japan desk dominated the formulation of Japan policy in the U.S. government. That was no longer the case after Nixon came to power and Kissinger came to the White House. It was no longer possible, and it is not possible today, to talk of a single "Japan policy" in the U.S. government in the sense of a coherent, comprehensive, bureaucratically well-coordinated strategy for dealing with Japan.

Another characteristic of U.S. policy making with respect to Japan that can be traced back to Kissinger and other key players in the Nixon administration, such as Secretary of the Treasury John Connally, is the widespread acceptance of the idea that Japan is somehow unique, that its economic institutions and basic cultural characteristics make it an outlier among trading nations, and that this uniqueness requires and justifies tailor-made approaches and policies. This view grew stronger and wider over time as the Japanese economy boomed, Japan's trade surplus with the United States became ever larger, and the view that Japan posed an economic threat to the United States perhaps greater in its long-term implications than the Soviet military threat became increasingly popular. The notion that Japan's competitive edge was rooted in unique cultural features that made it impossible for other countries to engage with Japan on a "level playing field" gave rise to the popularity of so-called revisionist thinking in the United States, thinking that was to become the ideational basis for the Clinton administration's trade policy toward Japan. Although revisionism became a buzzword only in the late 1980s, the roots of this kind of thinking about Japan can be traced back to the attitudes of the men who made Japan policy in the Nixon administration.

THE CHINA ISSUE

It has become rather fashionable to speak of a U.S.-Japan-China "triangle," but the notion that these three countries have some kind of triangular relationship has far less analytical utility or historical relevance than the constant invocation of the triangular metaphor might lead one to suspect. It is true of course that relations among the United States, Japan, and China involve three countries and that the policies that one of those countries pursues toward another one will be of concern to the third. But if implicit in the idea of a U.S.-Japan-China triangle is the assumption that each country in the triangle formulates its policies toward another on the basis of a careful consideration of the way it will affect relations with the third, then the triangular imagery is quite misleading.

Until Nixon initiated an opening to China in 1971, the singular goal of postwar American East Asian policy was to balance Soviet power and contain communist influence. Japan was incorporated into the U.S. military alliance structure, a junior partner of the United States in the cold war whose role was to facilitate the projection of American power into East Asia as provided for by the Security Treaty. China was regarded as a member of a unified communist bloc, and continued to be so regarded even in the face of evidence of a serious Sino-Soviet split. U.S. policymakers saw the world in bipolar, not multipolar, terms. There was no room for a U.S.-Japan-China triangle in this worldview; indeed, the United States firmly rejected Japanese efforts to break out of the rigid bipolar mold in developing Japan's policy toward China.

Prime Minister Yoshida Shigeru, the Japanese architect of the postwar peace settlement that Japan made with the United States and most of the Allied powers, had a quite different view of China from that of the American architect of that settlement, John Foster Dulles. Yoshida believed that nationalism was stronger than communism in China, and he also assumed that access to the China market would have to be an important element in Japan's economic recovery. Yoshida was anxious to recognize the new People's Republic of China government, quickly resume trade relations with Beijing, and possibly gain some diplomatic maneuvering room vis-à-vis the United States by developing ties with China. The U.S. government spared no effort to dissuade Yoshida from pursuing this course, including a threat issued by key U.S. senators at Dulles's request that Japan's failure to recognize Chiang Kai-shek's government on Taiwan as the legitimate government of all China might cause the Senate to fail to ratify the San Francisco Peace Treaty. Until the Nixon administration's "China shock" freed Japan from the constraints on its China policy that the United States had imposed, the Japanese government pursued a policy known as "separation of politics and economics" *(seikei bunri)*, namely, the development of rather low levels of trade relations with China through private and semiofficial channels and support for the U.S. policy of diplomatically isolating China.

There was of course a triangular relationship involved in President Nixon's decision to send his national security advisor, Kissinger, on his famed secret mission to Beijing in July 1971, but the triangle was a U.S.-Chinese-Soviet one. The United States hoped to use its new relationship with China to nudge Moscow toward acceptance of the concept of détente, and China hoped to use its new relationship with the United States to strengthen its power position vis-à-vis its communist-camp adversary.

That the U.S. decision to end China's isolation had everything to do with the Soviet Union and nothing to do with Japan was made all too obvious to the Japanese by the manner in which the opening was accomplished. It may have been unrealistic to expect that Kissinger would consult with the Japanese about a shift in China policy—after all, Kissinger did not even consult with Nixon's own secretary of state—but Prime Minister Satō was embarrassed nonetheless that his government was not given advance notice of the public announcement of the opening of U.S.-China normalization talks. Kissinger has admitted in his memoirs to a "serious error in manners" in not finding a way to moderate the shock that his secret mission to Beijing caused in Tokyo (1979, 762). He has not admitted to any error in strategy, however, for the perfectly good reason that he believed then and later that Japan had no option but to adjust to the new American line on China.

Others took quite a different view at the time. U. Alexis Johnson, the U.S. ambassador to Japan just prior to Nixon's coming to office and one of the most influential Japan hands in the State Department, drew a much more severe conclusion in his memoirs, noting that Kissinger's "passion for secrecy, combined with his contempt for the [State] Department and disdain for the Japanese, threw a devastating wrench into our relations with Japan on the question of China" (Schaller 1997, 225).

In the light of developments in U.S.-Japan-China relations over the three decades since Kissinger's first trip to Beijing in 1971, it would be difficult to make a convincing case that the Nixon administration's secret diplomacy with the Chinese had a "devastating" impact on U.S.-Japan relations with respect to China. No doubt it sowed seeds of suspicion in Tokyo about U.S. policy and established a pattern of playing down the importance of consultations with the Japanese on China policy. Embarrassed and angry as they were at Nixon for his failure to notify the United States' key ally in East Asia about his new China policy, however, Japanese government leaders, who had suspected for months before Kissinger's visit that U.S. China policy was going to change, quickly made their adjustment to the new situation. They moved with remarkable speed to catch up with the United States and then moved out ahead of it by establishing formal diplomatic relations with China in 1972, seven years before the United States did so.

The historical record suggests that we should not make too much of the adverse impact of the Nixon administration's failure to give advance warning to the Japanese about the U.S. opening to China. Far more important than not giving prior notice to Japan about the U.S. shift in China policy is what Nixon and Kissinger said about Japan in their meetings with Mao Zedong and Zhou Enlai. Nixon and Kissinger did not try to convince the Chinese leaders that postwar democratic Japan was determined to pursue a peaceful foreign policy and prevent a resurgence of military power. The thrust of their remarks was that the best way to prevent Japan from once again becoming an important military factor in the region was to keep it allied with and subordinated to the United States.

In Nixon's and Kissinger's geopolitical perspective, it was imperative that the United States remain a military power in East Asia and that it continue to be able to forward deploy its forces on bases in Japan. Thus, Nixon and Kissinger saw as one of their most important tasks convincing the Chinese leaders that it was in China's vital national interest to have the Security Treaty remain in force and to have U.S. military forces continue to be stationed in Japan. They did so by playing on Chinese fears of a revival of Japanese militarism.

Kissinger notes in his memoirs that he stressed to Mao that "China's fear of Japan could best be assuaged by a continuing U.S.-Japanese alliance" (1979, 756). Both Kissinger and Nixon stressed the role that the U.S.-Japan alliance played in keeping a lid on Japanese military power, as serving as a "rein on Japanese unilateralism," as Kissinger put it (1979, 1089). Here is Nixon, for example, talking to Zhou: "[T]he United States can get out of Japanese waters, but others will still fish there. If we were to leave Japan naked and defenseless, they would have to turn to others for help [a warning that the Japanese would look to the Soviets?] or build the capability to defend themselves. If we had no defense arrangement with Japan, we would have no influence where they were concerned." Since a Japanese-Soviet military alliance was too far fetched for Zhou or anyone else to take seriously, this was a thinly veiled warning that the only alternative to a U.S.-Japan alliance was an independently militarily powerful Japan.

Nixon went on to drive the point home: "If the United States is gone from Asia, gone from Japan, our protests, no matter how loud, would be like firing an empty cannon. We would have no effect, because thousands of miles away is just too far to be heard" (Nixon 1978, 567).

Nixon and Kissinger, in other words, worked hard to convince the Chinese leadership that it was in China's interest to avoid a U.S.-Japan-China triangular relationship in East Asia. It would be far better to keep Japan in the snug embrace of the United States, which would delay for a considerable time if not avoid altogether Japan's revival as a military power. They no doubt took this posture in part for opportunistic reasons, seeing it as a persuasive argument to use with the Chinese to gain their acquiescence to the continuation of the Security Treaty and the presence of U.S. forces in the region. It was easy for them to do so, however, because both Nixon and Kissinger viewed Japan in ways that were remarkably compatible with Mao's and Zhou's views.

Nixon and Kissinger prided themselves on being realists in international affairs, and realist theory demanded that as Japan became economically stronger it would seek to become more powerful in its region and in the world in political and military terms, as well. Realists have argued for years that Japan was about to become a "normal" country. Kissinger did so when he was in public office, and he has continued ever since to adhere to the view that Japan will soon decide to develop a military posture commensurate with its economic capabilities. That may happen one day, and if it does realists will be quick to claim that their theory has been confirmed. One has to wonder, however, about the utility of a theory that has been so spectacularly wrong with respect to Japan for at least the past thirty years. It is not enough to say, as its defenders do, that the theory seeks to explain general characteristics of the international system rather than the policies of any particular country. Given its economic power and its military potential, Japan is too important a case to be dismissed as simply an exception to the rule.

Both Nixon and Kissinger believed that pressures emanating at the international level would overwhelm pacifist opinion in Japan and drive it in the direction of major rearmament. They may not have shared the Chinese fear of the Japanese as being somehow inherently militaristic, but their penchant for realist thinking gave them a perspective on Japan that was far more compatible with views they heard in China than any they heard in Tokyo.

In February 1970, shortly after agreeing to return control over Okinawa to Japan, Nixon predicted that Japan would no longer be reluctant to involve itself in world affairs and that he "wouldn't be surprised if in five years we didn't have to restrain them" (Schaller 1997, 220). This was a rather astounding statement for someone who had gained a reputation for being a brilliant analyst of international affairs. Nixon later boasted that he was tough with the Chinese, telling them that if they did not agree to strategic cooperation against the Soviets on American terms, the United States would encourage Japan to develop nuclear weapons. "We told them that if you try to keep us from protecting the Japanese, we would let them go nuclear" (Schaller 1997, 230), as if the only thing holding the Japanese back from becoming a nuclear power and a menace to the region was the United States and its Security Treaty with Japan.

The popularity of the idea that the Security Treaty is the "cap in the bottle" of Japanese militarism is a legacy of the Nixon-Kissinger era, even if the phrase itself is not. (It was coined in March 1990 by Major General Henry Stackpole III, the commander of Marine Corps bases in Japan). The Chinese accepted this interpretation and gave passive if not open support for the Security Treaty until the mid-1990s. Their views turned decidedly more negative with the issuance of the 1996 Joint Declaration on Security by President Clinton and Prime Minister Hashimoto and a subsequent revision of the Guidelines for U.S.-Japan Defense Cooperation that called on Japan to play an expanded role in supporting U.S. forces engaged in hostilities in "areas surrounding Japan." Chinese leaders appear to have viewed these developments as an attempt to pull the cap at least partway off the Japanese military bottle.

Nixon's and Kissinger's readiness to reinforce Chinese fears of revived Japanese militarism as a means of getting the Chinese to accept the Security Treaty drew sharp criticism from U.S. officials responsible for managing relations with Japan. The U.S. ambassador to Tokyo at the time, Armin Meyer, warned Nixon and Kissinger against trying to "persuade the Chinese that the United States–Japan security relationship had a restraining effect on Japanese 'militarism.' This would inevitably get back to Japan, undermining Japanese confidence in the U.S. and weakening the U.S.-Japan relationship just as Beijing desired" (Schaller 1997, 242).

It must be emphasized that Nixon and Kissinger, who understood that the Japanese did not have much choice but to acquiesce to American policy toward China, were more realistic about the short-term consequences of their position than were the U.S. ambassador and the Japan hands in the State Department. Nixon and Kissinger were not inclined to pay much attention to Japanese sensitivities when there was little Japan could do to upset U.S. China policy and when the United States was engaged in a historic effort to mobilize China to create a new balance of power with the Soviet Union.

It should also be noted that if Nixon and Kissinger had opted for a strategy that involved close consultation with Japan, they almost certainly would have been frustrated by the Japanese government's reluctance to engage in such consultations. It is difficult to imagine that Japanese political leaders, if Kissinger had solicited their views, would not have voiced the concerns of the ruling party's powerful Taiwan lobby or that they would not have leaked information about an impending U.S. opening to China to protect themselves from attack by this lobby. Whatever their embarrassment at being ignored, Japanese political leaders surely found it easier to break relations with Taiwan and establish them with Beijing once they were faced with the *fait accompli* of the new U.S. China policy.

U.S. unilateralism proved to be convenient for Japanese political leaders with respect to China and many other foreign-policy issues as well during the cold-war years. By claiming that the United States had acted without consulting Japan and that as a result Japan had no choice but to adjust its own policies to the new situation, Japanese political leaders were able to shift the burden of responsibility for politically controversial decisions off their own shoulders and onto those of the U.S. government. It is doubtful that senior officials in Washington ever understood this dynamic or grasped the point that consultations are not simply an issue of etiquette but also a way to get Japan to take positions on important issues, and to assume public responsibility for the positions taken.

FROM KISSINGER TO BRZEZINSKI

The election of Carter as president in 1976 and his appointment of Brzezinski as his national security advisor, even though it meant a shift from a Republican to a Democratic administration, did not alter the basic lines of U.S. policy toward Japan with respect to China that had been established by Nixon and Kissinger. Brzezinski was intent on pushing the U.S.-China strategic relationship further than Kissinger had been able to take it. Japanese leaders for the most part were ignored by the new leaders of the U.S. government on China matters, as they had been by the administrations of Nixon and Ford. Kissinger's success when he was national security advisor in grasping control over China policy and cutting out the State Department set a precedent that Brzezinski was all too eager to continue. It was not long before he and Secretary of State Cyrus Vance were engaged in a struggle for influence with the president on a range of foreign-policy issues, including China.

"Consultations" with Japan about China amounted to little more than Brzezinski's stopping in Tokyo on his way back from Beijing to urge Prime Minister Fukuda Takeo to get on with signing a formal peace and friendship treaty with China and to accept China's demand for the inclusion of an "anti-hegemony" clause aimed at the Soviet Union if that is what it would take to bring the negotiations to a successful conclusion. The Carter administration was pushing hard to establish formal diplomatic relations with China, and Brzezinski wanted Japan to be fully in line with U.S. strategy in East Asia.

The Japanese government, concerned about aggravating its relations with the Soviet Union, hesitated to accept the antihegemony language that the Chinese proposed. By August 1978, however, anxious that it might miss the latest bus to China if its own negotiations for a peace and friendship treaty remained stalled while U.S.-China normalization moved forward, the Japanese government reached agreement on a treaty that included an antihegemony clause. The treaty language made a concession to Japanese sensibilities by referring to hegemony "by any country," which supposedly enabled the Japanese government to tell the Soviets that it was not aimed against them.

Brzezinski's lack of attention to the Japan relationship during the time he served in the Carter administration is somewhat surprising. He had written a book about Japan (Brezezinski 1972), and before entering the government he had been a key figure in establishing and providing the intellectual leadership for the Trilateral Commission, which was created in the belief that there needed to be a broader dialogue and closer consultations between Americans and Europeans on the one hand and Japanese on the other. Perhaps all that this neglect of Japan indicates is that policymakers, unlike university professors, become preoccupied with immediate issues that need resolution. The Carter administration had decided to make an all-out effort to establish formal diplomatic relations with China, and it saw little reason to involve Japan in that effort. Japan, after all, had established diplomatic relations with China several years earlier.

To the extent that there was a difference in U.S.-Japan relations with respect to security issues in the Carter-Brzezinski years from what they were when Nixon and Ford were in power and Kissinger was in charge of foreign policy, it was a difference that grew out of the Carter administration's skepticism about détente. Kissinger tried to play a China card to draw the Soviets into accepting the premises of détente. Brzezinski was a severe critic of détente and saw his China card as a way to maximize the power of forces opposed to Soviet expansionism.

Because of this concern about containing Soviet power, the Carter administration put more emphasis on the importance of Japan's strengthening its own military capabilities and taking over more of the burden of its own defense. Pressures to strengthen the military component of the alliance resulted in a Japanese proposal that the two countries establish clear guidelines for U.S.-Japan defense cooperation. The U.S. responded positively to this initiative, seeing the adoption of the guidelines as a way to integrate Japanese defense forces more closely with U.S. forces. Japan saw them as a way to specify the limits on its own security role. The guidelines did not change Japan's "defensive defense" strategy but they did consolidate an evolving change in relations between the U.S. and Japanese militaries. Instead of Japanese forces supplementing U.S. power in the event of an attack on Japan, now Japan was to take primary responsibility for its own defense, while American military actions would focus on threats to regional security. The guidelines agreed to by the Carter administration remained in effect until they were revised by the next Democratic president, Clinton, nearly twenty years later.

Unlike their surprise at the "China shock" in 1971, Japanese leaders were well aware in 1978 that the new president would press forward to complete the task of normalizing relations with China. They were far more nervous about other aspects of the new administration's policy in East Asia than its China policy. Japanese looked on with alarm as candidate Carter staked out a position during the presidential campaign in favor of removing U.S. troops from South Korea. After coming into office, Carter did not consult with Japan on his troop-withdrawal plan, even though it struck at the heart of Japanese security concerns, nor did he consult with Japan when he decided to reverse himself and keep U.S. troops there.

On top of the uneasiness the Korean troop-withdrawal issue created in Tokyo, the United States and Japan found themselves in a heated argument because of Carter's nuclear nonproliferation policies. As the only country ever to suffer a nuclear attack, Japan was particularly sensitive to anything having to do with nuclear weapons. As a country almost totally bereft of natural energy sources, it also had a major peaceful nuclear energy program in place. Carter believed that Japanese plans to build a nuclear fuel reprocessing plant at Tokaimura (which became the site of a nuclear accident, and near nuclear disaster, in September 1999) raised proliferation dangers, and he sought to get the Japanese government to suspend construction. This issue sparked a great deal of hostility among Japanese leaders toward the Carter administration. The U.S. policy was seen as reflecting a lack of trust in the Japanese commitment not to develop nuclear weapons and as an effort to restrict the development of peaceful nuclear energy production in a country that had few alternatives. The matter was eventually resolved, but President Carter's one term in office, far from ameliorating the tensions that had resulted from the China policies pursued by Nixon and Ford, generated further difficulties in relations with Japan due to the Korean troop-withdrawal issue and the flap over nuclear reprocessing.

THE RON-YASU RELATIONSHIP

Reagan's election as president produced important changes in the Japan policy line that had been laid down by Nixon and Kissinger and that had been continued by Carter and Brzezinski. Reagan was not enthralled with China, as Nixon and Carter and their national security advisors had been, and he did not have to deal with the problems of opening a dialogue or establishing formal diplomatic relations with China, since his predecessors had accomplished those tasks. Unlike Nixon, the conservative practitioner of Realpolitik, Reagan was an ideologue whose sympathies for Taiwan made him less than enthusiastic about embracing the Chinese to fight the "evil empire" of the Soviet Union.

Reagan was more inclined to embrace Japan, and he found himself dealing with a kindred soul in the person of Prime Minister Nakasone Yasuhiro. Nakasone was a well-known nationalist who took pride in his knowledge of international affairs and in his ability to think in global and strategic terms. The two leaders established a "Ron-Yasu" relationship that seems to have been genuinely warm, based on a common view of the Soviet threat, and rooted in an understanding of the importance of their two countries' having the closest possible relationship.

Few observers would have guessed, when they first came to power, that Reagan and Nakasone would get along so well. Reagan and his secretary of defense, Caspar Weinberger, believed in confronting the Soviet Union with over-whelming military power and, at least in Reagan's first term, in strengthening ties with Taiwan. It would have been reasonable to expect that Reagan would pressure the Japanese government to increase its defense budget and take a larger security role and to move closer to the Reagan administration's position on Taiwan. Nakasone, for his part, came into office with a reputation of being something of a Japanese-style Gaullist. He had worn a black tie to every National Diet session during the Allied Occupation because he believed the nation was in mourning until the U.S. occupying army left Japan. Many people both in Japan and in the United States believed that he wanted to see a loosening of Japan's bonds with the United States in favor of a more "autonomous" defense.

Reagan's and Nakasone's behavior confounded these expectations. The Reagan administration fundamentally shifted U.S. strategy toward Japan on defense matters. Rather than try to negotiate how much the Japanese government should increase its defense budget, it focused its attention and its negotiations with Japan on missions and roles. The idea was that if agreement could be reached with Japan on defining new roles and missions for Japan's Self-Defense Forces, then the Japanese themselves would decide how much it would cost to live up to the terms of the agreement. The earlier emphasis on budgetary expen-ditures had been a carryover from the Occupation, involving American offi-cials in a domestic decision-making process in ways that were highly inappropriate. The "roles and missions" approach quickly produced positive results, the first being the decision by the short-lived Suzuki Zenkō govern-ment that preceded Nakasone's selection as prime minister in 1982 to expand Japan's defense perimeter to sea lanes extending a thousand miles southeast and southwest from Japanese shores.

Quite contrary to his image as a proponent of autonomous defense who wanted to put greater distance between Japan and the United States on security matters, Nakasone sought every opportunity to demonstrate to the Japanese public that Japan's security was ineluctably linked to U.S. power and that U.S. and Japanese policies must be formulated in the context of a global, not simply a regional, balance of power. Nakasone succeeded in convincing Reagan that it was essential that an agreement with the Soviet Union to remove SS-20 missiles aimed at Western Europe should also prohibit their redeployment to East Asia. Nakasone declared that Japan was an "immovable aircraft carrier" in the cause of free-world security and openly criticized the pacifism-in-one-country mentality so dominant in Japan. The sharp differences over China policy and tensions in defense relations that had characterized U.S.-Japan relations in the 1970s were muted during the years that Ron and Yasu were in charge.

Another reason for the positive turn in U.S.-Japan relations during the Reagan years was the role played by George Shultz. Shultz succeeded Alexander Haig as Reagan's secretary of state in 1982 and remained in that post until the end of the Reagan era. He was a professional economist whose worldview seemed to be formed more by considerations of relative economic power than by the kind of geopolitical thinking that Kissinger and Brzezinski favored. Shultz was skeptical about China's importance to the United States, arguing that fascination with China "has tended to make U.S. foreign policy in Asia Sinocentric.... For me, the centerpiece has always been Japan. By far the largest economy in Asia, Japan is a key strategic partner and a dramatic example of successful democratic governance in an area where that is scarce" (Shultz 1993, 173). Shultz insisted that his first trip as secretary of state to Asia should be to Japan rather than to China, and he made a point of stopping off in Tokyo, as his predecessors had not done and as his successors would not do either, after visiting China to report to Japanese government leaders on his discussions there (Shultz 1993, 185).

Shultz, his economist view of the world driving his views on Japan, was against Japan becoming a major military power. "America must ensure that Japan is not tempted, because of Western neglect, shortsightedness, or hostility, to build an economic and military zone of its own in Asia. A strong Japan severed from America would be unnerving to Asia and the rest of the world. The other side of the coin is that Japan, through its intense competitive challenge, can help keep the massive potential and achievements of the American economy from declining through our own complacency" (Shultz 1993, 174). Together Reagan and Shultz, with their close working relationship with Nakasone and his minister for foreign affairs, Abe Shintarō, repaired some of the damage that had been done to U.S. relations with Japan by the preceding administrations. But they were unable to stem the tide of anti-Japanese sentiment that was rising in the country because of the gross imbalance in trade, as we shall see later in this chapter, and they were no longer in office when the Tiananmen Square Incident posed new challenges to the U.S.-Japan relationship with respect to China.

THE IMPACT OF TIANANMEN SQUARE

The Tiananmen Square Incident of 1989 played out in a curious way in terms of U.S.-Japan relations. Bush, who succeeded Reagan as president in 1989, had been ambassador to China and, unlike Reagan, was enthusiastic about developing closer ties with China. The Tiananmen Square Incident upset his plans because of the intense criticism in Congress and among the general public provoked by the Chinese government's brutal suppression of prodemocracy demonstrations. The Japanese imposed sanctions on China, along with the United States and European countries, but they did so reluctantly and looked for the first opportunity to remove them.

Japan's seeming lack of outrage over the actions of the Chinese government, and its alleged indifference to human-rights issues in China, produced a chorus of criticism in Congress and the American media, but Bush did not join in this criticism. The Japanese prime minister at the time, Kaifu Toshiki, found himself in a politically rather advantageous position. He was able to pursue a China policy that at one and the same time served Japanese economic interests, made Kaifu look like a leader who would stand up to the Americans for Japanese interests, and enjoyed the quiet blessing of President Bush. When Kaifu proclaimed at the July 1990 Houston Group of Seven (G7) summit Japan's intention to resume loans to China, he was announcing the kind of policy that Bush would have liked to pursue if domestic political pressures in the United States had not prevented him from doing so. Kaifu had discussed China with Bush on the phone before traveling to Houston,[1] and I remember him telling me at the time that he had secured Bush's blessing for his policy, the assumption being that Japan would ease the way for the United States to resume normal relations with Beijing, as well. Bush's public comment on Kaifu's announcement that Japan would move forward with a US$5.6 billion package for China was more supportive than a lot of Americans wanted. Japan "is a sovereign nation," Bush remarked, "that can make up its own mind on a lot of questions" (Mann 1999, 240). Kaifu almost certainly would not have been the first leader from a G7 country to visit China after Tiananmen Square without the implicit support of the U.S. government. What appeared to be a breaking of ranks with the West (Mann 1999, 247) was rather the consequence of close if not exactly public consultations with the United States.

It was unavoidable that U.S. leaders from Nixon to Bush would give far more attention to China than to Japan. The president, national security advisor, and secretary of state, with the singular exception of Shultz, saw foreign policy almost exclusively in political and military terms. Economics was a second-order issue. Japan was a given in the context of the cold-war struggle with the Soviet Union, while China offered an opportunity for innovative diplomacy. Strategists could design a China policy that could be expected to strengthen the U.S. position vis-à-vis the Soviet Union. Major changes in relations with Japan, however, could only cause problems, domestically in Japan and in U.S. relations with China and with South Korea and Southeast Asia, as well. Thus, a great deal of thought and energy went into designing a new China policy. There was no comparable incentive for innovative thinking about relations with Japan.

Moreover, in the 1970s in particular, American leaders were not concerned about Japan's taking actions that would complicate their relations with China. Given Japan's weak power position, Nixon and Kissinger, and later Carter and Brzezinski, could safely assume that Japan, which after all had wanted to normalize relations with Beijing back in 1950, would follow in the tracks the Americans laid down, grumbling about not being consulted but accommodating itself to the new U.S. position.

Another factor, whose importance is impossible to measure, was that strategists like Kissinger and Brzezinski obviously enjoyed discussing global issues with the Chinese and were bored to tears by discussions with the Japanese. Kissinger had enormous difficulty engaging with the Japanese and chalked it up to Japan's being "a society whose structures, habits, and forms of decision making are so unique as to insulate Japan from all other cultures" (Kissinger 1979, 322). Since there was little worry that Japan would do anything to upset the United States' evolving China policy and little to be learned from listening to Japanese leaders' views, there was little incentive for busy officials to take the time to discuss China policy with Japanese leaders, even if they did represent the United States' most important ally in East Asia.

THE CLINTON ADMINISTRATION AND "JAPAN PASSING"

The Clinton administration came into office with one set of policies toward China and went out with another entirely different one. Clinton criticized the Bush administration in the 1992 presidential campaign for coddling the "butchers of Beijing" and committed himself to make most-favored-nation (MFN) treatment of China conditional on improvement in its human-rights policy. Within a year, he had discarded that policy and pushed for unconditional MFN treatment of China and a policy of "engagement." By Clinton's second term, engagement had been expanded to a substantively vague but rhetorically robust emphasis on a "strategic partnership" with China. Like its predecessors, the Clinton administration paid scant attention to consultations with Japan in developing its policies toward China or in assessing the way each twist and turn in U.S. policy might affect U.S. relations with Japan or Japan's relations with China.

Bypassing Japan on the way to China was hardly a feature of U.S. diplomacy new to the Clinton administration. But its consequences for U.S.-Japan relations were considerably different from what they had been during earlier administrations. For one thing, it produced for the first time sharp divergence in U.S. and Japanese policies and strategies for dealing with China. In the 1970s, when Nixon opened relations with China and Carter normalized them, Japan made sure to stay in step with U.S. policy. Then for most of the 1980s China policy did not impinge directly on U.S.-Japan relations. The differences that did emerge in U.S. and Japanese responses to the Tiananmen Square Incident were more apparent than real, Kaifu's show of independence from the United States in ending sanctions against Beijing actually having been carefully orchestrated with President Bush, as mentioned earlier.

U.S.-Japan relations with respect to China during the Clinton years were another matter. When Clinton came to power, then–Prime Minister Miyazawa Kiichi urged him to avoid a confrontational stance with regard to human-rights issues in China and to accord China unconditional MFN treatment. Later the Japanese reacted with caution to the Clinton administration's embrace of a new policy of strategic partnership with China, concerned that Clinton seemed to be playing down the importance of the one truly meaningful strategic partnership that the United States had in East Asia, the one with Japan, in favor of developing a new one with China.

Chinese President Jiang Zemin received a warm welcome when he visited Washington in October 1997 after making a stop at Pearl Harbor that was full of intended symbolism about the old friendship between the United States and China and old enmities between the United States and Japan. He received anything but a warm welcome when he visited Japan in November 1998. Jiang went back to Beijing from that Tokyo trip without the written apology for Japanese wartime behavior that he had asked for. The Japanese government seemed determined to teach him the lesson that China could not simply make demands on Japan but would have to give something in return, as South Korean President Kim Dae Jung had done in a visit to Tokyo a month earlier, when he had received the kind of written apology that the Chinese wanted and in turn stressed the importance of looking forward rather than continuing to dwell on the past. The Japanese were taking a hard line toward China when the Clinton administration was pursuing a soft one, just as earlier they had taken a soft line when the Clinton administration had taken a hard one on human rights.

By the time the Clinton administration came to power the cold war had ended, Sino-Japanese economic ties had grown strong, and the Japanese were no longer worried about missing the bus to China, as they had been in the 1970s. Now they seemed determined to avoid having Japanese policy whiplashed by Washington's erratic steering of U.S. China policy. As the 1990s unfolded, U.S.-Japan-China relations began to evince a "triangular" quality that had been missing in earlier years. With the United States' and Japan's China policy no longer being designed with the Soviet Union in mind, the relations among the three countries took on a new dynamic. China viewed the Clinton-Hashimoto Joint Declaration on Security of April 1996 and the decision to revise the Guidelines for U.S.-Japan Defense Cooperation with suspicion. It demanded unsuccessfully that the United States and Japan publicly state that Taiwan lay outside the area to which the guidelines applied and expressed concern that the security declaration was intended to encourage Japan to play a regional military role.

After the Asian financial crisis broke out in the summer of 1997, the Clinton administration became increasingly agitated at Japan's failure to take the drastic actions the administration believed were necessary to restore soundness to Japan's banking system and to get its economy back on the road to growth. In a joint press conference with Jiang in Beijing on June 27, 1998, President Clinton applauded China for its "great statesmanship and strength in making a strong contribution to the stability . . . of the entire region by maintaining the value of its currency." He then went on to publicly point an accusing finger at Japan and to imply that Japan was a common problem for the United States and China. "The United States, as you know," Clinton remarked, "has worked hard to try to support the stability of the Japanese yen and to help growth resume in Japan. . . . The key here, I believe, is for the plans to reform the financial institutions in Japan and take other steps that will get growth going and get investments going in Japan to be made." He then added, "I think that ultimately while President Jiang and I would give anything to be able to just wave a wand and have all of this go away, we are not the only actors in this drama. And a lot of this must be done by the Japanese government and the Japanese people. And we can be supportive but they have to make the right decisions." The imagery of Clinton and Jiang hand in hand with a magic wand that they wished they could use to deal with Japan caused considerable consternation in Tokyo, where it was interpreted as further evidence of the U.S. "passing" Japan in its China policy. Clinton was the first president in the postwar period to raise serious doubts in Tokyo about the objectives of U.S. China policy.

If differences over dealing with China had arisen in the context of otherwise positive relations between the United States and Japan, the issue might not have seemed so important. But it emerged in what was perhaps the most bitter confrontation between the United States and Japan in the postwar period over trade policy and Japan's financial and economic policies.

THE TRADE CONUNDRUM

It hardly seems necessary to note that the most difficult and contentious issue in U.S.-Japan relations over the past three decades has been trade. Japanese trade surpluses were on an inexorable climb throughout the 1970s and 1980s. Japanese economic power grew while the United States confronted mounting budget and trade deficits. No administration, whatever its ideological inclination, could afford to ignore intense domestic pressures that it "do something" about the United States' ballooning trade deficit with Japan and about what was widely believed to be Japan's unfair trade practices.

Yet as politically controversial as trade relations with Japan were, it was not until the Clinton administration, or arguably until the last year of the Bush government, that the president and his top foreign-policy advisors put trade with Japan high on their foreign-policy priority list. Pressures to do something about Japan traditionally came from Congress and from agencies within the executive branch such as the Commerce Department and the Office of the U.S. Trade Representative (USTR), for which doing something about trade was an important part of their bureaucratic mission. There is no evidence to suggest that any of the presidents prior to Clinton thought about trade as a vital national security concern or that any of their chief foreign-policy advisors—Kissinger, Brzezinski, Richard Allen, Robert McFarlane, Colin Powell, Brent Scowcroft, and others—or secretaries of state other than Shultz thought of trade policy, or international economic relations more generally, as a necessary part of a comprehensive foreign-policy strategy.

Trade relations were to a considerable extent more a matter of relations between the administration and Congress than between the U.S. government and Japan. The Japanese understood this situation quite accurately and did what they could to support the administration in fighting off Congressional demands for action against Japan while keeping their concessions to the United States to a minimum. This caused intense frustration, to put it mildly, among many U.S. trade negotiators. Clyde Prestowitz, who was involved in trade negotiations with Japan in the 1980s, emerged from the trenches of U.S.-Japan trade battles to complain that "[t]he negotiation thus changed direction: originally a matter of U.S. government requests, it became one of mutually calibrating just how much action would be necessary to keep Congress leashed. Instead of a negotiator, the U.S. trade team became an adviser to the government of Japan on how to handle the U.S. Congress" (1988, 281). The consequence was increased hostility toward Japan and growing frustration with the state of bilateral economic relations in the Congress and in public opinion.

Neither Nixon nor Kissinger was much interested in trade, except in Nixon's case to the degree that it affected his domestic political power base. International economic relations did not figure in the calculus of the United States' top strategic thinkers. Kissinger in his memoirs makes light of his ignorance of trade issues, but the fact that the president's senior advisor on international affairs had little interest in or knowledge of international economics was particularly unfortunate with respect to U.S.-Japan relations. Little attention was paid to thinking about ways to manage trade relations or to deal with the tensions being produced by important structural changes that were then taking place in the world economy.

Nixon's "textile wrangle" with Japan was the most politically charged trade dispute up to that point in postwar U.S.-Japanese history. It was not, however, the first time that the United States and Japan had had to deal with a serious bilateral trade problem, nor was it the first time that the United States had sought a solution to a trade problem by asking for Japanese voluntary export restraints. What made the textile case significantly different from earlier trade disputes was that it came in the context of a fundamental change in the U.S. position in the world economy. In 1971, the United States experienced its first overall merchandise trade deficit—US$2.27 billion—in nearly a century. The deficit with Japan swelled to US$3.2 billion on two-way trade of almost US$11.5 billion. Ten years later, the U.S. bilateral trade deficit with Japan was US$16 billion. In 1987, it reached a staggering US$59 billion.

The appearance of red ink on the current account of the U.S. balance of payments led to the second "Nixon shock" (the first being the rapprochement with China), the New Economic Policy announced on August 15, 1971. Among other things, it imposed a 10 percent surcharge on all imports and suspended the convertibility of the dollar into gold. The failure of the Smithsonian agreement that was signed three months later (and that pegged the dollar at ¥308 instead of ¥360) to stabilize exchange rates produced a new regime of floating exchange rates. It also produced a new phase in U.S.-Japan economic relations in which the U.S. administration tried to use macroeconomic measures, multilateral trade negotiations, sector-specific trade agreements, results-oriented managed-trade agreements, and other strategies in an effort to contain the growing, and increasingly politically explosive, Japan trade problem.

Through the 1970s, that is, through the Nixon, Ford, and Carter presidencies, Congressional hostility toward Japan over trade issues grew at an exponential rate. All three administrations tried to deal with it in essentially the same manner. They strong-armed Japan to adopt voluntary export restraints, they threatened to unleash Congress and impose harsh protectionist measures against Japan if it did not comply with U.S. demands, and they kept a high fire wall between trade and the security dimensions of the U.S.-Japan alliance.

This was still an age when trade was considered to be a matter that could be left to the trade specialists in the government, and to those in the White House who were responsible for managing relations with Congress. The State Department had not emphasized economic expertise in training its foreign service officers and, whether under Rogers, Kissinger, or Vance, it did not aggressively seek to exert influence over trade policy. The National Security Council did not consider economic relations to fall under the rubric of national security. Given the exigencies of the cold war and the critical role the Japan alliance played in U.S. strategy in Asia, there was no enthusiasm among the president's foreign-policy advisors for supporting a policy toward Japan that would put that alliance at risk in order to achieve a better balance in the flow of imports and exports between the United States and Japan.

Yet Nixon, Ford, and Carter did little to try to reduce the growing hostility toward Japan that was being generated by trade relations. In rhetoric, if not in real policy terms, the presidents during the 1970s echoed the criticisms of Japanese trade practices that were being voiced in the Congress. They did not develop coherent strategies to engage Japan over trade conflicts, and they did not contest the popular view that the villain of the piece was the Japanese government's trade policies. The result was a pattern of piecemeal protectionist measures adopted in order to avoid Congressional imposition of harsher measures.

Presidential rhetoric changed when Reagan came into office. He was a committed free-trader, and, just as important, so were the key people in his administration, none more so than Shultz. Shultz's equanimity in the face of the growing U.S. trade deficit reflected his training in modern economic theory, but his views were far from those that were gaining strength in the Congress and in the business community and mass media: "As an economist and a believer in the benefits of free trade, I worried less about such developments [Japan's trade surplus and overseas investment] than did most people in Washington. If the Japanese, as a producer-dominated and protected society, want to pay astronomical prices for goods that are cheaper elsewhere, that is more their problem than ours. . . . If we are worried about foreign financing of investment in the United States, let us increase our own savings to finance our own investment. In other words, I felt, if we wanted to see our real problems, we should look in the mirror" (Shultz 1993, 190).

But precisely because Reagan and Shultz did not see the bilateral trade imbalance with Japan as the burning issue so many others believed it to be, they came into office without any strategy for dealing with it. So they found themselves in much the same position as their predecessors: They had no strategy for dealing with Japan over trade, but they had to improvise one to deal with a Congress that was threatening protectionist measures to contain Japanese imports. A failure to head off Congress over the Japan trade problem would not only produce Congressional action that Reagan considered unwise but also demonstrate the Democrat-controlled Congress's power over the Republican administration and thus weaken the president politically.

The result was that the Reagan administration's inclination to treat the trade problem with Japan with benign neglect produced policies toward Congress that resulted in demands on Japan for further voluntary export restraints. Within months of coming into office, Reagan sought voluntary export restraints on

Japanese automobiles. Later in his first term, he did the same with respect to steel. In the meantime, the politics of U.S.-Japan trade relations escalated and became ever more bitter.

THE MOSS TALKS

However much he might have agreed with Shultz that trade-account imbalances are a symptom rather than a cause of economic problems, politically Reagan could not afford not to try to get out in front of the trade problem with Japan. In 1985, the Reagan administration announced that it was initiating a new round of negotiations with Japan over trade that were called the MOSS talks. MOSS involved an enormous commitment of time on the part of high-ranking officials to negotiate with the Japanese the removal of barriers to foreign access to the Japanese market in electronics, telecommunications equipment and services, medical equipment and pharmaceuticals, and forest products.

The MOSS talks produced some modest progress, but the talks themselves did not accomplish their goal of relieving tensions in bilateral trade relations. Shultz evaluated them as having "produced positive results in a painful, tooth-pulling effort that left everyone a little ragged and frustrated" (Shultz 1993, 190). A strategy that required intense involvement by senior officials over an extended period for modest results could not be sustained, given the structure of the U.S. government. By contrast, it could be sustained by the Japanese government because it had many senior officials to deploy whose entire raison d'être was to deal with trade issues.

Whatever modest success the MOSS talks had, they did not accomplish the task of reducing Congressional criticism of Japan. They did, however, have an important impact on, or at least reflected a shift in, the focus of that criticism. Through the administrations of Nixon, Ford, and Carter, the major objective of trade negotiations with Japan had been to restrain Japanese imports into the U.S. market. Complaints had been voiced about the difficulties foreign companies faced in exporting to or investing in the Japanese market, but the policy emphasis had been on getting Japan to restrain exports rather than to encourage imports. The MOSS talks shifted the focus of concern to Japanese market access. In the MOSS negotiations, the United States emphasized the importance of Japan's changing rules and procedures that created structural barriers to foreign firms seeking to enter the Japanese market. MOSS represented an important turning point in U.S. trade policy toward Japan, and was a kind of leading indicator of a basic change in emphasis in U.S. trade policy more generally. Reagan and Bush (and Clinton as well) argued that the core challenge in U.S.-Japan trade relations was not how to protect U.S. companies against Japanese (or other foreign) competition in the U.S. market, but how to give U.S. and other foreign companies a fair chance to compete in the Japanese and other foreign markets. Market access became the key objective, and threats to restrict Japanese access to the U.S. market were used as leverage to pry open Japanese markets.

By emphasizing expanding trade through increased market access rather than restricting it through voluntary or coercive restraints on Japanese exports, the policies of the USTR and the Commerce Department came into somewhat better sync with the macroeconomic policies that were being pursued by the Treasury Department and that were supported by the Council of Economic Advisers. The coordinated intervention to force a depreciation of the dollar vis-à-vis the yen and other major currencies that was achieved by the Plaza Accord in 1985 removed the handicap that an overvalued dollar put on American manufacturers in the world market. It sought to drive policy in the same direction that "market access" advocates in the USTR wanted to take it: toward an expansion of U.S. exports rather than a contraction of U.S. imports.

Neither the MOSS talks nor the Plaza Accord were sufficient to calm the roiled waters of anti-Japanese opinion in Congress and in the business community, however. Demands for more and tougher measures against Japan continued to mount at roughly the same pace as the increase in the U.S. trade deficit with Japan. In March 1985, the Senate passed by a vote of ninety-two to zero a resolution condemning Japan for unfair trade practices and urging retaliation if U.S. exports there did not increase significantly. In Reagan's last year in office, 1988, the Senate passed the Omnibus Trade and Competitiveness Act, which included the so-called Super 301 provision, compelling the administration to compile a list of countries maintaining a consistent pattern of unfair trade practices and requiring it to negotiate the removal of barriers within a set period of time.

In the midst of these growing pressures, the Reagan administration forged an agreement with Japan that violated its own strictures about free trade and provided a model for the kind of "results oriented" trade agreements that the Clinton administration would later make the heart of its strategy for dealing with Japan over trade. This was the 1986 Semiconductor Agreement.

The agreement sought to prevent dumping of Japanese semiconductors abroad and to facilitate increased sales of foreign semiconductor firms in Japan through Japanese government efforts to promote relationships between Japanese firms and foreign semiconductor manufacturers. The most important provision of the agreement came in the form of a confidential side letter (that was quickly leaked) that committed Japan to seek to increase the share of foreign semiconductor sales in Japan from 10 percent to more than 20 percent of the market by 1991. Although the Japanese government denied that the agreement amounted to a government guarantee of market share, the United States insisted that there was a firm commitment on the Japanese part to see that the goal was attained. The Japanese failure to live up to what the United States thought Japan had agreed to do led to the imposition of economic sanctions in 1987, when the U.S. government determined that dumping had not ceased and that access to the Japanese market continued to be restricted. The dumping portion of the sanctions was lifted the same year, but the market-access portion of the sanctions was suspended only in 1991, when the Bush administration revised and extended the agreement.

Supporters of the Semiconductor Agreement argued that trying to get Japan to change its rules and procedures would be time consuming and would produce little to benefit American exporters. A new "revisionist" theory now became a prominent part of the debate over trade relations with Japan. Japan should be free to organize its economy any way it prefers, these critics argued. What matters to the United States is results, not how Japan achieves them. Simply sticking to the mantra of free trade will get the United States nowhere in terms of access to the Japanese market. The only sensible strategy for dealing with a mercantilist country like Japan that stacks the deck against foreign competitors in its domestic market through methods both formal and informal is to set targets industry by industry, identify measurable indicators of progress, and demand results. The Reagan administration, with its ideological commitment to free trade, did not accept this revisionist theory. But in its efforts to manage the domestic political problems generated by trade tensions with Japan, it ended up forging a semiconductor agreement that became the darling of the revisionist community and the model invoked by those who advocated managed-trade deals with Japan.

FROM MOSS TO SII

The Bush administration's trade policy toward Japan, like that of its predecessors, reflected the tensions between the White House and Congress, between the trade-specialized agencies and the macroeconomic-oriented Treasury Department and Council of Economic Advisers, and between the State Department, with its concern about keeping political relations on an even keel, and the administration's trade hawks. The public debate over Japan trade relations during the Bush administration became polarized. On one side were those who adopted the revisionist position that the organization of the Japanese political economy was so fundamentally different from that of every other country that special results-oriented measures were imperative. On the other were those, derided by some as members of a "Chrysanthemum Club," who argued either that bilateral trade imbalances were unimportant or that the relevant issue was the lack of competitiveness of U.S. companies rather than Japanese barriers to imports, and that trade relations should not be permitted to threaten the all-important U.S.-Japan political and security relationship.

Japanese trade relations posed a difficult domestic political issue for the Bush administration, and it responded by trying to accommodate all these conflicting pressures. It came to evince the same pattern as earlier administrations of tough rhetoric toward Japan combined with a concerted attempt to derail strongly protectionist measures in Congress, by an emphasis on multilateral trade negotiations to reduce barriers to trade globally along with the pursuit of bilateral sector-specific agreements.

Multilateral negotiations to reduce barriers to market access through the Uruguay Round of the General Agreement on Tariffs and Trade was at the top of the Bush administration's list of trade priorities, the goal being to conclude an agreement by December 1990. The Japanese government joined European countries in opposing U.S. proposals for agricultural liberalization since farmers made up the core constituency for the ruling Liberal Democratic Party (LDP). Where it "chose to be vocal on specific issues," as the deputy assistant U.S. trade representative during the Bush years put it, "it took positions that were either opposed to outcomes sought by the United States or less ambitious than those hoped for by the United States (Janow 1994, 59). The negotiating parties eventually compromised, leading to the successful conclusion of the Uruguay Round in 1994 when neither Bush nor the LDP was in power.

The Japanese government's performance in the Uruguay Round reinforced its image as being determinedly protectionist. Japan was not primarily responsible for the slow progress of the Uruguay Round, and in the end, once the Americans and the Europeans had cut a deal, Japan quickly got on board with the concessions needed to conclude an agreement. But Japan took no initiatives to hasten the round's successful conclusion. Consequently, its performance in those talks did nothing to weaken the anti-Japanese sentiment that was growing ever stronger on Capitol Hill.

In terms of dealing bilaterally with Japan on trade, the Bush administration introduced a new approach, and one that signaled how far U.S. trade policy had evolved since the Nixon administration's "textile wrangle" with Japan. Specifically, the Bush administration sought to get Japan to implement reforms in policies and institutional arrangements that the United States believed posed structural barriers to the expansion of foreign penetration of the Japanese market. This included macroeconomic policies, the organization of the distribution system, bidding practices for public works projects, relations among group firms *(keiretsu)* and other issues. This was the SII negotiations.

SII was based on an optimistic assumption, quite contrary to the views of the revisionist school, that changes in Japanese practices and institutions could level the playing field of trade relations. It was also rooted in the belief that simply negotiating sector-specific agreements, as Reagan's MOSS talks had sought to do, would just wear out the American negotiators and could never get to the nub of the problem. Accomplishing the latter meant attacking the entire panoply of Japanese economic practices that had created a system which produced trade policies the world economy could not sustain and the American political system would not tolerate. So the USTR set out with a limited staff but with unlimited energy and enthusiasm to do just that. At one point in the SII process the Japanese media countered 240 separate American demands for change in Japan (Schoppa 1997, 11).

SII had mixed results in achieving its stated goals, but it had a positive longer-term impact that was generally underestimated at the time. A key assumption behind the SII strategy was that the United States had to go over the head of the Japanese government and appeal directly to the Japanese public if it hoped to create a domestic constituency in Japan that would press for the kinds of changes the United States wanted to see Japan adopt. As Lynn Williams, the chief U.S. negotiator in the SII talks, put it, "The only way we were going to succeed was if we could appeal to the [Japanese] public interest (Schoppa 1997, 82).

Through the coverage it received in the Japanese media, SII educated the Japanese public about outrageous pricing practices that made it cheaper to buy some Japanese goods in New York than to buy them in Tokyo. It provided graphic examples of how much more expensive it was to live in Tokyo than in other major metropolitan cities and how inferior Tokyo living conditions were in terms of public infrastructure and housing. And it revealed patterns of oligopolistic practices and government-business collusion that not only were disadvantageous to foreigners but also penalized the Japanese people themselves. SII had a great deal more to do with triggering a debate in the 1990s about the need for structural reform in the Japanese economy than it is usually given credit for.

If, however, one of the purposes of SII was to significantly reduce political demands emanating from Congress and elsewhere in the United States for tougher action against Japan, it must be judged a failure. Because of the domestic pressure he faced, President Bush, while pursuing SII, also pressed hard for agreements that he could use to show the business community and Congress that he was able to get "results" from Japan. This led to his ill-fated trip to Tokyo in January 1992 with a score of American businessmen in his wake, where he became ill and threw up in Prime Minister Miyazawa's lap.

The Bush administration scored some success in opening the Japanese market to further U.S. exports. Exports in the sectors covered by the thirteen bilateral sectoral agreements that the United States and Japan signed increased about twice as fast as exports to Japan overall, according to some estimates (Janow 1994, 68). But the Bush administration, despite its rhetorical emphasis on results, remained committed to a process-oriented approach. Its modest achievements did little to stem the rising revisionist demand for a results-oriented, managed-market approach to dealing with Japan.

Even former Secretaries of State Kissinger and Vance, neither of whom had exercised any leadership over or even evinced much interest in international economic relations when they were in the government, jumped onto what was now a rolling revisionist bandwagon. In a 1988 *Foreign Affairs* article, they declared that the United States and Japan should seek to "establish an overall trade balance the United States would find tolerable; within that balance, Japan would have the choice of either reducing its exports or increasing its imports, thus removing the need for sector-by-sector industrial negotiations" (913). They did not spell out what the United States should do if Japan did not agree to go along with this scheme. Nor did they explain why they considered a reduction of Japanese exports to the United States equivalent to an increase of U.S. exports to Japan in terms of the impact on the U.S. economy. Indeed, they seemed to be unaware of the significance of the shift in U.S. trade policy in the 1980s from import protection to export expansion.

In February 1989, the Advisory Committee on Trade Policy and Negotiations, the USTR's most senior private-sector advisory committee, issued a report calling on the government to adopt a "results oriented trade strategy." The advisory committee recommended that the United States identify those sectors where "an increase in U.S. exports could be expected if Japan were to act like other industrial countries with similar economic attributes" and "insist on appropriate sectoral import levels that properly reflect the international competitiveness of U.S." and other foreign suppliers (Advisory Committee on Trade Policy and Negotiations 1989, 5). This report was issued near the end of the Bush presidency. Bush did not act on it, but Clinton did, leading to the most contentious and least productive period in postwar U.S.-Japan trade relations.

The Reagan administration's Semiconductor Agreement embodied what was to be the guiding spirit of the Clinton approach. In an extension of that agreement negotiated by the Bush administration in 1991, the Japanese government explicitly recognized the U.S. industry "expectation" that foreign semiconductors would secure more than 20 percent of the Japanese market by the end of 1992. The Japanese added that it "considers that this can be realized," which was all but a promise that the government would make sure it was realized.

The 1991 accord emphasized that the 20 percent figure was not a floor, a ceiling, or a guaranteed market share, and that other "quantitative and qualitative factors" would be taken into account in measuring progress under the agreement. Given the decided lack of enthusiasm for this agreement later expressed by Carla Hills, the U.S. trade representative responsible for negotiating it (Hills 1993), it seems quite clear that it reflected not the Bush administration's view of what was desirable in terms of trade policy but its view of what was politically unavoidable or expedient. It was left to Clinton and to his trade representative, Mickey Kantor, to design a managed-trade strategy for dealing with Japan that took its inspiration from the Semiconductor Agreement.

THE PLUSES AND MINUSES OF TRADE FRICTIONS

Before examining the Clinton years, it is important to look back over the rocky road of U.S.-Japan trade relations in the 1970s and 1980s and recognize that the Japan trade problem had significant salutary effects on the United States. Japanese economic success truly scared American business leaders and forced them to focus hard on issues of productivity and competitiveness. American managers became avid students of just-in-time inventory systems and other Japanese management techniques. Corporate boards of directors became more concerned about what management was doing to improve quality to compete with high-quality Japanese goods. Competition from Japanese automobile companies forced the U.S. Big Three to take decisive steps to improve the quality of the cars they produced. Little did anyone suspect at the time that Japanese competition would strengthen American industry but that continued Japanese restrictions on foreign competition in its markets would contribute to weakening both Japan's manufacturing and its financial industries.

Japanese success and the opportunities that SII in particular provided to the Japanese to tell Americans what was wrong with their economy also had a positive impact. SII gave both governments the opportunity to raise issues of concern regarding structural issues in the other country. The Japanese harped on the importance of the United States' reducing its budget deficit if it hoped to enjoy economic growth and a declining trade deficit. Japanese lectures about the way the United States should run its economy, which were often delivered with the same kind of hubris that Americans now exhibit when they deliver their advice to Japanese on the way they should rebuild their economy, were not responsible for, but surely contributed to, the determined American effort to get the budget deficit under control.

Another positive effect of the Japan trade problem emerged from the complicated domestic politics that trade disputes engendered. Each administration wanted to avoid protectionism, and yet each felt the Congressional pressure to do something about Japan. The response that became dominant by the mid-1980s was to emphasize market access to Japan, channeling protectionist pressures so that they became a wedge, or a crowbar in Trade Representative Hills's apt phrase, in breaking down barriers to access to the Japanese market.

Through MOSS and SII, the United States could plausibly claim to be pressing for an expansion of a rules-based liberal trading regime while insisting to those sectors of the U.S. economy most intensely concerned about Japanese competition that it had their interests at heart. Through SII, moreover, the United States was able to strengthen domestic constituencies in Japan in support of market-liberalizing measures. In the end, despite popular assumptions about Japan's responsiveness to *gaiatsu*—foreign, namely U.S., pressure—if exercised intensely and long enough, SII demonstrated quite persuasively that the way for the United States to elicit meaningful change in Japanese commercial and economic policies was to ally with domestic constituencies in Japan strong enough to demand it.

The negative side of the ledger of two decades of trade wars hardly needs elaboration. U.S.-Japan trade disputes exacted a heavy price in terms of American attitudes about Japan, especially among the policy elite. By the time the Clinton administration came into office, the revisionist view of Japan as an unfair trader and a threat to the United States had become the dominant view in Washington, and it was to have a substantial impact on the thinking of top officials in the new government. Persistent trade tensions with Japan and the resort to ad hoc bilateral agreements and unilateral actions to deal with those tensions also weakened support in the United States for a rules-based multilateral trade regime. In terms of its impact on the overall tenor of the U.S.-Japan relationship, the trade conflict produced no winners. Although not much is to be gained by constructing counterfactual arguments about what might have been if trade disputes had been handled differently, there is no doubt in my mind that many opportunities for cooperative action on a range of issues of common interest were lost because of the animosity generated by the failure of the two governments to manage trade relations more effectively.

THE CLINTON ADMINISTRATION'S "JAPAN PROBLEM"

In Tokyo on July 10, 1993, Prime Minister Miyazawa and President Clinton announced the successful conclusion of a new agreement, officially called the United States–Japan Framework for New Economic Partnership that, according to Miyazawa, would "improve the bilateral relationship and benefit the world economy (Finkle 1993). What it provided was a framework for the most bitter and ultimately the most unsuccessful period in the entire postwar history of U.S.-Japan trade negotiations.

Clinton had gone to Tokyo determined to come home with nothing less than an agreement that would provide a framework for results-oriented trade negotiations. Miyazawa was intent on finding some language that would allow the U.S. president to leave Japan with an agreement but without Japan's accepting the U.S. demand that there be "qualitative and quantitative measurements" to be used in setting targets and evaluating Japan's market-opening actions.

Clinton believed that the Japanese had agreed to do what he wanted them to do, and Japanese leaders were relieved that they had sent him home with a face-saving agreement that enabled them to avoid a nasty confrontation. Clinton had no sooner claimed success in getting Japan to agree to using measurable indicators than the chairman of Keidanren (Japan Federation of Economic Organizations) praised the accord for not including numerical targets. While the Clinton administration claimed victory in obtaining Japanese concessions on matters related to autos and auto parts, high technology, and medical equipment, the Japanese government claimed success for having avoided making any commitments that went much beyond the "series of seminars to encourage automakers to purchase U.S. auto parts" that Ministry of International Trade and Industry (MITI) officials had offered to set up (Finkle 1993).

For years, the United States and Japan had been engaged in trade "wars" that actually amounted to elaborate war "games" in which the goal was to contain Congressional pressures for protectionist measures and avoid a serious rupture in the relationship.[2] In the course of developing the games' rules, and as part of the more general phenomenon of economic globalization, the two countries had moved from an emphasis on restricting Japanese access to the U.S. market in the 1970s to expanding U.S. access to the Japanese market in the 1980s. Although market access remained the goal of the Clinton administration, the Japanese were slow to realize that Clinton had decided to change the rules of the game. Rather than work with the Japanese to contain Congress, Clinton was eager to enlist Congress to contain the much talked about Japanese economic threat.

The negotiations were led on the American side by Kantor, the trade representative, and on the Japanese side by Hashimoto, the minister of international trade and industry. Having decided to follow the revisionists' script, Kantor insisted that Japan agree to quantitative targets, as it had done in the earlier Semiconductor Agreement. He seemed to be convinced that Japan would eventually cave in under American pressure despite strong statements by Hashimoto and other Japanese officials that the Japanese government would never again sign an agreement that would guarantee market share to foreign companies. They had learned their lesson in the Semiconductor Agreement, and they were not about to repeat the mistake.

Trade officials in the Clinton administration, and the president himself, had become so captivated by the revisionist view of Japan that they refused to heed warnings that U.S. policy was likely to fail and that the effort itself would prove to be counterproductive. They ended up giving the Japanese government a kind of public relations bonanza, enabling it to make what otherwise would surely have been viewed as a ludicrous claim that Japan was defending the principles of free trade against a U.S. government intent on imposing managed-trade agreements. U.S. policy with respect to trade with Japan provoked a strongly negative reaction around the world, and especially in Asia, where leaders worried that if the U.S. effort to establish a results-oriented trade regime with Japan succeeded, the United States would use the same approach to strike bilateral deals with other countries in the region that were much less powerful than Japan. It also proved to be a boon to Hashimoto, whose toughness in Japanese eyes in staring down Kantor and standing up for Japan helped build the political support that took him from MITI minister to prime minister.

Clinton was unlike any earlier president in the importance he attached to international economic issues. Convinced that the United States' future well-being depended on its being the leader of a global economy, he seemed far more interested in economic issues than in the geopolitical ones that were the staple of the foreign-policy establishment. He was the first president who seemed to understand instinctively that economic relations were an integral component of national security. But he was woefully ill informed about Japan and surrounded himself with advisors who believed that Japan would do what they demanded and who had prepared no fallback position if their demands were rejected.

Clinton personally and aggressively advanced the administration's revisionist agenda with Japan. When Prime Minister Hosokawa Morihiro, the leader of the governing coalition that had replaced the long ruling LDP in August 1993, visited Washington in February 1994, Clinton greeted him with demands that Japan accept quantitative indicators and market-sharing guarantees. Hosokawa refused and went back to Japan with a new reputation as the first prime minister who could say no to the United States. Although he remained in office only a couple of months longer, other Japanese political leaders and senior bureaucrats in MITI and the Ministry of Foreign Affairs continued to resist U.S. demands and to insist that trade negotiations focus on multilateral agreements rather than bilateral deals. Clinton had tried unilaterally to change the rules of the game, and the Japanese had refused to play.

The Clinton administration approached the end of its first term with the effort to pursue a results-oriented trade policy toward Japan having produced little more than frustration, disappointment, and bitter feelings all around. By this point, however, Japan was no longer the perceived threat that it had been when Clinton came to office. The stock market and real estate bubble of the late 1980s had collapsed, leaving Japan with economic problems that grew only more serious as the new decade unfolded. The revisionist assumption that Japanese global economic dominance could not be stopped unless the United States departed from the normal rules of international trade and imposed a managed-trade regime on Japan looked rather silly in the face of America's economic renaissance and Japan's financial and economic mess. After spending his first four years trying to use a misguided trade policy to restrain Japan's global economic "hegemony," President Clinton and Treasury Secretary Robert Rubin spent most of the next four years badgering Japanese leaders to change their economic and financial systems to avoid precipitating a worldwide depression.

FACING THE FUTURE

The U.S.-Japan relationship has survived remarkable changes in economic circumstances in the two countries, foreign-policy shocks, bitter bilateral trade disputes, and at times inept diplomacy. Security relations have grown closer, even with the loss of the "glue" of the cold-war confrontation with the Soviet Union. Every American president has understood that vital U.S. national interests are at stake in the relationship with Japan, and every Japanese prime minister has viewed the U.S. alliance as the cornerstone of Japanese foreign policy.

Economic interdependence has increased dramatically, and seems certain to grow deeper faster in the coming years than in the past. The marked decline in the political salience of bilateral trade disputes in the second half of the 1990s no doubt owes a lot to the fact that the U.S. economy was booming. However, it was also the consequence of changes in Japanese economic policies that led to significant increases in foreign direct capital investment in Japan. There is every reason to believe that this trend will continue and probably accelerate in coming years.

It seems self-evident that the United States has nothing to gain, and potentially a great deal to lose, from a weakening of security or economic ties with Japan and from an increase in tensions between the countries that would reduce their willingness to cooperate in a variety of multilateral settings. It is one thing, however, to recognize that maintaining strong and positive relations with Japan is in the U.S. national interest and quite another to design a coherent strategy that serves that goal in the changed international and domestic contexts of the early twenty-first century.

We have seen from our discussion of U.S. interactions with Japan over China how changes in the international political system have undermined some of the key assumptions that U.S. policymakers virtually took for granted for decades in dealing with Japan. President Nixon's "China shock" in the early 1970s was embarrassing to the Japanese government and left it scampering not to miss the China bus. There is no doubt that Japanese leaders were irritated that Nixon and Kissinger played up the Japanese militarist threat with the Chinese. Precisely because there was not a hint of a U.S.-Japan-China triangle in U.S. strategy, however, Nixon's China initiative and Carter's formal recognition of China did not create fear in Japan of abandonment by the United States. Quite to the contrary, Nixon and Kissinger, and then Carter and Brzezinski, emphasized to the Chinese the critical importance of the U.S.-Japan Security Treaty. Japanese may have found the rationale not entirely pleasing, but because of it they obtained credible assurance that this key prop of postwar Japanese security policy would remain in place.

The nervousness created in Tokyo by Clinton's China policy is an important indicator of how much the dynamics of the China issue in U.S.-Japan relations has changed. Without the cold war to hold the U.S.-Japan alliance together, with China's economic rise and growing political influence, and with what many Japanese perceive as an American romanticized exaggeration of China's economic and political importance, the possibility not so much of outright abandonment as of a kind of drifting away from Japan by the United States seems far more real to Japanese today than it did before 1990.

Thus, actions that might have been just irritating in earlier years, such as not stopping in Japan on the way to or from China, now raise uneasy questions in Tokyo about U.S. intentions. When the president of the United States stresses the importance of a "strategic partnership" with China instead of the one the United States enjoys with Japan, and uses the opportunity of a joint press conference with the president of China to reflect on their common problem of Japan's inadequate economic performance, it is hardly surprising that Japanese speculation about a shift in U.S. strategy in East Asia should result.

The manner in which the United States from Nixon to Bush conducted its China policy set a pattern of bypassing Japan that the Clinton administration all too readily adopted as its own. If the United States had developed habits of consultation with Japan over China policy instead of habits of unilateralism, the two countries might have been better prepared to avoid frictions as they developed their respective China policies in the aftermath of the cold war and to maximize their combined leverage over China. In any case, the United States can no longer take it for granted that Japan will adjust its China policy to keep it in line with U.S. policy. Enhanced consultations and far greater attention among U.S. policymakers as to the way policies toward China might affect Japanese policy seem to be more urgent now than in the past. The triangular metaphor is becoming a more realistic image of relations among the United States, Japan, and China, and it is important that the United States and Japan consciously seek to keep their two corners of that triangle close.

We have seen how every administration has kept a high fire wall between economic and security affairs, refusing to let anger with Japan over trade issues spill over to adversely affect security ties. I do not believe that there is much danger that this fire wall will be breached in the foreseeable future. Trade disputes no doubt will arise in coming years, but unless one posits a disastrous collapse of the U.S. economy, there is every reason to believe that the United States will keep its markets open and that Japanese markets will also become increasingly open. Rather than shake the foundation of the bilateral relationship, as they sometimes threatened to do in the past, trade disputes in the future are likely to become a normal if unpleasant part of the relationship, as they are between the United States and Europe, to be dealt with in a pragmatic manner and contained from threatening broader national interests. It is difficult to imagine a scenario in which U.S. anger with Japan over matters of economic policy would translate into confrontation over security policies.

It is not so difficult, however, to imagine scenarios in which friction arises between the United States and Japan over issues that lie on the security side of the fire wall. The U.S.-Japan security relationship is sustained by a Japanese belief that the U.S. commitment to Japanese security is credible, and by an American belief that alliance with Japan serves vital U.S. national interests. Both these convictions could come under unprecedented challenge in the coming years.

The United States and Japan have to manage their alliance in a context in which it is no longer an entirely safe assumption, as it was during the cold war, that any external threat to Japan would necessarily be perceived as a threat to the United States. This new reality is reflected in the fact that Japanese confidence in the U.S. commitment to Japan's defense and to sustaining a regional balance of power seems to be more tentative than before. The North Korean launch in August 1998 of a missile that passed over Japanese territory, and what was perceived in Japan as a too-tepid U.S. response to that missile launch, raised new security concerns in Japan. Fortunately, subsequent efforts to coordinate U.S., Japanese, and South Korean policy with respect to North Korea, led largely by President Clinton's special emissary, former Secretary of Defense William Perry, were successful in ameliorating Japanese concerns and in ensuring that U.S., Japanese, and South Korean policy toward the North proceeded on the same track. Perry's consultations with Japan and South Korea constitute an approach to dealing with regional problems, and with regional allies, that is different from traditional bilateral approaches and different again from traditional multilateral approaches. Close U.S.-Japan–South Korean consultations on North Korea amount to a kind of "enhanced bilateralism" that may well offer a new model for regional dialogue and cooperation in a setting in which there is unlikely to be the development of regional multilateral security institutions such as exist in Europe.

The dangers posed by such issues as Taiwanese independence, conflicting claims among countries in the region to the Spratly Islands, competing Chinese and Japanese claims over the Senkaku, or Diaoyutai, Islands, and the division of the Korean peninsula underscore the importance of a strong U.S.-Japan security alliance. It is an alliance, however, that is inherently and unavoidably asymmetrical. It commits the United States to defend Japan, and it limits Japan's role to self-defense and to facilitating the projection of U.S. power into the region by giving it the right to maintain military bases in Japan.

A key challenge to effective alliance management results from the reality that it is not possible to eliminate the asymmetry in rights and obligations under the Security Treaty in a manner that would satisfy both American and Japanese views of what is in their country's national interest. As long as the U.S. commitment to remain the predominant military power in the East Asian region remains credible, Japan's own military commitments will remain highly restricted. A decline in confidence in the U.S. commitment to remain a military power in East Asia and in the essential commonality of U.S. and Japanese interests in the region might produce a more robust Japanese military effort. But it is not in the United States' interest to encourage doubts about its commitments in order to build political support in Japan that does not now exist for a Japanese military role in the region.

It is also questionable whether the American public would support a security arrangement with Japan that involved an open-ended U.S. commitment to Japanese defense but did not provide the United States with the military-base structure in Japan that has made possible the timely projection of U.S. power into the region and beyond. At the moment it seems highly unlikely that Japan will elect a government that will demand U.S. withdrawal from bases in Japan. But there are important Japanese political leaders who argue for a "Security Treaty without bases" arrangement under which U.S. forces would have access to Japanese bases only when the two governments concluded that it was necessary. If a government committed to carrying out such a policy were to come to power in Japan, a crisis in relations with the United States would result. But such a political development in Japan in the foreseeable future seems improbable in the extreme.

The possibility of a major clash between the United States and Japan over the nature of the security alliance must be judged to be extremely low. Far more dangerous is the possibility that the dynamic and ambiguous international political situation in East Asia will produce misperceptions, misunderstandings, and differences in priorities and political strategies between the United States and Japan. The challenge to American and Japanese leaders in this post–cold war era is to figure out how to minimize the risk that differences of this kind will emerge and produce friction between the two countries over regional issues and how to maximize the opportunities to mobilize their combined strengths to serve what are overwhelmingly common interests in the region.

The economic issues that pose the most serious challenges to U.S.-Japan relations in the future are far more likely to be regional than bilateral in scope and to be as political as they are economic. The Japanese government's unsuccessful, and indeed rather halfhearted, effort in 1998 to create an Asian Monetary Fund (AMF) may have offered a preview of the kind of issue that will challenge U.S.-Japan cooperation over issues related to the regional economy.

The Japanese Ministry of Finance floated the idea for an AMF to help Asian countries recover from the financial crisis that broke out in the late summer of 1997. It was vigorously opposed by the U.S. government. One reason was concern that it would provide a "soft" alternative to the tough conditionality the International Monetary Fund (IMF) imposed in giving loans and thus undermine the IMF's authority. Another was that it was seen as a gambit by Japan to seek a more powerful political voice in East Asia by means of a policy agenda that conflicted with U.S. policy goals.

U.S. opposition, and the fact that the AMF idea was floated before a strong consensus had been secured in Japan, led to its rather quick abandonment. But Japan does aspire to play more of a leadership role in East Asia, especially with respect to regional economic affairs. There is no necessary reason why it should not be able to do so in a manner that is consistent with U.S. interests in the region and that contributes to greater regional economic integration and growth. What needs to be avoided are U.S. government actions that support a Japanese perception that the United States is determined to block Japan from taking regional initiatives except when asked to by the U.S. government, and Japanese actions that support an American perception that the goal of Japanese diplomatic activity in the region is to wrest "autonomy" from the United States. There are enormous opportunities for complementary if not always coordinated policies between the United States and Japan to strengthen the regional as well as the global economy and to build stronger regional economic institutions.

The U.S.-Japan alliance has proved enormously valuable to both countries. There are no compelling reasons for the United States to want to change it fundamentally. While there is more vigorous debate in Japan today than at any time since the early 1950s about what course its foreign and defense policies should take in the future, there is a broad consensus among both its leadership elite and the public that alliance with the United States should be maintained as the centerpiece of its foreign policy. The challenge to U.S. leaders is not to devise policies or employ an antagonistic rhetoric that suggests that the United States is less committed to sustaining this relationship than is in fact the case.

American national interests will best be served by continuity rather than radical change in U.S.-Japan relations. A close and positive relationship with Japan is of critical importance in dealing with a host of regional and global issues. But given the changed economic and political context of U.S.-Japan relations, sustaining and strengthening this relationship will require innovative thinking and leadership by the president and the senior members of the administration. More has to be done to involve people with expertise about Japan when making important decisions with respect to East Asia. Greater attention needs to be paid to engaging top Japanese policymakers in consultations about regional issues. The United States needs to think strategically about East Asia and place Japan at the center of that strategic thinking.

The U.S.-Japan relationship is not in crisis, and it does not have to be "fixed" in some basic or far-reaching manner. What it needs is the sustained attention of top policymakers and a better understanding among the American public as well as political leaders of how relations with Japan can serve U.S. vital national interests in the twenty-first century as well as they did in the last half of the century just concluded.

NOTES

1. Kaifu apparently consulted so often with Bush that the joke in Tokyo at the time was that instead of a "push phone" (a push-button telephone) Kaifu had a "Bush phone."

2. On U.S.-Japan trade relations as a well-structured game, see Campbell (1994).

BIBLIOGRAPHY

Advisory Committee on Trade Policy and Negotiations. 1989. *Analysis of the US-Japan Trade Problem.*

Brzezinski, Zbigniew. 1972. *The Fragile Blossom: Crisis and Change in Japan.* New York: Harper and Row.

Campbell, John Creighton. 1994. "Japan and the United States: Games That Work." In Gerald L. Curtis, ed. *The United States, Japan, and Asia.* New York: Norton.

Finkle, James R. 1993. "Japan, US OK New Framework." *Daily Yomiuri* 11 July.

Hills, Carla. 1993. "Targets Won't Open Japanese Markets." *Wall Street Journal* 11 June: A10.

Janow, Merit. 1994. "Trading with an Ally: Progress and Discontent in U.S.-Japan Trade Relations." In Gerald L. Curtis, ed. *The United States, Japan, and Asia.* New York: Norton.

Kissinger, Henry. 1979. *The White House Years.* Boston: Little, Brown.

Kissinger, Henry, and Cyrus Vance. 1988. "Bipartisan Objectives for American Foreign Policy." *Foreign Affairs* 66(5): 899–921.

Mann, Jim. 1999. *About Face: A History of America's Curious Relationship with China.* New York: Knopf.

Nixon, Richard. 1978. *RN: The Memoirs of Richard Nixon.* New York: Grosset and Dunlap.

Prestowitz, Clyde V., Jr. 1988. *Trading Places: How We Allowed Japan to Take the Lead.* New York: Basic Books.

Schaller, Michael. 1997. *Altered States: The United States and Japan since the Occupation.* New York: Oxford University Press.

Schoppa, Leonard. 1997. *Bargaining with Japan: What American Pressure Can and Cannot Do.* New York: Columbia University Press.

Shultz, George P. 1993. *Turmoil and Triumph: My Years as Secretary of State.* New York: Scribner.

2

Market Opening in Japan:
Deregulation, Reregulation, and Cross-Sectoral Variation

Robert W. Bullock

DESPITE THE HISTORIC STRENGTH OF THE U.S. ECONOMY and the chronic recession and "deregulation fever" in Japan today, many American analysts have never been more pessimistic about the prospects for opening Japan's markets. In a 1998 position paper for the Council on Foreign Relations, Edward Lincoln, former special economic advisor to the U.S. Ambassador to Japan, concludes that we should simply lower our expectations for opening Japanese markets. Progress has been slow and difficult and there are few signs that things will improve.[1] In some ways, trade expert Leonard Schoppa is even more pessimistic. He argues that the prospects for the United States to win trade concessions from Japan sharply deteriorated with the change in Japanese "social context" in the early 1990s. With the end of the cold war, the establishment of the World Trade Organization (WTO), and a new generation of bureaucrats who "can say no" to unilateral U.S. demands, American trade negotiators face tougher conditions than ever (Schoppa 1999).

Recent works by American scholars on deregulation in Japan offer similarly pessimistic assessments. In the Brookings study *Is Japan Really Changing Its Ways?*, contributors stress the slow pace of reform, the persistence of industry cartels and bureaucratic governance of markets, and limited market opening. As coeditor Mark Tilton remarks, "The regulatory reform movement must be understood as a corrective and complement to Japan's system of developmentalist capitalism rather than an attempt to overthrow it" (Carlile and Tilton 1998). Even the "Big Bang" of financial-market reform, Elizabeth Norville tells us, is "mostly cosmetic," with little impact on traditional policy-making practices

The author wishes to thank Jennifer Holt Dwyer, Len Schoppa, and Steve Vogel for their advice on this chapter. Special thanks to Gerald Curtis, Greg Noble, T. J. Pempel, and Bob Uriu for their detailed comments and criticism.

(Norville 1998). Steven Vogel's recent article takes a similar line, stressing continuity in national regulatory style: "Japan's distinctive approach to liberalization has been characterized by slow and incremental change; elaborate political bargains, typically involving compensation for the potential losers from reform; considerable efforts to prepare industry for competition; and continued bureaucratic monitoring and manipulation of the terms of competition" (1999a).

This caution is understandable. It is undoubtedly true that the Japanese economy—especially manufacturing—remains dominated by well-organized, oligopolistic industries that are ambivalent at best about deregulation and market opening. Tilton, Lincoln, and others document enduring domestic-overseas price differentials (*naigai kakusa*) and the persistence of formal or informal market barriers in a range of important markets. Japan's trade negotiating strategy is still mostly one of, as Lincoln puts it, "deflect, delay, and diminish" (Lincoln 1999, 141; Tilton 1996). And government claims of success in deregulating the overall economy are suspect when the total number of regulations continues to increase.[2]

And yet, we cannot let these macro-oriented reservations obscure striking variation across Japanese markets. The fact is that we have already seen substantial regulatory change and market opening in some of Japan's most notoriously protected industries. It is striking that some of the most influential voices in Japanese studies and trade policy exhibit such skepticism at a time when the Japanese economy (or parts of it) is opening up at record speed. The Japanese economy is not, and probably never was, a united front. Japan can no longer be characterized as a "reactive state" where domestic actors merely respond, usually defensively, to external challenges (see Calder 1988b).

The first objective of this chapter is thus to document that in certain sectors, regulatory change—both deregulation and reregulation—has already been substantial and has facilitated market opening, while in other sectors it has not. We find "successes" among even the sectors most politically and economically central to Japanese politics and industrial policy, those which we would expect to be the toughest markets to crack. Among the politically central sectors, we have seen the relaxation and then abolition of the notorious Large Scale Retail Store Law and the subsequent explosion of new retail investment. Among the economically central sectors, we have seen substantial regulatory and market changes in telecommunications—in long-distance and cellular phone service in particular—and the Big Bang in financial services, which, while not quite a revolution, is the most important set of financial deregulatory measures of the postwar era.

The second, more ambitious objective of the chapter is to attempt to explain this variation. Clearly, what is occurring in Japan is neither across-the-board change, as convergence theory would have it, nor a unified resistance to change, as some historical institutionalists or developmental-state theorists might claim.

We must develop a more nuanced approach, moving beyond case-specific explanations. This chapter argues that the critical formula for market opening is external pressure (*gaiatsu*) plus internal, intra-sectoral conflict: more specifically, the existence of a substantial domestic constituency for reform that is composed of producer groups seeking strategic advantage via regulatory reform, with the support of at least some elements of the state bureaucracy as well.[3] This is perhaps most striking in the case of finance, where the more competitive elements of the sector, backed by elements of the Ministry of Finance (MOF) and Prime Minister Hashimoto Ryūtarō's Administrative Reform Council, have driven wide-ranging deregulation.

Of course, one might argue that the enormity of the banking crisis made financial reform, if anything, overdetermined. But we find significant regulatory change and market opening elsewhere, in sectors untouched by crisis: in telecommunications, where the divide is between the mammoth Nippon Telegraph and Telephone Corporation (NTT) and comparatively small, up-and-coming firms (often joint ventures or foreign firms) that are backed by the Ministry of Posts and Telecommunications (MPT) in its efforts to contain NTT dominance and encourage competition; and in retail, where competitive elements of the sector, backed in the end by the Ministry of International Trade and Industry (MITI), have aggressively pushed for regulatory change and liberalization, with U.S. *gaiatsu* playing an important supporting role.

The chapter explores four sectors in pairs—rice and retail, finance and telecommunications—and puts each paired comparison to slightly different use. In rice versus retail, the most interesting variation is in terms of market opening, which is significant in retail but token in rice. In retail, as noted above, business interests, with the support of American pressure and ultimately of MITI itself, drove significant regulatory change and market opening. In rice, by contrast, the Liberal Democratic Party (LDP), the Ministry of Agriculture, Forestry and Fisheries (MAFF), and organized agriculture—notably, the Japan Agricultural Co-operatives (JA), formerly known as Nōkyō—have presented a united front of resistance. To be sure, there is domestic dissent—particularly from competitive, large-scale farmers and (to a lesser degree) from big business—but it is disorganized and muted. The only major force for change has been American *gaiatsu*. Lacking domestic allies, American trade negotiators have won only minimal concessions and only by dint of concerted political pressure.

In finance versus telecommunications, regulatory change and market opening are important in both, but there is significant variation in the *style* of regulatory reform. In finance, reform is now primarily deregulatory, as a weakened MOF is losing control over the sector. In telecommunications, regulatory change remains primarily reregulatory, and the MPT as yet retains undiminished control of the sector. In short, internal market splits plus external pressure drive market opening, while the decline of bureaucratic power favors deregulation.

These outcomes are broadly consistent with the argument made by Leonard Schoppa in his 1997 book: *gaiatsu* fails without the support of domestic interests (which help also to legitimize policy change and to monitor results). But at the same time, it is difficult to argue that the United States did more than complement these actors. In other words, Schoppa's emphasis on "synergistic strategies"—that is, where the actions of one player shape the behavior and even the preferences of the other—is intellectually interesting but difficult to verify empirically, at least in the cases discussed here. Take, for example, "participation expansion," the main such tactic explored in Schoppa's study of the Bush administration's trade negotiations with Japan.[4] Consumers were one of the primary targets of this tactic, but in Japan (as elsewhere), the problems inherent to collective action render consumers ineffective as political actors.[5] Further, what consumer groups do exist in Japan tend to be just as protectionist as producer groups (Vogel 1999b).[6] While a consumerist strategy may help to legitimize market-opening demands, much more central to explaining market opening and regulatory change are the preferences and capabilities of producer interests. Among them, there may be mavericks—low-cost producers who believe that they will do better with more open markets or greater deregulation. Mavericks may exist even among the "insiders" who dominate the sector. But these producers were not *created* by U.S. pressure, nor did their preferences suddenly shift from protectionism to free trade. These actors were present all along, and they were far from silent in advocating regulatory change and market opening.

In short, the effectiveness of *gaiatsu* depends not only on tactics but also—and perhaps even more importantly—on the domestic political economy. Simply put, some markets are easier to crack than others. Each side's "win sets" (i.e., the range of acceptable agreements) can be tweaked only so far. And the bigger the gap between them, the less likely are tactics of any sort to close it. However, where win sets do not overlap but are nonetheless close, international pressure may help to move them together and to tip the balance in favor of market opening. External forces like the U.S. government or American firms may form, implicitly or explicitly, transnational alliances with domestic mavericks.[7] Needless to say, the domestic approach developed here does not contradict the emphasis on international tactics but complements it. Nonetheless, it makes sense to think first about which sectors are vulnerable to market-opening pressures before deliberating on the tactics most likely to work.

What is more, much of the new trade with Japan is coming in the form of foreign direct investment (FDI), not simply merchandise or service trade. While we cannot be sure whether or how long the influx will continue, there are already powerful new players in the Japanese market—Trojan horses, as it were—with a vested interest in continued opening. And as Dennis Encarnation (1992) argues, additional trade tends to follow investment. Related to this point, Helen Milner (1988) argues that as a national industry becomes more internationalized, it is likely to reduce its political demand for protection and, indeed, to pursue liberalization.

This chapter has several implications for U.S. policy. The most important recent successes for U.S. exporters have come less via bruising, bilateral conflict than through regulatory change, where *gaiatsu* was but one of a host of pressures. These successes demonstrate that market opening need not come from managed trade alone. While numbers-based managed trade deals have been more successful than detractors claim, the approach is deeply unpopular in Japan today and remains controversial in Washington.[8] In the current atmosphere of deregulation fever in Japan, the United States would do well to focus its attention on regulatory change and to consider managed-trade demands only in those sectors that appear impossible to crack otherwise—that is, where sectoral divides are weak or absent, where actors on the American side are relatively unified, and where the United States is sufficiently competitive to benefit.

RICE AGRICULTURE AND SMALL RETAIL

Rice agriculture and small retail served as the chief social bases of postwar conservative rule for some forty years—from the 1950s into the 1990s. The two sectors survived decades of double-digit, industry-led growth, demographic change that was nearly as rapid, and international liberalization pressures that only mounted with time. In the economic recession of the 1990s, however, small business began to be squeezed out of the coalition, while agriculture's place in conservative politics became ever more secure.

First, the political bottom line: together, the two sectors supplied some three-quarters of the LDP vote in the 1950s and nearly one-half in the late 1980s. The relative contributions of each sector have been roughly comparable over time. The two sectors owe their electoral clout not only to their numbers but also to their high turnout, stable conservative support over time, organizational strength, and bloc-like voting behavior. On all counts, they stand in contrast to the urban majorities, who are less likely to vote, less interested in or involved in organized politics, and whose party/candidate preferences are weak and volatile over time.

There are additional similarities between the two sectors. First, each has a powerful ministry advocate—MAFF in the case of agriculture, and MITI's Small and Medium Enterprise Agency (SMEA) for small business. Both are major players in bureaucratic politics. The SMEA is on equal terms with other MITI bureaus that are more devoted to developmental policies (i.e., it is not outclassed by divisions that oversee high-growth/high-tech sectors).[9] Second, each is politically well organized. Organizational structure is not perfectly analogous—that of agriculture is highly concentrated and pro-LDP, while that of small business is more fragmented and politically split—but there is no reason to believe that the small-business split would make the LDP less sensitive to the sector's demands. (Indeed, one could well argue the opposite.) Third, each sector has strong, entrenched public support, not least among urban consumers; this support is strongest and most obvious for rice agriculture, given the importance of rice as Japan's staple food and as a locus of the country's cultural identity, but holds also for small retail and its importance in everyday neighborhood life.[10] Fourth, in terms of international pressure, the United States was at least as aggressive in demanding rice-market liberalization as in pursuing retail reform. I describe each sector in more detail below.

Agriculture

To an overwhelming extent, Japanese agriculture remains predominantly rice agriculture. Even today, rice is grown by more than 80 percent of Japan's four million farm households, occupies half of Japan's farmland, and provides one-third of its agricultural income. Agriculture has been rationalized largely through the spread of part-time farming (now 90 percent of the total), rather than through the exit of inefficient farmers. The average farm size in Japan today is just over two acres—virtually the same as in the 1930s. The logic is both economic and political: small-scale rice farming remains economically rational for individual farmers (if not for the sector or economy as a whole), and farmland consolidation would erode the political base of the LDP and the jurisdictional base of MAFF.

Ninety-nine percent of farmers are members of the agricultural cooperatives, the JA. Total JA membership, more than nine million today, is increasing despite agricultural decline, making it the largest mass-membership organization in Japan. Rice farmers have profited from two state policies in particular: a virtual ban on rice imports (partly lifted in 1993, as will be explained below) and a state-set rice price that is some seven to twelve times comparable prices on the world markets.

Small Retail

Small retail constitutes by far the largest and most politically active subcategory of small business. Like agriculture, small retail engages about 8 percent–9 percent of the labor force today, with about four million workers in each. Of the 1.3 million retail businesses in Japan in 1987, small businesses accounted for 970,000, including 704,000 single-shop operations (Patrick and Rohlen 1987, 339). In 1982, the number of retail stores per capita was 75 percent higher in Japan than in the United States, while the value-added per employee was 28 percent less. Stores with one or two employees accounted for just 14 percent of sales but 60 percent of all stores (Upham 1996, 278–279; see also Riethmuller 1994a, 131–143). Small-retail numbers have expanded over the postwar era, particularly from the early 1970s. The primary reason for this growth is state protection, and the primary reason for protection is the sector's electoral importance for the LDP.

Small-business organizations, unlike those of farmers, are not combined under a single peak association. Instead, hundreds, even thousands, have proliferated. Minshu Shōkōkai (or Minshō, for short), an organization for small businesses that has close ties to the Japan Communist Party (JCP), has enjoyed particular success, notably in undergirding decades of Communist Party dominance of Kyoto city politics (see Krauss 1980, 383–424; see also Calder 1988a, 200, 344–345). Local chambers of commerce and shopping-district (shōtengai) associations tend to be much closer to the LDP.

Small retail has been served by a range of subsidies—mostly in the form of low-interest loans—that expanded over the rapid-growth period even as similar loans to big business rapidly declined.[11] The centerpiece of small-retail support, however, has been the Large Scale Retail Store Law (Daikibo kouri tenpo hō), which created entry barriers for large retailers seeking to open new shops.

The Large Scale Retail Store Law was introduced in 1973 to replace the Department Store Law (Hyakkaten hō) of 1956 (originally passed in 1937). According to Kusano Atsushi (1992, 228), MITI had no plans of its own to introduce new legislation, but the Socialists and Communists had picked up new small-retail support in the 1972 election. The LDP therefore stepped up its efforts to win back the sector by demanding that the Department Store Law be enhanced or replaced. The new law was entirely political in intent.[12]

Under the Large Scale Retail Store Law, local retailers themselves held the power to grant or deny permission for the construction of large retail stores ("large" being defined as 500 square meters or more).[13] Typically small shopkeepers, these local interests tended to be unsympathetic to large-store proposals, and many localities imposed effective bans on the establishment of new large stores. With no time limits set for the process, even successful applicants could be forced to wait ten years or more for approval.

Under the new law, the number of new large- and medium-sized stores dropped to a trickle. In 1974, retail shops with one or two employees accounted for 62.5 percent of the total number of retail stores. By 1988, their share had fallen by just 5 percentage points. Over the same period, large stores (with more than twenty employees) increased their share of the total by just 1.1 percentage points (Schoppa 1997, 236).

In sum, there are strong similarities across rice agriculture and small retail and thus reason to expect policy change to be similar for each. Indeed, if anything, there are a number of factors that might lead one to predict that agriculture, not small retail, would be the more likely to be sacrificed: the Uruguay Round (concluded in December 1993) was regarded by many in Japan, and notably by the media, as virtually synonymous with rice-market liberalization, whereas in the 1989–1990 Structural Impediments Initiative (SII), where the United States sought Large Scale Retail Store Law reform, retail was just one of a host of issues[14]; farmers' political power was a central target of the 1994 electoral reforms (which substantially reduced the malapportionment favoring rural districts); the policy payoff in agriculture depends more heavily on budget outlays than does small-business payoff, which depends more on entry barriers, making agriculture more vulnerable to attack amidst the ongoing recession and rapidly increasing state budget deficits; and, finally, small retail is largely a full-time occupation whereas farming is overwhelmingly part-time, meaning that retail cuts would hit constituents harder than equivalent cuts in agriculture. Nonetheless, the Japanese government has increased supports for rice even as it has cut those for small retail.

Policy Change in Agriculture

Subsidies for rice have continued to climb through the 1990s and liberalization efforts under the Uruguay Round resulted in "minimum access" rice imports—a "minimal" concession where imports are controlled by MAFF, which buys them at cheap international prices, sells them at expensive domestic prices, and uses the proceeds to fund additional farm subsidies (as will be discussed below).

Since the Uruguay Round's 1993 conclusion, moreover, the conservative commitment to agriculture has only increased. Returning to power in the spring of 1994, the LDP's first priority was to push through a massive ¥6.01 trillion (US$60 billion) farm subsidy package, which even MAFF found excessive.[15] Soon afterward, the party and the JA co-ops won a ¥685 billion bailout for JA losses in the housing-loan companies (jūsen) debacle, Japan's version of the U.S. savings and loan crisis. They were even able to mask the political motivations behind the bailout somewhat by having it labeled a "contribution" (zōyo) (Nihon Keizai Shimbun 20 February 1996, 1).[16] In 1997, the Ministry of Finance organized a study group to consider ways to reduce the growing state budget deficit. Although the ¥6.01 trillion in post–Uruguay Round farm subsidies was one of the reasons the group was formed in the first place, in the end it recommended cuts in defense and official development assistance (ODA) rather than touching the farm grants (Nihon Nōgyō Shimbun 23 February 1997, 1).

Some analysts argue that the 1995 scrapping of the old Food Control Law

(Shokuryō kanri hō), which had been in place since 1942, and the introduction of the new Staple Food Law (Shokuryō hō, or Shin shokuryō hō) promise at last to free up the farm sector. The new law has won praise as "drastic deregulation" and an important step toward rehabilitating Japanese agriculture (*Nihon Keizai Shimbun* 30 October 1995, 2).[17] This author, however, takes a slightly different view. Although recent agricultural policy reforms are important and have achieved a great deal, their nature has often been mischaracterized and overstated. Specifically, market liberalization has progressed domestically, but not internationally. Domestic market liberalization does not mean deregulation. MAFF has redefined its control over the rice economy (via reregulation) but it has reduced that control only marginally.

The new Food Supply Law has five main features:

1. MAFF's role as a direct participant in the rice economy has been reduced. Government purchase of rice is now limited to foreign rice imported under the Uruguay Round minimum-access arrangement and domestic rice for stockpiling (food security) purposes.

2. In place of the old system of "government-controlled rice" (*seifu mai*) and "semi-controlled rice" (*jishu ryūtsū mai*) distribution routes, under which 20 percent–30 percent of rice ended up being sold through an illegal black market (*yami-gome*), the new law established a new set of routes. The first is for "government rice" (*keikaku ryūtsū mai*), including both the government-controlled rice, which the government itself buys from the farmers, and semi-controlled rice, which licensed buyers purchase from the farmers. The second is for "voluntary-marketed rice" (*keikaku-gai mai*), which farmers and the JA cooperatives are now permitted to sell directly to retailers and wholesalers. The major significance of this shift is that, after deciding it could not eliminate the black market, MAFF decided to "recognize" and legalize the market, thereby bringing it under ministerial oversight.

3. Japan's rice reserves are to be increased to 1.5 million tons. This change reflects, above all, the experience of 1993–1994. A 25 percent shortfall in the 1993 rice harvest led to shortages on the legal markets and spectacular price increases on the black market. The prices of the most popular varieties shot up nearly threefold, with would-be sellers withholding their stock in the hope of further increases, and with pundits describing the confusion as the "*Heisei kome sōdō*"—the "rice riots of Heisei (post-1989) Japan."

4. Rice-production control, formerly ad hoc in nature, has been incorporated into the legal framework. Coercive measures, such as withholding subsidies from areas that do not fulfill their reduction quotas, have been abolished. Concern remains, however, that the text of the law leaves room for informal pressure, particularly from JA.

5. Most significantly, the law provides for substantial deregulation of rice

retailing. This appears to be the single most consequential measure of the new law. Prospective retailers are no longer required to apply for permission to enter the market but need only register with the Food Agency. By all accounts, this is no small change. Registration applications are being approved almost automatically. The number of stores selling rice is projected to triple. By the end of 1996, the number of retail rice outlets had already reached 175,600, nearly twice the number in existence the previous year (*Japan Agrinfo Newsletter* August 1997, 2). Many analysts have remarked upon the new "warring states period" (*sengoku jidai*) in the rice trade and anticipate that the number of wholesalers and rice specialty shops will plummet (*Asahi Shimbun* 2 April 1996, 9).[18]

With the exception of retail, however, the new law is a clear case of reregulation. While the new Staple Food Law has significantly liberalized retail trade, in the areas of production and distribution, the *Shūkan Tōyō Keizai*, for example, dismisses the MAFF-proclaimed "deregulation" as a "big lie." Instead, the new law constitutes a "new form of control from above [. . .]. MAFF has introduced new, clever mechanisms" ("Nōkyō to nōsei" 1996). Price controls remain on rice. With domestic rice prices that are at least ten times higher than international prices, production control to limit rice supplies remains essential. MAFF withdrawal from production control has been matched by JA's advance. Indeed, one common criticism of the new law is that it simply represents a shift "from government food management to JA food management" (Nōsei Jānarisuto no Kai 1996, 14; Ouchi and Saeki 1995). Again, 99 percent of Japan's farmers are members of the JA (which is closely involved in national agricultural policy making and implementation), and its co-ops overwhelmingly dominate rice distribution and marketing. Overall, the new law represents far more an accommodation to long-term changes in the agricultural economy than a positive program for reshaping it.[19]

MAFF handling of rice imports since 1993 is also best characterized as reregulatory and of limited significance for market opening. In December 1993, under the auspices of the Uruguay Round negotiations, Japan agreed to a U.S. offer of a "minimum access" formula for rice imports: Japan would import 4 percent of its rice demand in 1995, increasing the share to 8 percent by the year 2000, with renegotiation to follow. Although the market-opening deal is a clear case of managed trade both in terms of who sells to Japan and how the imports are handled (i.e., via state trading), the United States and GATT (General Agreement on Tariffs and Trade) accepted this as a step toward complete liberalization. The results, however, have proven disappointing for would-be rice exporters.

MAFF's Food Agency holds the responsibility for importing rice, and the import system will remain "state trade until the very end" (*aku made kokka bōeki*) in the words of one agency bureaucrat (Saitō 1995). And while the agency is required to buy rice from abroad, it is not required to sell it to Japanese consumers. The problem is that selling foreign rice (*gaimai*) at anywhere near international prices would mean stiff new competition for domestic producers. Instead, the government decided to set artificially high prices on imported rice, at just under the prices for domestic rice. It is no surprise, then, that very little foreign rice has appeared in the table-rice market. Consumer preferences may be one problem, but the more immediate issue is that wholesalers earn little profit in the foreign-rice trade and thus have no incentive to expand their operations. As a result, although rice imports are mostly of table-rice quality, they are being diverted into processing (e.g., rice crackers), food aid for developing countries, and even animal feed. Of the 940,000 tons imported in the 1995–1996 fiscal year, for instance, 38 percent was used for processing, 31 percent for animal feed, and 13 percent for overseas food aid. Just 7 percent was sold as table rice. The remainder (11 percent) lies in storage.[20] Thus, imported rice is rarely available in retail establishments, even as rice retail is booming in a newly liberalized environment.

Under the minimum-access agreement, Japan has had to import increasing shares of foreign rice even as domestic production (the 1993 shortfall excepted) has continued to exceed demand, leading to mounting rice surpluses. An increasing share of the backlog is of foreign origin. Between 1995 and 1997, Japan imported 920,000 tons of rice; just 200,000 tons of this had been sold by May 1997. Over 700,000 tons of this rice (about half from the United States) remains in government warehouses. Between the fall of 1996 and the summer of 1998, Japan's total rice stock jumped 40 percent to 3.7 million tons, with imports constituting at least 1 million tons (*Asahi Shimbun* 26 July 1998). The new Staple Food Law was billed as introducing market principles into rice agriculture—that is, to allow prices to reflect the laws of supply and demand. These numbers make it clear that, as yet, the attempt has failed.[21]

In early 1999, Japan converted its rice import policy from minimum access to tariffication, which was the original U.S./GATT demand. It did so not because the United States demanded it, but because MAFF bureaucrats determined that tariffication would allow Japan to import even less rice. In effect since April 1, 1999, the tariff amounts to ¥351.17 per kilogram. On the basis of current import prices, this translates to a tariff of 300 percent–400 percent.[22] The new policy has drawn little opposition from Japanese farm interests, who cite consumer loyalty to high-quality domestic rice. They are doubtless also calmed by the high tariff rates. The price of rice imports ranges from ¥60 to ¥100 per kilogram, but with the tariffs added it costs more than every "brand rice" in Japan except one—Uonuma Koshihikari, which is grown in a single village in northern Niigata prefecture and is the most expensive rice in Japan. This means that for the time being there is a virtual ban on imports (*Nikkei Ryūtsū Shimbun* 6 April 1999; *Nikkei Weekly* 21 April 1999).

The United States has protested the high rates and the methods used to calculate them. It has not, however, lodged a formal complaint with the WTO, perhaps for fear of jeopardizing its current market share. Rumors abound that the United States has negotiated a secret market-share agreement under the new arrangement, just as it allegedly did in 1993, for half of the minimum-access market.[23]

Policy Change in Retail

If the Big Bang is the most dramatic expression of the new deregulation movement, regulatory change in retail is perhaps the most surprising. Protection of small retail, in contrast to that of agriculture, has declined dramatically as a result of the reform, and then abolition, of the Large Scale Retail Store Law over the past decade. The 1990 reforms to the law returned the authority to grant large-store operating permits from localities to MITI and the application approval process was limited to a maximum of eighteen months.[24] As a result, the number of large-store openings jumped from 132 in 1989 to 617 in 1990. Subsequent openings declined somewhat (following an initial burst of pent-up demand), but exceeded 2,000 in 1995 and 1996, falling to 1,928 in 1997 (*Sankei Shimbun* 15 April 1997, 1; unpublished MITI data 1998). Meanwhile, the number of small retailers fell by 6.6 percent between 1991 and 1994, with the 1994–1997 drop expected to be similar (*Nihon Keizai Shimbun* 27 February 1998). The Japan Retailers Association (Nihon Kourigyō Kyōkai) predicts that small retail numbers will drop 30 percent by 2010 (*Nikkei Ryūtsū Shimbun* 10 March 1998).

No major new subsidies were introduced to compensate for the Large Scale Retail Store Law relaxation. The only new package—for shopping-district revitalization, computers, parking facilities, and other physical improvements—provided just ¥10 billion per year (Ministry of International Trade and Industry 1997, 50). In a 1997 interview, a MITI official specializing in small business agreed that the amount was both minuscule and insufficient compared with what rice farmers received (again, US$60 billion over six years) in compensation for a far less significant market opening.[25]

The reforms have provoked cries of distress from small retailers that "our neighborhood stores will collapse" (*Yomiuri Shimbun* 15 March 1997, 1). Surveys show declines in small-business numbers and growing vacancy rates in small-business districts.[26] Contemplating these changes, even the *Nihon Keizai Shimbun* felt moved to quote from Karl Polanyi's *The Great Transformation* on the destructive forces of the market and the need for society to set limits on its power (*Nihon Keizai Shimbun* 12 May 1997, evening edition).[27]

As MITI moved toward further relaxation of the Large Scale Retail Store Law with new reforms in 1992 and 1994, even some big-business beneficiaries thought this was adding insult to injury. In late 1993, when the abolition of the law was being considered by a study group reporting to Prime Minister Hosokawa Morihiro, leading chain stores and supermarkets made no calls whatsoever in support of that policy. One large retailer was quoted as saying, "It would be unwise to provoke small- and medium-sized retailers by touching the Large Scale Retail Store Law, which [now] has little impact" (*Nihon Keizai Shimbun* 15 December 1993, evening edition). And despite its early enthusiasm for reforming the law, MITI itself grew ambivalent about further relaxation, given that changes to date seemed to be working (*Shūkan Daiyamondo* 11 October 1997, 40–42).

Not surprisingly, small retailers have defected from the LDP in droves. An *Asahi* survey on party preferences by sector, conducted just after the October 1996 House of Representatives (Lower House) election, found that on a preference scale ranging from –6 to +12, the LDP's scores were as follows: farmers, 6.0; small business, 3.8; commercial labor, –1.8; industrial labor, –0.5; and office/administrative workers, –4.5. The only score that was higher than the farmers' support for the LDP was a 6.5 given by office/administrative workers to the newly formed Democratic Party (*Asahi Shimbun* 24 October 1996, 9).[28] While small-business support for the LDP remained positive, in previous elections it had been approximately equal to farmers' support. Meanwhile, membership in the Communist-affiliated Minshu Shōkōkai is said to be surging.[29]

What do these changes mean for foreign exports? Needless to say, neither regulatory change nor market opening necessarily benefits U.S. interests. And there is concern that recent regulatory tightening will hurt U.S. exports.[30] Even so, Toys "R" Us—the very symbol of the U.S. market-opening drive in 1990—has become Japan's largest toy retailer. After opening its first store in Japan in 1991, it had established sixty-four branches by the end of 1997, with sales topping ¥100 billion (Tilton 1998, 166).[31] Gap, after opening its first branch in 1995, now has thirty-eight outlets nationwide. Starbucks is spreading faster in downtown Tokyo than in Manhattan. Eddie Bauer now has thirty outlets in Japan, while L.L. Bean has twenty (*Focus Japan* November 1998). Mail-order business is also booming, with foreign firms now holding 10 percent of that market. Major retailers like WalMart are also gearing up to enter the Japanese market. In office supplies, Office Depot and Office Max are rapidly expanding, having entered the Japanese market in 1997. They are staging aggressive discounting drives to break into a sector long dominated by Kokuyo Co., which controls more than sixty wholesalers and some twenty thousand outlets (*Nikkei Weekly* 3 May 1999).

For the overall economy, it appears that regulatory change in retail has had positive, if unspectacular, effects. The Organization for Economic Cooperation and Development (OECD) finds that Japan's retail prices have dropped around 1 percent annually since 1990. The Economic Planning Agency (EPA) finds that price declines have been appreciably stronger in sectors undergoing regulatory change than in those which are not (Organization for Economic Cooperation and Development [OECD] 1999, 38). As Lincoln and Tilton observe, *naigai* (domestic versus foreign) price disparities are a good indicator of protection, whether formal or informal. This slow, steady decline is a sign of progressive change—even if the decline starts from high levels even by Japanese standards (OECD 1999, 38; Tilton 1998, 163–164).

Explaining Change in the Two Sectors

How do we account for this new divergence between agricultural and small-retail policy? As summarized above, the sectors are similar in political clout, ministry representation, public attitudes, and external challenges.

The most striking difference between the two sectors lies elsewhere: their position in the overall economy, particularly vis-à-vis big business. From the perspective of big business, small-retail protection is considerably more zero-sum than that of agriculture. In the latter, concentrated producer gains from protection are balanced by diffused losses, born by millions of poorly organized, politically weak consumers. There are no Japanese agribusinesses scheming to enter the agricultural sector, and no foreign powers have ever threatened to target Japanese industrial exports in retaliation for agricultural protection. Food processing, the only significant agriculture-related industry, is highly concentrated, low in productivity by manufacturing standards, and the most protected of all manufacturing sectors in Japan.[32] Due to border protection and oligopolistic organization of the industry, this sector has easily passed on high input costs to consumers. In this way, food processing resembles Japanese industries that tolerate the protection of intermediate goods industries, such as concrete, steel, and petrochemicals, despite the fact that this protection substantially increases their production costs (see especially Tilton 1996).

By contrast, Japanese small retail has come under direct assault from powerful domestic retail interests, particularly from the late 1980s. The timing can be attributed in part to economic slowdown, and in part to the emergence of chain stores as the most dynamic force in Japanese retail. Significantly, these pressures *predate* the 1990 U.S. demand for Large Scale Retail Store Law change. In other words, Japan's inefficient distribution system was not an issue for the United States alone; it represented a huge opportunity for aggressive Japanese retailers—one that was all the more attractive in a time of increased competition and sluggish overall sales. This new generation of retailers was anxious to win new markets. While small retail gained or retained benefits under the old Large Scale Retail Store Law, the chain stores (especially mid- and large-sized stores) were bearing the costs of the law and were thus pressing for its reform. Convenience-store and supermarket chains like Seven-Eleven Japan, Lawson, and Itō-Yōkadō have been among the most dynamic and aggressive Japanese firms of the 1980s and 1990s (see Kawabe 1994; Yahagi 1994).

Convenience-store chains are owned by large corporations like Itō-Yōkadō and Daiei, the largest retail concerns in Japan (far outpacing the traditional leaders such as Mitsukoshi, Takashimaya, and Seibu). They have used their market power as leverage over wholesalers and are seen as the principal force behind the modernization of Japanese retail.[33] Recent retail innovations—driven especially by computerization—include the JIT (just in time) delivery system, high-tech distribution networks, VANS (value-added networks), EOS (electronic ordering system), and POS (point of sales) systems record-keeping.[34] As the number of mom and pop stores decline, they are replaced less by huge "super-stores" than by mid-sized stores, convenience stores, and specialty stores.

A supporting reason for change is that MITI itself was pressing for Large Scale Retail Store Law reforms from the late 1980s, again predating U.S. demands. In the summer of 1989, MITI proposed the abolition of all local regulations on retail-shop opening, but backed down in the face of opposition from prefectural governments. Around the same time, the EPA and the Administrative Reform Council also issued reports critical of the law. In 1989, two MITI advisory councils, the Industrial Structure Council and the Small and Medium Enterprise Policy Making Council, prepared for the ministry its "Vision for Distribution in the 1990s," which also called for a relaxation of the law's provisions. MITI initially planned to make a number of the regulatory changes in the fall of 1989, but after releasing the report to the LDP government, MITI took no action on the proposed revisions. For the first time since 1955, the LDP had lost control of the Upper House in the 1989 election and it was not anxious to risk making any changes to the Large Scale Retail Store Law. In light of the Lower House election scheduled for February 1990, LDP leaders intervened and asked MITI to hold off. MITI agreed and delayed its announcement of the reforms until three days after the elections (Kusano 1992, 161–194).

By 1990, however, Kusano Atsushi finds that the LDP was no longer mounting any resistance to these reforms, and that in the late stages of negotiations, party figures simply refused to meet with any small-business representatives. Business *zoku* (members of the so-called "policy tribes") within the party were divided between supporting small shops and supporting supermarkets and convenience stores. The more powerful among them, including Noda Takeshi, Watanabe Hideo, Mutō Kabun, and Tahara Takashi, tended to back the latter. While evidence concerning LDP preferences at this time is thin, it is clear that the LDP offered little defense of small-business interests against the attacks of big business, MITI, and the United States (Kusano 1992, chap. 5). Nor did LDP members publicly object to further Large Scale Retail Store Law changes by MITI in 1992 (see below, however, on the recent "backlash").

Finally, while the *timing* of the 1990s reforms can be partly attributed to U.S. pressure, which was considerable during SII, it was domestic pressure that made the reforms inevitable. Within the conservative coalition, LDP ambivalence was overpowered by MITI and large-retail commitment to reform. The latter enthusiastically, if tacitly, supported American pressure. After 1990, the United States put the Large Scale Retail Store Law on the back burner (although it still favored further relaxation), but the reforms to the law continued nonetheless. (Changes in 1992 and 1994 limited the application-processing period to one year, increased the floor-space definition of "large stores" from 500 to 1,000 square meters, etc.)

In the spring of 1998, retail reform went a step further—or backward, critics would say—with the abolition of the Large Scale Retail Store Law and the introduction of the new Law Concerning the Measures by Large Scale Retail Stores for Preservation of the Living Environment (Daikibo kouri tenpo ricchi hō). The new law, dubbed the "crown jewel of deregulation" by the *Sankei Shimbun*, was passed by the Diet in May 1998, and took effect in June 2000. In addition to specifying transparent store-opening procedures and a one-year time limit on the application-approval process, the law sets new restrictions on large stores in terms of parking, noise, and garbage removal (*Sankei Shimbun* 28 May 1998). In conjunction with this, the Law on Improvement and Vitalization in City Centers (Chūshin shigaichi kasseika hō) was enacted in July, providing ¥1 trillion of small-retail funding to support downtown shopping districts. The Ministry of Construction also prepared a third law, the Revised City Planning Law (Kaisei toshi keikaku hō), to allow local governments to restrict areas in which large stores may be opened. Together, the stated intent of these "three laws for town-building" (*machi-zukuri kanren sanpō*) is to shift the emphasis from economic protection of small retailers to a positive program of community development—one that includes large retail.

Large retail interests worry that the new laws mean a return to the old days. In early 1998, the small-business-dominated Japan Chamber of Commerce and Industry had a "terrible reaction" to the proposed Large Store Location Law and stepped up its lobbying of the LDP and MITI. Small-retail pressure resulted in the devolution of regulatory authority from MITI back to the localities, where small-retail power is most potent. "With [the changes], the group's influence was clearly written into the final draft of the law as vested interests crept into the process" (*Nihon Keizai Shimbun* 28 February 1998; see also *Asahi Shimbun* 12 March 1998 and Tilton 1998, 168).[35] That devolution, along with the strict new regulations on parking lots, garbage removal, and noise restrictions represent new hurdles for large stores and constitute more, not less, regulation.[36] As one large retailer put it, "the details of the new law are more severe than we had expected" (*Nihon*

Keizai Shimbun 27 February 1998, 13 May 1999).[37] Another observed that "the regulatory means have simply become more ingenious" (*Nihon Keizai Shimbun* 28 February 1998).[38] In support of this take on the law, the *Nihon Keizai Shimbun* quoted one local chamber of commerce member from Fukushima prefecture as saying, "Shifting authority to the localities is rather beneficial in that we can prevent disorderly store openings" (14 May 1999).

Still, it is easy to overstate the backlash. Despite the concessions they won, small retailers see the new law as a poor substitute for the old Large Scale Retail Store Law. They turned against the LDP in the July 1998 Upper House elections just as they had done in 1996. Although Prime Minister Hashimoto, along with the Japanese media, was confident of an LDP victory, in the end the party won just 25 percent of the vote. The loss came partly from small-business defection (one small-retail specialist at MITI believes this was the single most important cause of the LDP's poor showing) and more generally from dissatisfaction—especially among uncommitted voters who would be unlikely otherwise to turn out—with Hashimoto's weak, contradictory program for economic recovery.[39] And although the media has widely publicized the new (¥1 billion) funding to revitalize shopping districts, only 10 percent of the monies are in fact new. The remainder had already been appropriated. On balance, MITI officials seem to be committed to regulatory opening and claim to be more concerned about large-retail interests overpowering localities (with information, money, and so forth) than the converse.[40] More concretely, tens of thousands of large stores have opened over the 1990s, already making for a hugely changed balance of power in the sector. No regulatory tightening can reverse these changes.

FINANCE AND TELECOMMUNICATIONS REFORM

We have seen even more rapid regulatory change and market opening in the economically central sectors of finance and telecommunications. In finance, most striking are the new policies for restructuring the banking sector, which constitute a sharp break with the old MOF-dominated regime, and the Big Bang financial reforms begun in 1998, which significantly liberalize financial services, are primarily deregulatory, and reduce MOF powers. In telecom, dramatic changes have occurred in the long-distance and mobile markets, and may potentially occur in the local telephone market as well. The long-distance and mobile markets are characterized by rapidly declining prices and service improvements as a result of regulatory change and increased competition, including an influx of foreign firms and joint ventures. Nonetheless, the MPT retains firm control of the sector, even as MOF appears to be losing control of finance.

Why has telecom reform proceeded differently from that of finance? First, this variance is not in the degree of market opening—which is significant in both—but in regulatory *style*, despite many reasons to expect reforms to proceed similarly in the two sectors. Each has been under heavy and increasing international market pressures. Indeed, the two are the very definition of high-growth, high-technology sectors, where globalization is driven by not only political pressure but also by rapid technological change and international firms looking for new markets. Both sectors have been targeted by heavy U.S. (and EU) political pressure as well. Indeed, the pressure focused on telecom is probably even stronger than that on finance, given that external political pressure had minimal influence on the Big Bang reforms. Both sectors, further, are critically important to the ruling LDP, though less in terms of votes than financial contributions. In addition, each sector is marked by increasing sectoral splits: in telecom, fierce competition between the mammoth NTT and aggressive new upstarts, and in finance, a gap between strong and weak financial institutions that became unbridgeable with the banking crisis.

In explaining the divergent style of regulatory change, perhaps the chief reason is simply this: unlike MOF, the MPT has not been tarred by scandal or by massive policy failure. Nor was it punished in Prime Minister Hashimoto's administrative reforms, in which MOF was perhaps the biggest single loser. And powerful ministries tend to prefer reregulation to deregulation because the latter means, by definition, less control of the sector. In short, Steven Vogel's (1996) characterization of telecom reforms as reregulatory remains apt in the late 1990s, whereas regulatory change in finance has become largely deregulatory in nature.[41] To repeat: sectoral splits, driven by the emergence of maverick, competitive firms, mean the emergence of a domestic constituency for market opening. This we have seen in both telecom and finance (with the latter crippled by the banking crisis as well). At the same time, the decline of bureaucratic dominance favors deregulation and, arguably, accelerates the pace of change as well. This we see in finance alone.[42]

At the same time, it is important to stress that as foreign firms and joint ventures take root in the Japanese market—in telecom no less than in finance—both sectors are likely to become increasingly difficult for the ministry, or anyone, to control. These rapidly changing and internationalizing sectors are likely to move increasingly beyond the control of national policymakers. As Frieden (1991) and many others contend, convergence theory works a lot better for some sectors than for others.

MOF, the Big Bang, and the Financial Crisis

Vogel (1996, 1999a) argues that, even in the most dynamic and globalizing industries, governments are not necessarily overwhelmed by international market pressures. To the contrary, he finds that Japan's "national regulatory regime" is to manage liberalization, resist devolution of regulatory power, protect ministry discretion, and implement necessary reforms in a smooth and coordinated fashion.

In finance, MOF prided itself until recently on a record of zero bank failures since 1945. The ministry arranged private mergers or bailouts on a case-by-case basis for any troubled financial institutions. It strove to protect all financial institutions from failure and to thereby maintain public confidence in the overall financial system. MOF closely managed the process of regulatory reform, deliberately opting for slower, smoother, and more coherent policy change than in the United States. Policy reform was kept slow in order to persuade any dissenters to accept the changes, to arrange compensation packages, and to enable firms to prepare for the new conditions. "The ministry has orchestrated political bargains between industry groups—with market segmentation keeping the industry economically protected but politically divided—filtered its own agenda into the reform legislation, and continued to redefine the reform at the stage of implementation. MOF officials have not only dictated the pace (slow) and the quality (tidy) of policy change, but they have been powerfully influential in its content" (Vogel 1994, 220).

MOF retained this approach for as long as it could, but the banking crisis of the 1990s marked the beginning of the end for the old regime. By the early 1990s, a combination of loose monetary policy, lax ministry oversight, and an explosion of risky, high-stakes investment (especially in real estate and equities) made for a bad-loan problem impossible even for optimists to ignore. MOF stonewalled, however, and resisted major policy change until 1997, when it at last allowed several major financial institutions to fail. Earlier that year, the ministry had managed to save the Nippon Credit Bank by arranging capital infusions from healthy banks. It then tried to save Hokkaido Takushoku Bank and the Long-Term Credit Bank of Japan (LTCB) in the same manner, by arranging for mergers and providing financial assistance from the Deposit Insurance Corporation and the Bank of Japan. But faced with growing opposition from comparatively healthy banks, growing alarm from international investors and MOF's fiscal arm, and the sheer volume of nonperforming loans—with current estimates running at US$1 trillion or more—the old system simply no longer worked. The ministry was forced to ask the Diet to pass bills allocating public monies to liquidate failing banks and support comparatively healthy ones. Enacted in February 1998, the Emergency Measures Law for Stabilization of Financial Functions (Kinyū kinō anteika kinkyū sochi hō) allocated ¥13 trillion to improve the capital adequacy of healthy financial institutions (those with capital-asset ratios of 8 percent or higher) and in part to enable them to absorb insolvent institutions, while the Revised Deposit Insurance Law (Kaisei yokin hoken hō) allocated ¥17 trillion to protect the depositors of failed banks. But because these monies were nowhere close to being enough to deal with the crisis, the ministry also began courting foreign firms. Simply in order to survive, the sector requires the infusion of foreign capital and best-practices talent to restructure the sector in an already internationalized, intensely competitive industry. This restructuring has begun in earnest.

A stream of bribery, *sōkaiya* (racketeer) payoffs, *tobashi* (the practice by brokerages of shifting losses from one client to another with the understanding that the paper losses would be covered), and other corruption scandals, together with MOF mismanagement, have undermined the ministry's reputation and credibility and have led to its worst nightmare: loss of jurisdiction, dismemberment, and even renaming. For the first time in fifty years, the Bank of Japan Law was revised in 1998, granting the bank new autonomy from MOF. A new, independent regulatory body, the Financial Supervisory Agency (FSA), was established in June 1998 to oversee financial institutions. It took over the Securities and Exchange Surveillance Commission (SESC), which had been established in 1992 within MOF to monitor the securities industry. At the beginning of the decade, with the financial sector already weakened and scandal-ridden, MOF had been able to resist the creation of an independent securities regulator, creating the SESC under its own jurisdiction. But by 1998, it was no longer able to resist. The crisis had worsened by orders of magnitude. Opposition parties (especially the Democratic Party of Japan), emboldened by the LDP's defeat in the 1998 Upper House election, pursued an aggressively anti-MOF line to distinguish themselves from the LDP and attempted to exploit public discontent. Opposition parties also proved instrumental in overcoming LDP ambivalence and MOF opposition to establish the Financial Reconstruction Commission (FRC) in the fall of 1998.[43] The Commission is charged with overseeing the resolution of failed loans, financial-crisis management, and other supervisory work with the support of the FSA (see Asahi Shimbun Keizaibu 1998).

While some observers have expressed concern that the FSA (and FRC) would function as a vehicle of old-guard MOF policy, especially as many of its staff are seconded MOF officials, early practices suggest not. The agency forcibly nationalized one bank in November 1998 and fired the management. In another case, it agreed to support the merger of two troubled institutions only after they committed to substantial downsizing. It has been hiring up financial experts from the private sector (especially foreign securities firms) and building, even among outside observers, a reputation for smart, creative sleuthing (*New York Times* 17 September 1999).[44] In early 1999, Minister of State and FRC Chair Yanagisawa Hakuo publicly stated that he would like to see LTCB or Nippon Credit Bank—both of which were nationalized due to their debt problems—sold off to foreign institutions, arguing that this would promote restructuring within the sector. (In September 1999, it was decided that U.S.-based Ripplewood Holdings would in fact buy out LTCB. The agreement, signed by the two parties in February 2000, became the first sell-off of a nationalized financial institution.) Yanagisawa also made clear that he would "show no mercy" to banks that fail to meet restructuring pledges they made in order to receive government funding (*Japan Digest* 29 March 1999, 8–9).[45]

To be sure, the story is hardly one of total defeat for the ministry. MOF retains sole authority over taxation and the budget. Even in terms of financial regulation, a compromise was reached. Although the FSA was established as an independent agency, MOF was to retain authority in policy planning for bank failures and crisis management. How this division of labor will work in practice remains unclear. A recent article in the *Nikkei Weekly* comments, "This marks a significant victory for Finance Ministry bureaucrats in that it keeps the ministry's old discretionary regulation powers alive even as it sows the seeds of serious confusion later on" (26 April 1999; see also Mabuchi 1997).

Nonetheless, overall policy changes amount to a radical shift in MOF authority and policy toward troubled banks. Failing banks are no longer to be propped up with cross-subsidization or public funds but are to be liquidated, with public funds used to support only those on sound footing. This marks a huge decline in MOF's discretionary authority and a corresponding increase in the importance of formal, juridical regulation.

The Big Bang reforms constitute a similar shift. In November 1996, Prime Minister Hashimoto ordered MOF and other relevant government bodies to begin discussion on the Japanese version of the United Kingdom's Big Bang financial reforms with the basic goal of establishing "free, fair, and global" financial markets. Not incidentally, the administration also hoped to make the Japanese market competitive with New York and London and to reestablish Tokyo as the financial center of Asia. Hashimoto stacked his Administrative Reform Council with reformists and chaired it himself. Past deregulation and administrative reform efforts have often been bold in rhetoric but weak in substance. Those under Hashimoto have been the most substantive since the Rinchō administrative reforms implemented under Prime Minister Nakasone Yasuhiro (see e.g., *Nihon Keizai Shimbun* 8 December 1995; *Yomiuri Shimbun* 8 December 1995; Carlile and Tilton 1998, 76–110).[46]

In June 1997, reports outlining the proposed reforms were published. Among the most important measures: removing entry restrictions between banking, securities, and insurance; liberalizing insurance premiums and stockbroker commissions; liberalizing securities derivatives; easing the registration process for new securities companies; promoting an asset-backed securities market; deregulating new financial products and reforming the financial supervisory system for financial institutions; legalizing financial holding companies; and establishing new rules for transparency, accounting, acceptable business practices, and investor protection.[47] The reforms mark a clear transition from MOF's old, informal, collusive practices to new, formal, codified regulations—reregulation—as well as substantial deregulation. The changes undermine MOF's traditional regime of informal oversight over a segmented financial market. Henceforth, the industry will become less divided, more powerful, and more internationalized, while MOF policy will be less discretionary and more legalistic.

The Big Bang began on April 1, 1998, with the liberalization of foreign exchange transactions. To date, measures are being implemented on schedule. In December 1998, banks and insurance firms were allowed to begin selling over-the-counter investment trusts (similar to mutual funds in the United States). In the past, investment trusts have accounted for just 2 percent–3 percent of personal financial assets (which totaled ¥1.2 trillion in 1998), with bank deposits and cash comprising about 50 percent (*Nihon Keizai Shimbun* 30 March 1998, 24 November 1998). But there has been a surge of new interest as consumers look for better returns. (A ¥1 million bank deposit yields a measly annual return of ¥500 today.) Some analysts predict that investment trusts will grow to account for 10 percent of personal financial assets. This growth is expected to disproportionately benefit foreign firms. Many customers believe that foreign asset-management firms, in addition to their proven record in money management, are more trustworthy in terms of information disclosure ("Investment Trusts" 1999).

To encourage increased competition and more diversified products, MOF has introduced a series of new regulations on transparency, accounting formulas, insider trading, investor protection, and capital adequacy. Henry Laurence has aptly described a "race to the bottom" in Japanese (and British) deregulation as international financial markets struggle to become more competitive. On the other hand, he finds a "race to the top"—reregulation—to tighten disclosure laws, protect investor rights, and so forth (Laurence 1996). In short, the rules governing the financial sector have become more transparent and formal, with implementation expected to be more juridical than in the past. However, this sort of reregulation, far from enhancing ministry authority, promises to reduce it.

Once described as the "world's most powerful bureaucratic institution" (Pempel 1998, 66), MOF is perhaps the biggest loser in the administrative reforms and, in some ways, in the Big Bang as well. Not only has it lost its exclusive jurisdiction over banking and securities, but it has suffered perhaps the ultimate insult: MOF is to be renamed as the Zaimushō (tentatively to be called the Ministry of Treasury in English) in January 2001. At the same time, the financial industry, once highly segmented, is on its way to becoming more unified, powerful, and foreign-penetrated, further undermining the old order.

Nonetheless, MOF as a whole has grudgingly supported the Big Bang reforms. The continuing stock-market slump persuaded the ministry, along with stronger players in the financial sector, that the only path to recovery was to make the Tokyo market more accessible and attractive internationally by reducing sectoral barriers and increasing competition. Moreover, the yen, stock market, and economy—all flagging—made MOF's fiscal arm acutely aware that the inability and unwillingness of the Financial Bureau to fix the banking crisis was dragging down the overall economy. In this way, we can say that MOF came to accept the rearrangement of the existing financial policy regime. The ministry certainly did not want to be broken up, but it did know that policy had to change.[48]

Healthier elements of the financial sector have been among the reforms' most enthusiastic supporters, correctly seeing them as a means to expand their market presence. And even as some in the industry undoubtedly still have their heads in the sand, the crisis has provoked a remarkable candor among others. Consider the remarks of Kanzaki Yasuo, chairman of Nikkō Research Center:

> Why is reform of the financial industry spearheading Hashimoto's grand [deregulation] scheme? I can think of several reasons, not very flattering to the industry. First of all, the financial industry is regarded as—indeed is—one of the most heavily protected and regulated in Japan. Secondly, due partly to various recent scandals, the financial industry is among the least popular and least likely to receive public sympathy. Third, the industry has fallen far behind foreign competitors and the public is demanding better service from their bankers and brokers. Fourth, to revitalize the Japanese economy, restoring confidence in the financial industry is absolutely crucial (1997).

What will Big Bang reforms mean for other Japanese financial institutions, already weak and struggling to compete in an even tougher market? Some observers, notably Alicia Ogawa, Edward Lincoln, and Robert Litan, are not optimistic (Ogawa 1998; Lincoln and Litan 1998). While it is much too early to predict the winners and losers of the reforms, it appears likely that foreign firms and joint ventures will be prominent among the winners. As Iwata Kazumasa observes, "Foreign institutions have now in fact taken over the leading role in the Japanese Big Bang, overshadowing their local counterparts. The so-called Wimbledon phenomenon, the dominance of foreign players in Britain's financial markets after its own Big Bang, is becoming evident in Japan as well" (1999, 56). This, obviously, has made for a significant change in market outcomes already.

To date, foreign institutions have focused on mutual funds, foreign-currency deposits, and entry into the securities business. Morgan Stanley Dean Witter, for one, is betting that asset-backed securitization (e.g., mortgage-backed securities) in Japan will show the fastest growth of any market in the world (*Nikkei Weekly* 19 April 1999). Citibank has excelled in attracting foreign-security deposits. The number of its customers for foreign currency deposits grew 50 percent in 1997, and 39 percent in 1998 (*Nikkei Weekly* 5 April 1999).

The combination of the continuing recession, declining property values, and financial-sector reform has led to a surge of FDI into Japan. For years, foreign companies complained that it was too expensive to invest in Japan and that Japanese authorities made it very difficult for them to do so. Today, foreign firms are actively wooed by Japanese interests seeking both foreign capital and market skills. In fiscal year 1998, FDI into Japan by foreign companies more than doubled to a record high of US$10.95 billion. That by U.S. companies increased more than fivefold to US$6.6 billion. As expected, these increases were concentrated in finance.[49] Foreign concerns now account for nearly half of trading on the Tokyo Stock Exchange and have been buying up problem loans in bulk.

One of the principal means for foreign entry into the Japanese market is through alliances with and acquisitions of Japanese financial institutions. Recent examples include Bankers Trust's joint venture with Nippon Credit Bank, GE Capital's de facto acquisition of Tōhō Mutual Life Insurance, Salomon Smith Barney's 25 percent purchase of Nikkō Securities, and Merrill Lynch's hiring of more than two thousand employees and absorption of offices from the bankrupt Yamaichi Securities. In this way, *gaiatsu* can become *naiatsu* (internal pressure), gaining strength and arguably legitimacy in the process, and serving as a Trojan horse on behalf of continuing reform.

Indeed, it is FDI, not calls for managed trade, that has become the chief American irritant (in economics, at least) for Japanese nationalists today. Many worry that the economy will become hopelessly penetrated by outsider interests (ignoring at the same time that it is these outsiders who are propping up troubled Japanese firms). In 1998, LDP Secretary-General Nonaka Hiromu notoriously referred to these trends as the "second invasion of Asia." The Ripplewood Holdings takeover of LTCB drew charges of a "Jewish conspiracy" from the *Shūkan Post* (15 October 1999).[50] A short decade ago, of course, American alarmists were making similar charges against Japan. How times—and especially the rhetoric—have changed.

Still, these shifts should not obscure the huge investment imbalances that remain. American FDI in Japan is growing, but from a very low starting point. In 1996, it totaled US$6.6 billion (0.08 percent of gross domestic product), as compared to Japan's US$84 billion (1.4 percent of GDP) of investments in the United States. As of 1998, total FDI in Japan remained less than 1 percent of GDP, the lowest in the OECD (OECD 1999; Department of Commerce 1998). The same must be said of mergers and acquisitions (M&A). There was just US$2 billion of M&A investment into Japan in 1996, comprised mostly of buyouts by American firms of their Japanese venture partners. Compare this to a figure of US$60 billion in the United States for the same year (American Chamber of Commerce in Japan 1999, 14).

Nonetheless, and in conclusion, the old MOF regime is being toppled.

Whether these policy changes will revitalize the financial industry is an open question, but they have already weakened MOF, brought significant deregulation to the industry, and enabled a dramatically increased foreign market presence. Reregulation has occurred as well, but in a manner that has constrained, not enhanced, ministry power.

Telecommunications Reform:
Mobile, Long-Distance, and Local Services

Japan is the world's second largest telecommunications market, with annual revenues of US$110 billion in 1998. Far from being in crisis, telecom is one of the hottest, most dynamic industries in Japan today, projected to displace manufacturing as Japan's largest industry early in the next century. NTT overwhelmingly dominates the market, with 1997 revenues of US$77 billion (including those for NTT DoCoMo, the dominant cellular phone provider)—about eight times those of its nearest rival, DDI. Indeed, the NTT Group is the largest telecommunications company in the world, with 1997 revenues of US$7.6 billion—50 percent larger than AT&T ("The Global 500 Survey" 1998).[51] But its services are expensive and it is vulnerable to competition. High NTT usage fees have long been an irritant to foreign users, with the cost of leased lines as much as seven times higher than in the United States. Telecommunications equipment is typically 50 percent–400 percent more expensive in Japan than in the United States and telephone calls can be three times as expensive (Katz 1997).

Nonetheless, the market has seen important regulatory change and market opening in recent years as market segmentation has been eroded by technological and market changes, new providers have been allowed to enter, and NTT has been forced to scramble. The telecommunications market has come under strong international challenge from the United States (and the EU). For its part, the big-business federation Keidanren (Japan Federation of Economic Organizations) is said to be planning proposals modeled on the 1996 telecom deregulation in the United States, aimed at promoting competition and reducing NTT dominance.

What is probably the chief driving force, however, is the MPT's long and ongoing battle with NTT. Prior to its 1985 "privatization" (only one-third of the company's shares were sold off that year and the state retains majority control today), NTT was the dominant force in the sector as the monopoly carrier, the primary sponsor of research and development, and the de facto market regulator until the MPT won rights to the sector (see Vogel 1996). The two have been at odds ever since. The MPT has sought the breakup of NTT but the telephone giant managed to resist it for twelve years, until 1999. Moreover, the "breakup" deal that was finally worked out leaves the three new NTT entities under a single hold-ing company. NTT "family consciousness," according to the *Nihon Keizai Shimbun*, is unlikely to diminish (24 June 1999).

But even as the MPT's effort to break up the giant has been thwarted, the min-istry holds other levers, including licensing requirements, authority over price and service changes by NTT and its competitors (known as the new common carriers, or NCCs), and low-interest loans. The ministry has consistently used these levers to favor the NCCs, limit NTT power, and improve the sector's competitiveness overall. In doing so, it has both retained its regulatory authority over the sector and enabled the entry of new players, including foreign concerns.

MOBILE TELEPHONE SERVICES

One example of this power game is in the mobile telephone market. In the mar-ket's infancy, the MPT itself arranged a consortium of private firms (IDO Corporation) to compete with NTT, but using already available NTT technology. Faced with U.S. pressure to use Motorola technology, it then put together a second consortium led by DDI Corporation, which used the Motorola format. At first, DDI was assigned to the Osaka region, while IDO was assigned to Tokyo. Under continued U.S. pressure, the MPT pushed IDO to make investments in Motorola technology as well. Doing so both placated the United States and helped to reduce NTT dominance, preserving an MPT-brokered balance in the sector.[52]

In recent years, the number of cellular phone subscribers has exploded, jumping from two million in 1993 to nearly forty million in 1998. In 1994, NTT DoCoMo abolished the ¥100,000 deposit requirement and allowed sales of cel-lular phones in retail stores. Following heavy U.S. pressure that year, tight gov-ernment restrictions on transmission terminals lifted in 1995. As of May 1999, there were 42.5 million cellphones and 5.79 million Personal Handy Phone (PHS) subscriptions.[53] New cellphone competitors, notably J-Phone and TU-KA, have expanded aggressively and hold NTT DoCoMo to a 60 percent market share today.[54] Technological change has helped to drive the cellphone boom, with rapid improvements in miniaturization, battery life, and available func-tions, including e-mail capacity on the newest models (*Nihon Keizai Shimbun* 23 September 1998; *Japan Digest* 17 May 1999, 22). Perhaps even more impor-tantly, rate wars between cellphone providers have driven prices down rapidly. Between 1994 and 1996 alone, consumer prices in cellphones fell by more than 80 percent (OECD 1999, 86).

Young single people are increasingly likely to subscribe to mobile tele-phone services rather than install expensive fixed-line telephones at home (which require deposits of some US$800) (*Yomiuri Shimbun* 12 March 1999). Indeed, the new phones have started to have substitution effects. Since 1994, mobile subscriber growth has outpaced that of fixed-line service and the number of fixed lines (now sixty million) actually began to decrease in 1997 (OECD 1999, 86).

In 1997, mobile phone services generated revenues of ¥5.28 trillion, up 29.9 percent from 1996. To keep up with soaring demand, 1997 telecom industry investment totaled 10 percent of Japan's total capital investment—second only to Japan's electric power companies—and will increase further as the industry prepares for the next generation of cellphones. New investment is estimated to run to ¥1 trillion (Asano 1999, 7; *Nihon Keizai Shimbun* 22–23 September 1998). Given these rapid advances, Japan appears to be moving into the position of market leader. Although Europe is currently leading the cellphone market with a 50 percent market share, the next generation of cellphones (capable of transmitting sound, pictures, and high-speed data) will be marketed first by Japan, indicating that Japan is quickly becoming the technological leader in the industry (see *Nihon Keizai Shimbun* 22–23 September 1998).

The Long-Distance Market

We also find this combination of MPT objectives—managing competition and managing NTT—in the long-distance market. Over the past ten years, the average long-distance rate has fallen from an average of ¥400 to ¥100 for a three-minute call (*Japan Digest* 16 February 1998, 21). The cost of long-distance calls between Tokyo and Osaka declined by 77.5 percent—from ¥400 to ¥90 for three minutes—between April 1985 and February 1998 (OECD 1999, 84). Long-distance service has been shaken up by a range of new upstarts—notably, Tokyo Telecommunication Network (TTNet), DDI, IDO, and Japan Telecom—and by rate wars as the new competitors fight it out. The MPT has consistently allowed the upstart NCCs a rate advantage over NTT, although the amount of this advantage has fallen over time.[55] The NCCs' share of the market has risen steadily with time and now amounts to about one-third of domestic long distance, and one-half of calls between Tokyo, Osaka, and Nagoya. But even this success has been difficult to achieve because of NTT reluctance to provide adequate and reasonably priced interconnections (Arthur D. Little, Japan 1998, unpublished report). And even today, the United States charges that interconnection fees are as much as eight times the charges in the United States and that they are well above NTT's actual costs (*Nihon Keizai Shimbun* 22 September 1999).

Local Markets

The MPT is now challenging NTT on its strongest ground: the local telephone market, in which it holds more than a 99 percent market share. Consider, for example, the MPT plans for wireless local-service networks. The wireless local service will connect homes and offices to relay bases and regional phone networks like cellphones but without being mobile. It will provide an alternative to NTT's hard-wired local phone service monopoly and is expected to be cheaper to install and maintain, and fast enough for Internet use. To give NCCs a head start on establishing service, the MPT will bar NTT from entering the wireless local phone market until April 2001. KDD, DDI, and Japan Telecom, in addition to several foreign firms, are expected to enter the market (*Nihon Keizai Shimbun* 16 September 1998; *Japan Digest* 21 September 1998, 21).

NCCs and other firms are also mounting a strong challenge to NTT in the Internet service market. Due to high NTT access charges and the difficulties of using Japanese-language computers (PC penetration is only 25 percent in Japan), Internet use in Japan remains low—perhaps 15 percent of the population. NTT currently charges ¥10,000 per month (plus ¥2,800 in line charges) for unlimited Internet access. The MPT had pushed for the giant to offer lower prices, but NTT refused and the ministry countered in July 1999 by allowing other providers direct connections to NTT's main distribution frames—bypassing NTT's metered (and costly) switchboards. This move is expected to cut the cost of the rivals' Internet connections by half. *The Japan Digest* concludes that the MPT's decision is "a major step toward breaking NTT's longtime monopoly on the so-called last mile—connections into homes and offices" (26 July 1999, 22).

NTT is facing a similar challenge in the fiber-optic market, aimed at servicing data transmission (projected to exceed voice-transmission traffic early in the next decade). Cross Wave Communications leases fiber-optic networks from KDD (the leading international-telephone-service provider, having had a monopoly until 1989) and offers data transmission services for half of the NTT rates. KDD itself plans to lay a new loop through the Tokyo business district. PowerNets Japan, an association of local telecom companies established by ten local electric utilities, has 160,000 kilometers (km) of local fiber-optic networks—more than NTT. The Tokyo Electric Power Company (TEPCO) is planning a 5,000-km fiber-optic network in Tokyo.[56] Among foreign firms, MCI WorldCom and British Telecommunications are laying their own fiber-optic lines in downtown Tokyo (*Japan Times* 3 July 1999; *Japan Digest* 20 August 1999, 24, and 30 August 1999, 24).

The battle between NTT and its competitors is raging in political circles as well, although as yet this battle is entirely underground—unlike the more visible political fights in agriculture and retail, where large, mobilized vote blocs are at stake and openly assert their interests. The NCCs argue in particular that NTT should be broken up because its monopoly control of local phone networks allows it to charge its competitors exorbitant access fees and to restrict interconnection. A new group of telecom *zoku* is emerging in the Diet that have allied themselves with newcomer firms against the older *zoku* who are tied to NTT. A great deal of money is said to be involved in the fierce political battle now being waged over this sector.[57] Just as we saw in retail, then, telecom's sectoral split has manifested itself inside party politics as well.

In addition to cash payoffs from the industry, some politicians also hope that the impressive price reductions that have resulted from market opening will win them new consumer support. While it is true that in cases like rice, imported rice may be cheaper (though not by much, after passing through MAFF's hands), rice accounts for a tiny and declining share of household budgets (about 1 percent today). Moreover, opinion surveys demonstrate that consumers *increasingly* support the protection and subsidization of domestic rice and strongly prefer Japanese rice to foreign varieties, whether short-grained or not.[58] In telecom markets, however, consumer services of different companies are more or less identical and there is little love lost between consumers and the reigning firms, NTT and KDD, which have long been known for their high prices. Everyone (as the line goes) may love a farmer, but the telephone company is an altogether different matter. And again, price declines in the market have already been substantial.

While the numbers are less dramatic than in finance, there have been surges of telecom FDI into Japan as well (*Nikkei Weekly* 17 May 1999). DDI has entered into a tie-up with the Canadian carrier Teleglobe to provide international services. In order to enter the domestic long-distance market, AT&T and British Telecommunications have each bought 15 percent stakes in Japan Telecom, the third-largest domestic long-distance carrier (see *Nikkei Weekly* 26 April 1999). At the same time, NTT has entered into a linkup with AT&T, and, in what some describe as a hostile takeover, the British firm Cable and Wireless plc defeated NTT in a bidding war for control of IDO. Last fall, MCI WoldCom began investing several tens of billions of yen to begin laying a 100-km fiber-optic network in Tokyo. Altogether, as of July 1999, there were thirty-two Type 1 telecommunication carriers (of some one hundred thirty-five total) in which foreign investors held stakes of 5 percent or higher. Eight of these were wholly foreign owned (*Look Japan* October 1999, 14).[59]

As in finance, transnational alliances in telecommunications are producing a new domestic constituency for continued market opening, both domestic and international (see Kusano 1999). Although not as quickly as in finance, market segmentation is breaking down and foreign firms are becoming players in the market. But as yet—and in contrast to MOF—the MPT remains in control of regulatory reform and market change. The ministry maintains an informal consultation process in allowing new business entrants. For instance, it continues to use "public interest" standards in evaluating applications of potential market entrants but refuses to provide clear information on the minimum requirements for receiving a license. While processing periods for license applications are limited to one to two months, the MPT's discretion can result in lengthy delays (OECD 1999, 88).

The ministry also allows favored firms advance access to new markets (e.g., the wireless local telephone market discussed above). Similarly, it has allowed these firms to cut rates below those of NTT (although this lever disappeared in 1998, when the MPT converted the approval system for rate changes into a notification system).[60] Finally, such firms have also been favored with low-interest loans channeled through the Japan Development Bank to fund R&D and infrastructure projects. The MPT, long a student of MITI and MOF administrative guidance and industrial policy, has learned its lessons well enough to outlast its teachers.

CONCLUSIONS—IMPLICATIONS FOR U.S. POLICY

So, is Japan really "changing its ways"? This brief review has found that in certain sectors it is. One of these sectors has been a core support base for LDP rule. Others have been at the center of economic and industrial policy. Nonetheless, a combination of sectoral splits, foreign pressure, and, in finance, near collapse has combined to drive significant regulatory change and market opening.

Current trends in Japan mean unprecedented opportunities for further market opening and regulatory change. The prolonged recession has shaken people's faith in the old economic formulas and has prompted even some insiders to call for change. The LDP has survived the recession—despite the common belief that growth was a necessary condition for its rule—but it has lost its position of unassailable dominance. The bureaucracy has been tarred by scandals that have undermined its credibility and authority. Free-market economists like Nakatani Iwao and Takenaka Heizō are pressing for system-wide deregulation and the media has endorsed much of their agenda. In addition, maverick producers and retailers are exploiting the climate of deregulation fever, making them key constituents for continued change.

In this atmosphere, the United States is well advised to join in the chorus and call for continued regulatory change. Kusano (1999) argues that the United States has concentrated its efforts on sectoral, market-opening negotiations, viewing deregulation as an important but longer-term process. This chapter suggests that deregulation, and sometimes reregulation, have already brought trade gains in the short term. The U.S.-Japan Enhanced Initiative on Deregulation and Competition Policy, begun in 1997, should most definitely be continued. In sharp contrast to managed trade, deregulation has become a fully legitimate policy option in Japan—and one endlessly discussed in the press today. Related to that point, U.S. advocacy of deregulation would seem less likely to provoke divisions on the home front as well. Divisions among the United States Trade Representative (USTR), Department of Commerce, State Department, and Congress remain a chronic weakness in U.S. trade policy. If anything, managed-trade tactics have exacerbated these divisions.

And, as it happens, the United States is extremely competitive in the sectors subject to the greatest regulatory change and market-opening pressures today—finance and telecommunications. Moreover, ongoing FDI into Japanese markets promises to serve as a Trojan horse in support of continued change.

This chapter has focused on inter-sectoral differences because these differences, although often overlooked, are striking, and because variation facilitates the building and testing of theories. The "successes" reviewed here—finance, telecommunications, and retail—suggest that, above all, sectoral splits count. All are marked by weak or declining concentration or cartellization, accelerated by the crisis in the financial sector and by the emergence of new, competitive forces in retail and telecommunications. Seconding Schoppa, I think the general message for the United States is clear: look for domestic allies, but do so especially among low-cost producers dissatisfied with the status quo. Potential exporters to Japan would do well to look for interest-based conflicts among producers and to cultivate ties with maverick figures like Daiei's Nakauchi Iwao, Tokyo Steel's Iketani Masanari, Summit's Arai Shinya, Softbank's Son Masayoshi, or rice trader Kawasaki Isonobu. However, the importance of "participation expansion" and other "synergistic strategies" can be easily exaggerated. First, efforts to draw consumers into the process have failed or backfired. To the degree that they are organized at all, consumers have generally been as protectionist as producer groups. Second, maverick producers such as those mentioned above were not created by U.S. strategy. They were there all along, and they were far from silent. The international politics that matter most have centered on transnational alliances, not participation expansion per se. Ongoing restructuring, the emergence of upstart firms, and the increased presence of foreign firms and joint ventures mean new cracks in Japanese markets and new domestic support bases for further market opening.

Allies can sometimes be found in the ministries as well. They exist at the MPT, which seeks to counterbalance NTT dominance by encouraging rival firms, and at MOF, which has opted (with great reluctance) to back substantial reforms in a context of sheer economic necessity. At MITI, the fierce battles between the "internationalist" and "nationalist" factions ended a long time ago with the victory of the former (Johnson 1982, chaps. 7, 8). Today, the battle is over deregulation versus reregulation, with the line of division more generational than bureau- or personality-based. This divide is at least as important as the one Schoppa highlights: that between an older, more deferential generation of bureaucrats who began their careers in the early postwar era and a new generation that regards Japan as the United States' equal (Schoppa 1999).

At the same time, the rice case provides a cautionary example of what can go wrong and what the United States should not do. It reminds us that regulatory change does not always mean liberalization, and that partial market opening need not beget further market opening (i.e., by creating a constituency for further change). Interestingly, the case also suggests that Japan is not always averse to managed trade. Just as Japan was pronouncing its much-publicized rejection of Clinton's managed-trade demands in the automobile sector (1993–1994), it was in fact concluding a managed-trade deal for rice. Finally, the rice case shows that consumer preferences themselves may sometimes constitute Japan's ultimate "non-tariff barrier," where even complete liberalization would promise few gains for U.S. exporters. In sum, one is hard-pressed to find a trade issue where the United States has tried harder and achieved less. More careful analysis of Japanese politics and markets might help in avoiding such mistakes in the future.

Generally, managed trade is deeply unpopular in Japan today and has become harder to justify in the WTO era. Even successful managed-trade efforts may well cause more harm than good over the long term, undermining both Japanese trust in the United States and the credibility of the WTO (Schoppa 1997; Abels 1996). Given these dangers, any such demands should be made sparingly and be targeted at sectors where the potential benefits are great, where U.S. actors are unified, and where the market is unlikely to open otherwise (i.e., pronounced sectoral splits are absent). They should not be wasted on sectors like rice, which is of limited economic importance to the United States and politically central in Japan. Amazingly, the USTR continues to list rice as among the U.S. economy's "best export prospects."

To be sure, none of this is meant to deny what pluralists like E. E. Schattschneider and I. M. Destler have long argued: American trade politics is strongly shaped by the demands of domestic lobbies, not just the probability or significance of changes in trade outcomes. Similarly, one of the more elementary truths of political science is that reelection-minded politicians tend to want their results in the short term. Given this, concern over long-term credibility with Japan or the WTO may not rate high in Congress. Nonetheless, U.S. negotiators would be well advised to consider the "supply-side" factors this chapter has stressed—i.e., the sectoral conditions of Japanese markets—in addition to those on the demand side.

The approach developed in this chapter is incomplete. It is necessary to think more about how to measure sectoral splits, what causes them, and how much of a split is necessary to make a sector ripe for change. As a first effort, I have chosen to study sectors marked by extreme variations in sectoral split—virtually none in rice, large and growing splits in retail and telecom, and an enormous divide in finance—and where there are clear successes and clear failures with respect to regulatory change and market opening—successes in retail, telecom, and finance, and relative failure in rice. Likewise, successful regulatory change and market opening were seen in the case faced with the least external political pressure (the Big Bang in finance) and failure in the case with the most (rice). I have also focused on successes in parts of the economy that one would imagine to be most sacrosanct: core LDP support bases (small retail), and strategic sectors at the center of developmental/industrial policy (finance and telecom).

To refine the argument on market opening, the literatures on industrial organization and endogenous tariff theory may help. Obvious areas for exploration include the speed of technological change, production-cost spread within the sector, degree of market organization and cartellization, degree of product differentiation, and the strength of industry associations. Adding new cases to obtain further variation is also necessary to test these ideas.[61]

In addition, while this chapter has argued that consumers are too weak and poorly organized to have much influence on policy, the same cannot be said of intermediate (corporate) consumers. Some analysts claim, for instance, that large manufacturing firms, seeking cheaper and more flexible access to capital, have been a critical constituent for financial-sector change. Intermediate users are also likely to figure large in MITI's attempt to deregulate the electric power industry, mobilizing big users like the steel and auto industries against that powerful, highly-concentrated but high-cost sector.[62]

The domestic focus taken here should also be integrated with Schoppa's focus on international tactics. As argued above, market-opening tactics should target not the broad public but producer interests vulnerable to division. They can be used, for instance, to break united fronts and widen market splits—as the United States tried, for instance, in the 1986 semiconductor dispute, where it cited some Japanese firms but not others in anti-dumping complaints (see Krauss 1993, 272).[63] Japan, for its part, proved adept at exploiting American divisions over the Clinton administration's demands for managed trade (Schoppa 1997, chap. 9). Interesting new work focused primarily on U.S. trade policy has moved in this integrative direction.[64] This, indeed, was Putnam's prescription in his seminal 1988 article on two-level games, where he stressed that any two-level theory of international negotiations must be rooted in a theory of domestic politics.

NOTES

1. Council on Foreign Relations position papers by Ira Wolff and Jim Southwick send much the same message as Lincoln's 1998 "Whither Trade Policy with Japan?" Lincoln amplifies this thesis in his *Troubled Times: U.S.-Japan Trade Relations in the 1990s*, in which, it should be noted, he identifies finance as "the one partial exception to the general thesis of weak deregulation and structural change" (1999, 199).

2. Lincoln (1999) notes that from 1996 to 1997, the number of regulations rose by 223, for a total of 10,983. As of March 1998, the Prime Minister's Office found that the number had increased to 11,117 (*Tokyo Shimbun* 2 March 1999).

3. An analogous argument is made by Anne Krueger (1996), who finds that the most effective defense against protection is division within the industry in question.

4. "Participation expansion" refers to attempts by one country to increase participation in the other's decision-making process and, more generally, to "increase public awareness of a problem and sometimes serve as a rallying point for the unorganized and ignored general public" (Schoppa 1993, 372). The other tactic Schoppa studies—alternative specification—is intended to influence domestic politics by linking and building on policy proposals already in existence. While participation expansion is attempted in four of the cases Schoppa studies, alternative specification is used in only one: U.S. demands for change in Japanese land laws (characterized by Schoppa as a partial success). Here, the United States linked proposals by Japanese scholars that had previously been considered only in isolation. In Schoppa's research on the Framework Initiative negotiations conducted by the Clinton administration, the main tactic under review is managed trade (Schoppa 1997, chap. 9; 1999).

5. As many political economists argue, consumers are many in number and tend to derive only small benefits from organizing to attack high prices, whereas the producers are relatively few in number, tend to be organized already, and derive considerable individual (not only collective) gains from protection.

6. Consumer-movement specialist Patricia Maclachlan confirms that consumer groups remain wary of deregulation and market-opening moves today (Personal communication, October 1999).

7. For an early, important analysis of transnational alliances in U.S.-Japan trade negotiations, see Kusano (1983).

8. In a 1997 study, the American Chamber of Commerce in Japan (ACCJ) finds that of forty-five major U.S.-Japan trade agreements since 1980, just thirteen were producing the intended results, while ten were judged a complete failure. "Numbers-based" deals are among the most highly rated. The 1986 and 1991 semiconductor agreements were scored 8 out of 10, as was the 1995 auto parts agreement. These sectors, like rice agriculture in this chapter, are marked by high producer organization and minimal sectoral divides.

9. Personal interviews with various MITI officials (Tokyo, 1996–1997).

10. For excellent survey data on public opinions on rice, see the Prime Minister's Office "Public opinion surveys concerning the roles of food and farm villages" (*Shokuseikatsu, nōson no yakuwari ni kansuru yoron chōsa*, various years). Among other things, the surveys show high and increasing shares of respondents saying they will buy expensive domestic rice even if cheaper foreign imports are available. On consumer attitudes toward retail stores, see the 1997 "Public opinion survey concerning small-retail shops" (*Kouri tempo tō ni kansuru yoron chōsa*, also from the Prime Minister's Office). In terms of small, independent stores, for instance, the most important qualities are, in descending order, a friendly atmosphere, good service, low prices, and good merchandise quality. (Elsewhere, consumers stress convenience, familiarity, and trustworthiness as important small-store qualities.) For superstores, price is most important, while for specialty stores, product quality is the critical factor. Sensibly, consumers have different preferences with respect to different kinds of stores. Consumer groups are neutral or opposed to retail deregulation in general. See, for example, the *Nikkei Ryūtsū Shimbun* interview with the secretary-general of Shufuren, the Housewives' Association (29 May 1997). A second source is Maclachlan (Personal communication, October 1999).

11. Most of these subsidies are funded by the Fiscal Investment and Loan Program, Japan's "second budget" (see Noguchi 1995).

12. MITI official Amaya Naohiro confirms that the Large Scale Retail Store Law had little to do with improving competitiveness in the sector: "The Large Scale Retail Store Law is the result of a compromise between supermarkets, which insist on free competition, and small retailers, who insist on the restriction of competition. It is impossible to find the consistency in such a law in terms of economic rationality. It is a product of a power balance between [existing] supermarkets and small retailers" (as quoted in Kusano 1992, 113).

13. The owner of a proposed store was required to submit documents detailing the proposed opening date, floor space, operating hours, required vacation days, and so forth to the local Commercial Activities Adjustment Boards. These boards were formed within local Chambers of Commerce, which are dominated by small-retail interests, and their purpose was to evaluate the proposals and to submit recommendations to MITI.

14. Schoppa (1993, 1997) identifies public investment, the distribution system (including the Large Scale Retail Store Law), land policy, exclusionary business practices, and *keiretsu* organization as the main U.S. targets in SII. By February 1990, the United States had made more than two hundred separate demands.

15. In the words of an *AERA* article, the agricultural budget is "overflowing" (*dabutsuki*). Twenty to 30 percent of the annual agricultural budget is being passed forward into the next fiscal year budget because there is more than can be used ("Hitori ichimanen" 1997, 24–27). The *Sankei Shimbun* reports that the ¥6.01 trillion figure was fixed via political pressure, without any needs-based calculations. It claims that ¥10 billion was added to the initial ¥6.01 trillion in order to give the appearance that the amount was worked out through such calculations (*Sankei Shimbun* 29 April 1997, 1).

16. No other financial institutions received state funds. The decision to bail out JA was of course politically motivated. Interestingly, the details were worked out by MAFF and MOF via administrative guidance (*kanryō shudō*), circumventing the LDP. One MAFF bureaucrat said, "If they learned of the figures beforehand, we thought they'd just get upset and make it difficult to resolve" (*Nihon Keizai Shimbun* 21 February 1996, 1).

17. For an English-language analysis that takes a similar line, see Francks (1998).

18. From March 1996 to March 1997 alone, the number of rice specialty shops fell from 30,000 to 20,000 (*Nihon Keizai Shimbun* 7 January 1998). The most enthusiastic entrants into rice retailing have been supermarkets and, in particular, convenience stores. The Japan Rice Market projects that the number of rice wholesalers will drop from three hundred down to seventy or eighty, with perhaps just ten active nationwide (*Nikkei Ryūtsū Shimbun* 3 November 1998).

19. Personal interviews with MAFF officials (May 1997) confirm this assessment.

20. For details, see *Nihon no kome shijō* (8 April 1998) on the website of the Japan Rice Data Bank <http://www.japan-rice.com>. Storage costs for rice are expensive—an annual cost of ¥12,000–¥14,000 per ton.

21. The emphasis on farmer protection and local production continue today. Although even MAFF calls their goals unrealistic, JA and the LDP are now pushing for new farm-income supplements to increase Japan's overall food self-sufficiency, which is now 42 percent, to 50 percent by 2010 (*Nihon Keizai Shimbun* 18 December 1998).

22. Japan calculated the tariff on the basis of the price differences between imported

and domestic rice during 1986–1989. The main imports at that time were low-cost Thai rice used for processing, hence the high tariff. Tariffs will remain at the same level for 2000 (*Nikkei Weekly* 22 February 1999). One Democratic Party member charges, "While there was no debate in the Diet or among the Japanese people, the tariff levels were forced through by an agreement between the ruling party, the bureaucracy, and some of the agricultural organizations [i.e., JA]." The MAFF vice-minister agrees, saying, "Public debate was insufficient" (*Yomiuri Shimbun* 28 March 1999).

23. While no Japanese government member has been willing to confirm this agreement (illegal under GATT/WTO), an official at South Korea's Ministry of Agriculture and Forestry openly acknowledged that the United States forced exactly the same deal on Seoul. But unlike Japan, South Korea subsequently said, in essence, "What deal?" and bought the cheapest foreign rice it could find (from China and India) to fulfill its minimum-access obligations (Personal interview, Seoul, November 1997). By contrast, the United States has consistently held a 50 percent share of Japan's rice imports, despite the fact that American rice is neither the cheapest (Indian, Thai, and Chinese rice being the least expensive) nor the most highly regarded foreign rice in Japan (Australian *koshihikari* is according to the *Nihon Keizai Shimbun* 2 June 1999). All of these details add credence to the allegation. (On rumors of the 1999 renewal, see *Mainichi Shimbun* 24 March 1999).

24. The reforms also increased permissible hours and days of operations for large stores and improved the transparency of the approval process.

25. Personal interview with a MITI official (Tokyo, August 1997).

26. The *Yomiuri* article summarizes a survey by the Japan Chamber of Commerce and Industry that found that in the mean *shōtengai* (small-business district) of 57 stores, 5 are now vacant. The vacancy rate has risen fairly steadily over the 1990s—from 4 percent of stores in 1990 to 8.1 percent in 1997 (*Asahi Shimbun* 30 May 1998). In one-third of the *shōtengai* today, 10 percent or more of the shops are vacant ("Shōtengai hōkai" 1998).

27. The article continued to say, "Before a further relaxation of Large Scale Retail Store Law restrictions results in only large-scale retail stores and the destruction of local shopping districts, Japan must prepare a system that can function as a self-defense mechanism for society."

28. Note that the survey measures support for parties, not particular candidates; in Japan, party support tends to lie below candidate support, especially for the "hard vote" of farmers and retailers. Finally, regarding the Democratic Party's high level of support, note that new parties in Japan often undergo booms in their early days, doing particularly well among the "floating vote"—those voters unattached to particular parties or candidates.

29. Personal interview with MITI officials (Tokyo, June 1997); Personal interview with Kikkawa Takeo, Professor, Tokyo University (Tokyo, June 1997).

30. Personal interview with representative of the American Chamber of Commerce in Japan (ACCJ) (Tokyo, May 1999).

31. In fiscal year 1998, despite the recession and the shrinking number of Japanese children, the chain registered a 17 percent sales increase (*Japan Digest* 10 May 1999, 15).

32. At the close of the Tokyo Round, the effective rate of protection for agriculture as a whole was 20 percent; that for food processing was 50 percent (Riethmuller 1994b, 3–6).

33. In 1998, Lawson (owned by Daiei) was raided by the Fair Trade Commission of Japan for violating the Antimonopoly Law. Reportedly, the chain has used its market

power to wrest concessions from wholesalers. Daiei itself was targeted for squeezing Suntory on beer prices (*Asahi Shimbun* 18 August 1998).

34. The Japanese press has been full of reports on the "convenience store wars" and "*kakaku hakai*" (price destruction) in the 1990s (see, e.g., *Shūkan Tōyō Keizai* 27 March 1996, 13 April 1996, and 31 August 1996). The latest conflict (fall 1999) is a "beer war" provoked by 9 percent price cuts at Seven-Eleven, with other chains following suit. Despite such conflicts, and in contrast to department stores and supermarkets, convenience stores have increased profits and sales throughout the 1990s and earned a reputation for being "recession-proof." In fiscal year 1998, all convenience-store chains posted sales gains of 4 percent–6 percent and all except Lawson posted record pretax profits (*Japan Digest* 27 April 1998, 10; *Asahi Evening News* 12 April 1999). For background, see Kawabe (1994) and Yahagi (1994).

35. In the House of Representatives, since the 1994 introduction of the single-member district system (*shō senkyoku sei*), politicians have become even more beholden to local interests, including the well-organized small retailers (*Nihon Keizai Shimbun* 14 May 1999). In the House of Councillors (Upper House), too, backbenchers are wary. As one put it in early 1998, "We're facing [Upper House] elections this summer and it is taboo to oppose the views of the large vote base of the small retailers" (*Nihon Keizai Shimbun* 28 February 1998).

36. The United States has publicly complained about the new law for these reasons (*Japan Digest* 31 May 1999, 24).

37. Some chains are racing to open currently planned stores before the new laws take effect (e.g., Toys "R" Us and Itō-Yōkadō). In recent years, the Life Supermarket chain has been opening around twenty large supermarkets annually but expects the figure to fall to around five under the new law (*Sankei Shimbun* 28 May 1998).

38. Daiei's Chairman Nakauchi Isao similarly comments: "We demand the creation of transparent and fair procedures that will keep the new law, which scatters authority among the local governments, from becoming as restrictive as the Large Scale Retail Store Law" (*Sankei Shimbun* 28 May 1998).

39. Personal interviews with MITI officials (Tokyo, July 1998 and November 1999). Still, it is unclear, stated the same MITI official a year later, that the LDP made the wrong choice in pushing through the law. "If the LDP had failed to pass the law, that would have been damaging, too." See also Curtis (1999, 208–210).

40. But even MITI bureaucrats are unsure what the new law will mean. When I asked another official whether he thinks the Law Concerning the Measures by Large Scale Retail Stores for Preservation of the Living Environment (Daikibo kouri tenpo ricchi hō) marks a return to the old Large Scale Retail Store Law, he replied, "As a MITI bureaucrat, no, but as a political scientist, yes." Personal interviews with MITI officials (Tokyo, June and November 1999).

41. For a related argument focused on television broadcasting, especially the emerging cable and satellite markets, see Noble (2000). Like Japan's telephone markets, broadcasting is marked by rapid technological change, market desegmentation, and internationalization pressures, but the MPT nonetheless remains the gatekeeper mediating the impact of these forces on Japanese markets.

42. Jennifer Holt Dwyer suggests that asset-specificity—higher in telecom than

finance—is likely also relevant. This hypothesis deserves more attention but is beyond the scope of this paper (Personal communication, July 1999).

43. On the centrality of opposition parties in driving MOF restructuring, see Hiwatari (2000).

44. Moreover, there is at least an informal understanding that seconded MOF bureaucrats will remain at the FSA rather than be returned to the ministry (Personal interviews with MITI and MOF officials, Tokyo, June and August 1999).

45. On the other hand, Yanagisawa was succeeded in the fall of 1999 by Ochi Michio, who has distanced himself from Yanagisawa and appears likely to take a more moderate approach.

46. Beginning in 1981, the Second Provisional Commission on Administrative Reform, known as the Second Rinchō (Rinji gyōsei chōsakai), and subsequent administrative reform efforts succeeded in introducing a program to reduce Japan's growing budget deficit without tax increases as well as to privatize a range of government-owned corporations. See especially Carlile (1998, 77–85).

47. Note that the "Big Bang" moniker is something of a misnomer. Regulatory changes do not occur all at once but are spaced out over three years (1998–2000). More importantly, they constitute only the latest—although much more thoroughgoing—measures in a series of financial reforms that date back two decades. Desegmentation and internationalization of the industry began in the 1970s, foreign ownership of bank shares has been increasing since the early 1990s, and by some accounts, financial reforms have been largely deregulatory since the early 1980s.

48. Personal interview with MOF official (Tokyo, June 1999).

49. While inward foreign direct investment in fiscal 1998 was double that of fiscal 1997, at the same time, outgoing investment by Japanese firms fell to US$42.6 billion in fiscal 1998, representing a 20 percent drop from the previous year (*Journal of Commerce* 28 May 1999).

50. At the same time, a 1999 editorial in the *Nikkan Kōgyō Shimbun* observed that Japanese firms in the United States now employ 2.9 million workers, almost as many as are unemployed in Japan. "It's time for foreign capital to help create jobs [in Japan too]" (as quoted in Doi 1999).

51. At the time of the *Fortune* survey, NTT and NTT DoCoMo were a single company. For more on NTT's reorganization, see the *Nihon Keizai Shimbun* series "NTT saihen" (24–26 June 1999).

52. Note that today, Motorola is focusing less on hardware, where its competitive advantage has eroded, than on phone units (*Japan Digest* 16 November 1998, 23).

53. PHS initially boomed when introduced in 1995, but is being eclipsed by advances in cellphone technology, price drops, and density/coverage of transmitter stations. Unlike PHS, cellphones can also be used in moving cars or trains. Japan's Telecommunication Technology Committee forecasts that by 2010, the number of mobile phone subscribers will reach eighty-one million—two of every three Japanese people. That is double the current total, with a majority likely to use a new generation of digital phone service that will become available in 2000. The council predicts that the total mobile phone market will reach ¥9.3 trillion a year and employ 563,000 people (*Japan Digest* 4 October 1999, 24).

54. This is the smallest advantage NTT holds in the different telephone markets (NTT

market share is about two-thirds of the domestic long-distance market and virtually the entire local market). Even with cellphone rates deregulated today, competitors offer lower rates, although DoCoMo continues to lead in the provision of new services.

55. The ministry has used selective access to cheap capital as an additional lever. As Vogel observes, "Ironically, at a time when MITI was publicly renouncing industrial policy, the MPT was just getting started" (1996, 138).

56. TEPCO also plans to develop a low-cost Internet service using transmitters mounted on its utility poles, with prices again one-half those of NTT for unlimited access.

57. Personal interview with MITI official (Tokyo, June 1999).

58. See the Prime Minster's Office surveys cited previously.

59. Type 1 licenses are for facilities-based carriers; Type 2 licenses allow carriers to use Type 1 carriers' facilities.

60. Although the notification system is more lenient, it still leaves room for MPT discretion. Almost immediately following the regulatory change, for instance, the ministry intervened against DoCoMo rate-setting on behalf of competitors (*Asahi Shimbun* 6 January 1999).

61. On industrial organization, see especially Tilton (1996) and Uriu (1996). Unrelated to Japan but conceptually rich is Bowman (1989). On endogenous tariff theory, see especially Nelson (1988) and Magee, Brock, and Young (1989).

62. Personal interview with MITI official (Tokyo, October 1999).

63. In 1995, the United States used a similar tactic, threatening to target Japanese luxury-car exports with punitive tariffs. That time, MITI and the industry remained united and denounced the Clinton administration's heavy-handedness and managed-trade agenda.

64. For several recent efforts to combine two-level game analysis with models of domestic politics (drawn heavily from collective action and endogenous tariff theory), see Milner (1997); Gilligan (1997); and O'Halloran (1994).

BIBLIOGRAPHY

Abels, Tracy M. 1996. "The World Trade Organization's First Test: The United States–Japan Auto Dispute." *UCLA Law Review* 44(2): 467–525.

American Chamber of Commerce in Japan. 1994. *U.S.-Japan Trade White Paper*. Tokyo: American Chamber of Commerce in Japan.

———. 1997. *Making Trade Talks Work: Lessons from Recent History*. Tokyo: American Chamber of Commerce in Japan.

———. 1999. *U.S.-Japan Trade White Paper*. Tokyo: American Chamber of Commerce in Japan.

Asahi Shimbun Keizaibu, ed. 1998. *Kinyū dōran* (Financial disturbance). Tokyo: Asahi Shimbunsha.

Asano Ayu. 1999. "Mobile Nation." *Look Japan* (October): 7.

Bowman, John. 1989. *Capitalist Collective Action: Competition, Cooperation, and Conflict in the Coal Industry*. Cambridge, England: Cambridge University Press.

Calder, Kent C. 1988a. *Crisis and Compensation: Public Policy and Political Stability in Japan, 1949–1986*. Princeton, N.J.: Princeton University Press.

———. 1988b. "Japanese Foreign Economic Policy: Explaining the Reactive State." *World Politics* 40(4): 517–541.

Carlile, Lonny E. 1998. "The Politics of Administrative Reform." In Lonny E. Carlile and Mark C. Tilton, eds. *Is Japan Really Changing Its Ways?: Regulatory Reform and the Japanese Economy*. Washington, D.C.: Brookings Institution Press.

Carlile, Lonny E., and Mark C. Tilton, eds. 1998. *Is Japan Really Changing Its Ways?: Regulatory Reform and the Japanese Economy*. Washington, D.C.: Brookings Institution Press.

Curtis, Gerald L. 1999. *The Logic of Japanese Politics: Leaders, Institutions, and the Limits of Change*. New York: Columbia University Press.

Doi Ayako. 1999. "Foreign Investment: Trading Places All Over Again." *Japan Digest* (19 July): 24.

Department of Commerce, Trade Compliance Center. 1998. *1998 Japan Country Reports on Economic Policy and Trade Practices*. Washington, D.C.: Department of Commerce.

Encarnation, Dennis J. 1992. *Rivals Beyond Trade: America Versus Japan in Global Competition*. Ithaca, N.Y.: Cornell University Press.

Francks, Penelope. 1998. "Agriculture and the State in Industrial East Asia: The Rise and Fall of the Food Control System in Japan." *Japan Forum* 10(1): 1–16.

Frieden, Jeffry. 1991. "Invested Interests: The Politics of National Economic Policies in a World of Global Finance." *International Organization* 45: 425–451.

Gilligan, Michael J. 1997. *Empowering Exporters: Reciprocity, Delegation, and Collective Action in American Trade Policy*. Ann Arbor, Mich.: University of Michigan Press.

"The Global 500 Survey." 1998. *Fortune* (3 August): F-25.

"'Hitori ichimanen' zeikin yamawake: Nōgyō yosan musaboru riken kōzō" (Ten thousand yen in taxes for each person: The structure of agricultural budget greed). 1997. *AERA* (28 April–5 May): 24–27.

Hiwatari Nobuhiro. 2000. "The Reorganization of the Japanese Financial Bureaucracy: The Politics of Bureaucratic Structure and Blame Avoidance." In Takeo Hoshi and Hugh Patrick, eds. *Crisis and Change in the Japanese Financial System*. Boston: Kluwer Academic.

"Investment Trusts: Banks Race to Join New Market." 1999. *Focus Japan* (April): 2–5.

Iwata Kazumasa. 1999. "The Japanese Big Bang and the Financial Crisis." *Japan Review of International Affairs* 13(1): 55–73.

Johnson, Chalmers. 1982. *MITI and the Japanese Miracle: The Growth of Industrial Policy, 1925–1975*. Stanford, Calif.: Stanford University Press.

Kanzaki Yasuo. 1997. "Deregulation in Japan: Big Bang or Big Whimper?" Paper delivered at the Woodrow Wilson International Center for Scholars, The Smithsonian Institution, in Washington, D.C., on March 7. Transcript taken from the Internet: <http://www.nmjc.org/jiap/dereg/papers/kanzaki.html>.

Katz, Richard. 1997. "Japan's Self-Defeating Trade Policy." *Washington Quarterly* (March): 153–181.

Kawabe Nobuo. 1994. *Sebun-irebun to keieishi: Nichibei kigyō, keieiryoku no gyakuten* (Seven-Eleven and management history: The reversal of management power between Japanese and American companies). Tokyo: Yūhikaku.

Krauss, Ellis S. 1980. "Opposition in Power: The Development and Maintenance of Leftist

Government in Kyoto Prefecture." In Kurt Steiner, Ellis S. Krauss, and Scott C. Flanagan, eds. *Political Opposition and Local Politics in Japan*. Princeton, N.J.: Princeton University Press.

———. 1993. "U.S.-Japan Negotiations on Construction and Semiconductors, 1985–1988: Building Friction and Relation-Chips." In Peter B. Evans, Harold K. Jacobson, and Robert D. Putnam, eds. *Double-Edged Diplomacy: International Bargaining and Domestic Politics*. Berkeley: University of California Press.

Krueger, Anne O. 1996. "Implications of the Results of Individual Studies." In Anne O. Krueger, ed. *The Political Economy of Trade Protection*. Chicago: University of Chicago Press.

Kusano Atsushi. 1983. *Nichibei orenji kōshō: Keizai masatsu o miru atarashii shiten* (U.S.-Japan orange negotiations: A new perspective on economic friction). Tokyo: Nihon Keizai Shimbunsha.

———. 1992. *Daitenhō: Keizai kisei no kōzō: Gyōsei shidō no kōzai o tou* (The Large Scale Retail Store Law: Questioning the structure of economic regulation). Tokyo: Nihon Keizai Shimbunsha.

———. 1999. "Deregulation in Japan and the Role of *Naiatsu* (Domestic Pressure)." *Social Sciences Japan Journal* 2(1): 65–84.

Laurence, Henry. 1996. "Regulatory Competition of Financial Market Reform in Britain and Japan." *Governance* 9(3): 311–341.

Lincoln, Edward J. 1998. "Whither Trade Policy with Japan?" (A Position Paper for the CFR Study Group). New York: Council of Foreign Relations.

———. 1999. *Troubled Times: U.S.-Japan Trade Relations in the 1990s*. Washington, D.C.: Brookings Institution.

Lincoln, Edward J., and Robert E. Litan. 1998. "The 'Big Bang'?: An Ambivalent Japan Deregulates Its Financial Markets." *Brookings Review* 16(1): 37–40.

Mabuchi Masaru. 1997. *Ōkurashō wa naze oitsumerareta no ka: Seikan kankei no henbō* (Why was the Ministry of Finance cornered?: Transformation in government-bureaucracy relations). Tokyo: Chūō Kōronsha.

Magee, Stephen P., William A. Brock, and Leslie Young. 1989. *Black Hole Tariffs and Endogenous Policy Theory: Political Economy in General Equilibrium*. Cambridge, England: Cambridge University Press.

Milner, Helen W. 1988. *Resisting Protectionism: Global Industries and the Politics of International Trade*. Princeton, N.J.: Princeton University Press.

———. 1997. *Interests, Institutions, and Information: Domestic Politics and International Relations*. Princeton, N.J.: Princeton University Press.

Ministry of International Trade and Industry. 1997. *Chūshō kigyō hakusho* (SME white paper). Tokyo: Ministry of International Trade and Industry.

———. 1989. *90-nendai no ryūtsū bijon* (A vision for distribution in the 1990s). Tokyo: Research Institute of International Trade and Industry (Tsūshō Sangyō Chōsakai).

Nelson, Douglas. 1988. "Endogenous Tariff Theory: A Critical Survey." *American Journal of Political Science* 32(3): 796–837.

Noble, Gregory. 2000. "Let a Hundred Channels Contend: Technological Change, Political Opening and Bureaucratic Priorities in Japanese Television Broadcasting." *Journal of Japanese Studies* 26(1): 79–109.

Noguchi Yukio. 1995. "The Role of the Fiscal Investment and Loan Program in Postwar Japanese Economic Growth." In Hyung-Ki Kim et al., eds. *The Japanese Civil Service and Economic Development: Catalysts of Change.* Oxford: Clarendon Press.

"Nōkyō to nōsei" (Agricultural co-operatives and agricultural policy). 1996. *Shūkan Tōyō Keizai* (20 April): 72.

Norville, Elizabeth. 1998. "The Illiberal Roots of Financial Regulatory Reform." In Lonny E. Carlile and Mark C. Tilton, eds. *Is Japan Really Changing Its Ways?: Regulatory Reform and the Japanese Economy.* Washington, D.C.: Brookings Institution Press.

Nōsei Jānarisuto no Kai (Society of Agriculture Policy Journalists), ed. 1996. *Sutāto shita shin shokuryō hō* (The new Food Supply Law has started). Tokyo: Nōsei Jānarisuto no Kai.

Ogawa, Alicia. 1998. "Japan's Banks More Vulnerable to Competition from Abroad." *Japan Quarterly* (April–June): 10–14.

O'Halloran, Sharyn. 1994. *Politics, Process, and American Trade Policy.* Ann Arbor, Mich.: University of Michigan Press.

Organization for Economic Cooperation and Development. 1999. *OECD Review of Regulatory Reform in Japan.* Paris: Organization for Economic Cooperation and Development.

Ōuchi Tsutomu and Saeki Naomi, eds. 1995. *Seifu shokkan kara nōkyō shokkan e: shin shokuryō hō o tou* (From government food control to Nōkyō food control: Questioning the new Food Supply Law). Nihon nōgyō nenpō 42. Tokyo: Nōrin Tōkei Kyōkai.

Patrick, Hugh T., and Thomas P. Rohlen. 1987. "Small-Scale Family Enterprises." In Yamamura Kōzō and Yasuba Yasukichi, eds. *The Political Economy of Japan: Vol. 1, The Domestic Transformation.* Stanford, Calif.: Stanford University Press.

Pempel, T. J. 1998. *Regime Shift: Comparative Dynamics of the Japanese Political Economy.* Ithaca, N.Y.: Cornell University Press.

Putnam, Robert D. 1988. "Diplomacy and Domestic Politics: The Logic of Two-Level Games." *International Organization* 42(3): 426–460.

Riethmuller, Paul. 1994a. "Where do Japanese Consumers Buy Their Food?" *Agribusiness* (March–April): 131–143.

——. 1994b. "Food Processors, Retailers, and Restaurants: Their Place in the Japanese Food Sector." *Pacific Economic Paper* (Australia-Japan Research Centre) no. 230: 3–6.

Saitō Takao. 1995. "Kome bijinesu to shōsha" (The rice business and trading companies). *Shokun* (May): 133–142.

Schoppa, Leonard J. 1993. "Two-Level Games and Bargaining Outcomes: Why Gaiatsu Succeeds in Japan in Some Cases But Not Others." *International Organization* 47(3): 353–386

——. 1997. *Bargaining with Japan: What American Pressure Can and Cannot Do.* New York: Columbia University Press.

——. 1999. "The Social Context in Coercive International Bargaining," *International Organization* 53(2): 307–342.

"Shōtengai hōkai" (The collapse of small-business districts). 1998. *AERA* (10 August): 42–47.

Tilton, Mark. 1996. *Restrained Trade: Cartels in Japan's Basic Materials Industries.* Ithaca, N.Y.: Cornell University Press.

———. 1998. "Regulatory Change and Market Opening in Japan." In Lonny E. Carlile and Mark C. Tilton, eds. *Is Japan Really Changing Its Ways?: Regulatory Reform and the Japanese Economy*. Washington, D.C.: Brookings Institution Press.

Upham, Frank. 1996. "The SII and the Japanese Retail Industry." In Suzanne Berger and Ronald Dore, eds. *National Diversity and Global Capitalism*. Ithaca, N.Y.: Cornell University Press.

Uriu, Robert M. 1996. *Troubled Industries: Confronting Economic Change in Japan*. Ithaca, N.Y.: Cornell University Press.

Vogel, Steven K. 1994. "The Bureaucratic Approach to the Financial Revolution: Japan's Ministry of Finance and Financial System Reform." *Governance* 7(3): 219–243.

———. 1996. *Freer Markets, More Rules: Regulatory Reform in Advanced Industrial Countries*. Ithaca, N.Y.: Cornell University Press.

———. 1999a. "Can Japan Disengage? Winners and Losers in Japan's Political Economy, and the Ties That Bind Them." *Social Science Japan Journal* 2(1): 3–21.

———. 1999b. "When Interests Are Not Preferences: The Cautionary Tale of Japanese Consumers." *Comparative Politics* 31(2): 187–208.

Yahagi Toshiyuki. 1994. *Konbiniensu sutoa shisutemu no kakushinsei* (Reformism in convenience stores systems). Tokyo: Nihon Keizai Shimbunsha.

3

U.S.-Japan Financial-Market Relations in an Era of Global Finance

Jennifer Holt Dwyer

THIS CHAPTER EXPLORES THE POTENTIAL for change in U.S.-Japan relations emanating from the financial-market revolution that has swept the world these past three decades. Specifically, I investigate the ways in which the process and product of globalization affect the prospects for U.S.-Japan cooperation and conflict in the financial-issue area. I conclude that although there is ample reason to expect that the United States and Japan will continue to manage their financial-market affairs within a fundamentally cooperative framework, most notably in regard to efforts to maintain basic international financial system stability, globalization has fostered changes in the international and domestic contexts informing these relations that will complicate some aspects of cooperation in the future. In particular, globalization has fostered greater rivalry over whose policies and ideas will influence ongoing market restructuring in Asia, and has led to domestic institutional reforms that are altering the way financial issues are negotiated both domestically and internationally. I begin with an overview of the factors facilitating continued U.S.-Japan cooperation and follow with a more detailed discussion of the ways in which the impact of globalization on both economic and political competition, as well as on domestic institutional structures, is redefining the set of problems associated with various types of cooperation in the financial-issue area.

I preface this examination with two caveats. The first is that while this chapter addresses anticipated changes in U.S.-Japan relations, the part of my argument concerning the impact of domestic policy and institutional change is built predominantly on evidence drawn from the Japanese side of the equation. My reasons for this approach are both empirical and methodological. On the one hand, although the United States is finally moving toward a legislated overhaul of depression-era banking laws, over the past few decades the degree of change in both the domestic regulatory arrangements and the political interactions and institutions that shape national financial policies has been significantly greater in Japan than in the United States.[1] Accordingly, change in U.S.-Japan financial-market relations in the near future is more likely to be explained by these developments in Japan than by the relative continuity of U.S. financial-market policies. On the other hand, in terms of methodology, the arguments I present about the impact of globalization on domestic politics, such as those concerning increased politicization and pressures behind regulatory competition, are generalizable across open economies rather than particular to the Japanese case.[2] A parallel examination of these impacts on the U.S. side of the equation should support rather than call into question my conclusions.[3]

The second caveat is that although financial issues have become quite prominent among international news topics over the past three decades, financial globalization is not the primary factor informing the U.S.-Japan relationship. Broader changes in both nations' economic and geopolitical circumstances continue to set the stage on which the role of financial affairs is played out. In particular, Japan's continued dependence on the United States for national security serves as a tremendous constraint on Japanese leaders' ability to aggressively challenge the United States in other policy areas. In addition, as we enter the new millennium, China's and North Korea's economic and strategic postures, the still nascent face of European unification, uncertainty over the restoration of Asia's economic dynamism, Russia's political and economic fragility, and political instability in much of Eastern Europe, Central and Southeast Asia, and elsewhere are just some of the additional factors that could dramatically limit the relative importance of financial-market affairs in the U.S.-Japan alliance. Nevertheless, financial issues have been at the center of many of the most dynamic and dramatic changes seen in the international political economy over the past three decades and have introduced a number of particularly challenging problems into the U.S.-Japan relationship. This chapter seeks to identify how and in what form the effects of globalization will become manifest in U.S.-Japan financial relations, and thereby encourage policymakers to base future decisions not on the assumption of an unchanging pattern in U.S.-Japan relations but rather with the impacts of globalization in mind.

THE GLOBALIZATION OF FINANCIAL MARKETS

The globalization of economic relations refers to the increasingly close integration of domestic markets into a larger international marketplace. The term also suggests increased marketization because, compared with the past, financial-market developments not only are taking place on a much broader geographical scale but also are influenced more by nonstate actors.[4] In short, globalization describes the process creating an increasingly interdependent international political economy that is no longer shaped only by relations between states.

The globalization of finance and the associated increase in capital mobility were promoted through the confluence of several identifiable developments during the past several decades.[5] First came the breakdown of the Bretton Woods system of fixed exchange rates in the early 1970s and the shift to a flexible monetary system, which allows nations to float, peg, or otherwise manage their exchange rates as they see fit. Second, increased institutionalization of savings and investments, combined with considerable growth in international trade facilitated by a series of bilateral and multilateral agreements, led to significantly larger funds pursuing trade and diversified investments across borders. Third, advances in telecommunications technology, as well as in the theory and practice of finance, enabled these increasingly large financial-market actors to take advantage of cross-national opportunities at speeds and levels of efficiency never before possible. And fourth, a powerful wave of financial deregulation affecting virtually all open-market economies significantly reduced government control over capital flows and financial-market developments both within and across national borders. These forces continue to feed off one another and have expanded the internationalization of financial activity and the sensitivity of domestic markets to outside circumstances to such an extent that the financial world appears to be moving towards a fully globally integrated market environment.[6] The effects of globalization are made manifest in shifting opportunity costs arising predominantly from the associated greater potential for capital to move across borders.[7] Some of the obvious consequences of this process include greater volatility in foreign-exchange markets, large international-payments imbalances, and participation in financial markets by not only banks but also a larger number of nonfinancial institutions.[8]

This chapter's exploration of the ways in which American and Japanese interests in the financial-issue area intersect or diverge in the context of the globalization of finance begins with an overview of the factors supporting continued cooperation between the two countries. These include the salience of the financial-issue area, the role of bargaining across types of cooperation, and the institutionalization of cooperation. These factors point to my general conclusion that regardless of the difficulties introduced through globalization, to be discussed below, neither the United States nor Japan is likely to allow future conflicts to escalate to the point where they threaten their fundamentally cooperative relationship.

GLOBALIZATION AND COOPERATION

As is well recognized, the globalization of finance has deepened international interdependence, heightened national economies' sensitivity to international market conditions, and amplified political cognizance that these increasingly "free" international markets must be supervised through international cooperation (Bank for International Settlements 1986; Organization for Economic Cooperation and Development 1987; Underhill 1991, 197). Specifically, globalization has led to a shift in the relative focus of cooperative efforts away from the coordination of macroeconomic policies by the Group of Seven (G7) seen in the late 1970s and throughout the 1980s and toward cooperative crisis management and prevention rooted in more marked attention to internationally standardized rules and regulations designed to protect basic financial system stability (Bergsten and Henning 1996, 5). The shift reflects a growing consensus that these formerly somewhat successful means of economic cooperation are no longer feasible because increased capital mobility often precludes governments from effectively influencing currency markets or using fiscal policy flexibly.

Greater attention to ensuring basic stability is required because the shift in monetary systems from the early 1970s onward has introduced tremendous volatility into foreign-exchange rates, enabled the persistence of large payments imbalances, and added currency risk to the many other risks associated with international trade and investment. Advanced telecommunications has further complicated the picture by spreading news and facilitating transactions almost instantaneously, largely negating the role of geography as a buffer against overseas developments. Greater institutionalization of funds means fewer actors can make a larger impact on the market as a whole. And deregulation has generally left individual governments fewer means with which to autonomously manage the impact of financial-market developments on their domestic economy and constituents. Thus, although there is overwhelming evidence that globalization has increased levels of efficiency in many markets, there is equally widespread agreement that many aspects of this process, including the commodification of foreign exchange, the rapid transmission of volatile prices, and the remaining inadequacies of supervisory practices, underscore the extent to which cooperation among financial authorities is crucial for maintaining the soundness and stability of the international financial system. In short, greater internationalization not only increases the likelihood of some forms of crises but also virtually ensures that the effects of crisis will spread farther and faster than before (Portes and Swoboda 1987).

Accordingly, the incentives to cooperate to maintain a healthy international financial system increase with globalization. This is particularly true in the case of the financial centers and economies most deeply integrated into international financial markets. Whether those facing incentives to cooperate actually achieve cooperation, however, depends on a variety of factors. Here we discuss how cooperation between the United States and Japan is facilitated by a strong mutual interest in reaching some cooperative agreement, relatively convergent preferences concerning the general form of that cooperation, and common involvement in institutionalized arrangements that reduce the costs of negotiating and enforcing such agreements (Axlerod 1984; Fearon 1998, Keohane 1984).

Although globalization implies that financial markets span and therefore affect the entire globe, clearly the distribution of both activities and their consequences is far from uniform. The United States and Japan in particular hold unique positions in this network of financial ties that give them unusually large stakes in the international financial system. Most obviously, they are the two largest economies, host two of the world's most prominent financial centers, and are seemingly bound in a symbiotic relationship as major debtor and creditor.[9] In addition to the United States being the largest debtor nation, the U.S. dollar is the world's dominant currency, playing a substantial role in investments, invoicing, foreign-exchange transactions, and foreign reserves and intervention. Japan, the largest creditor nation, serves as the major international financial center for the formerly dynamic economies of Asia, has a currency that is growing in international use, and for many years could claim that its major players dominated nearly every ranking of international financial institutions. Even as Japan is grappling with its own banking crisis, the relationship between its domestic problems and the crisis in Asia, as well as the extent to which both domestic and greater Asian financial reconstruction depend on the coordination of U.S.-dominated International Monetary Fund (IMF)– and Japan-proposed programs, only underscores the tremendous role these two nations play in maintaining international financial stability.

In sum, for both the United States and Japan cooperation designed to maintain international financial market stability is absolutely critical to their achievement of virtually every other political objective. At this point, their economies are so integrated into international financial markets that a breakdown in this system, or a retreat from the international system through the reassertion of capital controls, for example, would inflict inestimable damage on their domestic economies as well as their governments' domestic and international authority. As one U.S. Department of the Treasury official has explained, financial-market relations between the United States and Japan parallel the structure of the MAD paradigm in security studies; both sides are well aware of the mutually assured destruction that would ensue if there were a serious breakdown in their cooperation to maintain international financial-market stability.[10] In short, because both have a large stake in international financial stability and are major players in that system, the United States and Japan have equally high stakes in preserving the cooperative framework of their relationship.

The United States and Japan share a nearly uniform view of this overarching goal of maintaining international financial-system stability through international cooperation: Financial system stability is a necessary condition for sustainable economic development. And because the nature of financial linkages is such that instability in one area can be readily transmitted to others through contagion, financial-market stability is seen as inherently fragile. Finally, since only states or international institutions supported by states have the ability to inject sufficient liquidity or impose needed regulation during financial crises, maintaining stability is virtually uncontested as a worthy objective of U.S.-Japan, as well as broader G7, cooperation. Cooperative efforts over the past three decades readily illustrate the extent to which this goal is shared and aggressively pursued.[11]

Fearon provides a framework for understanding why international cooperation may be more forthcoming in efforts to maintain financial stability than in some other areas. He explains that the difficulties associated with reaching an agreement to cooperate vary depending on how much those involved in the negotiations discount their future payoffs from cooperation. And because the nature of the proposed agreement affects the estimation of future payoffs, the type of cooperation pursued influences the likely success or failure of these bargaining situations. In particular, if the time available for bargaining over the specific details of cooperation is short because the window of opportunity to resolve a particular problem is perceived as very small, or when agreements involve repeated but often short-lived cooperative behavior, then incentives to bargain hard over the distribution of benefits from cooperation are diminished (Fearon 1998, 295). Consequently, we expect quick settlement of bargaining issues and a more rapid move to cooperative action in such circumstances, which encompass a large number of international financial-market cases, including foreign-exchange interventions and crisis-response situations. This framework suggests that, complementing the MAD analogy discussed above, the United States and Japan have responded quickly and cooperatively to a number of financial crises because their governments recognize that if they waste time haggling over the exact distribution of the costs and benefits of their proposed action the opportunity to achieve their shared objective may disappear.

On the other hand, accordingly to the same logic, the incentives for each actor to bargain hard for its preferred distribution of costs and benefits concerning cooperation increase significantly when cooperation involves longer-term commitments and thus less discounting of future payoffs. From this perspective, one can readily understand why U.S. negotiations with Japan over the liberalization of Japan's domestic financial market were so tortuous and largely unsuccessful.

Similarly, studies of the G7 economic summits show that negotiations over the distribution of the costs and benefits involved in macroeconomic policy coordination tend to be particularly difficult (see, for example, Putnam and Bayne 1984, Funabashi 1988, and Bergsten and Henning 1996). Accordingly, we expect that the United States and Japan will continue to have more contentious interactions when pursuing agreements that are expected to have a long-term impact on the distribution of benefits than when forced by circumstances to respond cooperatively to crises and periodic currency misalignments.

There are, however, institutional factors that facilitate cooperation even when agreements are expected to affect payoffs far into the future. The literature on international regimes, and more recently on varieties of institutionalism, highlights the importance of norms, rules, and procedures around which actors' expectations converge and the ways in which institutions that structure interactions bias outcomes. That is, institutional factors, such as established rules and procedures, which can reduce transaction costs as well as narrow the range of possible bargaining outcomes, increase the likelihood of agreement among members who have accepted those institutions as legitimate. Clearly, in the field of international finance there already exist a number of well-established and institutionalized cooperative solutions for a variety of financial-market issues, such as using IMF funding to restore liquidity. These institutions were themselves once the object of negotiations, but now policies pursued through these forums stand as institutionalized bargaining solutions and constrain any actor trying to deviate from the behavior prescribed through them.

One additional aspect of institutionalized cooperation that should be mentioned is the increasingly multilateral character of these endeavors. Although the United States and Japan are two of the most influential financial-center states, even their governments could not manage the international financial system through bilateral efforts alone. As the Bank for International Settlements (BIS) capital-adequacy negotiations and the limited past success of Group of Five (G5) and G7 agreements illustrate, effective financial-market cooperation requires that at least three major nations agree (Kapstein 1994; Bergsten and Henning 1996), and in many cases, such as regulatory cooperation to limit insider trading or other unlawful activities, far more widespread participation is needed to achieve effectiveness. This increasingly multilateral environment can be expected to affect U.S.-Japan cooperation in two ways. First, it may limit the extremes in either nation's policy prescriptions because the adoption of any proposal will require appealing to a larger number of participants. Second, it may facilitate Japan's playing a somewhat more independent role in international affairs by providing it with an international arena in which to air its own views and participate in coalitions that support alternatives to U.S. proposals. Moreover, if Japan were able to garner substantial support for an alternative proposal through a multilateral forum, any conflict with the United States would look less like a direct challenge by Japan (although it might in fact be) and more like an occasion on which the United States was out of step with the rest of the world.

The United States and Japan participate actively in a growing number of both formal organizations, such as the IMF, the World Bank, and the BIS, as well as less organization-defined assemblies, such as the G7 meetings, regional forums, and numerous bilateral negotiations. For the most part (that is, noting the impact of multilateralism mentioned above), these numerous institutional commitments, as well as the continuous organizational support and ongoing contact they require, reinforce the U.S.-Japan alliance by building a history of successes and fostering shared expectations about future behavior. In addition, and more particular to the financial-issue area, over the past fifteen years the United States and Japan have developed a variety of more mundane and personal relations that can be expected to facilitate cross-national communication and thus shared expectations among financial authorities. Examples include the participation of visiting U.S. Federal Reserve Bank employees in Bank of Japan (BOJ) research activities and the training of BOJ personnel at Federal Reserve Banks in the United States. These contacts are of course in addition to ongoing official communication between the Japanese Ministry of Finance (MOF) and U.S. Treasury staff at the U.S. Embassy in Tokyo and between the New York Federal Reserve Bank staff and the MOF and BOJ officials ensconced in offices just across the street from each other in New York.

These contacts between financial authorities exemplify a postwar shift in the management of U.S.-Japan relations more generally away from the domain of their foreign ministries and toward specialized functionaries (Curtis, introduction to this volume).[12] Recent changes in Japanese bureaucratic practices that are promoting greater specialization by career officials should also facilitate better communication with U.S. financial authorities, who in general have more specialized educational backgrounds or substantially greater practical experience.[13] And finally, to the extent that one believes communication is the foundation of all good relations, there is potential for greater cooperation in U.S.-Japan financial-market relations as careers advance in the generation of younger Japanese officials, many of whom have obtained some higher education overseas, have maintained relationships formed while away, and understand English well enough to keep abreast of U.S. debates and publications. Although the situation has improved significantly since the 1980s, the number of U.S. officials equally capable of reading Japanese and engaging in Japanese-language debates is unfortunately comparatively meager.

Taken together, these various institutional factors are generally expected to increase the likelihood of continued cooperation between the United States and

Japan.[14] Moreover, as discussed above, the United States and Japan have such high stakes in maintaining the international financial system that a breakdown in the alliance because of nonessential financial issues is virtually unthinkable. Accordingly, at this point, one might be inclined to paint a wholly optimistic picture of the prospects for U.S.-Japan cooperation concerning financial-market affairs. That would be a mistake, however. The common pursuit of financial-market stability sets the outer limit on how far each government can push in negotiations, and institutional factors assist efforts once a common objective is defined; neither factor precludes conflict.

CONFLICT IN U.S.-JAPAN FINANCIAL-MARKET RELATIONS

As we saw throughout the 1980s and 1990s, officials in the United States and Japan can find more than enough financial issues over which to disagree. During the 1980s, for example, U.S. representatives complained about the so-called over-presence of Japanese financial institutions in the U.S. and European markets and repeatedly admonished their Japanese counterparts for not going far enough or fast enough in their approach to domestic financial-market reform. Whenever possible, Japanese negotiators responded with criticism of the U.S. government's inability to reduce its twin deficits and the stresses they were placing on the world economy.[15] And, as if a sequel to a bad first run, the 1990s were similarly fraught with discord between the United States and Japan over the allocation of blame for the Asian and other currency crises and the appropriate prescriptions for recovery, as well as the pace and policy mix that should be used to pull Japan out of its own banking-sector quagmire and economic recession.

As any review of the past decade readily suggests, U.S.-Japan relations concerning financial issues are certainly more contentious now than during the Bretton Woods era, when domestic financial markets were largely isolated through the combination of domestic regulations and the fixed-rate foreign-exchange regime. The politics of finance inspires more heated battles now in large part because globalization has introduced or promoted a number of factors complicating the management of U.S.-Japan relations in the financial-issue area. Among the most salient are that (1) globalization in general, and capital mobility in particular, has created greater competition over the distribution of economic gains accruing through international finance, (2) globalization has opened the door to greater competition between the United States and Japan concerning which nation's ideas and policy proposals will shape the new architecture of international finance, and (3) globalization has led to domestic institutional change in Japan that is restructuring the way financial policies are negotiated both domestically and internationally. We will look at each of these below.

Competition Over Economic Gains

To a large extent globalization is the product of market-led competition. Private actors pursuing economic objectives created new technologies and financial products, forcing governments to respond to the demands of market constituents and the requirements of public policy by adjusting regulatory conditions to the new market environment. Because there was a bias in regulatory reform toward greater liberalization, ever larger numbers of participants joined in these activities, and competition intensified and expanded farther around the globe.

The main reason increased competition between market actors affects U.S.-Japan relations is that while in theory and sometimes in practice competition promotes market efficiencies, competition does not distribute these gains equally or according to any other politically responsive logic. And although U.S.-Japan relations are not predicated on a zero-sum view of the gains from trade, economic success certainly contributes to international political power and prestige; both the United States and Japan would prefer that their firms, financial institutions, and domestic financial centers emerged among the leaders in the financial-market race.[16] In addition, globalization increases conflicts over macroeconomic policies because domestic policy choices affect other states, as well. In sum, two ways in which globalization affects U.S.-Japan relations are macroeconomic policy conflicts and competition between governments as they try to increase their influence over these growing international market developments by enhancing their jurisdiction over international financial-market actors and activities.

To begin with, states disagree over macroeconomic policy mixes because the effects of one state's policies on another state's economy—and on the government's support networks—are not always complementary. Thus we see, for example, a history of cross-national complaints that one government's refusal to change interest rates or cut fiscal deficits is imposing costs on the other. Understandably, governments negotiate cooperative agreements concerning policy coordination based on their calculation of the domestic coalition needed to maintain their position, and agreements are thus reached only when they do not affect important domestic constituents in ways that will threaten an administration's hold on political authority. In cases of macroeconomic policy coordination and the attendant conflicts over whose constituents will best be served by any policy choice, the greater a nation's impact on international financial developments the greater weight its independent policy choices carry relative to those of other governments. Accordingly, even in cases of macroeconomic policy coordination, there are benefits to having greater financial-market power.

In addition, because the high degree of capital mobility and market integration inherent in financial globalization essentially allows market participants to do business wherever the conditions are deemed most attractive, running parallel to the well-examined competition between market actors is an equally important competition between governments trying to maintain jurisdiction over a strong and sound financial center, which in the context of globalization requires that it be internationally competitive (Bryant 1987; Kane 1987). Competition of this sort has been evident throughout the postwar history of the internationalization of finance, beginning with U.S. efforts to recapture jurisdiction over the dollar-denominated banking activities taking place in offshore European markets almost immediately after World War II. These efforts were soon countered by British financial reforms designed to reestablish London as the preeminent international financial center. As internationalization spread, the implicit threat of domestic financial-market "hollowing" if financial-market activities moved to more attractive markets compelled more governments to respond with policies that made them more competitive (Loriaux et al. 1997). Needless to say, over the past two decades the competition among the major centers, New York, London, and Tokyo, has become particularly intense (Moran 1991; Laurence 1996; Helleiner 1994; Dwyer forthcoming).

Although competition among financial centers may have been most evident in the 1980s, the heyday of deregulation, there is little reason for this competitive pressure to subside as long as capital is highly mobile. Thus, as evidenced by the three principles guiding Japan's recent financial-system reform package, even in the 1990s the government acknowledged that domestic financial reconstruction depended on Japan's offering through reforms what mobile financial-market participants found most attractive, namely, free, fair, and global markets (Ministry of Finance 1998, sec. 2, 1-2).[17] Similarly, Japan's recent big push to increase the internationalization of the yen was explicitly designed to increase the attractiveness of the Tokyo market, as well as to counter the dominance of the U.S. dollar in Asia and the increased draw of European markets due to the emergence of the euro (Ministry of Finance 1999).[18]

These two levels of competition have been at the root of U.S.-Japan financial-market tensions for at least two decades but have potentially very different effects on U.S.-Japan financial-market relations. On the one hand, competition to serve domestic interest groups through macroeconomic policies and other means remains intense. The United States in particular has aggressively pressed Japan for a seemingly unending list of financial-market reforms that U.S. officials have felt would improve the competitiveness of primarily foreign (read U.S.) firms. The Yen-Dollar Agreement, the best-known example, also represents a precedent-setting case of one country pressuring another to integrate its financial market with the rest of the world, supposedly to eliminate the severe misalignment of exchange rates seen as the cause of the United States' enormous and growing current account deficit (Frankel 1984). Although the logic of this endeavor was seriously questioned in regard to liberalization's likely exchange-rate effect, since that time the United States has continued to pressure Japan fairly relentlessly to adjust its domestic regulatory structure or monetary-policy stance because these policies have been viewed as providing unfair market advantages to Japanese firms and financial institutions. Until Japan's financial markets and policies perfectly suit the interests of U.S. firms, an outcome one cannot expect to arise soon if ever, this level of US-Japanese tension over the treatment of their respective constituents will continue.

Further encouraging this level of competition between the United States and Japan is an enduring perception by the public on both sides of the Pacific that, despite any arguments concerning mutual gains from exchange, the economic relationship between the United States and Japan is still fundamentally zero-sum. In the mid- and late 1980s, the self-congratulatory airs adopted by some Japanese over becoming "number one" were outdone only by the overreaction of some Americans to Japanese purchases of U.S. banks and "trophy real estate." Thus, we are reminded yet again that voters still identify themselves and their fortunes with their state—regardless of how global the marketplace or how multinational the firms in which they work. Not surprisingly, therefore, with the essential reversal of fortunes over the past decade, the United States riding a long-lasting economic boom while Japan languishes in recession, much bravado has returned to American discussions of Japan's poor performance, and both nationalistic and accusatory language has resurfaced in Japan (Ishihara 1998; Ogawa 1999).

On a more positive note, and somewhat counterintuitively, the competition between international financial centers that takes place in a global environment may eventually reduce the bilateral tensions perpetuated by this zero-sum view of market-level competition if what the United States demands of Japan is in line with emerging market trends. This is because the competitive pressure that capital mobility introduces into the financial-reform process effectively promotes greater cross-national convergence of regulatory environments (Dwyer forthcoming). As was evident in former Prime Minister Hashimoto Ryūtarō's repeated lamenting of the decline in Tokyo's status, the main goal of Japan's "Big Bang" financial-deregulation initiative was to revitalize Tokyo's sagging financial market.[19] Revitalizing the market means making it more attractive to mobile capital. Accordingly, recent reforms have been particularly focused on adjusting the Japanese market to emerging standards of internationally competitive markets. These unilateral efforts to create an internationally attractive market will reduce U.S.-Japan bilateral conflict because the more market pressure prods Japan to adjust domestic regulatory and administrative practices to bring them more in line with developing international standards, the less U.S. officials will feel compelled to do so. In other words, market pressure has been more successful than direct U.S. diplomatic pressure in pushing Japan toward reforms the United States wants.

During the early 1980s, Japanese officials were often unresponsive to U.S. demands for more drastic domestic reforms because they were reluctant to give up the means of influencing Japan's financial affairs that the deregulatory aspect of reform implied, they had to forge political compromises among competing interest groups and balance the costs and benefits of adjustment among their constituents, and they feared the uncertainty and instability that rapid reform might invite (Rosenbluth 1989; Vogel 1996; Dwyer 1997). A crucial factor enabling this incremental approach was that for much of that decade financial-market participants were attracted to Tokyo because of the surplus of available capital, that is, despite its unquestionably less attractive regulatory environment. In the early to mid-1990s, after the bubble had burst and Japan's economic situation had deteriorated, and then briefly recovered, Japanese officials acted as if the slow, incremental approach to reform practiced during the 1980s were still feasible and appropriate. Clearly, U.S. officials felt more dramatic action was needed.[20] The result was a period of considerable tension, primarily between MOF and Treasury, including Japanese complaints about American heavy-handedness and American complaints about the Japanese failure to face unpleasant realities (e.g., Saitō 1998).

By 1998, however, that earlier cushion of popularity and the façade of stability in the financial system had been ungraciously removed with the retreat of foreign corporate and financial institutions, the failure of Japanese financial institutions, and the gradual exposure of the magnitude of the bad-loan problem. Tokyo was quickly losing its reputation as an attractive international financial market, and the government recognized the danger. If the financial-market participants abandoned Tokyo for more stable ground, most hope for Japan's rapid economic recovery would be lost, as well. With this as background, by 1999 the Japanese government had finally begun taking bigger and more appropriate steps toward acknowledging the full extent of the problems, restoring some credibility to financial regulation through the creation of a new regulatory agency and commission, and resolving the banking crisis through the infusion of public funds, nationalization, and facilitated mergers. Although progress still seems slow, the Japanese government has finally recognized that it needs to respond to its problems in ways deemed satisfactory by the international financial community.[21] That is, the Japanese government is seeking to restore Tokyo's place as an attractive financial market by competing with other countries for financial-market share. This competition is evident in the government's adjusting regulatory policies, supervisory practices, and accounting and disclosure standards to replicate or at least approximate more closely those followed in other attractive markets.

This competition among governments trying to attract financial-market activities to areas within their jurisdiction is one new dynamic emerging from the increase in capital mobility that has accompanied globalization. As suggested above, however, in the narrow sense, if Japan adopts more market-responsive reforms that happen to fall closer in line with U.S. "suggestions"—then all the better for U.S.-Japan relations.[22] But this would not be a coincidence. Although financial markets are routinely described as global or at least international, the United States has played an unmistakably privileged role in shaping this environment (Strange 1986; Moran 1991; Helleiner 1994). The question we consider below is whether globalization will also increase political competition concerning who should set the standards for international finance in the future.

Competition over Political Leadership in Financial Affairs

Despite newspaper commentary on unbridled "free" markets, global finance does not take place in a vacuum; structure abounds, and which players win and lose is greatly influenced by the ideas and institutional biases informing the rules of the game. As stated above, for many years the dominant role of the United States in shaping international financial markets went largely unchallenged. Recently, however, more countries seem to be questioning the appropriateness of the existing international financial regime.[23] The reasons for this growing challenge to U.S. leadership are twofold. First, as the spate of financial crises in the late 1990s clearly illustrates, the potential for instability in a global market is great, and increased interdependence implies increased vulnerability, as well. More markets are integrated, more economies are exposed, and more governments want a say in how these powerful forces of economic growth or ruin will be managed. Second, global finance can be a tough game, and many developing nations, in particular, may be exposed to these markets before they are adequately prepared to handle the impact participation may have on their economies and political futures. Even if the so-called playing field is made level through the adoption of similar regulatory standards cross-nationally, the strongest market players tend to come out on top, leaving those less prepared caught off guard and smarting. In short, globalization has not only expanded the number of nations involved in this web of relations but also exposed them to the risks inherent in these markets. As a result, some national leaders are inspired by their bad experiences to think more seriously about alternative "rules" of the game, and there is now a more diverse community of nations involved with which to forge coalitions around these alternatives.

Criticism of a U.S.-dominated liberal market approach to international financial-market relations is not a new development; nor is any popular alternative visible on the horizon. Nevertheless, the extent to which major U.S. allies, including both Japan and Europe, are openly contemplating less radically open market arrangements suggests that this too is an area of potentially greater conflict in the future. A review of U.S.-Japan relations in response to the Asian currency crisis provides glimpses of this competition for influence over both the policies and the ideas shaping future international financial-market affairs.

The Asian currency crisis hit with a vengeance following the devaluation of the Thai baht in July 1997. One after another Thailand, Indonesia, Malaysia, the Philippines, and South Korea were shaken by speculative attacks on their currencies and were forced to expand or abolish exchange-rate bands and move to floating exchange rates. Although Indonesia and South Korea enjoyed better economic fundamentals at the time, their currencies suffered particularly from speculative contagion and continued to weaken through the end of the year. After the onset of the crisis, virtually all these countries experienced a severe credit crunch and associated economic contraction. Although several of these countries have already recovered quite substantially, the Asian currency crisis was a pivotal event informing international financial markets in the late 1990s. Here, however, I am not concerned with addressing the cause but rather exploring, in the contestation between the United States and Japan over the appropriate response to the crisis, the seeds of greater competition for political leadership, especially concerning financial affairs in Asia.[24]

First, as stated at the outset, the conflicts and competition between the United States and Japan concerning financial-market affairs are contained within the broader shared objective of maintaining international financial stability. It would serve neither's interest if financial disputes were allowed to escalate to a stability-threatening level. Thus, not surprisingly, the initial response by the United States and Japan, the two largest stakeholders in the region, was both quick and cooperative.[25] Within weeks, for example, most of the countries involved had requested and received IMF support under the usual conditions, such as fiscal or monetary restraint, financial system restructuring, or real-sector structural reform.[26] From that point on, however, conflicts between the United States and Japan over further steps revealed competition for political leadership. This contest had two dimensions. The first concerned which nation would shape the remaining policy responses to the Asian currency crisis. In this regard, Japan immediately stepped up to take a proactive role rather than simply wait for or defer to presumed U.S. leadership. The second dimension of the contest concerned whose ideas about international financial-market management enjoyed the support of Asian nations. In this regard, too, Japan made substantial efforts to been seen as on the side of its Asian neighbors.

Japan became a major international player in terms of its economic power several decades ago, but Asia remains the only place where Japan can possibly aspire to political leadership. Japan displaced the United States as the dominant economic force in Asia in the late 1980s, having invested more than twice as much as the United States in Association of Southeast Asian Nations (ASEAN) countries, exported and imported equal or greater amounts, and provided three times as much aid (Vogel 1994, 159, 161). Yet the legacy of Japanese behavior in Asia before and during World War II has long thwarted any embrace of Japan as a political leader in the region. Despite this history, Japan's postcrisis involvement in the Asian currency crisis was "uncharacteristically proactive" and displayed a clear intent to take on more political responsibility than usual (Fukui and Fukai 1998, 33). Given that in 1997 Japanese banks held approximately one-third of the outstanding commercial bank debt of the five ASEAN member countries (Pempel 1999, 8), Japanese interest and active participation in restoring financial stability were not surprising. Nevertheless, the behavior of Japanese leaders during this period gave greater credence to the possibility of Japan's challenging the role of U.S. leadership in the region.

During the early stage of the Asian crisis, Japan advocated establishing an Asian Monetary Fund (AMF). The idea for the fund was first publicly presented by Minister of Finance Miyazawa Kiichi during a World Bank–IMF meeting in Hong Kong in 1997 and met immediate and determined opposition from the United States and others (Bergsten 1998). Some Asian nations initially rejected the idea because it hinted at Japanese domination. The United States, meanwhile, used a "two birds with one stone" approach to topple it. U.S. representatives focused their criticism of the planned AMF on its potential to undermine the authority of the IMF. In particular, the AMF was maligned as enabling nations to avoid the discipline imposed by IMF conditionality by providing an alternative source of funds. In addition to these views, U.S. officials saw the proposal as threatening to divide the region down the Pacific, leaving the United States as an outlier.[27] Since their opposition to the plan, based on giving priority to the IMF, provided enough justification to derail the AMF suggestion, and because most other Asian nations did not want or politically could not afford to leave the United States out of the rescue operation, the United States did not have to dwell on its more political implications to topple the plan. In a similar fashion, a Japanese offer to provide substantial aid to Indonesia through a corporate debt rescheduling program was also quashed by staunch U.S. opposition. In this case, however, the reasons were related more to U.S. discomfort with Indonesia's political leaders at the time than with Japan's usurping U.S. leadership in the region.[28]

Clearly, Japan was unable to implement its proposals because of strong U.S. opposition. This failure was in large part due simply and unsurprisingly to the United States' greater influence in international financial-market affairs and Japan's general adherence to U.S. foreign and strategic policy prescriptions because of its dependence on the U.S. security umbrella. Nevertheless, two aspects of this period are worth special note. First, it is revealing that the United States did not greet Japan's more proactive efforts with greater enthusiasm; for many many years Americans had criticized Japan for "free riding" on a U.S.-provided international order and not pulling its weight in international affairs. The United States' abrupt and discouraging response to Japan's greater efforts suggests that Japan's proposals were viewed not as complementing U.S.-led efforts but as conflicting with them. Consequently, following the thread of existing American criticism concerning Japan's apparent inability to resolve its own domestic banking crisis and emerge from its recession, during this time U.S. officials publicly questioned whether Japan could be a responsible party in the global rescue of Asia if it could not even overcome domestic bickering over its own bailout packages.[29] In short, both Japan's uncharacteristically proactive efforts and the United States' unsupportive response reflected the contest between the United States and Japan over political leadership in Asia.

Japan was unable to follow through with the two policy ideas discussed above as originally planned, and thus is clearly not yet more influential than the United States in these matters. Nevertheless, Japan has persistently pursued the broad path set out in these early proposals, and through this perseverance has communicated to Asian leaders its commitment to the Asian cause. As mentioned above, for example, despite initial U.S. opposition to capital controls, the G7 eventually approved temporary controls over short-term capital flows at its summit in Germany in June 1999. In addition, although Japan's AMF proposal was rejected early on and replaced initially by the multilateral "Manila Framework" in December 1997, Japanese officials continued to design a more proactive response. Some are still working toward the eventual establishment of an AMF,[30] and recent news reports concerning the so-called Chian Mai Initiative suggest at least cautious U.S. support for what Asian leaders see as a step towards greater Asian financial cooperation. In the meantime, these efforts have begun to bear fruit through the "New Miyazawa Initiative" of October 1998.[31] Finally, Japan has packaged its promotion of the internationalization of the yen as fostering stability in Asia because Asian states' excessive dependence on the U.S. dollar is considered one of the factors that contributed to the currency crisis. Over time this evidence of Japan's persistence through primarily unilateral policies garnered praise from Asians as well as support from non-Asian members at later IMF meetings ("Japan Wins Praise" 1998; "Japan, S. Korean Lawmakers" 1998).

The importance of these Japanese policy responses for our broader discussion is that although Japan's efforts were initially dismissed by both non-Japanese Asians and Americans as self-interested attempts to improve the economies in which Japan had great exposure, Japanese officials persistently pursued a variety of plans, and some were eventually accepted by both the United States and other states.

Certainly in this process Japan accommodated U.S. interests to a considerable degree. Nevertheless, by creating and following through with these efforts, Japan relatively successfully portrayed itself as committed to contributing policies to the Asian cause in a way that improved its image in the eyes of at least some Asians, especially those unhappy with the IMF-led approach to recovery (Jomo 1998). This leads us to a second level of competition between the United States and Japan.

The second dimension of this competition for political leadership is ideational and was equally apparent in U.S.-Japan interaction during the Asian currency crisis. This competition concerns not which nation has the power to implement its preferred policies but rather which nation promotes ideas that speak to and are accepted by Asia's leaders. In this case, although Japan was surely outshone by the United States in terms of controlling policy for Asia's financial reconstruction, Japan nonetheless presented a set of ideas that identified Japan as being on the side of its Asian neighbors. At times these views clearly portrayed Japan as standing in opposition to the side of the United States and what was seen as its international financial-market policeman, the IMF. Whereas competition for power over policy leadership in Asia is unlikely to result in significant diminution of U.S. influence in the immediate future, competition over who best represents the interests of Asia may reveal the United States to be disadvantaged.

In particular, Japan is involved in a variety of Asian forums that do not include U.S. representatives and shoulders a large share of the burden in those that do. Looking at those most germane to the financial-issue area, one finds, for example, that while the BOJ is deeply involved in ongoing and institutionalized cooperation with Asian central banks, the United States was intentionally excluded from participation in this group from its inception.[32] Also, although Hong Kong is where the Asian BIS office was opened in 1998, Japan bears the major responsibility for managing that organization, just as it does the Asian Development Bank. In short, in addition to the obvious fact that Japan is an Asian nation and the United States is not, institutional arrangements like those mentioned above provide Japanese leaders with greater opportunities to influence the thinking of Asian officials who are looking for new ways to develop their financial markets and integrate them into the global economy. Specifically, Japanese leaders have wooed their fellow Asian counterparts through their profession of an alternative to "Western" capitalism. This competition over ideas is amply evident in the battle of words between two particularly assertive representatives of Japan and the United States, former MOF Vice-Minister for International Affairs Sakakibara Eisuke and Secretary of the Treasury Lawrence Summers.[33]

Sakakibara made a name for himself by being an outspoken proponent of a Japanese style of capitalism, one in which the government has a greater role to play in countering the excesses of free markets. "Mr. Sakakibara has also been a vocal advocate of governments taking more control of international markets to keep financial crises like the one that started in Asia two years ago from spreading around the globe."[34] He argues that the more liberal market approach to financial-market organization proposed predominantly by the U.S. Treasury leaves economies too exposed to "the inherent instability of liberalized international capital markets" (Sakakibara 1999, 2) and is more supportive of some types of capital controls than is his U.S. counterpart.[35] Sakakibara has also criticized parts of the IMF's programs for restoring Asia's economic health by questioning whether the IMF structural policy measures vis-à-vis the currency-crisis states were too ambitious, demanded more reform than was necessary to overcome the crisis, and ran the risk of causing "undue friction in society, because each country has its own traditions, history, and culture, which are reflected in the economic structure" (Sakakibara 1999, 3). Finally, in stark contrast to U.S., IMF, and Organization for Economic Cooperation and Development (OECD) arguments that economic recovery will occur only after substantial structural reform in both the real and financial sectors has taken place (IMF 1995), Japan has taken the position that requiring reform first is not always necessary and can be excessively painful.

In sum, through institutional affiliation, the words of Sakakibara and others, and various unilateral policies, Japan has taken up issues that resonate well among the Asian countries still dealing with both the crisis and the effects of IMF prescriptions: ideas not often expressed by the more free market–oriented U.S. Treasury.[36] If the recovery of the Asian economies does not go well, the frustration some Asians feel about their exposure to international markets may take on even more political expression. In that event, I expect continued tensions between the United States and Japan over how to deal with recalcitrant Asian governments and how fast those national economies should be integrated into the global economy.

This ideational competition or conflict over the appropriate role of government in the economy and the extent to which national circumstances deemed unique or special should be accommodated by other international market players was equally obvious in the tension between the United States and Japan concerning the most appropriate way for Japan to respond to its own domestic banking crisis. While in formal statements U.S. officials presented themselves as supporting Japanese efforts, in other forums it was obvious that many felt Japan was far too slow in identifying and disclosing the extent of the bad debt held by Japanese banks, too hesitant to commit public funds to uphold the banking system and provide domestic stimulus to the economy, and too generous and indiscriminate in sharing these public funds with poorly managed institutions that should have been forced to close. Competition on this ideational level is a good thing, however, and honest debate over alternative approaches among fundamentally cooperative allies may be the world's best hope for keeping up with ever changing markets, maintaining international financial stability, and managing financial crises when they inevitably strike.[37]

In sum, competition for political leadership between the United States and Japan has revealed itself in conflicts over both policies and ideas. As recounted above, Asian states' current dependence on U.S. participation for their recovery, together with Japan's inability to push too hard on these issues given its own dependence on the United States,[38] is likely to preclude these nations from either adopting policies that alienate the United States or ever actually experimenting with Japan's "recover first, reform later" ideas. Needless to say, Japan also has yet to convincingly prove the superiority of this model in its own struggles to recover from a domestic financial crisis. Nevertheless, persistent Japanese efforts to accommodate unique national circumstances rather than fully expose domestic markets to what is often depicted as a largely U.S.-envisioned liberal international economic order suggest that ideational competition between the United States and Japan concerning the ideas on which to base the new international financial architecture and manage domestic and international linkages will continue for the foreseeable future.

In several respects, the currency crisis in Asia provided Japan with one of the greatest opportunities to stand out and take a leadership role in resolving an international crisis. It occurred in Japan's Asian neighborhood, where Japan already had a substantial economic presence; it could be resolved with one of the few resources Japan had an abundance of, namely, capital; and because it concerned financial rather than military commitments, it would be significantly easier to sell to the Japanese public and posed none of the politically complicated moral judgements that many other international interventions involve, such as those concerning military or human-rights issues. Nevertheless, as the saying goes, "timing is everything," and given its own set of financial and economic problems, Japan was unable to present itself as a strong alternative to U.S. leadership. Had the Asian crisis occurred ten years earlier, when Japanese financial institutions were seemingly at their peak and the position of the ruling Liberal Democratic Party (LDP) was more secure, the competition between the United States and Japan might have been more severe. Whether this competition for leadership in Asia will intensify in the future depends on the recovery of Japan's financial sector, revitalization of the Japanese economy as a whole, and stabilization of Japanese party politics.

Finally, as I have said throughout this chapter, the extent to which Japan can promote policies or ideas that directly challenge or conflict with the United States is greatly constrained by the importance of the overall U.S.-Japan relationship. The more likely development is that in multilateral and especially regional settings Japan will seek to play a relatively greater role, but one that is portrayed as complementing rather than conflicting with U.S. interests in the region. Thus, for example, the greater acceptance by the United States of Japan's proposals concerning Asia's recovery after the currency crisis shifted to Latin America, where the United States sees its interests as more immediate, was interpreted as U.S. approval of a burden-sharing arrangement whereby the United States and Japan's common interests would be pursued by leaving the Asian recovery in Japan's hands (Shinohara 1999, 10). Whether Japan can parlay this role as the United States' assistant into something more autonomous remains to be seen.

GLOBALIZATION AND DOMESTIC INSTITUTIONAL CHANGE

One cannot fully understand the ways in which globalization affects the U.S.-Japan relationship without examining the significant influence these developments have had on domestic institutions.[39] As stated in the introduction, globalization has increased the sensitivity of domestic financial systems to international influence and fostered changes in a wide range of domestic policies and institutions in response to this pressure. One result of this domestic policy response to international change is that over time the extent to which domestic institutions can "block or refract" these international pressures also changes (Milner and Keohane 1996, 5). It is especially worthwhile to explore this possibility in the case of Japan because Japanese domestic institutions in particular have been portrayed as robust and slow to change in the face of international pressure.[40] The implication of this argument for U.S.-Japan financial-market relations is that patterns of political interaction both within and between the United States and Japan may change as globalization promotes change in both domestic policy preferences and institutional relationships.

Globalization implies that virtually all nations are increasingly exposed to changing international financial circumstances and many have adjusted domestic policies accordingly. The United States is no exception. In its case, however, domestic financial-market policy changes have not yet produced any major restructuring of institutional organization or financial-market authority. This may change soon, since Treasury and the Federal Reserve Board recently announced an agreement concerning jurisdictional issues that had been holding up any major overhaul of the U.S. financial system (Lebaton 1999). Globalization and the increased salience of financial-market developments for the U.S. political economy have created an increase in the relative political importance of Treasury, especially in matters concerning foreign affairs. This shift in the relative attention paid to Treasury preferences is also evident in U.S.-Japan relations. For many years trade issues dominated the U.S.-Japan agenda, and trade negotiators discussed financial issues as they related to trade. Since the late 1980s, however, financial issues have dominated this forum and have been largely delinked from trade concerns.

One implication of this change, as pointed out in Robert Uriu's chapter in this volume, is that U.S.-Japan relations as managed by Treasury are not influenced by the revisionist school of thought that once dominated trade-oriented relations. Overall, however, the impact of globalization on U.S.-Japan relations caused by domestic institutional change is much more evident when observed from the Japanese side.

In contrast to the United States, Japan is currently experiencing a period of tremendous turmoil and uncertainty, which has at least the potential to challenge and change Japan's political economy in significant ways.[41] Although it is difficult to see the direction in which things are headed from the eye of the storm, as it were, it is equally difficult to imagine that Japan will pass through this period of political and economic upheaval and emerge little changed by the experience. Thus, based on what we know today, and with the necessary caveats concerning predictions during periods of transition, I consider below some of the ways in which current political and economic circumstances in Japan can be expected to affect U.S.-Japan financial relations.

To summarize the turmoil, for most of the 1990s Japan's so-called ruling triumvirate, comprising the ruling LDP, the bureaucracy, and big business, was in disarray. At no other time in the postwar period had all three of the dominant forces shaping Japan's political economy been so unsettled at the same time. With the bursting of the so-called bubble economy at roughly the turn of the decade,[42] the economy, and therefore the big-business part of the triumvirate, experienced spectacularly less economic success; there was also a continued weakening in the commonality of interests within this broadly defined big-business group. Of particular relevance to this chapter is the increased dissatisfaction with government intervention and the greater divergence between the large and multinational corporate sector, with its preference for more rapid deregulation of financial markets, and the financial sector, in which conflicts of interest continue to hinder more proactive approaches to reform. In conjunction with a broad economic recession, Japan is struggling to manage the most recent in a series of spectacular financial-market crises, this one involving bad loans throughout the financial system that may account for as much as 10 percent of all loans outstanding ("Japan Banks" 1999). As a result, for the first time in decades Japanese financial institutions of all types have begun to fail. Given these events, confidence in Japan's economy as a whole, and in the financial system in particular, is extremely low.[43]

To this economic turmoil one must add significant political uncertainty. Since the early 1990s, when politicians began abandoning the LDP and in 1993 successfully seated the first non-LDP prime minister in almost four decades, the political situation in Japan has been unstable. The pace of the creation and dissolution of new parties and coalitions seen during the 1990s was extraordinary, especially when compared with most of the postwar period. Despite the LDP's having at times regained some semblance of effective rule by pulling in defectors from smaller parties or forming "alliances of convenience, it has not recouped its once unchallenged dominance and the threat of continued political uncertainty is great" (Fukui and Fukai 1998, 25).

Finally, Japan's bureaucracy is being reorganized and reconceived.[44] The financial bureaucracies (MOF and to a lesser extent the BOJ) in particular have been unceremoniously knocked off their pedestals and are under attack from the general public, politicians, and business in ways virtually unimaginable two decades ago. The public lost confidence in the capabilities of Japan's financial authorities after the asset-inflation bubble of the 1980s burst and eventually revealed the fragility of the financial infrastructure supporting the economy, first through the *jūsen*, or housing-loan company, crisis and more recently though the banking-sector crisis. Moreover, they lost respect for these officials as one scandal after another in the financial-services industry revealed bureaucrats' indifference, complacency, or even complicity and resulted in more than one official's being led from his office by prosecutors.[45]

Business groups, for their part, saw these events as creating an opportunity to further reduce bureaucratic intervention in the economy. Understandably, given the instability of political coalitions and the resulting overwhelming reelection imperatives, politicians from virtually all parties responded to this shift in business and public opinion and supported reorganization of MOF to varying degrees.[46] Thus, in 1998, after three years of debate, MOF, long considered one of the most powerful ministries in Japan, was formally relieved of a good portion of its regulatory and supervisory responsibilities. This major reorganization took effect just twelve months after the Bank of Japan Law was revised to provide the central bank with more open and formal independence from MOF. In short, the bureaucratic part of the financial-politics equation has also changed drastically in the past few years.

These changes in the fortunes and cohesiveness of the ruling party, the bureaucracy, and big business are expected to threaten the viability of long-standing patterns of politics. The extremely high level of uncertainty may well also call into question the government's future leadership capacity, both within Japan and internationally, as well as the continuity of financial policy and the credibility of commitments vis-à-vis the United States. The ramifications of all these domestic challenges may be extensive. Below I address only two of the ways in which the more indirect effects of globalization on domestic politics may influence U.S.-Japan relations in the financial-issue area: greater politicization of financial issues and decentralization of financial authority.

Politicization of Financial Issues

Globalization affects domestic politics because it increases the exposure of domestic constituents to international market developments (Milner and Keohane 1996, 16). Moreover, given the role deregulation has played in promoting globalization, governments now have less policy autonomy and fewer means to shield their constituents from overseas shocks (Bryant 1980; Goodman and Pauly 1993; Andrews 1994, Keohane and Milner 1996).[47] Specifically, in an increasingly global environment with extensive capital mobility, redistributive policy tools once commonly used to protect or compensate politically important groups (such as protective regulations and taxation) often conflicted directly with more competitive actors' interests and were eliminated in response to pressure to create a more internationally competitive economic environment (Stenmo 1996; Webb 1995). Accordingly, a common refrain of the internationalization literature is that governments can please voters or internationally mobile investors, but not both. That being said, fewer policy options do not mean fewer political obligations.

Domestic actors discontent with the distribution of the costs and benefits of international economic integration have commonly used political pressure on the government to try to change the terms of competition—or at least the distributive outcomes. In the context of globalization, as the domestic buffers against international shocks deteriorate, financial issues take on greater salience for a larger segment of the domestic population. In the case of Japan, the public has become painfully aware of the cost of accommodating mobile capital, as evidenced in fiscal policies, such as those increasing the consumption tax while reducing corporate and financial transaction–related taxes,[48] and of failed financial supervision, through the closure of financial institutions and the huge sums the government has pledged for the bailout of those remaining. Financial issues have been near the forefront of the political agenda in Japan for at least nine years now, and unlike the early 1980s, when financial reforms were debated almost exclusively among industry representatives, a handful of academics, and key politicians, these days financial policies influence party politics and public opinion matters. In short, globalization has pushed financial issues from the realm of "high politics," in which primarily sophisticated political actors or those with strong vested interests participate, into the realm of "low politics," in which the public is concerned and engaged.

Decentralization of Financial Authority

Three factors have fostered greater decentralization of financial authority in Japan. The first is the more active and overt role of politicians fostered by the politicization outlined above, the second is the revision of the Bank of Japan Law, and the third is the reorganization of MOF. Below I simply describe these changes. In the next section, I explore the implications of both politicization and decentralization for U.S.-Japan relations.

In 1993, the LDP's reign as one of the longest-running ruling parties in any contemporary democracy ended. This stunning loss of leadership was not caused by any single factor, but did take place at a time when public concern about political corruption and financial and economic mismanagement was intense. In fact, the early 1990s were a time in which both politicians and financial-market officials were near their nadir in terms of public support. In this environment, the opposition parties put forth a variety of proposals concerning reform of both the political system and the financial bureaucracies. Both political and financial reform were old issues in Japan and in their various manifestations had been debated but largely defeated numerous times over the years. Under these circumstances, however, a weakened LDP was barely able to save itself, let alone its longtime partner in economic management, MOF.

Given the myriad problems facing Japan and the LDP at the time, it was unclear whether the party would soon return to power or a new era of non-LDP administrations was just beginning. Faced with this uncertainty, some MOF leaders cooperated with the new leadership to an extent that antagonized their long-standing partner in governance, the LDP (Mabuchi 1998, 15; Brown 1999, 209–211). When the LDP did return to power, first in a coalition (1994) and then seating its own prime minister (1996), the party leadership was possibly less willing, and certainly less able, to defend MOF when pressured for reform. This is because the LDP's new dependence on coalition partners required that it consider, rather than simply dismiss, the more radical ideas to reform MOF proposed by less forgiving coalition partners.

This breakdown in the mutually supportive network between the LDP and MOF took place in the context of not only growing public criticism of MOF but also a broad financial reform process already in progress and propelled in large part by MOF itself. As a result, when the Hashimoto administration (1996–1998) promised it would curb the size and influence of the bureaucracy, it was both responding to global financial-market trends concerning financial liberalization and accommodating proposals that MOF be stripped of substantial power made by the two opposition parties in Hashimoto's coalition government (the Social Democratic Party and New Party Sakigake). In short, a supposedly all-powerful ministry, one that had withstood even the Supreme Commander for the Allied Powers' efforts at reform during the Allied occupation following World War II, was dismantled not by a strong LDP but, rather, by a seemingly weak and coalition-dependent one ("Under Attack" 1996; Mabuchi 1998; Hiwatari 1999).

The politics behind the reform process demonstrates that within a more politicized environment politicians, who are more desperate to please voters, and coalition members will more readily and more actively address areas of bureaucratic authority formerly left unchallenged. The postwar National Diet has always had ultimate authority to restructure ministries as its members see fit. Nevertheless, the extent to which politicians have been taking advantage of this power as it concerns the financial agencies is unprecedented, at least in the postwar period. Thus, while political intervention itself is a not a new factor in the political economy of financial policy making in Japan (Rosenbluth 1989), the past several years suggest that the Diet may become a more proactive and volatile source of decision making concerning financial policy than ever before.

The impact of this reform on MOF itself is obviously also critical to our story and clearly reflects the extent to which MOF is viewed as having mismanaged Japan's financial system.[49] The June 1998 reorganization of the ministry transferred authority for the inspection and supervision of financial institutions to a new Financial Supervisory Agency (FSA).[50] Within MOF, the Financial Inspection Department was eliminated and the Banking and Securities Bureaus were merged to create a new Financial Planning Bureau. Although MOF leadership failed in its efforts to have the FSA located within the ministry, as was the Securities and Exchange Surveillance Commission when it was created in 1992, the relationship between MOF and the new FSA is complicated, particularly in regard to personnel exchange, crisis management, and financial planning (Mabuchi 1998, 3–4).[51]

To begin with, over 90 percent of the FSA's starting staff came from MOF, and all but those reaching the position of department chief in the FSA will be eligible to return to MOF posts after two years at the new agency. This suggests that developing a cadre of FSA officials who do not feel beholden to MOF for career advancement may be difficult and thereby increases the FSA's susceptibility to MOF influence. In addition, while the FSA is charged with dealing with the failure of individual institutions, MOF must be consulted in cases where the repercussions of failure may cause system instability or require publicly funded assistance. Similarly, while the FSA was created in large part to reduce MOF's opaque administration based on close ongoing relationships with financial institutions' representatives, MOF is still able to maintain an open line to these institutions by requiring information from them for purposes of "planning." The extent to which MOF will use these last two ties to financial institutions as a way to emasculate the new FSA or pull it under its wing is something only time will tell.

Similarly, the revision of the Bank of Japan Law in June 1997 was designed to increase the central bank's independence, primarily vis-à-vis MOF.[52] The postwar relationship between the BOJ and MOF brought both costs and benefits to the central bank. On the one hand, many BOJ officials and economists considered MOF's influence over BOJ policy detrimental to both the central bank as an institution and the economy as a whole. The BOJ's ability to resist MOF influence was limited, however, because the old Bank of Japan Law provided MOF with significant legal influence. Moreover, the BOJ was beholden to MOF for "protection" from Diet pressure. That is, both MOF and BOJ officials recognized that one of MOF's roles was to stand between the Diet and the BOJ and buffer political demands regarding monetary policy and other financial affairs.

Given these preferences and institutional circumstances, over the years the central bank tried to resist MOF influence to the extent that its institutional capabilities allowed.[53] That is, BOJ officials pursued and achieved some level of de facto independence even though de jure the BOJ was one of the least independent central banks. For example, BOJ officials considered it a success that MOF was excluded from any participation in the formation of the Executives' Meeting of East Asian and Pacific Central Banks.[54] In addition, growing international agreement among scholars and policymakers concerning the economic benefits of central bank independence (Henning 1994)[55] were used to add credence to the BOJ's own pursuit of this goal and were brought to the public's attention through press accounts of various committee reports on central-bank reform (Brown 1999, 174–75; Mikitani and Kuwayama 1999, 2–3).[56]

In particular, supporters of greater BOJ independence focused on a body of economic literature examining the importance of central-bank independence in signaling to the international community a government's ability to uphold monetary-policy commitments.[57] This literature saw Japan as an anomaly because, although the BOJ ranked as one of the least independent central banks, Japan enjoyed one of the lowest inflation rates, which is an outcome expected only from countries with very independent central banks. This empirical outcome was explained by either the overwhelming influence of domestic interest groups that gain from low inflation or the BOJ's association with MOF, which was viewed as having enough autonomy from political forces that it could in turn protect the BOJ, thereby creating the same effect as BOJ independence.

While neither of these views is fully satisfying, it is true that the relative stability and constancy of political, bureaucratic, and business relations in the postwar period greatly reduced the pressures for drastic changes in monetary policy that often accompany changes in administrations or swings between left- and right-wing coalitions in other countries. Thus, as Lohmann argues, Japan's ability to maintain low inflation was a function of "non-institutionalized reputational means" rooted in the stability of the relations between a long-dominant ruling party, big business, and the bureaucracy (1997, 77). By implication, the extensive turmoil seen in each of these three sectors of Japan's political economy in the 1990s meant that the BOJ's commitment to price stability could no longer be assured by its political context; therefore, that commitment needed to be signaled through institutionalized means. This explains the logic behind the BOJ's continued efforts to "regularize" Japanese monetary institutions in line with other respected central banks, most notably the U.S. Federal Reserve Board. BOJ preferences do not necessarily explain policy change, however, and some have even argued that the BOJ did not play a large role in mobilizing support for the new Bank of Japan Law (Mikitani and Kuwayama 1999).

Revision of the law appeared on the political agenda more than once in Japan's postwar history but was always shunted aside, whether through MOF opposition or Diet indifference. This time, however, three circumstances contributed to its successful passage. First, BOJ reform came up as part and parcel of discussions of system-wide financial reform and, despite considerable opposition and some concessions to MOF, was pushed through by politicians as a critical part of Prime Minister Hashimoto's commitment to reform in response to the tremendous public outcry against government corruption, the government's (taxpayers') bailout of the jūsen, and other evidence of general financial-system mismanagement.[58] In other words, it was presented as part of a comprehensive plan for improving Japan's financial structure and not simply as a move by the BOJ to improve its status. Second, because MOF's reputation had been smeared by its involvement in various scandals and its apparent inability to pull Japan out of its financial morass, MOF officials were in no position to staunchly defend their continued influence over BOJ affairs. Many in fact blamed excessive MOF influence for the central bank's easy monetary policy in the late 1980s, which had contributed to the asset-inflated bubble economy and the later banking crisis (Ueda 1998).[59] For this reason, some see the passage of the revised Bank of Japan Law as simply another way to punish MOF. Considering the apparent willingness of LDP politicians to allow MOF to be the scapegoat for Japan's many woes, some have suggested that MOF officials' eventual lukewarm support for the new Bank of Japan Law was a diversionary tactic designed to deflect criticism and appease opposition politicians interested in more radical dismemberment of MOF (Cargill 1998, 19; Sapsford 1999, A14).

On the other hand, BOJ officials were not all behaving like angels, either. Several had been caught in a bribery scandal, and there was political pressure independent from anti-MOF sentiment to improve the central bank's transparency and public accountability. As one article put it, "The price of independence would be openness"(Sapsford 1999, A14). At this point, one must consider politicians' incentives for revising the law. The new law was discussed primarily in terms of how it would change the BOJ's relationship with MOF. But it would change the BOJ's relationship with the Diet, as well.

One expected implication of the new law was that less MOF influence meant more Diet influence. And the BOJ did recently create a new section to manage BOJ relations with the Diet, suggesting that the bank too expected it would have to deal with pressures from politicians once managed by MOF. But BOJ independence from MOF need not mean greater Diet influence. As Goodman (1991) has argued, politicians representing strong conservative social coalitions will vote to increase central-bank independence if they expect to lose their hold on political power.[60] The logic of this argument is that by granting the central bank independence while in power, the existing administration can essentially institutionalize its preferences for low inflation or price stability and effectively tie the hands of successor opposition parties, especially more liberal ones, that might prefer to use monetary policy to achieve more redistributive objectives. The underlying assumption is that politicians expecting to maintain their hold on power want freedom to intervene in monetary policy as they see fit but do not want to give those with different preferences the same opportunity. Although it may be an exaggeration to say the LDP *expected* to lose control of the Diet in the near future, certainly the political turmoil experienced in Japan over the previous eight years made that a much more likely scenario than at almost any time in the postwar period. Moreover, this argument explains why the LDP would not have felt compelled to grant the BOJ greater independence at earlier times.

As with the creation of the FSA, the impact of the new law on BOJ effectiveness and on the BOJ-MOF relationship is still far from clear. On the one hand, in their early analysis Mikitani and Kuwayama find the new law lacking. They point in particular to the law's impractical separation of monetary policy from other responsibilities and the several ways in which MOF might still wield influence over the BOJ, including BOJ responsibilities to keep "close contact" with MOF and submit parts of its budget for MOF approval, attendance by the minister of finance or his representative at meetings of the Policy Board, and continued treatment of the BOJ as the government's "agent" when conducting foreign-currency transactions. They summarize: "The muddying of the line between central bank and government responsibilities is unfortunately characteristic of the entire spirit of this law, which thus perpetuates exactly the kind of ambiguity that has kept the Bank of Japan from establishing its independence and accountability in the past" (1999, 11). On the other hand, despite these and other criticisms that the new law does not go far enough in ensuring BOJ independence, several commentators conclude that in the end it is not the legal institutional structure that will determine the extent of BOJ independence but rather BOJ policy practice.[61] In this regard, the BOJ is now in a better position to earn the public's trust and use greater transparency and accountability to its advantage as a means to reveal to the public any inappropriate efforts by politicians to intervene in BOJ affairs (Mikitani and Kuwayama 1999, 21). Although still very early, it is telling, therefore, that the BOJ has already publicly refused both MOF's and the prime minister's request that the BOJ raise interest rates or print money to reduce the value of the yen (Zaforin 1999).

IMPLICATIONS OF INCREASED
POLITICIZATION AND DECENTRALIZATION

Above I have outlined some of the changes in Japan's domestic economic, political, and bureaucratic circumstances that have affected financial politics. To reiterate, the most important of these 1990s developments were the decline in Japan's economic and financial health, volatility in political leadership, and reorganization of the financial bureaucracies. Here I consider some of the possible implications of these developments for U.S.-Japan financial relations.

First, increased politicization and decentralization are bound to complicate the policy-making processes in Japan and by extension any negotiations between the U.S. and Japanese governments. The reorganization of bureaucratic authority outlined above has increased the number of at least relatively independent institutional actors involved in financial policy making. Thus, whereas MOF was essentially in charge of managing the entire official response to failed institutions in the past, the FSA, MOF, and the BOJ may all bring different institutionally defined approaches to resolving such problems in the future. The unfortunate absence of clearer demarcation among these agencies' responsibilities further encourages their staffs to fight over jurisdiction and possibly feel compelled to participate in more types of negotiations than might otherwise be necessary. That is, if multiple jurisdictions are involved, conflicts among at least ostensibly independent Japanese agencies are sure to equal if not surpass those seen between MOF bureaus before the restructuring.

When one adds to this increase in institutional actors more intense competition among politicians, who are more motivated to respond to a wider range of opinions as they seek to solidify their voter base, the domestic politics of financial policy making looks much more contested than it did just a decade ago. Given the Japanese tradition of consultation and consensus building in policy formation, an increase in the number of powerful actors with a vested interest in the outcome almost ensures that resolving the domestic conflicts informing national policy decisions will become more difficult and time consuming.[62] The exception that proves the rule is that during times of crisis, such as Japan has experienced repeatedly in the past few years, surprisingly swift and radical policy change is sometimes possible.[63] Nevertheless, once a crisis has abated and the new institutional arrangements have fallen into place, only extraordinary leadership from the Diet prevents Japanese policy making from reverting to the incremental style that so often frustrates Americans. Given the unlikelihood of any radical change in Japan's policy-making style, the United States will just have to be patient with its often slow-moving ally. Fortunately, thus far the United States has been able to afford to be.

Although one would not generally characterize the U.S. government's standard approach toward Japan as gracious and patient, given the extent of the financial troubles Japan has faced over the past five years American officials have been less aggressive toward Japan than past relations would lead one to expect.[64] This greater patience with Japan is largely a function of the good fortune of a strong American economy.[65] In the words of the usually understated Federal Reserve Board Chairman Alan Greenspan, the performance of the American economy over the past seven years has been "truly phenomenal" (1999, 11). Its strength has been particularly pronounced in relation to the rest of the world, with the excess of U.S. growth over foreign growth in 1998 the largest in two decades and U.S. domestic demand–led growth accounting for almost one-third of the world total since 1996 (Greenspan 1999, 1; Meyer 1999, 2). Needless to say, this economic strength has also imposed on the United States the burden of pulling along the weaker economies almost single-handedly.[66] That role is quite clearly manifest in the United States' growing current account deficit, which reached nearly US$225 billion at the end of 1998 (Higgins and Klitgaard 1998, 1).

Although the current account deficit is a perennial sore spot in U.S.-Japan relations, for the time being the imbalance is not being highlighted as the most pressing problem. One reason is the U.S. government's recognition that attempts to crack down on imports now could threaten the fragile recovery taking place around the world and would thus prove to be a step backward over the long run. In addition, strong employment in the United States has virtually eliminated the usual channel of political complaints about the deficit. Formerly, the current account deficit was reviled as jeopardizing American jobs, because competitive imports meant U.S. exporters were hurting and might shut down or shift production overseas. During the 1990s, however, the current account deficit proved not to be a threat to overall employment in the United States, where the unemployment rate declined to a twenty-five-year low, in part because of capital investment from Japan.[67]

In this instance, the complementary aspects of the U.S.-Japan debtor-creditor relationship created a temporary buffer around the potentially strife-ridden topic of payments imbalances. But no one knows how long this buffer will last. For years Americans have insisted that the continuing current account imbalance could not be sustained without severe consequences, and yet it has lasted for quite some time and apparently without catastrophic effect. Nevertheless, economists and policymakers seem virtually unanimous in proclaiming that at some point the burden of the deficit, which of course represents foreign claims on the United States, will become too great and too destabilizing for the United States and the world economy to bear. One can only hope that currently favorable economic circumstances will sustain American patience long enough to facilitate Japan's economic recovery.

A second implication of increased politicization and decentralization is that communication and cooperative efforts between the United States and Japan may take place through new channels. Although this is purely speculative at this point, it is possible, for example, that continued politicization of financial issues in Japan will lead U.S. representatives to spend more time with their Japanese counterparts as Diet participation in policy debates becomes more visible. More likely, however, is an increase in what Keohane and Nye describe as transgovernmental relations (1977, 33–34), which is when bureaucrats or other government agents cooperate directly with their counterparts in other countries in ways that reflect their institutional complementarity of interests, as opposed to more all-encompassing national interests.[68] When power is decentralized and institutions become more specialized, as is happening through reform in Japan, the prospects for this process to take root also increase.

Looking at the U.S.-Japan case specifically, there has long been a great divide between the career generalists who reach the top of a Japanese bureaucracy charged with a broad agenda of responsibilities and the professionals with more hands-on experience running more narrowly charged U.S. financial agencies. Because of reform in Japan, however, this contrast has diminished somewhat in the past few years, and further changes in this direction are expected. Both globalization and decentralization have demanded greater expertise of financial supervisors and other officials, and since the late 1980s Japan's financial bureaucracies have been making career-track adjustments accordingly. The implications of decentralization and specialization for U.S.-Japan relations will depend on how far these two trends are carried (that is, whether the private-sector accountants recently hired to help out the primarily MOF-derived staff of the FSA will promote the development of FSA-specific expertise). In general, however, as officials on both sides of the table share an increasingly similar background and vocabulary in regard to financial matters, agreement among American and Japanese *specialists* should become much easier.[69] For example, one can readily anticipate that an official from the U.S. Security and Exchange Commission is more likely to find common ground discussing regulations to limit churning (the unnecessary trading of securities) with a similarly trained specialist in securities supervision working at Japan's new Securities and Exchange Surveillance Commission than he or she would have found with a MOF generalist whose institutional concerns ranged from securities supervision to the balance of regulatory burdens vis-à-vis banks and the impact of reduced transactions on the revenue gleaned from the securities transaction tax.

As the epistemic-community literature suggests, cross-national communities of specialists can often reach agreement more readily than can national representatives. Moreover, negotiators can at times use an internationally cooperative base as leverage to move their governments in the agreed upon direction (Moravcsik 1994). The greater efficiency of negotiations among more narrowly interested parties and their ability to pull governments into line is exemplified by the greater success of such groups as the BIS Committee on Banking Supervision than more broadly based efforts at macroeconomic policy coordination (Bergsten and Henning 1996). Thus, as long as the U.S.-Japan relationship continues to be strengthened through the resolution of many small specialized issues, decentralization accompanied by specialization and greater transgovernmental relations should contribute to overall financial-market cooperation.

In sum, politicization, and decentralization accompanied by greater specialization, can cut both ways, depending on the type of issue addressed. In the case of broad national policies with distributive effects obvious to the voting public, politicization and decentralization can be expected to complicate the process of reaching a domestic consensus and slow down the policy-making and policy-implementation process even more—unless, of course, political stability returns and the Diet proves able and willing to provide decisive leadership. On the other hand, in the context of the more technical and seemingly apolitical issues often associated with developing cooperative financial-market approaches in particular, decentralization accompanied by specialization should improve the chances of the United States and Japan reaching agreement more readily.

Conclusion

In this chapter, we have reviewed a variety of factors associated directly or indirectly with the globalization of finance and considered how they might shape U.S.-Japan financial-market relations in the future. It is far too early to tell whether the need for greater international financial-market supervision will be met by adequate cooperative efforts. Similarly, it is impossible to know with any certainty how the domestic turmoil in Japan's economic, political, and bureaucratic systems will play out over the next few years. Nevertheless, globalization is clearly a factor that will continue to influence the policy options available to both the United States and Japan.

Globalization is binding the two economies ever closer together and making each more sensitive to changes even in what were formerly considered small, and in terms of market share insignificant, financial markets. Due to their unique positions in international financial-market affairs, however, both the United States and Japan have a tremendously high stake in maintaining basic stability. Accordingly, I am confident that other conflicts will not be allowed to undermine this fundamental common interest.

One should not expect, however, that globalization will eliminate political competition to shape the rules of financial-market competition or the distributive outcomes these markets produce. As discussed above, sometimes the terms of financial-market competition can be adjusted in one's favor through unilateral regulatory or other policy adjustments. Both the Big Bang of financial reforms in London years ago and the ongoing Big Bang of financial reforms in Japan provide clear examples of governments taking unilateral steps to recapture lost international financial-market competitiveness. Sometimes, however, forcing other nations to adjust to terms more favorable to oneself seems the best, or at least the most politically expedient, route. The history of U.S.-Japan trade relations offers a seemingly endless parade of such occasions, with the list of bilateral demands embodied in the yen-dollar talks providing an obvious financial market counterpart (Frankel 1984).

Finally, economic conflicts between the United States and Japan in the past have been closely associated with payments imbalances, and financial politics cannot be permanently delinked from this issue. Thus, one should expect that significant changes in the balance of payments will change the context of the U.S.-Japan discourse in financial affairs. It is possible that this imbalance will lessen if the United States continues to make gains in regard to its fiscal deficit, the aging of Japan's population encourages more spending relative to savings, and Japan continues to welcome foreign direct investment. This scenario, however, is still years down the road.

Regardless of these possibilities, globalization will continue to affect U.S.-Japan relations. We have seen that it increases the importance of international cooperation for these uniquely positioned nations, especially in regard to financial-system stability. This basic level of cooperation, however, will limit but not eliminate the competition between the United States and Japan over the distribution of economic gains and over political leadership in Asia. In addition, the many changes taking place within Japan's political economy will continue to affect the political processes involved in U.S.-Japan negotiations. My prediction is that absent rarely seen commanding leadership by Japanese politicians, politicization and decentralization will make cooperation over broad financial-market issues more difficult because it will involve a larger number of actors and institutions, each with more narrowly defined interests. On the other hand, frank discussion of contending financial-system arrangements, greater institutionalization of existing cooperative arrangements, more transparent financial-market governance, and increased contact between similarly focused specialists will contribute to better management of the financial-market conflicts that will inevitably arise.

The conclusion I draw from this examination of the impact of globalization on U.S.-Japan relations is that cooperation in regard to stability-threatening issues will continue and develop further over the next decade. Continued cooperation designed to maintain international financial stability is well recognized as a first-level priority by both nations, and over time their repertoire of coordinated policy responses is expanding and becoming institutionalized through the IMF and other forums. On the other hand, cooperation involving agreements with longer-term distributional implications will remain difficult. Efforts aimed at this type of cooperation were clearly among the most contentious during the 1980s and included virtually all discussions concerning the regulatory, accounting, and other supervisory practices that ultimately define a new international standard. These issues, which are already difficult to settle because of their distributional and long-term implications, are expected to become even more difficult to negotiate. In addition to the problems that arise because of the competition between New York and Tokyo over financial-market jurisdiction and influence, distributional issues will become more difficult to resolve because of the increased politicization of financial-market issues at the domestic level and the restructuring of financial authority in Japan. In the long run, however, many of the issues in the latter category may essentially sort themselves out.

Today, many financial markets are in an awkward stage, and the politicians and financial authorities managing their development are still figuring out the proper balance between largely domestic markets with limited international exposure and more internationally integrated markets with some purely domestically oriented institutions. Accordingly, distribution-driven disagreements over what standards international market participants should follow are severe and concern a large number of issues. Of course, given the ever changing nature of markets, one cannot expect that even the standards worked out during this transitional phase will last forever. Adjustments will be ongoing. Nevertheless, over time the negotiation of standards will also become institutionalized and changes are more likely to be at the margin and affect all actors more equally than do contemporary agreements that are essentially defining international standards for the first time.

In addition, to the extent that market forces continue to pressure market actors, and through them government policies, to adapt to new market trends, whether this be through the offering of new products, new practices, or new organization forms, the number of issue areas requiring bargaining between governments may diminish, as well. That is to say, with the increased liberalization that has accompanied globalization, market actors themselves now play a larger role in defining international standards, and government agreements, while still very necessary, will concern more the market sustaining, supervisory, and crisis-management issues, where cooperation has proven to be more easily achieved.

The above conclusions are based on a broad view of the ways in which globalization is affecting the issues and institutions through which agreements concerning international financial issues are pursued, but should inform the U.S.-Japan relationship as well. To this broad perspective, however, we must add two factors unique to the bilateral relationship. First, for the time being Japan is the only nation in Asia that can support a regionally oriented alternative to a U.S.-based "Western" interpretation of how the globalization of finance should proceed.[70] Thus, as discussed above, disagreements between the United States and Japan over how best to integrate Asian economies into the global financial system may increase the ideational level of tension between the two nations over financial-market affairs. Yet a more straightforward exchange of ideas may ultimately strengthen U.S.-Japan understanding rather than threaten it.

Finally, throughout this chapter I have treated the common interest of the United States and Japan in maintaining international financial-market stability as defining the boundary limiting financial-market conflict between them. As stated in the introduction, however, without question the U.S.-Japan security relationship will continue to constrain the form of Japanese aspirations concerning Asian leadership, as well as the degree of assertiveness with which Japan can confront the United States over any financial issue. I am not in a position to guarantee that this security relationship is so central to each nation's national interest that neither government would breach it regardless of the severity of financial-market disagreements. But all obvious indications are that it is. Morever, most conflicts are of a much more limited nature. Accordingly, I conclude that even in the face of increased globalization the U.S.-Japan security relationship and the two nations' common interest in avoiding an international financial-system meltdown will provide ample assurance that while conflict and competition over financial issues will continue, they will be managed within an ongoing and fundamentally cooperative relationship.

Notes

1. Much of this variation in degrees of change is explained by the simple historical fact that the U.S. financial system was more open and exposed to international pressure from an earlier time, whereas the Japanese financial system was largely insulated from international pressures until the 1980s. Explanation of this variation is beyond the scope of this chapter.

2. This approach runs the risk of underrepresenting the role played by culture, history, and other variables closely tied to national identity, but puts us in a better position to understand how domestic political and institutional variables identified as causing patterns in national policy making in the past may themselves be subject to change.

3. This chapter only introduces these arguments. Testing the validity of the assumptions and causal inferences would, of course, require more rigorous examination, including a larger number of cases.

4. The literature on the causes, limits, and impact of financial globalization is vast and growing. A sense of this literature can be gleaned from Cohen (1996), Rodrik (1997), and Germain (1999).

5. As illustrative examples of financial globalization, by 1998 cross-border bank claims

had increased over five times the level fifteen years earlier, equaling more than 40 percent of the combined gross domestic product (GDP) of the Organization for Economic Cooperation and Development (OECD) countries. The annual issuance of international bonds more than quadrupled between 1988 and 1998, and between 1983 and 1998 securities transactions expanded from about 10 percent to around 70 percent of GDP in Japan and to "well above" 100 percent of GDP in the United States (Federal Reserve Bank of New York 1998).

6. The world has not yet seen, and may never see, a fully global market. Nevertheless, the trend in financial markets over the past several decades has unquestionably pointed toward greater interdependence.

7. Although Thomas (1998) provides an excellent argument concerning the equal importance of foreign direct investment in shaping the impact of increased capital mobility, this chapter focuses primarily on financial investment and portfolio forms of capital.

8. On the process and measurement of capital mobility and the internationalization of finance, see Cross (1998); Frankel (1991); Turner (1991); Goodman and Pauly (1993); and Bank for International Settlements (1998).

9. At the end of 1992 the net liabilities of the United States were approximately US$611 billion and the net foreign assets of Japan were approximately US$513 billion. Moreover, since the beginning of the 1980s a very substantial portion of Japan's current account surplus has been vis-à-vis the United States, which implies that Japan has been lending directly or indirectly to the United States (Hamada 1996, 79).

10. Interview, U.S. Embassy, Tokyo, June 1999.

11. One might begin a history of this type of cooperation with the establishment of the Basle Committee in 1974. Officially named the Standing Committee on Banking Regulations and Supervisory Practices, it was created after the failure of Franklin National Bank in the United States and, seven weeks later, the collapse of Bankhaus Herstatt in West Germany revealed how the failure of even a small institution conducting international (in these cases foreign-exchange) business could have significant and cross-national effects. Since that time, multilateral responses to financial crises have become if not routine, at least clearly expected, whether concerning Latin American debt in the 1980s or the recent currency crisis in Asia. As illustrative contrast, Eichengreen and Portes (1987) and Eichengreen (1996) examine financial crises before World War II.

12. The extent to which this serves or detracts from stable U.S.-Japan relations overall is discussed below.

13. A number of these changes are discussed in Dwyer (forthcoming). Brown has also pointed out, for example, that the recent routinization of the promotion of the director of the International Finance Bureau of MOF to the post of vice-minister for international affairs reflects greater recognition that this official should have expertise in not only international finance and English but also management of U.S. pressure (1999, 21).

14. This holds true whether one adopts a rational-actor model in which institutions embody repetition in strategic games, reduce transaction costs, and enhance the credibility of commitment; whether one focuses on the organizational characteristics of institutions that allow members increasingly to solve problems through standard operating procedures; or whether one highlights the importance of ideas and the role of institutions in facilitating the transmission of ideas, learning, and the development and empowerment of epistemic communities.

15. These cross-national complaints were amply evident in the Yen -Dollar Agreement (Frankel 1984).

16. In addition to the less tangible benefits of increased international prestige and power, there are very practical domestic benefits including tax revenues, employment opportunities, and greater influence over the players who shape international market developments.

17. For further discussion of what attributes market participants prefer and why competition does not lead to a "race to the bottom," see Kane (1988); Dwyer (forthcoming).

18. Interviews, BOJ, 1998. Numerous illustrations of the comparative decline of Tokyo vis-à-vis not only London and New York but also Singapore and Hong Kong can be found in Itō (1999).

19. See the Foreign Press Center newsletter *PressGuide*, March 1997, for details. To achieve this goal, the government is even moving to eliminate the long-standing ban on holding companies so that Japanese companies will be able to offer the range of financial products standard elsewhere.

20. Criticism of the Japanese approach to restructuring came not only from the United States but from most of the rest of the world, as well. A recent OECD report is particularly critical of the lack of rapid and forceful action in Japan. See "Japan Must Deregulate" (1999). Similar criticisms were well publicized in an earlier IMF report (International Monetary Fund 1995).

21. The interaction through which these evaluations are made is quite obvious. In addition to filling newspaper articles with quotations concerning whether the financial community considers a Japanese policy good or bad, these market actors make their preferences clear by moving funds out of Japanese investments when they do not like a government proposal and moving them back once sufficiently credible steps are in place. Thus, for example, the international financial community signaled its disapproval of the government's initial plan to disclose bad loans only on an aggregate basis, as opposed to bank by bank, by charging all Japanese banks a significant premium over and above market rates. More recent policies requiring disclosure at levels imposed in the United States and the United Kingdom are being well received, as were the aspects of the bridge-bank proposal modeled on the U.S. Resolution Trust Corporation. See, for example, *Wall Street Journal* Interactive Edition, 2 July 1998.

22. As one Department of State representative suggested, the United States does not have to push Japan to make these adjustments; it knows from the market what needs to be done (Interview, U.S. Embassy, Tokyo 1998).

23. This coincides with greater reluctance to follow the U.S. lead more generally (Huntington 1999).

24. Detailed discussion of the East Asian crisis already abounds and is beyond the scope of this chapter. It is often argued, however, that Japan helped create the Asian currency crisis, because the endless decline of the yen hurt the competitiveness of Asian countries, and is prolonging the crisis through its failure to address domestic reform and recovery aggressively enough.

25. Since the Asian financial crisis began in July 1997, Japan has contributed more than any other nation to the cause of East Asia's recovery (Castellano 1999, 1). Japanese exposure to the Asian region was estimated at US$100 billion in December 1998 ("Recessions in

Asia Mutually Reinforcing" 1998).

26. This assistance included pledges from not only the IMF but also the World Bank and the Asian Development Bank, as well as from individual countries, including Australia, Brunei, China, Japan, and other East Asian countries.

27. Interviews, U.S. Embassy, Tokyo, June 1999.

28. Interview, senior advisor, International Division, BOJ, June 1998.

29. See, for example, reporting on the summit between U.S. President Bill Clinton and Japanese Prime Minister Obuchi Keizō in the *Nihon Keizai Shimbun* 22 September 1998.

30. Not surprisingly, Sakakibara Eisuke, MOF vice-minister for international affairs at the time the AMF idea was broached, continues to tout the idea ("Mr. Yen Says" 2000). In addition, Japanese central bank officials are working on a payments system for Asian nations that could serve as the operational network for the AMF (interviews, June 1999).

31. Through this program, officially titled "A New Initiative to Overcome the Asian Currency Crisis," Japan committed itself to providing a package of support measures totaling US$30 billion to finance short- and long-term capital needs in Asia. The second stage of this program, called "The Resource Mobilization Plan for Asia," was established in May 1999, and "The New Miyazawa Initiative Short-term Financing Facility" was established in July of the same year.

32. Interview, senior advisor, International Division, BOJ, July 26, 1998. The group is the Executives' Meeting of East Asian and Pacific Central Banks (EMEAP). It has a three-tiered structure including regular governors' meetings, deputies' meetings, and working groups. Participants include representatives from Australia, China, Hong Kong, Indonesia, Japan, Malaysia, New Zealand, the Philippines, Singapore, South Korea, and Thailand. For details, see Oritani (1998) or visit the EMEAP website at <http://www.emeap.org:8084/>.

33. It should be noted that both Sakakibara and Summers have reputations of being more outspoken and blunt, and therefore less diplomatic, in their public comments than many of their predecessors. Consequently, their exchanges should not be viewed as representative of the usual tone of U.S.-Japan diplomacy.

34. Associated Press, New York, 28 June 1999.

35. This is an area in which the Japanese view actually won out, since the G7 countries later agreed to allow capital controls by developing nations in some instances.

36. Although U.S. representatives do not like Japanese criticism of the IMF, they run the risk of seeming too harsh if they aggressively counter these claims. With Japan poised to take the role now, and China expected to emerge someday as an Asian leader, the United States would not benefit from being seen as overbearing or unsympathetic in Asia.

37. A senior Japanese financial official who has accompanied Sakakibara on many occasions and defines him as a "close friend" has repeatedly described him as someone who just prefers straightforwardness and "would never take the chance of breaking with the United States." This description is based on numerous discussions between 1988 and 1999. The quote is from June 24, 1999.

38. One senior BOJ official recounted to me a discussion between Chinese and Japanese central bankers in which the Chinese asked why Japan backed down so readily in the face of U.S. opposition to its proposals concerning the Asian financial crisis. His comment to me was that the Chinese, being in a different position, just do not understand that Japan's dependence on the United States for security is in the background of every policy

decision (interview, 24 June 1999).

39. While some of these changes may not have obvious ties to the process of globalization per se, they all relate to financial-market developments, which cannot be taken out of their global context.

40. Most of the literature viewing the Japanese bureaucracy as the dominant player in Japan's political economy falls within this category (e.g., Vogel 1996), but even those who identify politicians as dominant have pointed out the political system's slow response to signals for change (e.g., Rosenbluth 1996).

41. For a broad examination of this transition, see Pempel (1998).

42. Although this chapter is not the forum in which to adequately analyze the causes of either the bursting of the asset-inflated bubble economy or the banking crisis that unfolded thereafter, there is no question that the globalization of finance was a factor in shaping the events of the 1990s in Japan. Increased pressure, thanks to globalization, for greater domestic deregulation, which was not always met with adequate reregulation; the BOJ's sacrifice of domestic monetary stability under pressure from the government, ostensibly to uphold its promises made in the context of G7 macroeconomic cooperation; and BIS agreements on capital adequacy, a cooperative response to globalization—all were factors in Japan's current financial morass (Ueda 1998).

43. Dentsu's bimonthly public opinion poll found that 80 percent of respondents described the economic situation as "bad," as reported in the *Asahi Shimbun* (19 November 1997, 10).

44. On administrative reform more generally, see Carlile (1998).

45. Scandalous activities plaguing the financial sector and MOF over the past decade are legion, including loss compensation by securities firms to important clients, fraud and failure to disclose enormous trading losses by Daiwa Bank in New York, payoffs to corporate racketeers by a variety of financial institutions, financial officials being disciplined for accepting lavish entertainment from clients seeking inside information, and the general crisis in the financial sector, which MOF was expected to prevent.

46. Not surprisingly, proposals from the LDP, which for so long governed in tandem with MOF, were less radical than proposals put forth by opposition-party members. As Hiwatari explains, "the splitting of MOF came only as a concession to its coalition partners" (1999, 1).

47. Keohane and Milner (1996) provides an excellent overview of the way internationalization affects domestic political economies through exposure to changes in terms of trade, as well as the way domestic institutions can shape the extent and quality of these influences.

48. The initial imposition of the consumption tax in 1988 drew much attention because it had been successfully defeated for so long. Nevertheless, it was only one part of a larger tax package that was designed to promote competitiveness through greater capital investment and included a reduction in corporate tax and a lowering of the securities transaction tax. Similarly, the increase in the consumption tax in 1996 was coupled with a large push by Japanese corporations to lower the corporate tax rate to a level similar to that in the United States (Okada 1996).

49. See Mabuchi (1998) for discussion of the role of the media in perpetrating this attack on MOF.

50. The FSA currently reports to a newly created Financial Reconstruction Commission (initially called the Financial Revitalization Commission) chaired by a cabinet minister but in April 2001 is expected to stand alone as the Financial Agency, with its own cabinet minister and at a level equal to MOF (MOF handout, June 1999).

51. As one BOJ official wrote recently, "The relationship between the MOF and the FSA is so complicated that it is very difficult to describe" (personal correspondence, 14 May 1999).

52. While the new law does not use the word *independence*, it does stipulate that the autonomy of the bank should be respected and transparency ensured (art. 3, par. 1, 2). Details concerning the Bank of Japan Law and the reorganization of the Bank of Japan can be found at the BOJ website: <http://www.boj.or.jp>.

53. Details of conflicts between MOF and the BOJ over money-market management and monetary policy can be found in Dwyer (1997, chap. 7).

54. Interviews, BOJ, 28 July 1998.

55. Taking exception to this commonly accepted view, Berman and McNamara (1999) argues that central-bank independence does not necessarily produce better economic outcomes and that central banks should be more responsive to politics.

56. The relevant committees were MOF's Financial System Research Council and the prime minister's Central Bank Study Group (the Torii Committee).

57. This discussion is based in large part on Lohmann (1997).

58. Interview with Shiozaki Yasuhisa, parlimentary vice-minister of finance at the time, June 1999. See also Brown (1999, 174–175) and Mikitani and Kuwayama (1999, 2).

59. The logic is that because of commitments the Japanese government had made concerning foreign-exchange rates in the Plaza Accord of 1985 and the Louvre Accord of 1987, the BOJ was pressured by MOF to place undue emphasis on the foreign-exchange implications of its monetary policy rather than attend primarily to domestic circumstances.

60. Boylan (1998) makes a similar argument.

61. Cargill in various publications has gone the furthest in arguing that despite its institutional dependence the BOJ began enhancing its political independence when it first successfully fought inflation in 1973 and "had achieved a considerable degree of political independence by the 1980s" (1998, 18.) See also Cargill, Hutchinson, and Itō 1997.

62. This statement obviously assumes that what I have characterized as typical Japanese policy-making style is a function of deeply embedded sociocultural traditions, as opposed to only institutional constraints, and thus is less likely to change quickly in response to institutional changes, such as administrative or electoral reform.

63. In the words of Gourevitch, crises create "open moments when system-creating choices are made" (1986, 34).

64. The relative lack of U.S. attention in the traditional form of "Japan bashing" even raised some concern in Japan and came to be known as "Japan passing."

65. This is not to suggest that the United States has not been critical of Japan's slow progress, just that, given the extent of the damage, the United States has been relatively restrained in its criticism of Japan in public, compared with U.S. posturing in the 1980s.

66. Europe's gains in GDP have been only modest; nevertheless Europe has also contributed to world economic recovery.

67. Japan's recession reduced domestic investment opportunities, pushing Japanese surplus funds into overseas investments. This flow of funds put downward pressure on world—and U.S.—interest rates, which in turn spurred investment and job creation in the United States to an extent that more than compensated for export-related job losses (Higgins and Klitgaard 1998, 1, 4).

68. Transgovernmental networks support bureaucrats' efforts to avoid politicization of issues under their jurisdiction (Keohane and Nye 1977, 33), a well-noted objective of MOF bureaucrats in particular (Horne 1985; Rosenbluth 1989; Vogel 1996).

69. This commonality of experience is already increasing as more Japanese officials attend graduate school in the United States.

70. Obviously China may someday take on this role, but not in the near future.

BIBLIOGRAPHY

Andrews, David. 1994. "Capital Mobility and State Autonomy: Towards a Structural Theory of International Monetary Relations." *International Studies Quarterly* 38(2): 193–218.

Axelrod, Robert. 1984. *The Evolution of Cooperation*. New York: Basic Books.

Bank for International Settlements. 1986. *Recent Innovations in International Banking*. Basle: Bank for International Settlements.

———. 1998. *Bank for International Settlements Sixty-Eighth Annual Report*. Basle: Bank for International Settlements.

Bergsten, C. Fred. 1998. "Reviving the 'Asian Monetary Fund.'" International Economics Policy Briefs No. 98-8. Washington, D.C.: Institute for International Economics. Report available at <http://www.iie.com/NEWSLETR/news98-8.htm>, 1–4.

Bergsten, C. Fred, and C. Randall Henning. 1996. *Global Economic Leadership and the Group of Seven*. Washington, D.C.: Institute for International Economics.

Berman, Sheri, and Kathleen R. McNamara. 1999. "Bank on Democracy: Why Central Banks Need Public Oversight." *Foreign Affairs* 78(2): 2–8.

Boylan, Delia. 1998. "Preemptive Strike: Central Bank Reform in Chile's Transition from Authoritarian Rule." *Comparative Politics* 30(4): 443–462.

Brown, J. Robert Jr. 1999. *The Ministry of Finance: Bureaucratic Practices and the Transformation of the Japanese Economy*. Westport, Conn.: Quorum Books.

Bryant, Ralph. 1980. *Money and Monetary Policy in Interdependent Nations*. Washington, D.C.: Brookings Institution.

———. 1987. *International Financial Intermediation*. Washington, D.C.: Brookings Institution.

Cargill, Thomas. 1998. "What Caused the Banking Crisis." Paper prepared for the conference "The Japanese Financial System: Restructuring for the Future." Columbia University, New York, 1–2 October.

Cargill, Thomas, Michael Hutchinson, and Takatoshi Itō. 1997. *The Political Economy of Japanese Monetary Policy*. Cambridge, Mass.: MIT Press.

Carlile, Lonny E. 1998. "The Politics of Administrative Reform." In Lonny E. Carlile and Mark C. Tilton, eds. *Is Japan Really Changing Its Ways?: Regulatory Reform and the Japanese Economy*. Washington, D.C.: Broookings Institution.

Castellano, Marc. 1999. *Japanese Foreign Aid: A Lifesaver for East Asia?* JEI Report 6.

Washington, D.C.: Japan Economic Institute.

Cohen, Benjamin J. 1996. "Phoenix Risen: The Resurrection of Global Finance." *World Politics* 48(2): 268–296.

Cross, Sam. 1998. *All About the Foreign Exchange Market in the United States*. New York: Federal Reserve Bank of New York.

Curtis, Gerald. 1999. *The Logic of Japanese Politics: Leaders, Institutions, and the Limits of Change*. New York: Columbia University Press.

Dwyer, Jennifer Holt. 1997. "Restructuring the Market—Restructuring the State: The Dynamics of Financial Market Reform in Japan." Dissertation University of Chicago.

———. Forthcoming. "Does Capital Mobility Cause Regulatory Convergence?: Illustrations from Japan." In Timothy Sinclair and Kenneth Thomas, eds. *Structure and Agency in International Capital Mobility*. London: Macmillan.

Eichengreen, Barry. 1996. *Globalizing Capital: A History of the International Monetary System*. Princeton, N.J.: Princeton University Press.

———. 1999. "The View From Economics." In Peter Katzenstein, Robert Keohane, and Stephen Krasner, eds. *Exploration and Contestation in the Study of World Politics*. Cambridge, Mass.: MIT Press.

Eichengreen, Barry, and Richard Portes. 1987. "The Anatomy of Financial Crises." In Richard Portes and Alexander Swoboda, eds. *Threats to International Financial Stability*. Cambridge: Cambridge University Press.

Fearon, James. 1998. "Bargaining, Enforcement, and International Cooperation." *International Organization* 52(2): 269–305.

Federal Reserve Bank of New York. 1998. *All About the Foreign Exchange Market in the United States*. New York: Federal Reserve Bank of New York.

Frankel, Jeffrey. 1984. *The Yen/Dollar Agreement: Liberalizing Japanese Capital Markets*. Washington, D.C.: Institute for International Economics.

———. 1991. "Quantifying International Capital Mobility in the 1980s." In Douglas Bernheim and John Shoven, eds. *National Saving and Economic Performance*. Chicago: University of Chicago Press.

Fukui Haruhiro and Fukai Shigeko. 1998. "Japan in 1997: More Uncertain, Less Hopeful." *Asian Survey* 38(1): 24–33.

Funabashi Yōichi. 1988. *Managing the Dollar: From the Plaza to the Louvre*. Washington, D.C.: Institute for International Economics.

Germain, Randall. 1999. *Globalization and Its Critics*. New York: St. Martin's Press.

Goodman, John. 1991. "The Politics of Central Bank Independence." *Comparative Politics* 23(3): 329–349.

Goodman, John, and Louis Pauly. 1993. "The Obsolescence of Capital Controls?: Economic Management in an Age of Global Markets." *World Politics* 46(1): 50–82.

Gourevitch, Peter. 1986. *Politics in Hard Times: Comparative Responses to International Economic Crises*. Ithaca, N.Y.: Cornell University Press.

Greenspan, Alan. 1999. Address. Thirty-fifth Annual Conference on Bank Structure and Competition of the Federal Reserve Bank of Chicago. Chicago, 6 May.

Haggard, Stephen, and Beth Simmons. 1987. "Theories of International Regimes." *International Organization* 41(3): 491–517.

Hamada Kōichi. 1996. "Capital Movements Between the United States and Japan in the

Context of Yen-Dollar Politics." In Noguchi Yukio and Yamamura Kōzō, eds. *U.S.-Japan Macroeconomic Relations: Interactions and Interdependence in the 1980s.* Seattle: University of Washington Press.

Helleiner, Eric. 1994. *States and the Reemergence of Global Finance: From Bretton Woods to the 1990s.* Ithaca, N.Y.: Cornell University Press.

Henning, C. Randall. 1994. *Currencies and Politics in the United States, Germany and Japan.* Washington, D.C.: Institute for International Economics.

Higgins, Matthew, and Thomas Klitgaard. 1998. "Viewing the Current Account Deficit as a Capital Inflow." *Current Issues in Economics and Finance* 4(13): 1–6.

Hiwatari Nobuhiro. 1999. "The Politics of Bureaucratic Structure and Blame Avoidance: Banking Crisis, Financial Globalization, and Reorganization of the Financial Bureaucracy in Japan." Draft paper.

Horne, James. 1985. *Japan's Financial Markets: Conflict and Consensus in Policymaking.* Sydney: Allen and Unwin.

Huntington, Samuel P. 1999. "The Lonely Superpower." *Foreign Affairs* 78(2): 35–49.

International Monetary Fund. 1995. *International Capital Markets: Developments, Prospects and Policy Issues.* Washington, D.C.: International Monetary Fund.

Ishihara Shintarō. 1998. "New Repel-the-Barbarian Argument in Asia: Japan Is Not America's Financial Slave." *Japanese Magazine Review* (September–October): 16–19. (Digest of article originally published in Japanese in *Bungei Shunjū* August.)

Itō Yōichi. 1999. "The Japanese Version of the 'Big Bang': Background and Outlook." Tokyo: Foreign Press Center.

"Japan Banks Have $171B in Bad Debts." 1999. Associated Press 25 May.

"Japan Must Deregulate to Put Economy Back on Track: OECD." 1999. Nikkei 14 April.

"Japan, S. Korean Lawmakers Agree on Asian Fund." 1998. Nikkei/Dow Jones 1 December.

"Japan Wins Praise from Asians at IMF Meetings." 1998. Nikkei/Dow Jones 9 October.

Jomo, K. S. 1998. *Tigers in Trouble: Financil Governance, Liberalisation, and Crises in East Asia.* London: St. Martin's.

Kane, Edward. 1987. "Competitive Financial Reregulation: An International Perspective." In Richard Portes and Alexander Swoboda, eds. *Threats to International Financial Stability.* Cambridge: Cambridge University Press.

———. 1988. How Market Forces Influence the Structure of Financial Regulation." In W. Haraf and R. Kishmeider, eds. *Restructuring Banking and Financial Services in America.* Washington, D.C.: American Enterprise Institute.

Kapstein, Ethan. 1994. *Governing the Global Economy: International Finance and the State.* Cambridge, Mass.: Harvard University Press.

Keohane, Robert. 1984. *After Hegemony: Cooperation and Discord in the World Political Economy.* Princeton, N.J.: Princeton University Press.

Keohane, Robert, and Helen Milner, eds. 1996. *Internationalization and Domestic Politics.* Cambridge: Cambridge University Press.

Keohane, Robert, and Joseph Nye. 1977. *Power and Interdependence: World Politics in Transition.* Boston: Little, Brown.

Krasner, Stephen, ed. 1983. *International Regimes.* Ithaca, N.Y.: Cornell University Press.

Lebaton, Stephen. 1999. "Treasury and Fed Reach Compromise." *New York Times* 15 October: C1.

Laurence, Henry. 1996. "Regulatory Competition and the Politics of Financial Market Reform in Britain and Japan." *Governance* 9(3): 311–341.

Lohmann, Suzanne. 1997. "Is Japan Special?: Monetary Linkages and Price Stability." *Bank of Japan Monetary and Economic Studies* (December): 63–79.

Loriaux, Michael, et al. 1997. *Capital Ungoverned: Liberalizing Finance in Interventionist States*. Ithaca, N.Y.: Cornell University Press.

Mabuchi Masaru. 1998. "The Political Economy of the MOF Reform." Paper prepared for the conference "The Japanese Financial System: Restructuring for the Future." Columbia University, New York, 1–2 October. First draft.

Meyer, Laurence. 1999. "The Global Economic Outlook and Challenges Facing Monetary Policy around the World." Remarks before the World Economic Forum USA Regional Meeting, National Chamber Foundation, U.S. Chamber of Commerce. Washington, D.C. 14 April.

Mikitani Ryōichi and Patricia Kuwayama. 1999. "Japan's New Central Banking Law: A Critical View." Draft paper.

Milner, Helen, and Robert Keohane. 1996. "Internationalization and Domestic Politics: An Introduction." In Robert Keohane and Helen Milner. *Internationalization and Domestic Politics*, eds. Cambridge: Cambridge University Press.

Ministry of Finance. 1997. *Financial System Reform: Toward the Early Achievement of Reform*. Tokyo: Ministry of Finance.

Ministry of Finance, Council on Foreign Exchange and Other Transactions. 1998. "Internationalization of the Yen: Interim Report" (provisional translation). Tokyo: Ministry of Finance.

————. 1999. *Nijūisseiki ni muketa en no kokusaika: Sekai no keizai kinyū jōsei no henka to Nihon no taisaku* (Internationalization of the yen for the 21st century—Japan's response to changes in global economic and financial environments). Tokyo: Ministry of Finance.

"Mr. Yen Says IMF Job Unlikely, Touts Asia Fund." 2000. Reuters 10 March.

Moran, Michael. 1991. *The Politics of the Financial Services Revolution: The USA, UK and Japan*. London: Macmillan.

Moravcsik, Andrew. 1994. "Why the European Community Strengthens the State: Domestic Politics and International Cooperation." Paper presented at the annual meeting of the American Political Science Association. New York Hilton, New York, 1–4 September.

Ogawa Akio. 1999. "Taken In by the Dollar Guys." *Asahi Evening News* (28 March).

Okada Motoharu 1996. "Finance Ministry Two-Faced about Tightening Belts." *Asahi Evening News* 14 August.

Organization for Economic Cooperation and Development. 1987. *Prudential Supervision in Banking*. Paris: Organization for Economic Cooperation and Development.

————. 1999. *OECD Reviews of Regulatory Reform: Regulatory Reform in Japan*. Paris: Organization for Economic Cooperation and Development.

Oritani Yoshiharu. 1998. "Payments and Settlement System in EMEAP Economies." Draft paper.

Owens, Cynthia. 1987. "Bringing It All Back Home." *Euromoney* (October): 61–65.

Oye, Kenneth, ed. 1986. *Cooperation under Anarchy*. Princeton, N.J.: Princeton University Press.

Packer, Frank. 1998. "The Disposal of Bad Loans in Japan: The Case of the CCPC." Draft paper.

Pempel, T. J. 1998. *Regime Shift: Comparative Dynamics of the Japanese Political Economy.* Ithaca, N.Y.: Cornell University Press.

———. 1999. "Introduction." In Pempel, T. J., ed. *The Politics of the Asian Economic Crisis.* Ithaca, N.Y.: Cornell University Press.

Portes, Richard, and Alexander Swoboda, eds. 1987. *Threats to International Financial Stability.* Cambridge: Cambridge University Press.

Putnam, Robert, and Nicholas Bayne. 1984. *Hanging Together: The Seven-Power Summits.* Cambridge, Mass.: Harvard University Press.

"Recessions in Asia Mutually Reinforcing." 1998. *Dow Jones Report* 22 December.

Rodrik, Dani, ed. 1997. *Has Globalization Gone Too Far?* Washington, D.C.: Institute for International Economics.

Rosenbluth, Frances. 1989. *Financial Politics in Contemporary Japan.* Ithaca, N.Y.: Cornell University Press.

———. 1996. "Internationalization and Electoral Politics in Japan." In Robert Keohane and Helen Milner, eds. *Internationalization and Domestic Politics.* Cambridge: Cambridge University Press.

Saitō Kunihiko 1998. "Listen America, Japan Is Not a Bunch of Fools." *Japanese Magazine Review* (September–October): 20–26. (Digest of article originally published in Japanese in *Bungei Shunjū* November.)

Sakakibara Eisuke. 1999. Address. Manila Framework Meeting. Melbourne, 26 March. (Draft.)

Sapsford, Jathon. 1999. "New Power Stirs Japan: Central Bank." *Wall Street Journal* (28 January): A13–14.

Shinohara Hajime. 1999. "On the Asian Monetary Fund." *Institute for International Monetary Affairs Newletter,* no. 4: 1–16.

Sinclair, Timothy, and Kenneth Thomas, eds. Forthcoming. *Structure and Agency in International Capital Mobility.* London: Macmillan.

Stenmo, Sven. 1996. *Taxation and Democracy: Swedish, British and American Approaches to Financing the Modern State.* New Haven: Yale University Press.

Strange, Susan. 1986. *Casino Capitalism.* Oxford: Blackwell.

Summers, Lawrence. 1998. *The US-Japanese Stake in a Free and Open Asian Capital Market.* Columbia University Center on Japanese Economy and Business Occasional Paper No. 38. New York: Columbia University.

Thomas, K. 1998. *Capital Beyond Borders: How Capital Mobility Strengthens Firms in Their Bargaining with States.* London: Macmillan.

Turner, Phillip. 1991. *Capital Flows in the 1980s.* BIS Economic Papers 30. Basle: Bank for International Settlements.

Ueda Kazuo. 1998. "Causes of the Japanese Banking Instability in the 1990s." Paper prepared for the conference "The Japanese Financial System: Restructuring for the Future." Columbia University, New York, 1–2 October.

"Under Attack: Japanese Financial Reform." 1996. *Economist* (7 December): 70–72.

Underhill, Geoffrey. 1991. "Markets Beyond Politics?: The State and the Internationalization of Financial Markets." *European Journal of Political Research* 19(2): 197–225.

Vogel, Ezra. 1994. "Japan as Number One in Asia." In Gerald Curtis, ed. *The United States, Japan, and Asia: Challenges for U.S. Policy.* New York: Norton.

Vogel, Steven. 1996. *Freer Markets, More Rules.* Ithaca, N.Y.: Cornell University Press.

Webb, Michael. 1995. *The Political Economy of Policy Coordination.* Ithaca, N.Y.: Cornell University Press.

Zaforin, A. 1999. "Worried About the Dollar." *Time* (11 October): 54.

4

The Transformation of Japan's Fiscal Orientation in the 1990s:
The Impact of External Pressure, Volatile Party Politics, and Recession

Katō Junko

UNTIL RECENTLY, JAPAN WAS A UNIQUE CASE of successful democratic capitalism outside the Western world. In the 1950s and 1960s, Japan achieved outstanding growth and industrialization in a benign global economic climate. In the 1970s, after the oil shock of 1973, the rapid-growth period abruptly ended, but Japan enjoyed good economic performance relative to other industrial democracies, with lower unemployment and a stable but higher growth rate than other industrial countries. In the 1980s, as Japan continued to enjoy good economic performance, its industrial products penetrated the markets of the United States and other industrial countries. This was regarded as a threat by other countries and intensified trade friction with Japan. The successful penetration of Japanese products was allegedly the result of "strategic trade" (pushing down export prices while keeping the domestic market closed) rather than international competitiveness. The yen appreciated massively after the Plaza Accord of 1985, but Japan's trade surplus did not decrease.

The "bubble economy" of the late 1980s seemed to confirm the strength of the Japanese economy and the advantages of Japanese-style capitalism. At the same time, the strategic and predatory nature of Japan's exports and the peculiarities of its industrial organization and business practices attracted criticism. Before the endless debate was resolved the bubble burst, and the Japanese economic downturn became apparent in 1992. Since then, the erstwhile high praise for Japanese capitalism has been reversed; yesterday's strength has become today's weakness. Japan's industrial structure and business practices, such as the *keiretsu* business groups, the seniority-based wage system, and lifetime employment, were once praised for cultivating loyalty among workers and continuity in business strategy. Now they are regarded as signs of a lack of flexibility and as obstacles to new solutions. The main-bank system and the allocation of industrial funds were once considered the reason for the flexible shift from one industrial sector to another. But as the number of failing financial institutions has increased, the government's supervision of the financial market and the tight organization of the industrial sector have become targets of censure.

Despite the ups and downs of the Japanese economy in the global context, Japan's economic policy, especially the style of economic cooperation with other industrial democracies, appears unchanged. Japan has been named a "reactive state" by Calder (1988), meaning that its foreign policy, including its economic policy, is determined more by response to other countries' demands and requests than the voluntary and independent action of the Japanese government. The United States in particular, as an economic hegemon, has demanded that Japan share the cost of maintaining the international economic order instead of just enjoying its fruits. Japan, the most privileged beneficiary of the order, has been accused of free riding on the provision of a public good (the international economic order) at the expense of the United States. Since consumption of a public good is indivisible, nonexcludable, and nonrival, the hegemon that can afford to provide it cannot directly demand payment from consumers.[1] Thus, the demands of the United States as a hegemonic power vis-à-vis Japan were focused on the coordination of economic policy as well as policy change in trade.

More specifically, the United States has demanded fiscal activism and expansion of domestic consumption. Japan's good economic performance and trade surplus in the 1970s and 1980s had led to these demands. Expanding public expenditures in Japan was believed to be desirable for the stagnant global economy, and increasing domestic consumption would serve to reduce the U.S. trade deficit. In the 1990s, with the declining fortunes of the Japanese economy, the necessity of economic recovery for Japan itself became the reason for such demands. This was urgently pursued by Japan and desired by other countries, which were afraid of a spillover of Japan's recession to the rest of Asia and elsewhere. In short, Japanese economic policy not only in trade and currency but also in public financial management was exposed to other countries' demands and, more importantly, looked as though it were reacting to such demands.

Against the above conventional view, on the basis of a brief examination of changes in the 1990s, I argue that the Japanese economic policy response has not been reactive. Although Japanese economic policy has seemed to follow external pressure (*gaiatsu*), the meaning of the interaction between external pressure and Japanese government action in the 1990s was distinct from that in the 1970s and 1980s. Two important factors that are likely to have influenced this change are the deep and long recession that replaced good economic performance and the increasing volatility of party politics that replaced the one-party dominance of the Liberal Democratic Party (LDP) from 1955 to 1993. After briefly describing the characteristics of the Japanese response to external pressure in the 1970s and 1980s, I will examine the interaction of Japanese fiscal policy and external pressure in the 1990s.

JAPAN IN THE 1970S AND 1980S

The oil shock in the autumn of 1973 was an event that symbolized the termination of post–World War II fast economic growth and also determined the style of interaction between Japanese fiscal management and external pressure. Although it is reasonable for foreign economic policy, such as trade and currency exchange, to be influenced by demands and requests from other countries, it does not automatically follow that external pressure influences fiscal orientation, which is a domestic economic policy. International coordination of economic policy is no longer a new subject of study in economics, and thus it is possible to conceive of a situation in which changing the fiscal orientation because of external economic considerations would bring optimal results for all. The external pressure on Japan does not appear to have been part of a "coordination," however, because the relationship has always been unilateral, that is, other countries have presented demands to Japan much more often than Japan has to other countries. Industrial democracies' policy response to the oil shock followed this basic pattern of interaction between Japanese fiscal policy and external pressure: Other countries demanded fiscal activism and the expansion of domestic consumption, and the Japanese government responded to the demand, though with reluctance and a time lag.

After the oil shock, the active fiscal orientation of the Tanaka Kakuei cabinet was expected to end with the appointment in November 1973 of Fukuda Takeo, who was a fiscal conservative, as minister of finance. Facing a soaring interest rate, which climbed to 24 percent in 1974, Fukuda tightened the budget, especially public works expenditures, though he left intact a ¥2 trillion income tax cut and an increase in social security expenditures. Despite fiscal consolidation as finance minister, Fukuda was forced to abandon his ideal of fiscal conservatism and shift to fiscal activism after he became prime minister in 1976. At that time, a relatively high growth rate and low unemployment rate were becoming apparent in Japan and West Germany. At the Group of Seven (G7) summit in Bonn in 1978, Fukuda accepted the "locomotive theory" (*kikansha ron*), according to which Japan and West Germany were capable of pulling along the faltering world economy, and he promised a 7 percent gross national product (GNP) growth rate. The United States, which was suffering from inflation, a trade deficit, and a weak dollar, had demanded this, and other countries had also become more critical of the inaction of Japan and West Germany. But Fukuda's decision was attributed to a sense of duty that countries with stronger economic outlooks, such as Japan and West Germany, had an obligation to pull along the global economy. Fukuda left an interesting commentary on his own decision. Domestic pressure from major business associations for a fiscal-stimulus package was also strong, but Fukuda asserted that he would not have launched an active fiscal program without taking into consideration the global economic situation (Andō 1987, vol. 2, 79–81). This pushed public works expenditures above the level of the 34.5 percent increase provided in the fiscal 1978 (April 1978–March 1979) original budget by adding another fiscal-stimulus package.

It is noteworthy that Japan was not necessarily in a position to indulge easily in fiscal expansion. After the first issuance of deficit bonds in the fiscal 1975 supplementary budget, the ratio of dependence on deficit bonds in the fiscal 1976 budget was 29.9 percent, and the ratio in the fiscal 1978 budget was 32.0 percent. The recession following the second oil shock in 1979 caused a large revenue shortfall, and deficit financing was inevitable. The bond dependence ratio hit a peak of 39.6 percent in fiscal 1979 and then started to decline, but until the late 1980s the dependence ratio was higher than the average in industrial democracies. For example, in fiscal 1984 it was as high as 25.0 percent, even higher than the worst case in the United States. Fukuda had been reluctant to respond to major business associations' demand for a fiscal stimulus but decided to shift to fiscal activism out of consideration for international economic management.

To sum up, Japan's implementation of a fiscal-stimulus package in the mid-1970s followed external pressure, but there remains the possibility that the decision was made voluntarily, according to the above evidence about Fukuda. As a fiscal conservative, he very likely expected that fiscal expansion would lead to chronic deficit financing. Despite this concern, Japan's good economic performance led Fukuda to accept the demands from abroad and launch an active fiscal program.

Japan's economic response to the oil shock illustrates the style of interaction between external pressure and fiscal management in the 1970s and the 1980s. Good economic performance in Japan intensified pressure from abroad. In the eyes of other countries, Japan could afford the fiscal expansion that was desirable for the international economy, and the United States felt that this was a cost that Japan had to pay while enjoying the stability of the international economic order. Its good economic performance despite the difficulties of other countries gave Japan a sense of guilt and caused it to implement the policies they demanded. If its performance had been even better, the external pressure would have been intense, and Japanese sensitivity to global economic conditions was high. In this regard, the Japanese response was not entirely forced by other countries and thus was not necessarily reactive.

The implementation of an economic stimulus desired by other countries was not necessarily a reasonable choice for Japan. The nation was suffering from a recession, but to a lesser extent than other countries, and there was a potential threat of chronic budget deficits. Japan was reacting to the fact that it was performing better economically than other countries rather than to their demands. Both the intensity of other countries' demands and the Japanese sensitivity to global economic conditions were functions of Japan's economic performance, and they worked in the same direction.

The decline in Japan's economic performance, which was worse than other countries' in the 1990s, provides a good test case of my argument. The next section will follow the changes in Japanese fiscal policy and external pressure since 1992, when the serious economic downturn became public knowledge.

DECLINING ECONOMIC PROMINENCE AND POLITICAL INSTABILITY IN THE 1990s

Economic Stimulation, 1992–1996: External Pressure and Japan's Response

At the beginning of 1992, when President George Bush visited Japan, the United States demanded an expansion of Japanese domestic demand and an economic-stimulus package. At that time, Japan was still regarded as the only country that could afford to implement an expansionary fiscal program for the purpose of global economic recovery. Germany was suffering from high inflation, and the United States had both budget and trade deficits. Bush especially desired an economic recovery led by Japan to strengthen his standing in an election year. Prime Minister Miyazawa Kiichi had been finance minister in the mid-1980s, when Japan had responded to a U.S. request to stimulate domestic demand and had entered the phase of the bubble economy. Thus, Japanese policymakers were afraid meeting the 1992 demand would lead to a return of the bubble economy and so did not consider seriously the need to stimulate the economy.

Meanwhile, it became apparent that the financial authorities had underestimated the adverse effects of the bubble's collapse on economic growth. Subsequently, the United States became concerned about the increasing Japanese trade surplus and intensified its demand for fiscal expansion to decrease the surplus. In April 1992, shortly after the Japanese government announced a fiscal-stimulus package, a top official of the U.S. Department of the Treasury said that further fiscal expansion was necessary to achieve the goal of 3.5 percent growth and decrease the trade surplus.[2] Japan's slowed growth and mounting trade surplus were the focus of the G7 meeting at the end of April, since Germany's high interest rates to cope with inflation were accepted. Despite the fiscal-stimulus package and the lowering of interest rates, pressure to expand domestic demand was increasing, but the Ministry of Finance (MOF) indicated that it would maintain the policy of eliminating the budget deficit.

In May, the trade surplus was at a peak. At the ministerial meeting of the Organization for Economic Cooperation and Development (OECD) countries that month and at the G7 summit in July, Japan was requested to make additional public expenditures to stimulate the economy. Japan's economic performance was still regarded as somewhat better than that of other countries. In August, the government introduced a fiscal-stimulus package financed by Fiscal Investment and Loan Program (FILP) lending and reserve funds as well as construction bonds. Total spending amounted to more than ¥2 trillion, although most funds went to land purchases. Toward the end of the year, the pressure from abroad increased, and the Japanese government attempted to intervene in the stock market with trust funds to stimulate the economy.

Nineteen ninety-three was a year of changes on both sides of the Pacific. In the United States, Bill Clinton was inaugurated as president and brought with him a team of economic experts, such as Lawrence Summers (deputy secretary of the treasury), Laura Tyson (chair of the Council of Economic Advisers), and Mickey Kantor (U.S. trade representative), who subsequently pressed Japan hard to eliminate the trade imbalance. On the Japanese side, the LDP lost power that summer and a non-LDP government was formed for the first time in thirty-eight years.

Simultaneously with this big political change, the economic situation in both countries was changing. At a meeting of the G7 ministers of finance and central bank heads in March, all other countries demanded that Japan stimulate domestic demand; the U.S. economy was showing signs of recovery, but not enough to revive the global economy. At the time of the G7 summit meeting in July, which Prime Minister Miyazawa chaired, Japan was enjoying a relatively good economic performance and presumably could afford to take measures to increase public spending (that is, without concern about high inflation and trade deficits) for the sake of the recovery of the global economy.

After the passage of the fiscal 1993 budget, Miyazawa introduced a package of "new comprehensive economic measures" (*shin sōgō keizai taisaku*). Aside from the supplementary budget (about ¥2.2 trillion) and tax cuts (¥2.25 trillion), most of the ¥13.2 trillion package was poured into public works. This package was regarded as a sign of the government's strong intention to stimulate the economy, but the spending included ¥11 trillion from the FILP that had been decided on earlier.

After Hosokawa Morihiro formed a non-LDP coalition cabinet in August, following the LDP's rout in the July general election, U.S. concern over the prolonged and deepening recession in Japan heightened. The demand for a more active fiscal orientation continued and became even stronger, but this was because the United States was concerned about the adverse effects of the recession in Japan and no longer expected that Japan could take a more active role bolstering global economic recovery. Economic stimulation was necessary for Japan, but its policy response appeared to be ineffective because of increasing constraints over policy options, not insensitivity to the worsening economic situation and increasing external pressure.

For example, immediately before the new government's announcement of emergency economic measures (*kinkyū keizai taisaku*) on September 16, Treasury Deputy Secretary Summers visited Japan to examine the expected effect of the measures and judge whether to demand additional measures. The measures included ¥6 trillion of public spending, but again most came from the FILP instead of the general account.[3] Thus, at the G7 ministerial meeting and at a meeting with the United States, a tax cut became a public promise to the international community. The concern of Japanese policymakers here was how to maintain the principle of zero issuance of deficit bonds with no financial source for a major tax cut other than deficit bonds. Generally speaking, the issuance of bonds for a tax cut is not classified as the same as the issuance of construction bonds for investment in economic and social infrastructure. The government announced its intention to issue temporary bonds (*tsunagi kokusai*). This name implies that they are different from construction bonds but also different from deficit bonds because they should not accumulate into chronic debt. A ¥5.85 trillion income tax cut was included in the comprehensive economic measures announced on February 8, 1994, and subsequently passed by the National Diet. These measures constituted the largest (¥15.25 trillion) stimulus package so far, providing ¥7.2 trillion for public works, financed by the FILP, as well as ¥2.19 trillion for small and medium-sized businesses, financed by bonds.

The government's initiative to stimulate the economy was neither clear nor assertive, however, and this was attributed to lack of stability in the coalition government. First, on February 3, 1994, Prime Minister Hosokawa announced that in fiscal 1996 he would raise the consumption tax from 3 percent to 7 percent and rename it the "national welfare tax" (*kokumin fukushi zei*). This proposal was supported by Ozawa Ichirō, then head of the Japan Renewal Party, and Saitō Jirō, MOF vice-minister. But it had not been known to, let alone agreed to by, all members of the ruling coalition, especially the Social Democratic Party (SDP) and New Party Sakigake (*sakigake* means pioneer), nor was it based on a firm consensus within MOF (Katō 1997).[4] Although the proposal was withdrawn immediately because of strong public opposition as well as criticism within the coalition, this incident showed that MOF's concern over the growing budget deficit was increasing and that there was disagreement within the coalition over fiscal policy. The passage of the fiscal 1994 budget was delayed until June by the disintegration of the coalition. It passed the House of Representatives on June 8 and the House of Councillors on June 23 as the LDP challenged the disintegrating coalition, although it did not necessarily oppose the content of the budget. Consequently, although fiscal policy was an issue that divided the coalition, partisan conflict also caused the delay and inconsistency of the fiscal program.

The coalition government was headed by Hata Tsutomu after Hosokawa's resignation in April. It passed the budget but was short lived because it was a minority government as a result of the defection of the SDP and Sakigake. In late June, the LDP returned to power in coalition with the SDP and Sakigake and supported SDP Chairman Murayama Tomiichi as the first socialist prime minister in more than forty years. The need to recover from the recession was the immediate concern of the new coalition. Its approach was tax reform, in which an income tax cut would precede a tax increase to be achieved by raising the consumption tax from 3 percent to 5 percent in fiscal 1997. Because of the expansionary fiscal orientation preferred by the SDP and Sakigake, the ¥5.5 trillion income and residential tax cut included a ¥3.5 trillion permanent cut and the consumption tax would rise only to 5 percent rather than 7 percent as previously planned. In addition, a New Gold Plan for the elderly, a welfare compensation package to cope with the regressive consumption tax increase, was to be introduced in fiscal 1995, and the revenue from 1 percent of the consumption tax increase was to be transferred to regional and local governments.

During the tenure of the non-LDP coalition, the LDP had become increasingly suspicious of the bureaucracy, which had cooperated with the coalition parties. MOF had apparently made concessions to the unstable coalition (Katō 1997). Despite substantial political intervention, specifically the SDP's desire to precede an economic stimulus with a tax increase, however, the fiscal authorities' optimism over the prospects for economic recovery were reflected in a tax-reform package that combined an income-tax cut with a consumption-tax increase. The fiscal authorities believed that the economy could recover well before April 1997, when the consumption tax would be raised. Thus, the government could avoid the loss of tax revenue and the unnecessary accumulation of budget deficits and pursue the two goals of economic stimulus and fiscal reconstruction. In line with this tax reform, in December 1994 the government decided on a fiscal 1995 initial budget that was 3 percent smaller than the fiscal 1994 budget and included ¥1 trillion less in total bond issues (¥200 billion in temporary-bond issues). This optimistic outlook for economic recovery was similar to the optimism over the prospects for resolution of the financial-market crisis that had led to a delay in pouring public money into the market. Loosening money was necessary for economic recovery, but in retrospect we can see that the unhealthy management conditions of financial institutions prevented firms from gaining investment money to build up their businesses.

The year 1995 started with the Great Hanshin-Awaji Earthquake on January 17. This increased the expectation that the economy would improve because of the necessity for reconstruction and rebuilding in the Kobe area. The government passed a ¥1.02 trillion supplementary budget in February aimed at increasing both general-account and FILP spending, but the growth rate was not as high as expected. Pressure from abroad to expand domestic consumption increased, due mostly to the rapid rise of the yen from approximately ¥100 to the U.S. dollar at the beginning of February to close to ¥80 to the dollar near the end of April. This nearly 20 percent increase in the value of the yen caused the government to issue a set of countermeasures (*kinkyū endaka keizai taisaku*) worth ¥4.62 trillion (¥2.73 trillion from the general account) in addition to an interest rate cut in April. The continuing strong yen led the government to implement another fiscal-stimulus plan in September, this one worth ¥14.2 trillion, including ¥5.3 trillion from the general account and ¥4.9 trillion in bonds.

The government's successive actions to stimulate the economy in fiscal 1995 had mixed results. That fiscal year the government issued a total of ¥21.25 trillion in bonds—far more than the initially planned ¥12.6 trillion. This was the highest level of spending for economic stimulus of the past decade, but at the same time the figures were often exaggerated. For example, actual general-account expenditure increased by only ¥4.95 trillion in fiscal 1995, and actual FILP spending increased by only ¥5 trillion. In other words, either the spending did not take place in that year or spending already budgeted was included in the stimulus packages.

The government's equivocal approach in fiscal 1994 and 1995 paralleled weakening pressure from other countries, especially the United States, to expand domestic consumption and stimulate the economy. The strong yen and the prolonged recession were reasons for other countries' demands, but at the same time troubles in Japan's financial market caused by failing financial institutions softened the pressure. The bankruptcies of Tokyo Kyōwa and Anzen credit cooperatives in March, Cosmo credit cooperative in July, and Kizu credit cooperative in August were the first symptoms. In August, Hyōgo Bank became the first bank during the post–World War II period that could not be saved by a merger with another bank, and went out of business. Moreover, in September it was revealed that Daiwa Bank's New York branch had hidden from the U.S. authorities losses amounting to US$1.1 billion. This was attributed to the wrongdoing of a young trader, but MOF, which had been informed of the situation in August, did not report it to the U.S. Federal Reserve Board until the scandal was revealed. While this series of troubles diminished confidence in Japanese financial institutions and the government's regulatory capability, other countries, especially the United States, shied away from being hard on Japan simply because they were afraid that the recession and financial-market crisis would spill over from Japan to the rest of the world.

The Shift to Fiscal Structural Reform, 1996–1997

In fiscal 1996, the climate in fiscal policy changed from an expansionary orientation to one of fiscal consolidation. The most important factor was a sign of economic recovery—annual growth in gross domestic product (GDP) rose to 2.4 percent and the economy was stable, with no signs of either inflation or deflation. In retrospect, this benign economic climate should not have been exaggerated, since the expected rise of the consumption tax from 3 percent to 5 percent in April 1997 increased the consumption of consumer durables. But at the same time, as MOF announced in July 1996, tax revenue in fiscal 1995 had increased for the first time in five years. Thus, there was another reason to believe that the economy was recovering. In this situation, the growing budget deficit turned the Hashimoto Ryūtarō cabinet, formed in January 1996, toward fiscal consolidation.

The necessity to mop up after failed *jūsen* (*jūtaku kinyū senmon gaisha*, companies specializing in housing loans) was put at the top of the economic policy agenda, along with restoring order in the financial market in general. Despite public criticism, in April the government decided to pour ¥685 billion into the market and passed the fiscal 1996 budget, which included this investment of public funds. Immediately after the passage in June of bills to implement the liquidation of the *jūsen* with the help of public funds, Prime Minister Hashimoto decided to relax the ceiling on ministry budget requests. The ceiling was not strictly imposed on the ministry budget requests made public in September, and thus general-account spending was expected to increase by 2.9 percent. But the fiscal authorities expected that increased tax revenue from a higher consumption tax and economic recovery would lower the budget's bond dependence rate from 28 percent to 21.6 percent.

Late that year, the government began to tackle fiscal consolidation from a long-term perspective. First, in December the Fiscal System Council issued a report articulating the goals of lowering the budget deficit ratio to GDP of local governments and the national government to 3 percent and eliminating the issuance of deficit bonds by 2005. The report was taken to the newly formed Conference on Fiscal Structural Reform headed by Prime Minister Hashimoto, whose members included former prime ministers, finance ministers, and executives of the LDP, the SDP, and Sakigake.

The conference began deliberations in January 1997, Hashimoto presented the principles for reform in March, and the conference issued its final report in June. The report was adopted immediately by the cabinet and legislation reflecting its recommendations was passed in late November. The legislation proclaimed the aims of reducing the budget deficit ratio to GDP of both local governments and the national government to 3 percent and eliminating the issuance of deficit bonds by 2003, and specified the details of spending cuts from fiscal 1998 to 2000.

Meanwhile, pressure from other countries was at least not thwarting the government's orientation toward fiscal consolidation, mainly because other countries' attention was focused on their own budget deficits in 1996. At the G7 meetings of finance ministers and central-bank heads in January, April, and September 1996, Finance Minister Kubo Wataru emphasized that Japan's budget deficit was the highest among the G7 countries and requested understanding of the need for fiscal consolidation.[5] At the OECD ministerial meeting in May, Japan pledged a 3 percent budget deficit ratio, which incidentally was the target for countries participating in European monetary union (EMU). Although the United States demanded further economic recovery, a distinction was made between the expansion of public spending and of domestic consumption, the United States emphasizing the latter at the expense of the former. Both the United States and European countries were forced to put the highest priority on the reduction of budget deficits. The U.S. government was faced with demands from Congress, while the European governments had to meet the requirements for participation in the EMU, and thus could not press Japan, which was still on the way to recovery.

This trend continued until the middle of 1997. Later that year, stagnant domestic consumption made other countries more doubtful of Japan's economic recovery. For example, at the G7 meeting in September the United States focused on Japan as well as the resolution of the Asian currency crisis. U.S. suspicions about the fragile nature of Japan's economic recovery appeared to be confirmed by the bankruptcies later that year of two financial institutions once believed invincible: Yamaichi Securities, one of the "big four" Japanese securities firms, and Hokkaido Takushoku Bank, a major city bank.

Deepening Recession, Faltering Financial System since the End of 1997

The failure of two major financial institutions interrupted the government's efforts toward fiscal structural reform. Only the issuance of deficit bonds, which ran counter to the aim of the fiscal-reform legislation, could finance the massive amount of public funds that were being provided to deteriorating financial firms through the Deposit Insurance Corporation of Japan. The Hashimoto cabinet finally decided to inject money into the financial market in December at the expense of fiscal reform. Japan faced a stalling bank system, the spread of the currency crisis, and the stock market collapse across East Asia; the international community believed that recovery of the Japanese economy was essential to help ailing Asian economies. It was decided to use at least ¥10 trillion of public funds to rescue shaky banks and deal with the financial-market crisis. In addition, without seeing any sign of economic recovery, the Hashimoto cabinet decided on a special cut of ¥2 trillion in income and residential tax in the fiscal 1997 supplementary budget. The tax cut was again financed by the issuance of deficit bonds. Consequently, both the financial crisis and the prolonged recession forced the Hashimoto cabinet to abandon the major economic reform aim of fiscal reconstruction. But the government's fiscal orientation did not shift immediately. The initial budget of fiscal 1998, drawn up at the end of 1997, abided by the requirements in the fiscal-reform legislation and thus decreased general expenditures for the first time in eleven years, and the general account increased by only 0.4 percent. The budget was ineffective for fiscal consolidation because the issuance of deficit bonds increased from ¥6.25 trillion, the upper limit set by the reform plan, to ¥7.13 trillion. The dependence ratio on deficit bonds, 20 percent, was the highest among major industrial democracies.

The first two years of the Hashimoto cabinet thus ended with declining popular support due to a stagnant economy and financial crisis. Opinion polls in the major newspapers around the turn of the year to 1998 reported the lowest support rates for the Hashimoto cabinet so far. An *Asahi Shimbun* opinion poll in December 1997 recorded a 36 percent support rate, comparable to that in September 1997, when Satō Kōkō, who had been convicted in 1986 for his role in the Lockheed bribery scandal of the mid-1970s, had to resign his cabinet post. The *Nihon Keizai Shimbun* reported a 30 percent support rate in January 1998 due to dissatisfaction with the weak economic-stimulus measures.[6]

The disclosure in January 1998 of a collusive relationship between MOF officials and financial institutions was a severe blow for the Hashimoto cabinet as well as MOF. Two MOF bank inspectors were arrested, whereupon first Minister of Finance Mitsuzuka Hiroshi and then the vice-minister, MOF's highest ranking bureaucrat, resigned. In March, two more MOF officials were arrested, including one who was on the fast track to high office. They had provided major securities companies and banks with inside policy-making information and given new licenses and permissions in exchange for money and lavish entertainment. This led to the humiliation of many high-ranking MOF officials, including resignations and pay cuts in April. At the same time as the MOF scandal, a bribery and corruption case involving the Bank of Japan (BOJ) was disclosed, and the BOJ governor resigned.

The loss of confidence in public authorities because of these scandals was problematic, in the light of the worsening Japanese economy. The previous year, there had been a minus growth rate (−0.7 percent) in GDP for the first time in twenty-three years and for the second time since 1951, when the government began to issue statistics. In 1998, economic growth continued to stagnate, and the rising unemployment rate, which was above 4 percent, also became a potential threat to economic recovery.

To cope with this situation, in April the government abandoned the priority of fiscal consolidation. Revised structural fiscal reform legislation was enacted at the end of May. The year to eliminate deficit bonds was postponed from 2003 to 2005, and the cap on social security expenditures was lifted. Based on this revision, on April 24 the government announced a package of comprehensive economic measures that included a ¥4 trillion special one-off income tax reduction beginning in fiscal 1998 and ¥7.7 trillion for public works. Altogether, spending (including tax expenditures) amounted to ¥16.65 trillion, exceeding the past record of ¥15.25 trillion in February 1994 and including a record ¥12.3 trillion in fiscal-stimulus expenditures. The Economic Planning Agency estimated that these measures would enable Japan to meet the target of 1.9 percent growth in fiscal 1998.

The prospects for economic recovery and fiscal consolidation were dim, however. At the beginning of June, when the -0.7 percent growth rate was disclosed, a revenue shortfall of more than ¥1 trillion in fiscal 1997 became apparent (the first such shortfall in four years). Economic recovery, especially an income tax cut, became the most important issue in the July House of Councillors (Upper House) election. The LDP, which had already terminated its coalition with the SDP and Sakigake, failed to win as many seats as it had in the previous Upper House election, held in 1995. When its 44 seats were combined with the 58 seats not up for election, the total of 102 seats was far short of a majority, 126 of the 252 Upper House seats. This dismal result was considered a sign of public dissatisfaction with the LDP government's efforts to stimulate the economy. Prime Minister (and LDP President) Hashimoto resigned, and in the ensuing election for a new LDP president economic policy was also an issue. The newly elected president, Obuchi Keizō, became prime minister. He appointed former Prime Minister Miyazawa finance minister in the expectation that his expertise in economic policy would help the Japanese economy recover from the prolonged recession. Because a former prime minister rarely becomes a minister in Japan, this appointment was considered an indication of the LDP's sense of crisis over economic management.

Miyazawa decided on another income tax cut in fiscal 1999 to revitalize the economy, but because of the fiscal 1997 revenue shortfall no financial source could be found except deficit bonds. Although the structural fiscal reform legislation had been revised, the issuance of deficit bonds was still against the government's principles. The government also decided to cut corporate tax. Tax reduction amounted to more than ¥7 trillion overall. But the government avoided structural change aimed at a permanent reduction of the tax burden, implementing a fixed-rate ¥4 trillion income tax cut. The highest tax rate at both the national and the local levels was lowered from 65 percent to 50 percent, but in the lower tax brackets a special one-off flat-rate tax reduction was implemented, that is, 20 percent in income tax at the national level (with an upper limit of ¥150,000) and 15 percent in residential tax at the local level (with an upper limit of ¥40,000). Since fiscal 1994, only the ¥3.5 trillion cut in fiscal 1995 had been a permanent reduction related to structural change. Other tax cuts—¥5.5 trillion in fiscal 1994, ¥2 trillion in fiscal 1995, ¥2 trillion in fiscal 1996, ¥4 trillion in fiscal 1998—were special one-off reductions, like the one in fiscal 1999.

In drafting the budget for fiscal 1999 in August 1998, Miyazawa combined the supplementary budget of fiscal 1998 with the initial budget of fiscal 1999 and incorporated more than ¥12 trillion for public works projects over fifteen months (January 1999 through March 2000) to stimulate the economy. General expenditure for fiscal 1999 increased by 11 percent, indicating an apparently active fiscal program.

Resolving the financial-market crisis was an even more urgent concern than stimulating the economy. In October 1998, the Diet passed bills to invest public funds in the financial industry to protect depositors from bankruptcy and to rectify the adverse management situations of financial institutions. Because of the LDP's weak hold on power, however, both houses amended the bills. A major LDP concession was to abandon the investment of public funds in the foundering Long-Term Credit Bank of Japan, one of the three major banks concerned with industrial lending, a bank that the LDP was keen to shore up. Another LDP concession to the opposition, specifically the New Kōmeitō, was agreement to provide merchandise vouchers worth ¥20,000 to thirty-five million people aged fifteen or under and sixty-five or over.

As the Japanese economy floundered, external pressure to stimulate it increased, especially from the United States. From the beginning of 1998, it was reported that the government had promised to implement a fiscal 1998 supplementary budget to stimulate the economy, although senior officials denied this.[7] In the G7 meetings in London in February and in Washington in April, other countries, especially the United States, strongly demanded an economic stimulus to jump-start the Japanese economy and stop the Asian economic downturn triggered by the currency crisis. It is going too far, however, to attribute the Japanese responses in 1998 exclusively to external pressure. The announcement of economic measures in 1998 was almost simultaneous with the demands of other countries, implying that the measures were voluntary rather than forced. Indirect evidence can be found in the fact that even the Diet, which is usually indifferent to external economic conditions, was eager to have Finance Minister

Matsunaga Hikari attend the G7 meeting in April, when the Diet was in session. The absence of ministers because of international meetings usually worsens sentiment in the Diet. This time, members of the opposition criticized the government because the finance minister skipped the G7 meeting to attend the Diet session. This was regarded as an expression of politicians' sense of crisis and their perception of Japan's adverse economic condition as a global economic problem, in sharp contrast to the situation in the 1970s and 1980s, when government officials were concerned about external economic considerations and were sensitive to external pressure, while Diet members were often critical of such attitudes.

CONCLUSION

More public and journalistic attention has been focused on international economic meetings, such as the G7 meetings and summits, in Japan than in any other country (Oshio 1999, 133–134). Government officials' public promises and other countries' demands on Japan have been extensively reported. This is considered a sign that Japan has been sensitive to external pressure. A brief examination of the way external pressure has worked from the 1970s through the 1990s, however, does not permit the easy generalization that Japanese economic policies are reactions to external pressure. It is true that policy changes have often been preceded by demands from other countries, most notably the United States, but this does not mean that external pressure makes Japan implement a policy that it would otherwise not implement. Rather, Japan voluntarily shifts to a policy based on the perception and anticipation of its own economic performance and global economic conditions.

Japan's good economic performance in the 1970s and 1980s was the reason external pressure appeared to be working. The United States legitimately demanded that Japan change its fiscal policy for the sake of global economic well-being because Japan was enjoying the fruits of international economic order at the expense of other countries, especially the United States. Japan could also afford to change its policy as demanded. Good economic performance made Japan respond to global economic conditions and also intensified external pressure. External pressure thus looked as though it were working on Japan.

The first major Japanese response to external pressure appeared to be at the time of the 1973 oil shock. Japan's economic performance after that oil shock was outstanding. Japan and West Germany were under strong pressure from other countries for fiscal expansion. Fiscal expansion was obviously not in Japan's own interest, witness the fact that Japan suffered large deficits in subsequent years, but Japanese policymakers complied as the duty of an economy that was performing well.

The dynamics of Japanese fiscal policy and external pressure in the 1990s demonstrate that poor economic performance delayed Japan's fiscal response to the global economic situation. Japan's economic performance began worsening in the early 1990s; for the first time in three decades, the performance of the United States exceeded that of Japan. In the 1990s, fiscal expansion was more necessary for Japan than for other countries. Despite this, U.S. pressure was less intense and Japan's response less sensitive than in earlier decades. This trend was especially apparent from late 1996 to early 1997, when the Japanese economic performance was improving and the budget deficit decreasing. With signs of economic recovery Japan quickly shifted from fiscal expansion to fiscal consolidation. As a result, Japan's response to the recession was delayed until 1998, when the government began massive and continuous infusions of money to stimulate the economy.

It is noteworthy that this shift corresponded with weakening pressure from other countries. Since Japan appeared to be on the road to economic recovery, the United States and other countries should have increased pressure to prevent Japan from shifting away from fiscal expansion. The United States as well as the European Union (EU) countries shied away from doing so, however, because they were afraid that Japan would point out their own inaction. The United States could not expand public spending, fearing both inflation and a budget deficit, and the EU countries could not because they had to hold down public debt to meet the criteria for participation in the EMU. These countries could have pushed Japan if its economic situation had been better than theirs, but given its poor performance, they feared that Japan might balk.

Seen in retrospect, the fiscal expansion in late 1996 and early 1997 was more consistent with both Japan's interest and global economic considerations than that during the post-oil shock period in the 1970s. The economic factor that differs most in the two periods is Japan's relative economic performance. In this regard, comparison of the two cases provides important evidence for the imperative of economic performance in determining the effect of external pressure on Japan. Another important factor that distinguishes the two periods has to do with party politics, that is, the stable one-party dominance before 1993 and the unstable coalition politics from 1993 onward. The volatile political situation was also a reason for the delayed economic response during the latter period. More precisely, during the period of unchanging LDP rule in the 1970s and 1980s, government officials could concentrate on coordinating policy in the light of global economic considerations, whereas political instability and poor economic performance delayed the implementation of an economic stimulus in the 1990s. Political instability worked in the same direction as the effect of economic performance on the behavior of government officials.

Japan is not a reactive state by nature. Until recently, Japan behaved as if it were reactive to external pressure because of its good economic performance. Good economic performance is likely to make a country vulnerable to demands from other countries whose performance is worse. If bad economic performance becomes the norm for Japan in the future, its economic policy will appear to be more independent from external pressure because Japan will not sensitively adjust policies to global economic conditions and other countries will rarely expect that Japan can afford to take action for the benefit of the global economy.

NOTES

1. For the concepts of a public good and free riding, see Olsen (1965), and for their ramifications for the U.S.-Japan economic relationship, see Gilpin (1987).

2. See *Asahi Shimbun* 5 April 1992.

3. The general account is the total amount of government expenditure except that in special accounts that the government establishes for specific purposes. General expenditure is the amount that excludes bonds and local allocation tax from the general account.

4. The SDP underwent several name changes in the 1990s. Originally the Japan Socialist Party (Nippon Shakaitō), it changed its English name to the Social Democratic Party of Japan in February 1991. In January 1996, it changed its name to the Social Democratic Party (Shakai Minshutō). In this chapter I use the current name for simplicity's sake.

5. See *Asahi Shimbun* 22 January, 23 April, and 30 September 1996.

6. See *Asahi Shimbun* 11 January 1998, *Nihon Keizai Shimbun* 13 January 1998.

7. See *Asahi Shimbun* 18 January 1998.

BIBLIOGRAPHY

Andō Hiroshi. 1987. *Sekinin to genkai* (Responsibility and limits). 2 vols. Tokyo: Kinyū Zaisei Jijō Kenkyūkai.

Calder, Kent. 1988. "Japanese Foreign Economic Policy Formation: Explaining the Reactive State." *World Politics* 40(4): 517–41.

Gilpin, Robert. 1987. *The Political Economy of International Relations*. Princeton, N.J.: Princeton University Press.

Katō Junko. 1997. "Tax Policy in Japan after the Demise of Conservative Dominance." In Purnendra Jain and Takashi Inoguchi, eds. *Japanese Politics Today*. Sydney: Macmillan.

Olsen, Mancur. 1965. *The Logic of Collective Action*. Cambridge, Mass.: Harvard University Press.

Oshio Takashi. 1999. *Shijō no koe* (The voice of the market). Tokyo: Chūō Kōron Shinsha.

5

Japan's Changing Attitude toward Adjusting Its Current Account Surplus:
The Strong Yen and Macroeconomic Policy in the 1990s

Kojō Yoshiko

SINCE THE LATE 1960S, imbalances in countries' external balance of payments positions have been an important item on the agenda of trade talks among industrial states. Specifically, the problem of current account imbalances—in particular, the large U.S. external deficit and Japan's large external surplus—has been a major issue in U.S.-Japan relations since the 1970s. The United States first started to experience a current account deficit in the 1970s, and has seen widening deficits since the 1980s. In contrast, Japan showed a current account surplus throughout most of the 1970s, and that surplus expanded rapidly from the mid-1980s on (see table 1). Every time Japan showed a large current account surplus, the U.S. government strongly pressed the Japanese government to eliminate the imbalance by applying macroeconomic policy, and particularly fiscal policy. The U.S. political pressure was based on the claim that there should be international coordination of domestic economic policies, and that industrial states—especially the United States, Germany, and Japan—should coordinate their domestic policies in order to reduce their external imbalances and related tensions.

In reality, however, this type of international coordination is difficult to achieve, mainly because few states are willing to alter their domestic policies solely for the purpose of adjusting external current account imbalances. Both economic and political considerations dictate that this be so (Gilpin 1987, 378–379). Macroeconomic policies, including monetary and fiscal policy, are traditionally formulated to achieve such domestic economic objectives as adequate growth, price stability, and full employment. It is therefore difficult for a state to alter its existing macroeconomic policy for the sake of external goals—in other words, adjusting the current account imbalance at the expense of domestic objectives—without provoking a domestic debate on the appropriateness of the state's policy choice.

Table 1. Balance of Payments: Japan and the United States 1970-1995 (US$ billions)

	Current Account Balance		Overall Trade Balance	
	Japan	United States	Japan	United States
1970	1.99	2.62	3.96	2.59
1971	5.80	-0.98	7.76	-2.27
1972	6.64	-5.26	8.94	-6.42
1973	-0.13	7.58	3.64	0.91
1974	-4.72	1.70	1.35	-5.51
1975	-0.68	17.88	4.94	8.91
1976	3.71	3.84	9.80	-9.49
1977	10.91	-15.10	17.16	-31.10
1978	16.53	-15.77	24.30	-33.95
1979	-8.74	-0.13	1.74	-27.54
1980	-10.75	2.15	2.13	-25.51
1981	4.77	4.84	19.96	-28.02
1982	6.85	-11.60	18.08	-36.48
1983	20.80	-44.22	31.46	-67.09
1984	35.00	-99.01	44.26	-112.48
1985	51.13	-124.47	55.99	-122.18
1986	85.88	-150.49	91.19	-145.05
1987	84.35	-166.47	91.58	-159.56
1988	79.25	-127.71	92.24	-126.96
1989	63.21	-104.26	80.12	-115.14
1990	44.08	-94.26	69.28	-109.03
1991	68.20	-9.26	96.08	-74.07
1992	112.57	-61.36	124.76	-96.10
1993	131.64	-90.57	139.42	-130.72
1994	130.26	-132.93	144.19	-164.14
1995	111.04	-129.19	131.79	-171.69

Source: International Monetary Fund (1998).

Indeed, this complex challenge facing states—the need to balance domestic objectives with the adjustment of international imbalances, is what Gilpin has termed the "clash between economic interdependence and political autonomy" (1987, 167).

In light of the constraints on altering domestic policy, under what circumstances might a state nevertheless decide to apply macroeconomic policy for the purpose of adjusting its external imbalances? Answering this question should prove helpful for evaluating the possibility of international macroeconomic coordination.

The cases of Japan in the 1970s and the 1980s are instructive for this purpose. More than any other industrial state in the post–World War II period, Japan chose to apply macroeconomic policy to adjust its balance of payments when it was faced with current account surpluses, even though the country was experiencing a budget deficit problem during that period. Since Japan was often regarded as one of the most stubborn states, resisting changes to its domestic policy in areas such as market liberalization even in the face of strong U.S. pressure, one wonders why Japan was more responsive to similar pressures to adjust its current account imbalance.

There were four time periods during which the Japanese government was pressed hard by the U.S. government to eliminate its current account surpluses by applying yen appreciation, macroeconomic policy, or a combination of the two: (a) 1971-1973, (b) 1977-1978, (c) 1985-1987, and (d) 1993-1995. In the first three cases, Japan was more willing to modify its fiscal policy to adjust its large current account surpluses—as was requested particularly by the United States—than was Germany, which was also under U.S. political pressure and which had a lower budget deficit and higher unemployment rate than Japan (Kojō 1996). However, by the early 1990s, Japan had become reluctant to pursue external surplus adjustments through fiscal policy. How can we explain this shift?

In a previous study I conducted of the first three cases, I concluded that domestic-level factors mattered more in Japan's policy choice of adjusting external surpluses than traditional approaches have assumed (Kojō 1995; 1996). In particular, I found that two domestic-level factors were important variables in understanding the state's choice of adjusting external imbalances. The first factor was domestic preferences regarding the exchange rate. The second factor was the domestic political structure that affected the formulation of national policy on the issue of adjusting the current account surplus.

From the late 1980s on, however, dramatic changes occurred in Japan's economic environment. Following the conclusion of the Plaza Accord in 1985, international capital mobility increased and the value of the yen rose, hitting a record high level in 1995. The Japanese economy recorded a 5 percent growth rate from 1987 to 1991. However, in 1993 the bubble burst, sending the Japanese economy into a prolonged recession. As a result, Japanese industry was forced to undertake structural changes in order to cope with both economic internationalization and the turmoil of the domestic economy.

How did these changes affect Japan's policy choices regarding the adjustment of its current account surplus? Did these economic changes alter the domestic preferences regarding specific policy instruments? The purpose of this chapter is, first, to explain the domestic sources of Japan's policy choices, and, second, to examine how changes in the international and domestic economic environment affected domestic preferences and state policy choices in the 1990s. The chapter is comprised of three parts. The first section will explain why eliminating current account imbalances has been an important issue in U.S.- Japan bilateral relations since the late 1960s and will summarize the policy choices that have been made in response to concerns over large external surpluses. The second section will examine the importance of domestic-level factors in explaining Japan's policy choices in the 1970s and the 1980s. And finally, the third section will analyze the case of the early 1990s by focusing on how domestic preferences regarding policy instruments for adjusting external surpluses changed as economic interdependence deepened from the mid-1980s on.

THE PROBLEM OF
CURRENT ACCOUNT SURPLUSES
Balance of Payments Adjustment as a Political Agenda

During both the gold standard era and the Bretton Woods era of the fixed exchange rate system, there was a framework or norm for making adjustments to the balance of payments. States experiencing unsustainable external imbalances were expected to eliminate those imbalances by modifying their own policies (Simmons 1994; Obstfeld 1993). In the floating exchange rate system of the post–Bretton Woods period, by contrast, no consensus has emerged among states on the degree to which imbalances should be adjusted. Many economists claim that it is not necessary to eliminate external imbalances because the imbalances in and of themselves are not detrimental to international economic welfare (Komiya 1993, 59; Krugman 1994, 44–48). Despite the attempts by a number of economists to define optimal policy choices, there is no single economic model that spells out how much external payment imbalances should be adjusted and under what circumstances states should apply various policy instruments.[1] As a result, since the early 1970s states faced with external payments imbalances tend to want other states to take responsibility for changing their policies and eliminating the imbalance. Individual states have not paid serious heed to calls to adjust their current account imbalances unless those imbalances seemed incompatible with their own economic objectives or undermined the international economy as a whole.

Despite the fact that there is no consensus among economists on the necessity of adjusting current account imbalances, however, the issue has been high on the international political agenda since the late 1970s. There were two phenomena that particularly attracted the attention of the international community during this period. One was the external debt of developing countries, which had become a serious problem even before being brought to the forefront by the Mexican crisis of 1982. The second phenomenon was the emergence of a large U.S. current account deficit, coupled with large current account surpluses on the part of Japan and pre-unification West Germany. Among industrial states—and particularly between Japan and the United States—the persistent imbalance of current accounts has been a cause of political disputes. The accumulation by the United

States of a huge current account deficit was attributed by many in the United States to Japan's large current account surplus, giving rise to protectionist arguments. Many in the United States claimed that since the U.S. trade deficit with Japan was a major cause of the U.S. current account deficit, Japan should eliminate its current account surplus, including its trade surplus, as a way of contributing to the reduction of the U.S. current account deficit.

In the four time periods I have listed above, the United States played a major role in placing international balance of payments adjustment on the political agenda among industrial countries, and in demanding that Japan and Germany use particular policy instruments. The first time period was 1971–1973, following the Nixon Shock. Until the late 1960s, Japan had experienced a cyclical external payment deficit. In 1968, however, that deficit turned into a surplus that continued to grow thereafter. In 1971, Japan posted a large current account surplus, while the United States was facing a significant external deficit compared to previous years. After the Nixon Shock, neither the temporary floating system nor the multilateral currency adjustments agreed upon by the Group of Five (G5) members could adjust the imbalances. In order to stabilize international monetary relations, international organizations such as the International Monetary Fund (IMF) and the Organization for Economic Cooperation and Development (OECD) proposed adjusting the international balance of payments imbalances, and the Japanese government was pressed hard by the international community to revalue the yen in order to cut its surplus.

During the period 1977–1978, the U.S. government urged the German and Japanese governments to apply macroeconomic policies to eliminate their current account surpluses, advocating a "locomotive theory" in which the expansion of the American, German, and Japanese economies would provide benefits for other nations. In the aftermath of the oil shock, these three countries were recovering from severe cost-push inflationary pressures and showed current account surpluses, while other industrial states such as Britain, France, and Italy still suffered from current account deficits. The unevenness of these current account balances among industrial states was recognized as a problem in the international economy and adjusting these imbalances topped the central agendas of international organizations, prompted mainly by the United States. The U.S. government's eagerness for adjustments was related to its concern over the country's changing external payments position. As it became more and more apparent that its current account balance was worsening, the U.S. government began to criticize Japan and Germany—the two countries running surpluses—for not taking appropriate measures to eliminate those surpluses. The U.S. government also emphasized the relationship between exchange-rate misalignment and its own external deficit, and pushed the Japanese and German governments to appreciate their currencies.

During the 1980s, the problem of balance of payments adjustment again became one of the most urgent issues confronting the international economy. The aggregate current account deficits of the OECD countries as a whole declined in 1981 but rose again to US$61 billion in 1984. External payment imbalances among industrial countries became prominent—particularly the large current account deficit of the United States and the increasing current account surpluses of Japan and Germany. As it became apparent that exchange-rate movements for major currencies were heading in a direction that would further widen these imbalances instead of eliminating them, a strong dollar and high U.S. interest rates provoked political debates internationally over the appropriateness of U.S. macroeconomic and exchange-rate policies in terms of the country's balance of payments.

In 1985, the U.S. government finally acknowledged the links among its budget deficit, a strong dollar, and its external deficit, and placed exchange rates and macroeconomic policies on the international agenda. The U.S. government once again asked the Japanese and German governments to adopt expansionary macroeconomic policies in order to adjust their external surpluses, which would reduce the U.S. external deficit.

During the period 1993–1995, the U.S. government also pressed the Japanese government to apply macroeconomic policy, calling in particular for tax cuts and increased public works spending to eliminate Japan's record-high current account surplus. Since the U.S. trade deficit with Japan had increased, the U.S. government was also eager to reduce Japan's current account surplus by pursuing aggressive bilateral trade talks with Japan, such as the Framework Talks.

In all four of these cases, the Japanese government was under political pressure from the United States to reduce its current account surpluses. However, the Japanese government did not have to eliminate its surpluses by applying macroeconomic policy, as was demanded by the U.S. government. Why, then, did the Japanese government decide to respond to the U.S. request and to apply fiscal policy to adjust the current account imbalance?

Policy Instruments for Reducing Current Account Surpluses

In order to understand the rationale for a state's choice of a particular policy instrument, it is first necessary to examine the alternatives available for shifting the current account position. The primary policy options can be divided into three categories.[2] The first category is direct control of international trade and capital transactions at national borders. Through the use of such measures as special taxes, tariffs, and quotas, deficit countries can restrict capital outflows and imports of merchandise and services, while surplus countries can restrict capital inflows and exports. The second category is exchange-rate policy. It is assumed that appreciation will reduce current account surpluses and depreciation will eliminate deficits (Bergsten and Noland 1993). Under a floating exchange rate system, the foreign exchange market mechanism was assumed to reduce current account imbalances automatically. However, after it became apparent that such automatic adjustments were not always occurring, exchange-rate policy came to be recognized as a useful policy option. Exchange-rate policy in a floating exchange rate system implies intervention in the foreign exchange markets.[3]

The final category is macroeconomic policy, which is usually used to achieve stable domestic economic conditions. In this area, monetary policy and fiscal policy are considered as useful tools for adjusting external imbalances. However, since monetary and fiscal policies have opposite effects on the capital account, fiscal policy might be directed to internal stability and monetary policy to external stability (Mundell 1962). It is generally believed that a current account deficit may be corrected by a more deflationary macroeconomic policy, while a surplus may be corrected by a somewhat more inflationary policy.

Of these categories of policy instruments, the first option is usually only useful—and thus only applied—for temporary imbalances. The latter two categories are considered as the main policy instruments for correcting persistent large current account imbalances.[4] Facing persistent external imbalances, a state can choose either to change its exchange rate, its macroeconomic policy, or both.

In the 1970s and the 1980s, as we have noted above, the Japanese government ended up applying expansionary fiscal policy (as was urged by the United States) despite its initial reluctance to do so. The question is why Japan consistently subordinated its macroeconomic policy to balance of payments considerations.

JAPAN'S POLICY CHOICES
IN THE 1970S AND 1980S

Domestic Anti–Yen Appreciation Preferences

Existing approaches in international political economy to explaining why and how states choose certain policy instruments to make such adjustments tend to emphasize the process of negotiation among or between states (Destler and Mitsuyu 1982; Henning 1987; Funabashi 1989; Iida 1990). There is no doubt that U.S. political pressure played an important role in urging Japan to deal with its current account surplus. However, it is important to know how and through what mechanism the government chose particular policy instruments to accomplish that objective. Choosing a certain policy entails the domestic allocation of the costs and benefits that derive from such a policy choice. Therefore, it can be assumed that there are societal preferences regarding that choice. A typical example is the impact of trade policies such as the lowering of tariff rates, which may cause a diversion of domestic preferences between import-competing industries and export-oriented industries.

The conventional understanding regarding the use of such instruments as exchange rates and macroeconomic policy for the purpose of adjusting current account imbalances is that exchange-rate policy is relatively easy to apply in this instance because changes in exchange rates do not provoke disputes in domestic politics (Kelly 1982; Krasner 1978; Odell 1982; Gowa 1988). By contrast, it is assumed that policymakers are constrained in the use of macroeconomic policy by domestic political pressures, since as noted above, the primary concern of macroeconomic policy is generally the domestic economy and objectives. Fiscal policy, in particular, is difficult to change for the purpose of adjusting a country's external payment position because it needs to be authorized by the legislature (Buchanan and Wagner 1977). The corollary usually drawn from this is that a state faced with the need to make such adjustments is likely to apply exchange-rate policy and to resist changing its macroeconomic policy. However, this corollary does not explain Japan's policy choices in the 1970s and the 1980s, when Japan tended to apply expansionary fiscal policy to adjust its balance of payments.

Since conventional explanations have tended to be based only on U.S. cases, they have missed the importance of domestic preferences. Recent studies, however, shed light on the significant role that domestic preferences play in regard to changes in exchange rates (Frieden 1991; Henning 1994). According to these economic models, changes in the exchange rate will result in costs and benefits for certain societal groups. Tradable sectors (i.e., export-oriented industries) are likely to be against the appreciation of currency, since it would undermine the competitiveness of exports. Industries that rely on imported intermediate products and raw materials, on the other hand, are more likely to be in favor of currency appreciation because the price levels of imported materials would be lowered. For the same reason, import-competing industries will generally be opposed to currency appreciation. A non-tradable sector like international banking would probably be for currency appreciation or volatility of exchange rates, since it can take advantage of those trends. Consumers also might be for currency appreciation, because appreciation stabilizes price levels by reducing the cost of imports (Frieden 1991, 444–449).

When Japan began to face both a stronger yen and an external surplus in the 1970s and 1980s, domestic preferences were predominantly against the appreciation of the yen and for fiscal expansion. As the yen appreciated, expansionary macroeconomic policy came to be focused on counter-*endaka* (strong yen, or yen appreciation) and counter-recessionary measures. Japan's export-oriented industries and small and medium-sized businesses were especially sensitive to exchange-rate levels and pressed the government to stop the acceleration of the yen's rise by applying fiscal expansion. In contrast, sectors of society that were expected to benefit from *endaka*, such as importing industries, service industries, and consumers, rarely voiced their preferences. Given that Japan's export dependence in the 1970s and 1980s was smaller than that of every other industrial state except for the United States, it seems puzzling that the negative effects of yen appreciation were emphasized and not the positive effects (see table 2).

Two factors are critical to explaining this puzzle. The first is the influential position held by Japan's export-oriented industries. Since the 1950s, export-oriented industries were regarded as essential for Japan's domestic economy. In the post–World War II period, and up until the mid-1980s, the Japanese government's economic policy emphasized export-led growth. The growth rate of exports during the 1960s was 16.9 percent, which was much larger than the average rate of 9.5 percent for all industrial states, although Japan's export dependence ratio was smaller than most industrial states in 1970. The growth rate of exports was highest in export-oriented industries such as steel, electronic products, textiles, and automobiles (Ishizaki 1990). Export-oriented industries organized politically influential industrial associations and were powerful members of peak business organizations.

Second, export-oriented small and medium-sized manufacturers were especially active in lobbying political parties and the government on exchange-rate policy (Kojō 1995). Since exports represented a larger percentage of their business than that of big enterprises, the export-oriented small and medium-sized enterprises were expected to be hit severely by the yen's appreciation.[5] Also, since more than 80 percent of the workforce was employed by small and medium-sized enterprises in the 1970s and 1980s, the associations of these businesses were able to voice their fears regarding the negative impact of *endaka* on not only their own jobs but also the Japanese labor market as a whole.

Table 2. Export Dependence of Germany, Japan, and the United States, 1965–1997 (percentage of exports in GDP)

	Germany	Japan	United States
1975	—	12.8	8.4
1976	—	13.6	8.2
1977	—	13.1	7.8
1978	25.7	11.1	8.1
1979	25.2	11.6	8.9
1980	26.4	13.7	10.0
1981	28.7	14.7	9.7
1982	29.8	14.6	8.7
1983	28.7	13.9	7.9
1984	30.7	14.5	7.8
1985	32.6	14.5	7.2
1986	30.2	11.4	7.3
1987	28.9	10.4	7.8
1988	29.5	10.0	8.9
1989	31.6	10.6	9.4
1990	32.3	10.7	9.7
1991	25.4	10.2	10.2
1992	23.7	10.1	10.2
1993	22.1	9.3	10.0
1994	22.7	9.3	10.4
1995	23.0	9.4	11.3
1996	23.3	9.9	11.4
1997	25.3	11.1	11.9

Source: International Monetary Fund (1999).

Political Institutions:
Responding to Domestic Preferences

Although there was clearly a predominant domestic preference against *endaka* in Japan, the ability of such preferences to affect a state's policy choice in terms of adjusting the balance of payments depends on the existing political institutions and the degree to which domestic preferences are reflected in the policy-making process (Garrett and Lange 1995; Frieden and Rogowski 1996).

The relationship between the bureaucracy and political parties plays an important role in determining policy in this area. Government officials generally prefer to form policy decisions autonomously from domestic political pressures, while political parties usually reflect domestic preferences in their policy choices. In macroeconomic policy, there is a common assumption that government officials and political parties have different interests. Whereas political parties tend to be more concerned with employment and economic growth, the financial ministry is usually much more concerned with balanced budgets, and the central bank is more concerned with stable price levels (Paterson and Rom 1988; Wildavsky 1984; Buchanan and Wagner 1977). In monetary policy, the independence of the central bank from political pressure is regarded as a significant determinant (Wooley 1985; Goodman 1992; Henning 1994). If the central bank is independent, monetary policy tends to be more price stability–oriented. In terms of fiscal policy, the financial ministry is usually reluctant to apply expansionary policy, while political parties are more likely to support such measures. In contrast, exchange-rate policy is usually regarded as being autonomous from political pressures because the exchange rate is so technical that only a limited number of government officials can formulate policy (Krasner, 1978; Odell 1982; Gowa 1988).

In Japan's case, there were two institutional characteristics that affected the issue of exchange-rate and macroeconomic policies. First, the country's central bank, the Bank of Japan (BOJ), was much less independent than the central banks of Germany or the United States in terms of influence from the financial ministry (Henning 1994). In the area of monetary policy, it was difficult for the BOJ to resist political pressure. Second, since the 1960s the Liberal Democratic Party (LDP), which was in power from 1955 through 1993, and other parties as well responded favorably to the preferences of export-oriented industries, and to those of export-oriented small and medium-sized enterprises in particular. The reason was that, since export-oriented small and medium-sized enterprises were essentially local businesses, they represented a significant share of the electoral bases of the political parties—both of the LDP and the opposition parties (Hiwatari 1991, 79–86; Calder 1988, 334).[6] As a result, small and medium-sized business policy has been one of the few issue areas with a low degree of partisan conflict since the 1960s (Mochizuki 1982, 333–334). Since all political parties in

Japan shared an interest in export-oriented small and medium-sized businesses, they also held a common stance on the appropriate policy instrument for balance of payments adjustment. As a result, the political parties succeeded in influencing policy formulation despite the fact that their preferences differed from the policy preferences of the BOJ and the Ministry of Finance (MOF). As the yen appreciated, the political parties tended to emphasize the negative effects of the strong yen and pressed for fiscal expansion as a means of curbing further appreciation.

The Cases

1971–1973

As noted above, Japan was faced with the problem of adjusting its external payments surplus in the 1970s and the 1980s. In December 1971, after the Nixon Shock, the cabinet of Prime Minister Satō Eisaku was forced to revalue the yen—an action Japan had long sought to avoid—under the terms of the Smithsonian Agreement, an agreement on multilateral currency realignment reached among the G5 nations at the Smithsonian Institution in Washington, D.C. The rate of revaluation, 16.88 percent, was the largest among the industrial countries. The following year, however, the Japanese government was faced with international political pressure to allow the yen to appreciate still further due to its continuing external payments surplus, and officials of MOF and the BOJ came to realize that Japan would have to accept a further revaluation. However, export-oriented industries, including small and medium-sized businesses, aggressively opposed any further strengthening of the yen.

In response to these domestic interests, political parties—all of which shared the same anti-revaluation preference—had an interest in provoking a political debate over the appropriate policy instruments for avoiding a further revaluation. The opposition parties blamed the LDP government for failing to avoid the revaluation of the yen. As a result, the government's policy choices were restrained and, in an effort to avoid revaluation, the government ended up relying heavily on expansionary macroeconomic policy to make the necessary adjustments to the balance of payments (Nakagawa 1981). In 1972, although the domestic economy had begun recovering and wholesale prices had been rising after the summer, the cabinet of Tanaka Kakuei (who had succeeded Satō) did not reconsider expansionary policy (Nakagawa 1981). Fiscal expansion in particular proved to be a policy instrument that was compatible with domestic preferences against *endaka*.[7]

1977–1978

In 1976, as it became increasingly apparent that the U.S. current account balance was worsening, the administration under President Jimmy Carter began to criticize Germany and Japan for not taking appropriate measures to eliminate their surpluses. At that time, the United States asked the Japanese and German governments to apply expansionary macroeconomic policy to their domestic economies.

The emergence of international criticism of Japan's current account surplus sparked a sharp rise in the yen from the end of September 1977. Over the subsequent two months, the value of the yen appreciated by about 10 percent. As the yen gained sharply against the dollar, the opposition to a strong yen became more vocal in the domestic political arena (Volcker and Gyohten 1992, 153). Business organizations and export-oriented small and medium-sized businesses demanded that Prime Minister Fukuda Takeo halt the yen's appreciation by applying expansionary fiscal policy. They responded not to the actual impact of yen appreciation on the economy as a whole, but to the rise in the exchange rate itself and the resulting fear of projected losses that they would incur.

With rapid yen appreciation and an increasing external payment surplus, the Fukuda cabinet was confronted with criticism on two fronts: from the international community, which complained about Japan's failure to stem its mounting surplus, and from domestic industries and political parties, which responded to industry's aversion to the strong yen. Since neither frequent intervention in the foreign exchange market in the autumn of 1977 nor a reduction in the official discount rate that same year appeared effective in preventing further yen appreciation, expansionary fiscal policy became the main focus of political debates (Kojō 1995). The sudden appreciation of the yen from a level of ¥266 to the dollar in September 1977 to a level of ¥240 to the dollar in November of that year strengthened industry's criticism of government policies as being ineffective. Despite MOF's strong opposition to an expansionary fiscal policy, which stemmed from the ministry's concern over the burgeoning budget deficit (the cumulative budget deficit had reached 16.1 percent of gross national product in 1976, up from 8.6 percent in 1974), the Fukuda government finally passed a large supplemental budget for fiscal year 1977, although this did not result in any decrease in the current surplus in 1978, nor did it stem the rise of the yen. In addition, in July 1978, at the Bonn G5 summit, the Fukuda cabinet acknowledged a 7 percent target growth rate (the target had previously been discussed only with the United States).

1985–1987

In the early 1980s, the huge U.S. current account deficit and large current account surpluses of Japan and Germany again became one of the most urgent issues confronting the international economy, as many industrial states (with the exception of the United States) began to fear that the U.S. dollar was overvalued. International negotiations took place continuously regarding which states should choose which policy instruments. At a G5 meeting held at the Plaza Hotel in September 1985, the Japanese government (at that time led by Prime Minister Nakasone Yasuhiro) agreed on exchange-rate realignment as the principal method of adjusting Japan's balance of payments in what is known as the Plaza Accord. As a result of this policy choice, the yen started to appreciate sharply. Between September 1985 and January 1986, the yen rose by about 20 percent, reaching the level of ¥190 to the dollar, which indicates that the Japanese government initially tried to maintain a strong yen to correct its external surplus. This initial policy choice can be explained by the fact that the Nakasone cabinet was firmly committed to a fiscal austerity policy, which was supported by MOF and by business leaders such as Dokō Toshio, chairman of Keidanren (Japan Federation of Economic Organizations).

Due to domestic sensitivity within Japan to the rise in the yen's value, international pressure for expansionary fiscal measures was able to influence Japan's choice of policy measures. In negotiations with the United States, which was concerned with the increasing U.S. trade deficit with Japan, the necessity of exchange-rate stability was accepted by the U.S. government in exchange for Japan's commitment to expansionary macroeconomic policy.

The yen appreciation actually had a number of negative effects on the domestic economy, such as lowering the growth rate and increasing unemployment. Since the yen continuously gained strength, the fear of recession remained strong among export-oriented industries. The Nakasone government did not begin to apply substantive fiscal measures for twenty months after the yen started to appreciate. Monetary policy was the main macroeconomic policy instrument used during this period to deal with external payments adjustment. The Nakasone government tried to avoid applying fiscal expansion, even while the economic slowdown was apparent. Moreover, the divergent views among business leaders on whether more expansionary fiscal policy was needed allowed the government to stimulate the economy through policy measures of privatization and deregulation.

In May 1987, however, the Nakasone government finally decided to introduce a fiscal stimulative package of more than ¥6 trillion, despite the negative impact of such a move on the budget deficit. This decision was a result of domestic preferences, especially those of small and medium-sized exporting businesses, which after January 1987 were increasingly against rapid appreciation of the yen. But by late in the spring of 1987, the domestic economy was already in the process of recovering, and thus, from the viewpoint of the domestic economy, the decision was made too late.

The policy orientations of the anti-Nakasone factions within the LDP and the opposition parties were similar with regard to macroeconomic policy: They were in opposition to MOF's fiscal austerity policy and provoked a debate over the deflationary effect of the strong yen on the domestic economy and its contribution to rising unemployment. They therefore focused on measures to stem the rise of the yen and to compensate small and medium-sized businesses hit by exchange-rate losses. Expansionary fiscal policy, which was urged by the U.S. government as a means of adjusting the current account surplus, was emphasized in domestic politics rather as a way to halt the yen's appreciation and to stimulate the domestic economy. In short, it was as a result of domestic sensitivity in Japan to the rise in the yen's value that international pressure was able to influence the Japanese government's choice of expansionary fiscal policy.

JAPAN'S POLICY CHOICE IN THE EARLY 1990S

Upsurges in the Current Account Surplus and U.S. Political Pressure

After 1987, there was a correlation between changes in Japan's overall current account surplus and its trade surplus with the United States on the one hand, and changes in U.S. political pressure on Japan on the other. Since the United States was faced with the problem of large twin deficits—i.e., a large current account deficit and a large budget deficit—the American trade deficit with Japan and Japan's current account surplus raised protectionist sentiments particularly in Congress, which then affected the U.S. government's policy toward Japan. From 1987 to 1990, Japan's current account surplus and its trade surplus with the United States in particular dropped drastically (see table 1). With the decline in external payment imbalances, the related political disputes among industrial states faded away.

In terms of U.S.-Japan relations, the U.S. current account and trade balances with Japan were still showing a deficit, although it was on the decline. The U.S. government continued to ask for Japanese government efforts to adjust those imbalances. In 1989, the administration of President George Bush proposed a new round of bilateral trade talks, termed the Structural Impediments Initiative (SII), in which the U.S. government proposed a new agenda that included a streamlining of the Japanese distribution system and revisions to Japan's Antimonopoly Act. However, until mid-1991, despite the aggressive attitude revealed in SII and other trade talks, the Bush administration took a middle-of-the-road approach to U.S.-Japan relations and did not resort to Super 301, which had been enacted by the Congress in 1988 (Hatakeyama 1996). From 1991 to 1995, as Japan's overall current account surplus and its trade surplus with the United States continuously increased, U.S. political pressure on Japan to reduce its surpluses intensified. In 1995, when Japan's surpluses dropped, the U.S. political pressure subsided.

In 1991, Japan's current account surplus climbed rapidly, jumping to US$42.74 billion in May—three times that registered a year earlier. As this upward trend became apparent, the balance of payments issue once again became a matter of concern to the U.S. government. At the Group of Seven (G7) summit meeting held in October, emphasis was placed on the importance of avoiding the reemergence of very large external payment imbalances. And although the G7 communiqué did not single out any country, it was interpreted as a warning to Japan about its growing surplus (*Nihon Keizai Shimbun* 13 October 1991).

Nonetheless, Japan's current account surplus continued to climb through 1992. In April of that year, economic management in Japan came under fire at a meeting in Washington, D.C., of G7 finance ministers and central bankers. The communiqué once again avoided mentioning Japan directly, but sent an unmistakable signal that Japan should take stimulative policy measures to strengthen its economy and eliminate its external payment imbalances (*Nihon Keizai Shimbun* 27 April 1992). At the same meeting, the U.S. government asked Japan to take expansionary fiscal measures and lower its interest rate. In 1993, Japan's current account surplus grew to a historical high of more than US$130 billion, or 3.3 percent of gross domestic product, jumping from US$44 billion, or 1.1 percent of GDP, in 1990 (see fig. 1). In January of that year, MOF also released trade figures showing that Japan's total overall trade surplus topped US$100 billion for the first time in history. Since the U.S. trade deficit with Japan also expanded, the American government took the initiative to place the problem of Japan's large current account surplus at the top of the agenda for U.S.-Japan relations.

President Bill Clinton, who took office in January 1993, and who gave his full attention to the recovery of the U.S. economy, took a tougher approach toward Japan's current account surplus than had his predecessor. In his first meeting with Minister of Foreign Affairs Watanabe Michio, he clearly stated that Japan's large surplus was a serious problem to be solved between the two countries and that Japan should make efforts to eliminate that imbalance and liberalize its markets (*Nihon Keizai Shimbun* 12 February 1993). The Clinton administration kept pressing the Japanese government (at that time, the cabinet of Prime Minister Miyazawa Kiichi) to undertake macroeconomic policy coordination to eliminate the current account and trade surpluses (*Nihon Keizai Shimbun* 14 April 1993).

In a Clinton-Miyazawa meeting in the spring of 1993, Clinton focused exclusively on the balance of payments problem and proposed two remedies: first, that the yen be further strengthened and, second, that Japan apply expansionary macroeconomic policy. Clinton also suggested to Miyazawa that Japan set a numerical target for the reduction of Japan's current account surplus. Miyazawa, however, refused (*Nihon Keizai Shimbun* 17 April 1993). Three months later, at the G7's Tokyo Summit, the discussions clearly showed that international pressure on Japan to adjust its current account surplus had intensified.

In November 1993, dissatisfied with big spending programs introduced in

Figure 1. Japan's Current Account Balance (percent of nominal GDP)

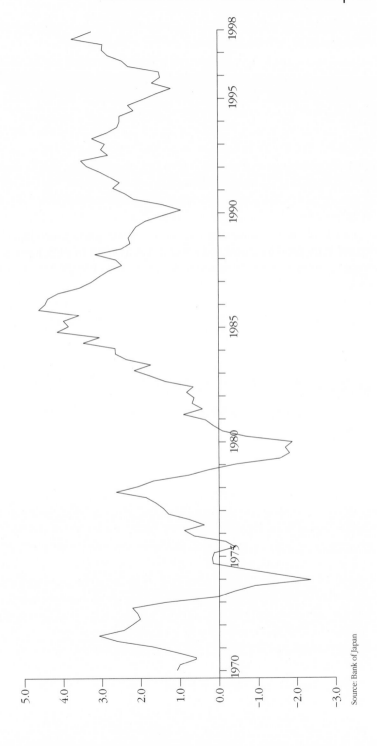

Source: Bank of Japan

September by the Japanese coalition government of newly installed Prime Minister Hosokawa Morihiro (the first non-LDP prime minister since 1955), the Clinton administration proposed to Hosokawa that his government use a specific policy instrument—namely, the introduction of a large income tax cut—to stimulate the domestic economy (*Nihon Keizai Shimbun* 12 November 1993). The U.S. pressure on Japan for fiscal expansion continued until 1995.

Along with its demand for macroeconomic remedies, the Clinton administration adopted a new strategy for trade talks with Japan that was aimed at reducing its bilateral trade imbalance. The two governments began new trade negotiations, known as the U.S.-Japan Framework Talks on Bilateral Trade, in July 1993. Through these negotiations, the United States attempted to pursue a results-oriented market access strategy, while the Japanese government continued to reject such an approach. Within the context of the Framework Talks, the Clinton administration also proposed once again to set a target of limiting Japan's current account surplus to within 2 percent of GDP, but the Miyazawa government steadfastly refused such an idea because the current account could not be controlled specifically by government intervention. After a Clinton-Hosokawa meeting in February 1994 failed to produce any agreement, the bilateral trade talks were further aggravated by the U.S. government's unilateral trade policies, such as threatening to impose sanctions under Super 301 on a number of Japanese luxury automobiles. (The U.S.-Japan automobile talks concluded the following month, in June 1995.)

The Exchange Rate and Macroeconomic Policies

The yen rate seemed to fluctuate according to changes in Japan's current account surplus in the early 1990s. The yen was undervalued relative to the dollar until the autumn of 1991. At the end of 1991, the yen rate was ¥125.25 = US$1, which was almost exactly the same as the year-end rate in 1988. In the first four months of 1992, the rate stayed close to the ¥133 = US$1 level. In May 1992, the yen started gaining against the dollar and rose steadily through April 1995, although there was some fluctuation during this period. The yen appreciated beyond ¥100 yen to the dollar in June 1994, passed the ¥90 to the dollar mark in March 1995, and hit the level of ¥80 yen to the dollar in April 1995, which was its highest level in the postwar period. It was not until August 1995 that the yen fell back below the level of ¥90 to the dollar (see fig. 2).

In early 1990, when the yen-dollar rate depreciated below ¥155 = US$1, the BOJ expressed concern about a low yen rate, fearing that the lower yen might push up price levels. The BOJ was frequently intervening in the foreign exchange market during that time, sometimes in coordination with the United States, to prevent further depreciation of the yen. The BOJ also raised the discount rate to 5.25

Figure 2. Nominal Foreign Exchange Rates (Yen/$)

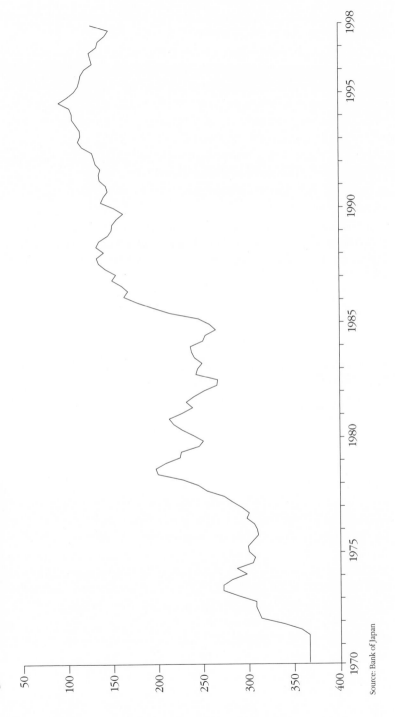

Source: Bank of Japan

percent from 4.25 percent in March, and to 6.00 percent in August 1990, in order to stabilize the level of the yen. However, the yen started to appreciate in late 1991, and rose rapidly in early 1993. The new Clinton administration took a more hands-off stance toward the yen-dollar exchange rate than had the Bush administration. The Clinton administration was more eager than the Bush administration to make a political issue of Japan's large current account surplus because of the widening of the U.S.-Japan trade imbalance, which had given rise to domestic protectionist arguments. This hands-off attitude was taken by the Japanese government as a sign of the United States' willingness to apply exchange-rate policy as a form of pressure on Japan to eliminate its current account surplus. Through 1992, the Japanese government also expressed its acceptance of yen appreciation in light of Japan's increasing current account surplus and trade surplus with the United States. In April 1993, however, the BOJ finally intervened in the foreign exchange market by selling yen and buying dollars to avoid further appreciation. This was the first use of this type of BOJ intervention to slow down the yen's rise since December 1988. After April 1993, the BOJ was a lonely player in its effort to stem further appreciation, and its intervention was not effective.

Under U.S. political pressure and foreign exchange market pressure, both of which favored a stronger yen, the Japanese government in the early 1990s had to deal with the problem of balance of payments adjustment in order to avoid further appreciation. After Japan's economic bubble burst, however, the country suffered from a sluggish domestic economy. In this new environment, what policy instruments did the Japanese government have?

Although exchange-rate policy was attempted, it was difficult for the Japanese government to reach an agreement on coordinated intervention among states to reverse the exchange rate moves. This difficulty was revealed at the G7's Naples Summit in July 1994. Prime Minister Murayama Tomiichi, who had been selected the previous month to head a new coalition government of the LDP, the Social Democratic Party of Japan, and the New Party Sakigake, sought to coordinate exchange-rate policy to reverse the yen-dollar exchange rate movement. However, the G7 countries failed to conclude an agreement on this issue. Instead, the final declaration called on countries where economic recoveries were not under way to take expansionary monetary and fiscal policy (*Nihon Keizai Shimbun* 9 July 1994). Although the BOJ continued to intervene frequently to depress the yen's value, for the most part its efforts proved futile.

In terms of applying macroeconomic policy, MOF did not feel that expansionary fiscal measures were feasible during this period. In the 1989–1990 SII talks, the Japanese government had agreed to budget ¥430 trillion for public works spending over the next decade. Despite its pledge, it was difficult for the Japanese government to apply additional expansionary policies. In March 1992, the

Miyazawa administration approved a "Seven-Point Plan" to boost the economy. The measures included front-loading fiscal 1992 public works spending, which would be 15.7 percent higher than the amount initially planned for fiscal 1991. In August, the Miyazawa administration also announced an economic stimulus package, the size of which (¥10.7 trillion) was nearly double the anticipated amount. Despite these packages, however, Japan's current account surplus continued to increase and the yen appreciated against the dollar.

The final policy option the government could use was monetary policy. In February 1993, the discount rate was reduced from 3.75 percent to 2.5 percent—equal to the postwar low—and there seemed little room for further reduction. The large-scale income tax cut proposed by the United States was opposed by MOF, which was concerned with the country's budget deficit and how to offset the loss of revenue that such a tax cut would entail. In mid-April, the Miyazawa administration announced a new ¥13.2 trillion economic stimulus package just before the prime minister flew to Washington to meet President Clinton. Despite the new package, which envisaged increased government spending amounting to 2.8 percent of GNP for one fiscal year, the U.S. government claimed that the Japanese measures were not enough. Japanese officials at MOF and the BOJ, however, tended to claim that the current account imbalances did not need to be adjusted and that Japan's current account surplus was useful because it enabled Japan to invest more overseas, thus helping the international economy (*Nihon Keizai Shimbun* 2 July 1993; Economic Planning Agency 1993, 290–294). This stance represented an apparent change in the Japanese government's attitude toward balance of payment adjustments.

Since further spending and tax cuts were difficult options for the government to take for balance of payments adjustment policy, monetary policy was the only remaining alternative. In September 1993, with the BOJ putting primary emphasis on the sluggish domestic economy, the discount rate was reduced to 1.75 percent (*Kinyūzaisei Jijō* 4 October 1993, 14–15). Reflecting MOF's strong opposition to an income tax cut, the economic policy package proposed by the Hosokawa administration that same month focused mainly on loosening government regulations and urging firms to pass the price benefits of the stronger yen on to consumers, and did not include a tax cut.

In April 1994, a temporary income tax cut was finally introduced. However, since this income tax cut was linked to a future increase in the sales tax, the United States expressed dissatisfaction with the plan. The fiscal 1994 budget included a mere 1 percent increase in overall spending from fiscal 1993's original level. Although two supplemental budgets for fiscal 1994 were approved in early 1995, the first supplement was designed mainly to help farmers affected by market liberalization under the Uruguay Round agreement and the second one was earmarked for helping the Kansai region, which had been devastated by the Great Hanshin-Awaji Earthquake in January 1995.

In light of a business survey that showed business confidence still deteriorating among Japanese firms in the spring of 1995, the BOJ, having resisted for a long time, finally reduced the discount rate from 1.75 percent to 1 percent in April, hoping to boost the economy. In May, the Murayama administration decided on the first supplemental budget for fiscal 1995 out of concern for the earthquake recovery efforts. Despite the Japanese government's application of expansionary monetary and fiscal policies in the spring, however, the yen appreciated rapidly, reaching a rate of nearly ¥80 = US$1. Faced with this rapid appreciation and a prolonged recession, the BOJ further reduced the discount rate to 0.5 percent in September.[8] Since the government realized that it was difficult to apply further reductions in the discount rate, the Murayama administration decided to introduce a second, large supplemental budget for fiscal 1995 in October. However, most of the money was earmarked for earthquake reconstruction and only limited amounts were tied directly to helping small and medium-sized businesses cope with the strong yen or to adjusting the external payment surplus. In other words, the decision to undertake fiscal expansionary policy was driven largely by domestic concerns about the earthquake and recession rather than by concerns about adjusting Japan's current account surplus in response to U.S. requests. The New Frontier Party, the largest opposition party, blamed the Murayama coalition government for taking no effective policy measures to halt the rising yen. The three coalition parties—the LDP, the Socialist Democratic Party, and Sakigake—finally agreed to set a target for reducing the current account surplus to within 1 percent of GDP over a period of three years, from 1996 to 1998 (*Nihon Keizai Shimbun* 25 April 1995).

Compared to the cases in the 1970s and the 1980s, then, the Japanese government was clearly less eager in the early 1990s to use expansionary fiscal policy, although Japan was faced with a "hyper-valued yen" that was reaching historically high levels. The Japanese government hesitated to implement expansionary fiscal measures despite requests by the United States to do so for the purpose of adjusting the bilateral trade imbalance (Webb 1995). Once again, this change in policy choice can be attributed largely to changes in domestic preferences.

Changes in Domestic Preferences regarding Adjustments to the Current Account Surplus

Looking at the 1993–1995 period, during which the yen appreciated sharply, both export-oriented industries and export-oriented small and medium-sized businesses expressed their preferences against the strong yen as they had in the three previous cases from the 1970s and the 1980s. Despite the rapid yen appreciation, however, there was comparatively less resistance in Japanese society to the strong yen in the early 1990s. In particular, industry preferences regarding the adjustment of external payments had become increasingly diversified. In the cases of 1971–1973 and 1977–1978, immediately after the yen started to appreciate the leaders of the four peak business organizations[9] urged the government to implement expansionary fiscal policy in order to avoid a revaluation or appreciation of the yen. In the 1985–1987 case, however, business leaders were not as active initially in pressing the government to apply expansionary fiscal measures, partly due to their firm commitments to fiscal reform and partly due to the diffusion of industries' attitudes toward a strong yen (Kojō 1995).

In the early 1990s, this diffusion of attitudes was further intensified as the effect of the strong yen became clearly divided by industry—especially between export-oriented industries such as steel and automobiles, and nonmanufacturing industries such as banking and telecommunications (Nihon Keizai Shimbunsha 1993). The diversity in profits among industries had already become apparent in the case of 1985–1987 and was even more apparent in the early 1990s (Economic Planning Agency 1997). For business leaders, it became increasingly difficult to represent a diffuse set of industry preferences toward a strong yen. For example, there were diverse opinions expressed regarding the yen rate during the 1994 meetings of Keidanren, Japan's most influential peak business association, and as a result their policy emphasis was instead put on deregulation (*Gekkan Keidanren* September 1994).

Small and medium-sized businesses were also quieter than in the past on the issue of the strong yen. The National Federation of Small Business Associations (NFSBA: Zenkoku Chūshō Kigyō Dantai Chūōkai), was not as vocal in urging the government to take expansionary fiscal policy as it had been in the 1970s and the 1980s as a means to avoid further yen appreciation. In 1993, although the yen had started to appreciate, the primary concern of the NFSBA was the sluggish economy (*Chūshōkigyō to Kumiai* December 1993, 40–42). As the yen continued to appreciate into 1994, however, the organization did call for coordinated intervention in foreign exchange markets to curb the rising yen rather than expansionary macroeconomic policy (*Chūshōkigyō to Kumiai* August 1994, 26). It was not until the spring of 1995, however, that small and medium-sized businesses began to urgently demand that the government provide a large supplemental budget for small-scale businesses.

Industry, in general, had shifted its business strategies to adapt to fluctuations in the exchange rate after the Plaza Accord, and had thus become less sensitive to the strong yen. This change affected their preferences regarding current account adjustments. In the 1970s and 1980s, with a large payment surplus, exchange rate movements that were triggered by the government's policy of exchange-rate realignment as a means of addressing its external payment surplus provoked domestic resistance to the high level of the exchange rate. The preferences of most sectors in Japan tended to be against yen appreciation and, in turn, to favor expansionary fiscal policy. In the early 1990s, most industries were less sensitive to the strong yen and there was no unanimous domestic preference against further appreciation. Given this change in domestic preferences, the government was rarely faced with a trade-off between autonomy of macroeconomic policy and exchange-rate stability. Therefore, it can be assumed that the Japanese government had less incentive domestically to apply macroeconomic policy for the purpose of external balance of payments adjustment.

The shift in industry preferences regarding the exchange rate can be attributed to structural changes implemented in response to the post–Plaza Accord period of yen appreciation. First, many industries shifted their focus from overseas markets to the domestic market. The export dependence ratio of Japan actually declined after 1986. The strong yen also led to an expansion of the service sector, which is usually less sensitive to the yen's appreciation than the export-oriented manufacturing industries.

Second, Japanese industries rapidly increased overseas direct investment in the late 1980s in order to avoid potential losses and to take advantage of the currency's new strength. For example, automobile manufacturers shifted production facilities to the United States, and many producers of machinery and electronic equipment moved their operations to Asian countries. In 1989, there were more than 1,800 cases of overseas investment undertaken by Japanese manufacturers—more than 2.5 times the amount in 1985.

Third, Japanese industry underwent major restructuring and rationalization to cope with the strong yen. The average level of the yen-dollar exchange rate at which firms could make a profit rose by 20 percent between 1991 and 1995. This demonstrates the degree of rationalization that Japanese industries went through to cope with the strong yen.

Small and medium-sized businesses were hit most severely by the rise of the yen because they did not have as much room for rationalization or restructuring. One survey showed that among local small business manufacturing regions that exported more than 20 percent of their products, the export dependence ratio declined to 36 percent in 1992, down significantly from the 1985 level of 49 percent, and the number of firms declined by about 30 percent. This shows that small and medium-sized businesses made efforts to shift to domestic-oriented businesses under these severe circumstances (Small and Medium Enterprise Agency 1994, 37–73, 195–198). Of course, not only export-oriented but also import-competing small-scale businesses suffered from the impact of the strong yen, but they generally undertook rationalization to be less sensitive to exchange-rate fluctuations.

Japan experienced a major political change in 1993, when the LDP government, which had led the country since 1955, was replaced by a coalition government. Between 1993 and 1995, three coalition governments came to office—the Hosokawa government in 1993, the Hata government in April 1994, and the Murayama government in June 1994. Of course, this change of government affected the government's policy choices in terms of balance of payments adjustment. For example, the Hosokawa government tried to emphasize deregulation and the need to pass on the benefits of a strong yen to consumers. However, since the attitudes of the various political parties toward the problem of the current account surplus were almost identical, it appears that the changes in domestic preferences had more influence on the formulation of policy in this area than these political changes per se.

CONCLUSION

This study has examined the differences that occurred in Japan's policymaking regarding the adjustment of its balance of payments between the 1970s–1980s and the 1990s. In conclusion, we can emphasize three points. First, domestic preferences clearly influenced Japan's policy choices regarding the method of making balance of payments adjustments in the postwar period. From the 1970s to the 1990s, when the current account surplus surged, yen appreciation occurred in the foreign exchange market at the same time. Under these circumstances, there was a predominant domestic preference for the adoption of alternative policy choices over a further appreciation of the yen. Export-oriented industries and small and medium-sized businesses were especially sensitive to the exchange-rate level and pressed the government to stop the rise of the yen. Political parties, in turn, were sensitive to such domestic preferences because all political parties relied on small and medium-sized businesses for important electoral support. Therefore, there was a domestic bias in Japan in favor of expansionary fiscal policy. This argument challenges the conventional understanding of exchange-rate policy, which holds that there are negligible domestic preferences regarding the exchange rate and minimal lobbying activities to influence exchange-rate policy.[10]

Second, economic internationalization affected the preferences of industries in Japan. Since the 1980s, financial liberalization and the easing of capital controls have led to the internationalization of capital movements. In a floating exchange rate system with massive capital mobility, exchange-rate fluctuations became a common occurrence. With a large current account surplus, the exchange rate for the yen tended to appreciate. In the 1970s and 1980s, Japanese industries—especially export-oriented industries—believed that a strong yen would reduce their competitiveness overseas. Therefore, they preferred that the government apply expansionary fiscal policy for external balance of payments adjustment. However, from the late 1980s, Japanese industries realized that the appreciation of the yen was a result of economic internationalization and began to implement strategies to cope with it. A review of the case of the early 1990s implies that this change in domestic preferences did indeed affect the policy choice of the government regarding external balance of payments adjustment.

Finally, the review of the early 1990s case shows that economic internationalization undermined the effectiveness of policy instruments for external balance of payment adjustment. In the 1970s and 1980s, expansionary fiscal policy was regarded not only by the U.S. government but also by the Japanese government as an effective instrument for reducing the current account surplus by expanding the domestic economy. Therefore, fiscal expansion was taken as an alternative policy choice to yen appreciation. However, since fiscal expansion was not as effective as expected, the argument was raised that—in keeping with the Mundell-Fleming model—with massive capital mobility, expansionary fiscal policy would lead to yen appreciation in the short run by putting upward pressure on the interest rates. The effectiveness of expansionary fiscal policy in stemming yen appreciation was therefore called into doubt. This may be one reason why industry was less eager to press hard for expansionary fiscal policy in the case of the 1990s.

In the late 1990s, Japan's current account surplus rose again and the United States current account deficit grew as well. The trade imbalance between Japan and the United States was large and widening. The U.S. government warned the Japanese government of the undesirability of Japan's current account surplus. Similarly, the IMF also expressed its concern over the danger of the growing current account imbalances between the United States and other industrial states (Warner 1999). However, since the Japanese economy remained stagnant, still suffering from the aftereffects of the collapse of the bubble economy and the Asian financial crisis, the Japanese government was more concerned with boosting the stagnant domestic economy than adjusting the current account surplus per se. Since the yen's value against the dollar had been gradually declining from the mid-1990s on, and since the domestic economy had become less sensitive to changes in the exchange rate as described above, there was less domestic pressure for the government to apply macroeconomic policy to avoid a stronger yen. In addition, the Japanese government was constrained in its use of expansionary fiscal policy by its huge budget deficit.

The government's policy choices in the late 1990s, however, were dominated by its concern over how to boost the domestic economy. As a result, in response to U.S. demands to reduce the current account surplus, the Japanese government put its emphasis on policies for deregulating markets. Since Japan's economy remains sluggish, the U.S. government has refrained from exerting too much pressure on the Japanese government. However, when the Japanese economy recovers, it is likely that the U.S. government will once again put Japan's current account surplus on the political agenda of the bilateral relationship, since the U.S. current account deficit and trade deficit with Japan will undoubtedly increase. At that time, if there is still limited domestic support for applying macroeconomic policy in Japan, it is unlikely that the U.S. government will experience the same success it did in the 1970s and 1980s in pressing the Japanese government to adopt this policy option to correct its external surpluses.

NOTES

1. Regarding the existence of various models for international macroeconomic policy coordination, see Frankel (1988).

2. Cooper defines three categories of policy instruments under fixed exchange rates: external, internal, and financing measures (1968, 13–23). Webb shows three categories: external policy, symptom management policy, and internal policy (1991, 314).

3. In a floating exchange rate system, with massive and rapid capital mobility, it has become much more difficult to alter exchange rates through a single country's intervention.

4. It should be noted that this categorization is based on conventional theory on policy instruments for current account adjustment, but there is no theoretical consensus on the effectiveness of each policy instrument.

5. In 1971, exports by small and medium-sized businesses comprised 40.2 percent of Japan's total exports and 43.5 percent of exports to the United States (Ohtsu 1971).

6. Rosenbluth (1993) focuses on the LDP's compensation policy for small-scale business in the period of the strong yen. However, it was not only the LDP but also other political parties that emphasized compensation for small-scale businesses.

7. The choice to use expansionary macroeconomic policy was also apparent in the making of the 1971, 1972, and 1973 budgets (Andō 1987; Yanagisawa 1985).

8. The BOJ was reluctant to reduce the rate. The bank's position, as expressed by the bank's president at that time, Matsushita Yasuo, was that it was not appropriate to apply monetary policy to stabilize exchange rates (*Nihon Keizai Shimbun* 8 March 1995).

9. The four peak business organizations are Keizai Dantai Rengōkai (Keidanren: Japan Federation of Economic Organizations), Keizai Dōyūkai (Japan Association of Corporate Executives), Nihon Keizaidantai Rengōkai (Nikkeiren: Japan Federation of Employers' Associations), and Nihon Shōkō Kaigisho (Nisshō: Japan Chamber of Commerce and Industry).

10. For an exceptional study, see Henning (1994). This study emphasizes societal preferences regarding exchange-rate policy in Japan, Germany, and the United States.

BIBLIOGRAPHY

Andō Hiroshi. 1987. *Sekinin to genkai.* (Responsibility and Limitations). 2 vols. Tokyo: Kinyū Zaisei Jijō Kenkyūkai.

Bergsten, C. Fred, and Marcus Noland. 1993. *Reconcilable Differences?: United States-Japan*

Economic Conflict. Washington, D. C.: Institute for International Economics.

Buchanan, James M., and Richard E. Wagner. 1977. *Democracy in Deficit*. New York: Academic Press, Inc.

Calder, Kent E. 1988. *Crisis and Compensation: Public Policy and Political Stability in Japan*. Princeton, N.J.: Princeton University Press.

Cooper, Richard. 1968. *The Economics of Interdependence: Economic Policy in the Atlantic Community*. New York: McGraw-Hill.

Destler, I. M., and Mitsuyu Hisao. 1982. "Locomotives on Different Tracks: Macroeconomic Diplomacy, 1977–1979." In I. M. Destler and Hideo Satō, eds. *Coping with U.S.-Japanese Economic Conflicts*. Lexington, Mass.: Lexington Books.

Destler, I. M., and C. Randall Henning. 1989. *Dollar Politics: Exchange Rate Policymaking in the United States*. Washington, D.C.: Institute for International Economics.

Economic Planning Agency. 1993. *Keizai hakusho* (Economic white paper). Tokyo: Ministry of Finance Printing Bureau.

———. 1997. *Keizai hakusho* (Economic white paper). Tokyo: Ministry of Finance Printing Bureau.

Frankel, Jeffrey A. 1988. *Obstacles to International Macroeconomic Policy Coordination*. Princeton Studies in International Finance no. 64 (December). Princeton, N.J.: Princeton University Press.

Frieden, Jeffery A. 1991. "National Economic Policies in a World of Global Finance." *International Organization* 45(4): 425–451.

Frieden, Jeffery A., and Ronald Rogowski. 1996. "The Impact of the International Economy on National Policies: An Analytical Overview." In Robert O. Keohane and Helen V. Milner, eds. *Internationalization and Domestic Politics*. Cambridge, England: Cambridge University Press.

Funabashi Yōichi. 1989. *Managing the Dollar: From the Plaza to the Louvre*, 2nd ed. Washington, D.C.: Institute for International Economics.

Garrett, Geoffrey, and Peter Lange. 1995. "Internationalization, Institutions, and Political Change." *International Organization* 49(4): 627–655.

Gilpin, Robert. 1987. *The Political Economy of International Relations*. Princeton, N.J.: Princeton University Press.

Goodman, John B. 1992. *Monetary Sovereignty: The Politics of Central Banking in Western Europe*. Ithaca, N.Y.: Cornell University Press.

Gowa, Joanne. 1988. "Public Goods and Political Institutions: Trade and Monetary Policy Processes in the United States." *International Organization* 42(1): 15–32.

Hatakeyama Noboru. 1996. *Tsūshōkōshō: Kokueki o meguru dorama* (Trade negotiation: The dramaturgy of national interest). Tokyo: Nihon Keizai Shimbunsha.

Henning, C. Randall. 1987. "Macroeconomic Diplomacy in the 1980s: Domestic Politics and International Conflict among the United States, Japan, and Europe." *Atlantic Paper* (no. 65). New York: Croom Helm.

———. 1994. *Currencies and Politics in the United States, Germany, and Japan*. Washington, D.C.: Institute for International Economics.

Hiwatari Nobuhiro. 1991. *Sengo Nihon no shijō to seiji* (Market and politics in postwar Japan). Tokyo: Tokyo Daigaku Shuppankai.

Iida Keisuke. 1990. "The Theory and Practice of International Economic Policy

Coordination." Ph.D. diss., Harvard University.

International Monetary Fund. 1998. *International Financial Statistics Yearbook, 1998*. Washington, D.C.: International Monetary Fund.

———. 1999. *International Financial Statistics Yearbook, 1999*. Washington, D.C.: International Monetary Fund.

Ishizaki Akihiko. 1990. *Nichibei keizai no gyakuten* (Reversal of U.S.-Japan economic relations). Tokyo: Tokyo Daigaku Shuppankai.

Kelly, Janet. 1982. "International Monetary Systems and National Security." In Klauss Knorr and Frank N. Trager, eds. *Economic Issues and National Security*. Lawrence, Kans.: Regents Press of Kansas.

Keohane, Robert O., and Helen V. Milner, eds. 1996. *Internationalization and Domestic Politics*. Cambridge, England: Cambridge University Press.

Kojō Yoshiko. 1995. *Keizaiteki sōgōizon to kokka* (Economic interdependence and the state). Tokyo: Bokutakusha.

———. 1996. "Domestic Sources of International Payments Adjustment: Japan's Policy Choices in the Postwar Period." Paper prepared for the 1996 Annual Meeting of the American Political Science Association, held in San Francisco on 29 August-1 September.

Komiya Ryūtarō. 1993. "Keijō kuroji berashi wa hitsuyōka ?" (Does the current account surplus need to be reduced?). *Tōyō Keizai* (10 July): 56-64.

Krasner, Stephan. 1978. "United States Commercial and Monetary Policy: Unraveling the Paradox of External Strength and Internal Weakness." In Peter Katzenstein, ed. *Between Power and Plenty*. Madison, Wisc.: University of Wisconsin Press.

Krugman, Paul. 1994. *The Age of Diminished Expectations: U.S. Economic Policy in the 1990s*, revised and updated edition. Cambridge, Mass.: The MIT Press.

Lincoln, Edward. 1988. *Japan: Facing Economic Maturity*. Washington, D.C.: The Brookings Institution.

Mochizuki, Mike. 1982. "Managing and Influencing the Japanese Legislative Process: The Role of Parties and the National Diet." Ph.D. diss., Harvard University.

Mundell, Robert A. 1962. "The Appropriate Use of Monetary and Fiscal Policy for Internal and External Stability." *IMF Staff Papers* 9(1): 70-78.

Nakagawa Yukitsugu. 1981. *Taikenteki kinyū seisaku-ron* (Financial policy from the viewpoint of personal experience). Tokyo: Nihon Keizai Shimbunsha.

Nihon Keizai Shimbunsha. 1993. *Chō-endaka* (Hyper-valued yen). Tokyo: Nihon Keizai Shimbunsha.

Obstfeld, Maurice. 1993. "The Adjustment Mechanism." In Michael D. Bordo and Barry Eichengreen, eds. *A Retrospective on the Bretton Woods System: Lessons for International Monetary Reform*. Chicago: University of Chicago Press.

Odell, John S. 1982. *U.S. International Monetary Policy: Markets, Power, and Ideas as Sources of Change*. Princeton, N.J.: Princeton University Press.

Ohtsu Takafumi. 1971. "Nikuson shokku go no chūshōkigyō kinkyū taisaku" (Emergent policy toward small and medium enterprises after the Nixon shock). *Finance*, no. 72: 13-19.

Paterson, Paul E., and Mark Rom. 1988. "Macroeconomic Policymaking: Who Is in Control?" In John E. Chubb and Paul E. Paterson, eds. *Can the Government Govern?* Washington, D.C.: The Brookings Institution.

Rosenbluth, Frances. 1993. "Japan's Response to the Strong Yen: Party Leadership and the Market for Political Favors." In Gerald L. Curtis, ed. *Japan's Foreign Policy After the Cold War*. New York: M.E. Sharpe, Inc.

Simmons, Beth. 1994. *Who Adjusts?: Domestic Sources of Foreign Economic Policy during the Interwar Years*. Princeton: Princeton University Press.

Small and Medium Enterprise Agency, Ministry of International Trade and Industry. 1994. *Chūshōkigyō hakusho* (White paper on small and medium-sized enterprises). Tokyo: Ministry of Finance Printing Bureau.

Volcker, Paul, and Gyohten Toyoo. 1992. *Changing Fortunes: The World's Money and the Threat to American Leadership*. New York: Times Books.

Warner, Rose. 1999. "IMF chief sees dangers in growing current account imbalances." USIA document <http://www.usia.gov/abtusia/posts/JA1/wwwh2200.htl#Services>.

Webb, Michael C. 1991. "International Economic Structures, Government Interests, and International Coordination of Macroeconomic Adjustment Policies." *International Organization* 45(3): 309-342.

———. 1995. *The Political Economy of Policy Coordination: International Adjustment Since 1945*. Ithaca, N.Y.: Cornell University Press.

Wildavsky, Aaron. 1984. *Politics of the Budgetary Process*, 4th ed. Boston: Little, Brown.

Wooley, John T. 1985. "Central Banks and Inflation." In Leon N. Lindberg and Charles S. Maier, eds. *The Politics of Inflation and Economic Stagnation: Theoretical Approaches and International Case Studies*. Washington, D.C.: The Brookings Institution.

Yanagisawa Hakuo. 1985. *Akaji zaisei no jūnen to yonin no sōritachi* (Ten years of budget deficit and four prime ministers). Tokyo: Nihon Seisansei Honbu.

6

The Media in U.S.-Japan Relations:
National Media in Transnational Relations

Tadokoro Masayuki

IT IS SELF-EVIDENT THAT THE NEWS MEDIA is an important element in today's domestic politics both in the United States and in Japan. Projecting images to the public and creating a favorable perception in the mind of the public through the media is a crucial part of the political game in any modern democracy. To run a successful election campaign, television and other media images are now such a critical factor that many even lament how little today's election campaigns differ from advertising for merchandise. And those in power pay a high price if they fail to maintain a good press image.

In international politics, however, the importance of the news media may be less clear. Some realists, for example, emphasize contrasts in the political processes between the international and domestic spheres. In the international sphere, they see power relations and strategic considerations as the central factors, not media images or public opinion; they therefore give limited, if any, importance to the media in shaping the relations between nations. Thus, the focus of traditional discussions on the news media's role in international relations has been primarily with respect to its role as a means of statecraft. In other words, the media was viewed as a means of international propaganda and as a subtle communication channel to other governments. A classic example was Otto von Bismarck's manipulation of the press in the nineteenth century. He deliberately doctored and leaked information on the ongoing Prussian-French negotiations to give the impression that the French position was unreasonable, thereby agitating public opinion in Germany and provoking the French into the Franco-Prussian War of 1870–1871 (Taylor 1995, 170). The media has also been viewed as a troublesome obstacle to the implementation of rational diplomacy. For Henry Kissinger, news reports on the Vietnam War, which were feeding bloody and hopeless images of the war to the American public, while not a negligible factor, were viewed basically as noise rather than as an essential factor in his quest of statecraft.

In contrast to the realist view, Wilsonian idealists have assumed a more important and constructive role of international public opinion. In a democracy, the media is supposed to be more than an object for policymakers to manipulate or an inevitable nuisance in conducting foreign policy. International public opinion, as represented by the media, is assumed to be largely enlightened and harmonious. It also is assumed that international public opinion significantly affects decisions made by foreign policymakers. Thus, the media, in the view of Wilsonian idealists, is an agent for enlightenment, pacifying international relations where there is no central government. By helping to form international public opinion, the media is expected to moderate the behavior of states. Many dissidents in authoritarian regimes rely on support from the international media in their fight against their domestic regimes. The fate of dissidents like Nelson Mandela and Kim Dae Jung would have been very different if there was no international media.

Whether or not the media's role is as benign as some liberals assume, it is difficult to marginalize the role of the news media in today's foreign policy, even of an authoritarian country with a highly traditional idea of statecraft. The Tiananmen Square Incident in China is an illustrative example of the impact of international news media in today's diplomacy. Chinese protesters wisely chose a time when the international media presence was strong because of President Mikhail Gorbachev's visit to Beijing and successfully put pressure on the authorities by fully mobilizing Western public opinion in their favor. The Statue of Liberty in Beijing, which was shown repeatedly by CNN, was highly effective in appealing to American sympathies and also in presenting the protesters as democrats who share basic values with the West (Hachten 1992, 79–80).

Those events also proved that the Chinese authorities could still choose to neglect the public opinions that were created and conveyed by the international media. But the suppression of the protesters, televised live all over the world, entailed a significant cost to China's international political position. For the following several years, China was diplomatically isolated and it took a great deal of effort for China to get its relations with the United States back on track. Thus, the traditional logic of "reason of states" had to give way to a significant extent to the logic of public opinion formed and conveyed by the news media. To assess the impact of the media, we should ask ourselves what would have occurred if the Tiananmen Square Incident had happened with no TV cameras rolling, as has been the case in Tibet, where more intensive suppression has been going on for much longer.

Given that both the United States and Japan are democracies with governments highly responsive to public opinion (as represented by the domestic media), it is natural to assume that the role of the news media in their bilateral relations is more significant than would be the case in authoritarian countries. In fact, both are democracies enjoying high levels of free speech and offering the largest media markets in the world. The two countries are major allies and economic partners, which results in information flows between not only the two governments but also the two publics. The governments of both countries always try to work with and react to the media. Thus, information flows across the Pacific are generally intensive in quantity and important in political processes.

At the same time, however, Japanese and American news reporting on one another involves important differences from reporting on domestic events, such as the long-standing disparity in the volume of coverage on each other, as well as completely different cultural and linguistic backgrounds. This chapter tries to analyze the role of media reports in the U.S.-Japan relationship. The first section will briefly discuss the general role of the news media in international politics. We then turn to the structural conditions in which the American and Japanese news media operate. Finally, we will examine how the connections between media reporting and politics have changed over the last several decades, and will touch upon the policy implications of this analysis.

The News Media in International Politics

In general, the news media's role is to mediate between sources and audiences. When considering bilateral relationships, four groups can be identified as sources and audiences, namely, the governments and the public in each of the two countries (fig. 1). We therefore can identify four types of interactions between these groups. First, the media serve to mediate information flows between the public and the government in a single country. This is a familiar function of the media in politics. Governments disseminate information and try to gain support from the public, while at the same time they have to react to a variety of voices channeled through the media. For example, when a government launches a policy, it has to sell it to the public while minimizing possible objections to it. The process, therefore, is a two-way flow between the public and the government.

In implementing foreign policy as well, the government tries to project images about international affairs and foreign countries to the public. But unlike domestic policy, that type of perception management is far less likely to be challenged by either foreign governments or public opinion abroad. One can therefore assume that perceptions about foreign countries can be more easily manipulated by the government at home. Being tough against an unreasonable foreign country usually can be an attractive option for a government wanting to gain quick popularity. But at the same time, perceptions created by a government to mobilize public support at home and to exercise pressure abroad can assume a life of their own.

Figure 1. Media in International Relations

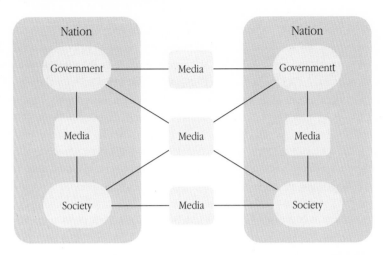

Once public opinion gets too tough, policymakers cannot strike a deal with their foreign counterparts without risking criticism at home. The vilification of foreign countries, therefore, reduces diplomatic maneuverability. For example, while American foreign policymakers needed public support as they fought the cold war with the Soviet Union, the anticommunist hysteria voiced by Senator Joseph McCarthy made the job of U.S. policymakers much more difficult. Similarly, the persistent Japanese territorial claim over the Kuril Islands controlled by Russia used to be a convenient symbol that enabled Tokyo to rally the Japanese public against the Soviet Union. But after the cold war, it turned into an awkward obstacle to improving relations with Russia.

Second, the media can be a supplementary communication channel between the two governments. Foreign relations are formally conducted through official communication channels, typically through diplomatic dispatch. But today's foreign relations are too intensive to rely solely upon these formal routes. Governments use the media extensively as a supplementary source of information to understand and analyze the behavior of their counterparts. In addition, officials sometimes find the media more convenient than the official channels. Comments made by high-ranking government officials to the press are often directed toward their counterparts abroad. This way of sending signals is a well-accepted practice in today's diplomacy, and, in fact, communication through the media has its own advantages. It is subtler, and is a noncommittal way of sending signals, which allows officials to see reactions from their counterparts by launching a "trial balloon." Publishing a journal article or a policy report can also work as a form of intergovernmental communication. It can bypass the cumbersome domestic policy procedures required before the message translates into an official cable. For example, the concept of the Marshall Plan was first presented at an address given at Harvard University because a negative reaction from the Congress was feared. By making sure of a positive European reaction first through ensuring media coverage of the proposed plan, the administration was able to go ahead and launch the program (Cohen 1986, 73–74). Similarly, low-ranking officials can go to the press as a way to attract the attention of a foreign government or the leader of their own organization. The very advantage of this method, however, can be a disadvantage as well; the subtle message can be misinterpreted or neglected. It may create confusion, misunderstanding, and distrust. Leaking information, therefore, is often a deliberate effort by an opponent within the government to disturb delicate negotiations with foreigners or quiet efforts by the government.[1]

Third, the media can be an intermediary between the public and the government of different countries. Sending a message to the public abroad in the hopes of creating a favorable international environment is a regular practice in foreign policy. If bilateral relations on an intergovernmental level are hostile, deliberate efforts by a government to foster antigovernment sentiment among the public abroad can be called propaganda or psychological warfare. In fact, during the cold war, the two camps were actively engaged in such propaganda campaigns, and the state media targeted at the other camp, such as Voice of America and Moscow Radio, were important means for these activities. This public diplomacy is not limited to cases between hostile countries. Even between two allies enjoying a peaceful relationship, improving one's public image abroad is a legitimate and common foreign policy goal. The United States Information Service, the British Council, and the Japan Foundation are major apparatuses through which the respective governments try to reach the public abroad.

For projecting information and views to the public abroad, however, it is more effective to utilize the foreign news media than governmental organizations. Local news media obviously can reach a far broader audience. Moreover, unlike information given directly by foreign governments, the public generally regards information given by an independent media as far more credible. Thus, government officials try to maintain contacts with the foreign press either through foreign correspondents or through embassies abroad.

Finally, the news media reports a great deal of nonpolitical information as well. In this case, both the audience and sources are private citizens rather than public authorities. In today's international journalism, the most intensive intersocietal information flows involve economic reporting. Business information such as share prices and stock indexes is intensively exchanged across borders. At the same time, social news such as crimes involving foreign nationals and other social phenomena sometimes create negative reactions from another society.

During the 1988 Olympic Games in Seoul, American television broadcast the scene of a Korean boxing coach punching a referee who penalized a Korean boxer. This drew severe criticism from Koreans, who felt that the U.S. media was unfairly focusing on the negative side of their country (Hachten 1992, 151–152). Intensive exchanges of information can sometimes develop into friction between different nations with different cultures.

The role of the media in any of the above-mentioned relationships is not limited to a passive interface mediating the sources and audiences. First, the media selects information according to its criteria of relevancy. No matter how important some information may be in terms of foreign policy, unless it has "news value," it will not be reported. On the other hand, a politically irrelevant incident, such as a nasty but isolated crime committed by one country's nationals in another country, may require a government to contain its bad public image abroad. Second, the media interprets the information. Although the Western media is based upon the principle of objective reporting, no media can ever be free of some degree of interpretation; whether a report will be presented in a negative or positive manner depends on choices made by the editor and/or journalist. In addition, the media carries opinions. Editorials clearly voice the position of the media, and while op-ed pieces, columns, and letters to the editor can be attributed to the individual authors, the selection of those pieces is completely up to the media.

In industrial democracies like Japan and the United States, the media is subject to commercial competition. This implies that it not only selects, reports, and interprets information and takes a position out of its institutional ideological principles, but it also entertains the audience. In other words, the media has an incentive to conform to rather than challenge existing stereotypes held by the audience in order to create a more sellable product. This can also mean that the media is subject to the danger of sensationalism. There is always a tendency toward simplification and exaggeration in reporting on the increasingly complicated world.

As Amrita Shah, a correspondent at *Imprint* magazine in Bombay who strings for the Time-Life News Service, has commented, stories from Asia that do not directly affect the United States "tend to be one of two kinds: stories that confirm stereotypes—for example, stories of widow burning or stampeding elephants that confirm the Western notion of India as a wild and exotic land are sure sellers, even if they are in actuality extremely rare occurrences. Or stories that indicate conformity to a familiar Western way of life. Stories about India's privatization programme or of a newly prosperous middle class investing in home appliances fall into this category" (Hess 1996, 77).

Thus, the media can play a variety of roles in international political processes by helping exchanges of messages among different players. Depending upon how something is reported or not reported, the media can be a means for propaganda or an agent for moderating intergovernmental relations. Even if the media does not take a clear position on a certain issue, the very act of reporting something and the way in which it is reported can have a strong impact on a political game by giving advantages and disadvantages to various actors in the political process. In a democracy, politics is very much a competition for controlling perception. It is therefore not difficult to infer that those with louder voices are better positioned. How, then, do these general assumptions apply to U.S.-Japan relations?

THE STRUCTURE OF
U.S.-JAPAN MEDIA INTERACTION
Media and the Authorities

It is often said that the Japanese news media is merely a corrupt government mouthpiece. It forms a cartel, monopolizing access to information and excluding outsiders such as foreign correspondents, while enjoying collusive relations with the government bureaucracy that controls information flows (Hall 1998, chap. 2; Wolferen 1990, 123–127). In fact, some practices of the Japanese political press surprise not only foreign observers but also many Japanese. Major Japanese media institutions assign political reporters to important politicians and those reporters, known as "*bankisha*," never conceal their close personal ties to influential political figures and other governmental sources. It is no secret that the *bankisha* are given special access to the private homes of the politicians, and they compete with each other for the privilege of gaining yet further access to the house's private zones—the politicians' living or sleeping quarters instead of just the rooms for receiving guests—to gain firsthand information.[2] This style of news gathering obviously casts doubt on the objectivity of Japanese political reporting.

Such close media-source relationships are even institutionalized in the form of the *kisha kurabu*, or press clubs. Reporters from the major Japanese media covering government institutions belong to press clubs and, by doing so, can enjoy exclusive privileges, including access to facilities like press rooms, telephone lines, press conferences, and press briefings. Many criticize this practice for several reasons. First, the club handicaps outsiders such as freelancers and foreign correspondents.[3] Second, it makes the press corps lazy by creating a cozy cartel that is assured of always being briefed by the sources. And finally, in exchange for that coziness, the media becomes susceptible to manipulation by its sources, which in the end makes the media merely a mouthpiece for the government.

For many who criticize the Japanese media, the American media has often been portrayed as a model to follow. It has been depicted as a democratic agent, checking the power of the government and contributing to an open and democratic political system. The uncovering of the Watergate scandals, which finally forced President Richard Nixon to resign, and the candid reporting on the Vietnam War despite the embarrassment to the American government were hailed as critical and heroic challenges to power. Interestingly, however, the credibility of the American media within the United States has significantly deteriorated over the last two decades or so, despite retaining its authority within Japan. According to a survey of public attitudes toward the press released in May 1995, "The news media has a generally positive view of itself in the watchdog role," but "the outside world strongly faults the news media for its negativism. . . . The public goes so far as to say that the press gets in the way of society solving its problems, an opinion that is even shared by many leaders" (as quoted in Fallows 1996, 46).

Among the reasons generally given in that survey for the media's declining credibility were its elitism, negativism, and cynicism. Many journalists today are graduates of elite universities, and as the media has become more influential, the average income of journalists has risen far above the national average. In particular, the anchors of the major TV networks or journalists appearing regularly on TV programs are now earning enormous sums of money. In addition, many high-profile "journalists" smoothly move through the revolving door between the political world and journalism. Pat Buchanan, for example, started his career as a journalist before entering politics by going to work for President Nixon. He subsequently shifted between his work as a syndicated columnist and TV talk show host, and his work for various administrations and as a presidential candidate. According to one American journalist, "To the public, journalists have crossed the line from being part of the public to being part of the political class. [We're seen as being] on the other side of the divide. . . . Increasingly journalists I think are seen as players in the process rather than as chroniclers of the process" (Chandler 1999, 27).

Thus, the relationship of the U.S. press with the authorities may not offer as much of a contrast with Japan as many tend to assume. It is believed that there is a tacit hierarchy among the roughly 15,000 journalists in Washington, D.C. At the top of this hierarchy is the "Inner Circle"—the *New York Times*, the *Washington Post*, the *Wall Street Journal*, the three major TV networks, the Associated Press (AP), and United Press International (UPI)—members of which are given special privileges in accessing information (Sasaki 1992, 32–43; Hess 1981). They are given more opportunities for press briefings and sometimes even exclusive interviews with important sources. Their phone calls to high-ranking officials are more likely to be answered, and they have more chances to receive leaks from government sources. Less important media are classified as the "Middle Circle," which includes such media institutions as the *Baltimore Sun*, the *Los Angeles Times*, and the *Chicago Tribune*. They have less access to sources, although depending upon the subject they may be chosen as the beneficiary of a leak. The rest, including the foreign press corps, belong to the "Outer Circle" and have very limited access to sources. While those with press passes for the White House may number 1,500—a very large number when compared to the small number of press club journalists in Japan who have access to the Prime Minister's Office—their ability to get information from key sources is in fact more limited.

With so many reporters competing with each other, it is inevitable and not surprising that sources are selective in deciding which members of the media will receive their information. While the relationship between the American news media and its sources is often contrasted with that in Japan in terms of its transparency, equality of access, and free competition, such comparisons are not so simple. The media-source relationship is always very complex and cannot be judged simply by a lack of institutionalized practices such as the *bankisha* or press clubs. Whether one is in Japan or in the United States, firsthand information cannot be obtained without getting sufficiently close to the source. But getting too close increases the chance of manipulation and even corruption. The source, by controlling access to hot information that is fiercely sought after by the media, can exercise power over the press. Thus, there is a universal dynamism at work that encourages the media to have some symbiotic relationship with the government, whether the relationship is institutionalized or not. In fact, something like Japan's press clubs can be found in Britain. A group of journalists covering Parliament who are known as "lobby correspondents" enjoy certain privileges and are bound by certain rules in covering members of Parliament that are fairly similar to those of the Japanese press clubs (Tunstall 1970; Seymour-Ure 1991, 171–179; Shimbun Hōdō Kenkyūkai 1995, 171–179).

While one can argue whether the media in the United States or Japan is less independent than the other, as long as perceptions matter in politics, political actors will always have an incentive to manipulate the media in their favor. And as long as the media has to compete for information, it is always vulnerable to being used by its sources. Thus, the media is inevitably involved in a delicate relationship with the government, full of dilemmas as it tries to stay close enough to the sources to win the competition for stories, but distant enough to be credible reporters.

What is important here is that the symbiotic relationship between the media and its sources is naturally formed more easily between the government and media within a country than between actors from different countries. Foreign correspondents posted in Tokyo or Washington, D.C., never belong to the Inner Circles in those capitals. Thus, both American and Japanese media are understandably more susceptible to the information given to them by their own governments than to that received from governments abroad. Although this structure does not make it necessarily pro-government, it is likely that the media is still very much bound by its nationality in its access to information.

Media and Audiences

A sharp contrast can be drawn between the media's ability to project information to a wide audience in Japan and the United States. In Japan, there is an influential national press, whereas in the United States, with the exceptions of the three national TV networks and CNN, even the most influential news media are local. Japan's major newspapers boast massive circulation rates. *Yomiuri Shimbun*'s circulation exceeds ten million, which is ten times larger than that of the *New York Times* or the *Los Angeles Times*. In fact, according to a 1999 survey by *Editor & Publisher* magazine, out of the top ten newspapers worldwide in terms of circulation, five were Japanese newspapers and none were American. The *New York Times* had a circulation of just over one million, which is smaller than even such local Japanese newspapers as the *Shizuoka Shimbun* or the *Hokkaido Shimbun*.[4] This means that Japanese newspapers serve a wide range of audiences ranging from intellectuals to the politically indifferent population. Thus, all of these national papers carry quite extensive international news and analysis, as well as practical and entertainment information. While major papers do take different political positions, they claim that their position is nonpartisan. Their basic attitude is focused less on trying to sway the public toward their position than on educating and enlightening the public. In other words, the major news media organizations in Japan, and particularly the major newspapers, are well-established social institutions that enjoy a fairly high level of respect as credible sources of information.

Their American counterparts, by contrast, are far smaller in terms of circulation. While major newspapers like the *New York Times* or the *Washington Post* may have a strong impact on the politically active elite and those who live in big cities like New York and Washington, D.C., the vast majority of American people read only the local press. These carry a very limited amount of international news compared to the "quality papers" widely read in Washington, D.C., unless a story directly relates to the local economy. Compared with the Japanese, fewer American households subscribe to newspapers and the number of subscribers is declining. Thus, even the local newspapers are having difficulties surviving and many cities that used to have both Republican and Democratic newspapers are now losing one of them.

Generally speaking, the American media outlets that are closely read and watched by the Japanese tend to represent and appeal to a relatively small segment of American public opinion in contrast to the catchall Japanese national press. The local press rarely reports about Japan, or more generally about international affairs, meaning that a great majority of Americans have a very limited chance to be exposed to news from Japan except for sporadic television images. But TV news coverage is shorter and less analytical than print media. In addition to the fact that television is more focused on entertainment than serious and analytical news, it naturally emphasizes image-oriented reports that are fit for the screen. Sensational images such as wars, famines, and natural disasters are more effectively presented to audiences through a visual medium than through print. Japan is handicapped in that sense because over the last fifty years or so, incidents of street violence or shocking bloodshed have been very rare. The Great Hanshin-Awaji Earthquake in the Kobe area and the Aum Shinrikyō cult's poison gas attack were widely covered, but everyday life in Japan is largely neglected by the TV camera. Japan, after all, may have become too modernized to be considered "exotic," and important issues concerning Japan like business and the economy do not lend themselves to powerful presentations through television images.

Some American media outlets have a fairly wide audience in Japan, as well. Many households now have access to CNN. The *Wall Street Journal* and the *International Herald Tribune* are read widely in Japanese financial circles and in the foreign policy community. But they are still members of the American media, serving an American audience. *Newsweek* has a Japanese edition aimed at the Japanese audience, but the editorial decisions are being made by Americans. For example, in 1989 *Newsweek* had to face a severe dilemma over how it should serve the Japanese audience when it ran a story on Sony Corporation's controversial purchase of Columbia Pictures Entertainment, Inc. They decided to use different titles on the front pages of the American and Japanese versions. The American version read "Japan Invades Hollywood," whereas the Japanese version was titled "Sony Advances on Hollywood" (*Sonī shingeki*) (*Newsweek* 9 October 1989, American edition; 12 October 1989, Japanese edition; the title on the international edition, which appeared on 9 October 1989, was "Japan Moves Into Hollywood"). The American version suggests that the purchase represents an attack by Japan as a country on the United States, whereas the Japanese version implies that it was merely a business transaction by a Japanese company. As this episode illustrates, it is difficult to run a binational press—to say nothing of a truly international press—given that Americans and Japanese are two peoples with different perspectives, cultures, historical backgrounds, and conceptual frameworks that affect how they interpret the world.

Organizational Characteristics of the Media

Japan's major news organizations are very popular employers for new college graduates, to the same degree as Sony or Honda. This means that media institutions are regarded as major corporations, offering decent and well-paying jobs to the graduates of elite universities. In fact, their recruitment and promotion patterns are typical of the "Japanese" style, which values seniority and hierarchical organizational lines. Most journalists identify more with the news organization they work for than with their profession of journalism. Once promoted, reporters become editors and, if they are lucky, move up to the editorial staff or to the management sector. It is rare that journalists remain reporters for their entire career. Japanese newspaper and magazine articles rarely carry bylines. This is symbolic of the fact that the editors' power in setting the tone of the articles is stronger than that of the reporters. There have been a number of publications, for example, that claim the tone of Japanese reporting on the United States is set in the Tokyo headquarters rather than by individual journalists posted in the United States (Fukushima 1992, 113; Andō 1991, 166–168).

The contrast between the U.S. and Japanese news media on these various points is obvious. Whereas Japanese journalists have been considered an elite trying to enlighten readers, in the United States until the mid-1960s, "journalism was essentially a high working-class activity. In big cities the typical reporters would make about as much as the typical cop. Many reporters had not gone to college" (Fallows 1996, 75). It was the Watergate scandal and the leak of the Pentagon Papers—two instances where reporters played a pivotal role in pushing the president into a corner—that promoted the status of journalism, making it an attractive profession for smart and ambitious graduates from elite universities. Most American media organizations are not as big as those in Japan, and journalists tend to identify themselves as journalists rather than as employees of a specific news organization. The career patterns of journalists are far more diverse than in Japan, and while some journalists remain reporters until they retire, others become freelancers or start completely new careers. Bylines are of the utmost importance for individual journalists since they are viewed as a mark of professional achievement. As a result, the pressure or control that media organizations can exercise upon an individual journalist's professional writing seems to be much weaker in the case of the American media.

This, however, does not mean that individual journalists are completely free to write whatever they believe to be important. Unless their piece is printed (preferably on the front page), their professional performance will not be appreciated. Thus, journalists compete with each other for a larger space on the front page. This involves editorial judgments over the news value of articles. Moreover, with the commercial competition in the American media market getting keener, journalists are under severe pressure to write something that will appeal to the audience in their news market. News value, therefore, involves a sense of what the audience would find enjoyable, appealing, and readable, as well as what is balanced and accurate.

In both countries, the media naturally is not free from the social and commercial contexts in which it operates. In Japan, the institutional and organizational structures within the industry are tightly defined. The content and tone of reporting are strongly constrained by editors and more generally by the policy of the organization. Japanese media organizations are highly "Japanese" institutions, with senior managers setting the general policy. The major American news media organizations generally give more freedom to individual journalists in the selection and content of what is to be written. But individual journalists are under stronger market pressure to write something appealing. The market, of course, is primarily American for the American media, while the Japanese media almost exclusively serves the Japanese audience. This means that both the American and Japanese media view the world through their respective national context and news values are set by national criteria.

International Reporting and the Media

Undoubtedly, the Japanese media pays much more attention to American news than their American counterparts pay to Japanese news. This is due at least partly to the relative importance of the countries to one another. As the United States is a dominant global power with interests and influence all over the world, it is inevitable that its attention is spread thin, covering many different countries and regions. It is also due to a general lack of interest in international affairs in the American media. As noted above, the American media has a stronger local characteristic than does the Japanese media, meaning that its attention is more focused on local affairs than on national or international affairs.

Even so, American media coverage of Japan has been disproportionately limited given Japan's importance as a security and economic partner. This can be explained by a lack of historical and cultural ties comparable to those with Europe. In addition, Japan may be a difficult place on which to report. First, in postwar Japan there have been few big spectacles like wars, street violence, or serious natural disasters. In Japan, things tend to happen gradually and in a subtle manner. Second, with the exception of those concerned with memories of World War II, most of the contentious stories about Japan have been related to business and the economy. These are somewhat technical and boring subjects when things are going well and become a hot news item only when there are trade disputes involved. Moreover, covering Japan involves special difficulties for foreign journalists. Language is still a big obstacle, although American correspondents with Japanese language capability have increased from the almost pathetic level of the 1960s (table 1). Highly institutionalized Japanese press practices like the press clubs have also been a source of irritation for American journalists covering Japan.

This, however, does not mean that the press club system is an impossible obstacle to overcome. According to interviews conducted by this author, most international correspondents from major media organizations have alternative

Table 1. American Foreign Correspondents' Language Proficiency, 1992

Country of Posting	High Proficiency (%)	Low Proficiency (%)	Number of Correspondents
France	93	3	144
Argentina	93	3	37
Mexico	91	5	58
Italy	70	13	60
Russia	58	21	114
China	52	29	42
Israel	37	53	62
Japan	28	49	109
Poland	26	65	31
Vietnam	24	69	45
Lebanon	15	70	33
Thailand	14	77	35
Egypt	5	80	39

Source: Hess (1996, 83).

means to access the information made available to press club members. One Japanese journalist complained that even after they opened the club to foreign journalists, they rarely showed up there, although with only two or three correspondents in Tokyo, they have neither the manpower nor interest in having a journalist hanging around the press club all the time (Tadokoro and Kimura 1998, 151–161). Moreover, journalists from major American media organizations enjoy special privileges in Japan that are totally unavailable to Japanese journalists in Washington. Ishizawa Yasuharu, who worked at the Tokyo bureau of the *Washington Post* from 1990 to 1994, comments as follows: "Japanese are afraid of the American media because they know that their coverage is influential enough to mobilize the American government. American correspondents consciously know about this awe towards them." Many Japanese officials and academics, knowing the international predominance of the American news media, welcome their approach. As Ishizawa notes, "I was surprised. If (the American journalists) wanted to, they could simply pass the time by sitting at their desks and waiting. Even still, they could write articles because key people— such as directors or counselors of the Ministry of Foreign Affairs and the Ministry of International Trade and Industry—would call of their own accord, and invite them to lunches. It is true that they usually interviewed people voluntarily in Japan." Some Japanese politicians, by having their comments printed in the *New York Times*, are able to gain prestige. At the very least, they make efforts to avoid negative coverage by the powerful American media. In sum, Ishizawa concludes, "The media is backed up by the power of the nation it belongs to. The American media is backed up by American power" (Zipangu 1998, 63).

By contrast, the Japanese media is expending far more energy to cover American news.[5] But Japanese journalists also have serious difficulties in operating in Washington. Although institutionalized obstacles are far fewer in the United States, getting access to independent sources in Washington is not an easy task. This is exacerbated by the fact that the Japanese media's international status is extremely weak, which means that Washington's important sources do not find Japanese journalists particularly useful for leaking information or sending messages. They find it easier to provide such leaks and hints to the American Inner Circle. It should also be added that, while the Japanese media expends more energy to cover international news in general, its coverage is disproportionately focused upon the United States (Andō 1991). Given the importance of the United States for Japan, this may not be surprising, but it is ironic that the same Japanese media that always criticizes the Japanese government for its "overly obedient" attitude toward the United States is equally preoccupied with American news.

In sum, even today, when exchanges of information across borders are tremendously intensive, the news media institutions in both Japan and the United States are highly national in nature. Because of their symbiotic relationship with sources, the audiences they serve, and their institutional characteristics, the criteria for their information selection and the way in which they interpret it are framed by their respective national perspectives. Although one can still argue that the international reporting by the media of one country is better than that of the other, there is no truly international media organization completely free from national prejudice and national perspectives.

There is also a paradox involved in this structure. While the American media pays limited attention to the world, and particularly to Japan, its international status is predominant. As a result, many third countries in Europe and Asia learn about Japan from American media reports, and thereby through an American conceptual lens. One South Korean scholar has argued that Japan has been misunderstood in South Korea because of the latter's dependence upon Western media for information about Japan. For example, the Western media in early 1998 criticized and ridiculed Japan for its unwillingness to contribute to overcoming the financial crisis in neighboring countries despite its enormous financial assistance and other initiatives. As a result, the South Korean media reported little about Japanese policy initiatives (which were in fact more sympathetic to the South Korean plight than those of the United States) or the massive financial assistance Japan provided during the crisis (Uhm 1998). As this example illustrates, what is not reported by the American news media has a very limited chance of being reported in third countries. What is worth reporting from Japan to the rest of the world is decided more by the American than the Japanese news media. In this sense, the increasingly inward-looking American media tends to play the role of a rating agency in terms of international news.

Because of the asymmetrical international impact of the media in the two countries, the very limited American media reports on Japan attract keen attention from the Japanese media, and "imported" American media reports, in turn, sometimes have a significant impact on Japanese politics. A classic example was Prime

Minister Tanaka Kakuei's bribery scandal. This scandal was first reported by a Japanese freelance journalist in an article in the monthly *Bungei Shunjū*. This story did not have any serious political impact, however, until it was picked up by the *Washington Post*, and the fact that the *Post* had reported on it was in turn reported by major Japanese newspapers. A short time later, in 1974, when Tanaka was invited to the Foreign Correspondents' Club in Tokyo, he was exposed to tough questions on the issue by foreign correspondents there. This triggered a flood of critical articles about the scandals that, in the end, forced him out of office. A similar case was Prime Minister Uno Sōsuke's sex scandal in 1989. When a Japanese weekly magazine reported on his relationship with a geisha, it was mostly ignored, but once that story was reported by the *Washington Post*, it developed into a major political issue that caused his humiliating resignation after only two months in office. These two examples illustrate how the American media can influence Japanese politics by reporting that is aimed at its own domestic audience.

MEDIA INTERACTION AND U.S.-JAPAN INTERGOVERNMENTAL RELATIONS

How have the basic characteristics of American and Japanese media described here affected political relations between the two countries? We will examine that issue by dividing the postwar era into three periods. The first period is a significant stretch of time during the cold war, which may be too long and too diverse to be treated as a single period, but nonetheless provides a useful reference for comparison with the two subsequent periods. The second period is the time when the Japanese economy looked to be outperforming that of the United States. And the third is the period during which America recovered its confidence in its economy, and Japan ceased to look like a major economic challenger.

Peaceful Coexistence of Different Perceptions (or Different Dreams in the Same Bed)

Japanese media attention toward the United States has been consistently intensive since the end of World War II. This may not be surprising in view of the fact that the United States was occupying Japan and that, even after Japan recovered its sovereignty, the country's relationship with the United States was critically important for Japan given the cold war context. What may be surprising, however, is that while the two governments were maintaining a largely smooth relationship, the Japanese media was highly critical of the United States on almost all issues, ranging from security to economic affairs. For example, the Japanese media was voicing very critical views of American intervention in Vietnam. While many Americans were also critical of the war, the views carried by the major media organizations in Japan, whose defense against communist countries was largely dependent upon the U.S. presence in the region, showed little sympathy toward the American dilemma.[6] This stance was probably due to the serious division of opinions within Japan. In a sense, Japan had a Berlin Wall of its own. Although in Germany the ideological division between the communist and noncommunist camps was more clearly demarcated by the line between East and West Germany, Japan similarly experienced a clear ideological schism at home. There was always a strong neutralist, pacifist, and anti-American element in the Japanese intellectual realm, and the Left clearly had a strong influence on the Japanese media.

While the Japanese government, ruled by the Liberal Democratic Party (LDP), stuck to a pro-American foreign policy that did identify Japan as a member of the "free world," the leading Japanese media organizations were generally sympathetic toward leftist and neutralist views during the long cold war period, and were always critical of Japan's cooperation with the American cold war strategy. They also tended to portray American demands on international trade and finance as unreasonable pressure. The Japanese media, rather than trying to explain to the public the American arguments behind its behavior, emphasized the unequal and awkward aspects of the alliance between the two states. The reversion of Okinawa and America's generous help in promoting the Japanese economic recovery in the 1950s and 1960s were not given fair weight, at least in the eyes of a great majority of Americans. Reading Japanese media accounts from this period, it is difficult to believe that the two countries were allies sharing common values and objectives.

For its part, American media coverage of Japan was consistently limited; the contrast between Japanese and American levels of attention to the other was almost staggering until the middle of the 1980s. Even in the early 1970s, the numbers were dramatic. At that time, a total of sixteen Japanese newspapers had bureaus in Washington and had forty correspondents posted there; in addition, fifteen newspapers sent a total of thirty-six correspondents to New York. Almost all of them could at least read English, and some of them (although not many) spoke English well enough to conduct interviews. In contrast, during the 1960s, apart from Oka Takashi, who worked as the Tokyo bureau chief for the *New York Times*, and Sam Jameson of the *Chicago Tribune* (later of the *Los Angeles Times*), there were no correspondents from any of the major American news agencies who could handle interviews in Japanese. And in the early 1970s as well, there were reportedly only three American correspondents who could read and speak Japanese at a professional level. The Associated Press had fourteen professional staff covering Japan, nine of whom were Japanese, but none of the American journalists spoke Japanese. United Press International also had a large

Tokyo bureau with sixteen journalists, but none of the three Americans there could function in the Japanese language either (Packard 1973, 228–231).

Blaming American foreign correspondents may be pointless because the demand for covering Japanese economic and social life was almost nonexistent. If what they had to cover was not Japanese society and daily life but its foreign policy, sources in the Japanese international circle could supply information in English. In fact, the limited media attention toward Japan during the cold war was directed toward Japan's role as a U.S. ally. Except for sporadic coverage of particular events like the Olympic games, royal marriage, or plane crashes, the American media tended to portray Japan as a developing American ally with a non-Western historical background. It was only in the late 1980s that economic issues came to be a central focus of American media attention toward Japan. After all, Japan was a remote country in the exotic Orient that had nothing to do with the day-to-day life of the great majority of Americans once it was defeated in World War II. Primitive stereotypes of geisha, Fujiyama, and hara-kiri were still strong among average Americans. Under such circumstances, the small number of foreign correspondents who were familiar with Japan's economic growth in the 1960s were having a frustrating time trying to convince their editors back home of Japan's potential importance.

Nonetheless, despite the fact that many American journalists came to Japan for only a few years, lived in a largely isolated foreign community in Tokyo, did not speak a word of the local language, and had very limited knowledge about the everyday life of the locals, they were still able to cover Japan because the limited attention of the American news media was focused upon "high politics." Of course, there were trade disputes from time to time and the media covered these aspects of the bilateral relationship as well. But during most of the cold war, the American national consensus gave priority to the global confrontation with the Soviet Union and, given America's economic supremacy, economic problems with Japan were not high on the national agenda. The American media naturally viewed Japan largely from a politico-strategic angle, and, accordingly, news sources were limited to the international circle in Japan, including a small number of key figures at the Ministry of Foreign Affairs and the American Embassy as well as some academics.

The unsympathetic popular perception of U.S. foreign policy and the critical views expressed by the largely left-wing Japanese press were generally swept under the carpet of the cold war. In fact, the U.S. and Japanese governments in many cases cooperated in downplaying the differences of public sentiment to make sure their bilateral relationship remained smooth and stable. In general, the two governments handled issues related to security and the alliance quietly, without mobilizing public opinion at home. This was partly because the positions of the authorities involved in security and foreign affairs were more cooperative with each other than were those in departments dealing with economic issues. But more importantly, the alliance between the two countries has never been a product of popular support. In Japan, pacifist-leftist antimilitary sentiment has been always an important element of popular opinion and, as a result, following the large-scale popular protests against the U.S.-Japan Security Treaty in 1960, the military aspects of the U.S.-Japan relationship have been constantly and successfully downplayed by successive Japanese governments.

For the American public, the security relationship with Japan has never been a hot topic affecting their everyday life, but they might have found the Japanese ungrateful for the generous protection the United States offered against the communist threat if they had known of the ambivalent attitude of the Japanese public toward the American military presence. Obviously, Article 9 of the Japanese Constitution (the "no-war" clause, written originally by the American occupation forces), the so-called sympathy budget (the host-nation support given by the Japanese government to the U.S. military in Japan), Japanese anti-nuclear sentiment, and other complicated regional conditions such as the strong anti-Japan sentiment in South Korea were far less striking than Japanese cars and videocasette recorders. While the Japanese government successfully played down its military contribution to the United States in the domestic context, the U.S. government in the 1980s had to play up Japan's contribution—particularly to the Congress—to cool down Congressional criticism of Japan's "free ride" on the U.S. defense commitment.

In short, while the perceptions held by the two publics are extremely different, the two governments actually took advantage of the American media indifference toward Japanese popular perceptions during this period. This enabled the two different views of foreign affairs to coexist without rocking the boat of the bilateral alliance against the communist bloc. Because the American media's focus was framed and constrained by the cold war agenda, there was no significant public interaction through the media of the two countries. If there had been keener and continuous attention on the part of the United States to reports by the Japanese media on the United States, there might have been a more negative reaction toward Japan among the U.S. public. This would have presented a serious challenge for the two governments in maintaining smooth bilateral relations.

The Rise of Japan as a Challenger to the U.S. from the Mid-1980s

The situation described above changed dramatically from the mid-1980s on. As the Japanese economy looked to be outperforming that of the United States in every respect, Japan started to be viewed by Americans as both an object of admiration and an economic threat. This led to a significant increase in the news value of Japan-related stories. In 1965, the number of articles classified under the heading "Japan" in the *New York Times* index was only 252 for the year. That number gradually increased over the next decades, climbing to 432 in 1975 and to 495 in 1985. From that point on however, it jumped dramatically, reaching 772 in 1990 and 938 in 1992 (Fujita 1994, 38). The 1980s also witnessed a significant increase in the number of American journalists who could speak Japanese.[7]

In fact, the sudden rise in the attention paid to Japan by the U.S. media was not only due to a newfound interest in Japan. At a time when the United States perceived itself to be experiencing an economic downturn, Japan seemed to represent a mirror in which the United States could view itself, often finding a not-so-flattering reflection. Japan looked as if it were free from many of the problems Americans were facing at the time. The Japanese school system seemed to be working better and at least seemed to be successful in creating higher literacy rates than in the United States. Japanese family values looked stronger and Tokyo seemed to be almost crime-free compared to America's large cities. More importantly, Japan's economic competitiveness looked almost unbeatable as Japanese cars, Japanese investments, and Japanese businessmen became increasingly visible in the United States.

Thus, the American media were not preoccupied with bashing Japan, as the Japanese media so often claimed during that time. Rather, the American media was projecting the country's frustrations with its own problems onto its reporting on and portrayal of Japan. This resulted in exaggerated images—either Japan was portrayed as wonderfully free from American problems or as an enigmatic threat to the American lifestyle. When one sees something better abroad, one can try to learn from it and copy it. In fact, some so-called Japanese business practices like the just-in-time system or quality control methods were seriously studied and successfully implemented by American manufacturers. But when one sees factors that one can never learn or copy, such as the alleged Japanese high savings rates, strong loyalty toward employers, or low crime rates, one is tempted to say that the other country is so fundamentally different that fair competition is impossible.

More importantly, whether it was bashing or admiring Japan, the American media clearly stressed the contrast between the two countries rather than the commonalties. Caricaturized images of workaholic Japanese businessmen, conformist practices, and hard-working children preparing for highly competitive university entrance exams were played up to emphasize the uniqueness and "otherness" of the Japanese. This is the background for the rising influence within American journalism of the so-called revisionist school on Japan.

In addition to Japan's perceived economic success, there was another important change: the end of the cold war had brought a fundamental shift in national priorities in the United States. Now that the global confrontation with the Soviet Union was over, the maintenance of Western alliances ceased to be an unquestionable top priority for Americans. Although the United States had clearly won the cold war, it found it difficult to completely savor the victory. Americans felt that the cold war preoccupation with a possible military confrontation had led to the country's poor economic performance, allowing Japan to surpass the United States. As a result, economic issues with Japan naturally increased in priority and salience. True, trade disputes over various products had been going on ever since the 1970s, and they had become almost a regular ritual between the two governments by the end of the 1980s. But now, the keener and broader American public focus on economic relations with Japan could no longer be checked or balanced by Japan's image as a cold war ally.

As public pressure on successive administrations to get tough with Japan became stronger, the U.S. government had less motivation to control specific domestic interest groups. While there was no serious attempt to terminate the U.S.-Japan security alliance, there was a clear shift in the national agenda away from security and toward the economy, which caused Americans to view Japan as an economic rival. This increased public attention to bilateral economic disputes made American foreign policy toward Japan far more sensitive to U.S. public opinion. U.S.-Japan economic issues could no longer be managed by a relatively small circle of interested parties but became a national issue, at times forcing American governments to react to, and sometimes manipulate, public opinion on U.S.-Japan trade issues in order to turn it to their political advantage.

During this period, Japan's media continued to pay keen attention to what was reported about Japan by its American major counterparts. Perhaps because of the expanded presence of the Japanese media in Washington, D.C., and its continued practice of emphasizing American pressure and "Japan bashing" in the United States, the sensitivity to negative reports on Japan seemed to be heightened. So-called revisionist literature, such as publications by James Fallows (1989) and Karel van Wolferen (1990), attracted more attention (and perhaps even sold more copies) in Japan than in the United States. This may not be surprising because their theses were largely made in Japan. The gist of the revisionist argument is basically the Japanese modernist argument that, despite Japan's modern surface, the country is basically a backward, pre-modern state in its essence. For example, Wolferen's thesis that Japan is a stateless country with nobody ruling responsibly fits very well with Maruyama Masao's (1964) lament about a lack of civil society in Japan in his analysis of Japanese politics as a system of irresponsibility. Similarly, a 1991 book titled *The Coming War with Japan*, written by two obscure authors, did not attract much serious attention by Americans, although James Fallows did write a review of it in the *New York Review of Books* (Friedman and LeBard

1991; Fallows 1991). The Japanese translation of the book, on the other hand, was quickly published and became a bestseller. The two authors were even invited to Japan to promote the book and enjoyed extensive media exposure there (Fukushima 1992, 103–106).

The Japanese mass media obviously overreacted as usual, but this time Americans were also overreacting to Japan rather than ignoring it. Under such conditions, the mutual reactions of the media in the United States and Japan often amplified negative messages between the two countries. A good example was the report of Prime Minister Miyazawa Kiichi's alleged remarks on American work ethics in February 1992. Miyazawa was reported by the AP to have said in a Diet session, "I have long felt that (Americans) lack a work ethic." This story made the front page of major newspapers all over the United States, including the *New York Times*, which reported that Miyazawa had said that Americans "'may lack a work ethic,' and that some of the country's ills came about because too many American college graduates headed to Wall Street in the 1980s rather than 'producing things of value'" (*New York Times* 4 February 1992). One headline in a U.S. paper said, "It's Time to Say, Knock it Off, Japan." And a "buy American" campaign kicked into high gear. Anti-Japanese feeling shot up in the opinion polls (Buress 1998, 41–42).[8] In fact, Miyazawa did not say anything to that effect and he had not even referred to "American workers." What he actually said was that ethics are lacking in the so-called money-game sector of both countries, and particularly in that context he was referring to the bubble economy in Japan. Interestingly, a few days later, the *New York Times* printed a full translation of Miyazawa's remarks at the bottom of the op-ed section (alongside an op-ed piece by Ezra Vogel arguing that Japan is a rival, but not an enemy). The text of those remarks is as follows:

> Looking at what things have come to over the past 10 years, we might say that the interpretation of producing things or creating value has become very loose; it's that no one doubts that value can be created in the money market. Creating things by the sweat of our brows, a kind of work ethic, is related to various things. There is probably even a connection with computers. People graduating from universities are going to Wall Street for high salaries. As a result, the number of engineers, who actually make things, is shrinking, something Representative [Kabun] Muto and I both see.
>
> While we were debating whether this situation was all right or not, the money market advanced and junk bonds appeared—junk bonds, just as their name implies, are very dangerous. We have these leveraged buyouts where those without their own money can buy up things, and then, unable to pay the interest on their debts, [the companies] fall into bankruptcy. It should be

obvious to anyone that such a situation could not continue long.

Yet, over the past 10 years, this very situation has continued. I have long felt that this might involve something like a lack of a work ethic. I think what you are worrying about is related to this situation. In one sense, there are many of these same elements present in what has been called Japan's bubble economy. After this bubble [burst], both [countries] now have a lot to clean up in the aftermath, and all of our people learned a lot from this. It is very important to build things of value with the sweat of our brows. This may sound like a sermon, but what I have said is what I feel. When President Bush talks about education, I believe he is trying to reiterate the above kind of message (*New York Times* 8 February 1992).

It is surprising how such completely nonprovocative comments could create such strong reactions from the United States. But even though the reported remarks were sheer misrepresentation and were later corrected, once it was reported by the U.S. media it ignited anti-Japanese reactions, which were then reported back to Japan by the Japanese media. Despite the lack of validity of the report, Miyazawa had to pay a significant political cost for the worsening of bilateral relations.

The classic distortion and sensationalizing of the Miyazawa remarks took place in this context when the American media was (like its Japanese counterpart) hypersensitive, and was busy looking for anti-American remarks by Japanese. Less than a month after President George Bush's unfortunate visit to Tokyo (where, to the embarrassment of the Americans, he threw up on Miyazawa's lap), Sakurauchi Yoshio, the speaker of the House of Representatives, stated that "about 30 percent of American workers are not even literate" (*Asahi Shimbun* 21 January 1992). Sakurauchi's remarks were indeed insulting, but no American newspaper would have cared about a Japanese politician's assessment of the American workforce before Japan looked like an economic challenger. In the context of that time, however, the impact of the remark was magnified, touching off some nasty exchanges between the countries. Several months later, while addressing employees at a factory in his home state of South Carolina, Senator Ernest Hollings fired back by saying, "You should draw a mushroom cloud and put underneath it, 'Made in America by lazy and illiterate Americans and tested in Japan'"—a comment that drew applause from the crowd (*New York Times* 4 March 1992).

Another victim of this transnational media process was an American sumo wrestler who used the professional name Konishiki. He was quoted by the U.S. media as saying that the reason he was not promoted to *yokozuna* (the top rank of wrestlers) was racism on the part of the Sumo Association. This story was carried in the major U.S. newspapers, including the *New York Times*, as a symbol of the closed Japanese society, which was again reported back to Japan through

198 | Tadokoro Masayuki

the Japanese media.[9] This put Konishiki in a difficult position with the Sumo Association. Although Konishiki claimed he never made the comment, and it seemed that it had been his assistant who had answered the telephone call from the American media, the leaders of the association took a serious view of the damage done to the international image of their organization. Interestingly, as of the fall of 1999, two out of the five current *yokozuna* are Americans—Akebono and Musashimaru—and they enjoy the same levels of popularity as their Japanese counterparts. But while some local press in the United States reported on this fact positively, the tone of both the *New York Times* and *Washington Post* accounts was somewhat satirical; when Akebono was promoted to *yokozuna*, they reported that the Japanese fears had become a reality, or that the sacred barrier was finally destroyed (Kondō 1994, 35).

The media-politics interaction at the international level is not limited to accidental damage done to the intergovernmental relationship by exaggerated reporting. In politics, trying to influence public opinion has always been an important part of the game. Heated exchanges between the people of two countries can be triggered as a result of deliberate efforts by a government to gain support from its domestic public. Government officials in both the United States and Japan claim that reporting by the news media of the other country distorts reality and that the media in the other country is being manipulated by their counterparts. The American news media, according to a Japanese diplomat who served in the Japanese embassy in Washington, repeatedly alleged that the Japanese market was closed and that Japanese trade practices were "unfair" without doing justice to the Japanese position on the point. The widely held assumption in the United States that Japan is closed, unfair, and cunning has been exploited by the U.S. government when it manipulates the media in order to impress the American public with its tough attitude toward Japan and to exaggerate the fruits of negotiations (Kondō 1997, 142–150). These tactics result in the perception that pressuring Japan always brings about the results Americans want. Even when the United States yields to Japan's position, it tends to further strengthen the perception in American minds that Japan is unfair or cunning—a perception that has been fostered through the cumulative effect of media manipulation. In fact, putting the desired spin on the news is part of the regular power game in Washington, and Japan, whose representation in the American media is obviously handicapped for a variety of reasons, can become an easy victim once it is targeted as the "villain" in the perception game.

Conversely, American trade negotiators make almost the identical observation about the Japanese media. Since the media and government officials have such a close relationship, when it comes to international negotiations, the media in Japan behaves like a cheering section for the government. This makes the

Americans feel as if they were, as Glen Fukushima has expressed it, "negotiating not only with Japanese trade officials but also with the Japanese media and public as well." The Japanese media, according to this view, usually portrays the United States as bullying Japan and rarely does justice to American claims. In many cases, when faced with a painful policy decision, the Japanese media and bureaucracy have encouraged the U.S. government to put outside pressure (*gaiatsu*) on Japan so that they could then place all the blame on the Americans. In a sense, the United States has been used as a scapegoat in order to preserve harmony among the Japanese. This may be a convenient way to make a decision in the short run, but in the long run it will distort mutual perceptions (Fukushima 1992, 180–181).

Given Japan's sensitivity to U.S. reporting, one might expect that the American government would have some advantage in terms of being able to influence Japan through the American media. In fact, such public diplomacy is not as easy as it may look. First, perception games in Washington, D.C., and in Tokyo are predominantly for domestic consumption. Being tough toward an unfair Japan might make the U.S. government popular with its domestic audience. Likewise, resisting unreasonable American demands can have the same effect for the Japanese government. However, if anti-Japan or anti-U.S. sentiment is allowed to get out of hand, it can actually constrain the government's negotiating position, since it can become difficult for either government to back down without losing face. Second, American efforts to mobilize public opinion at home to put pressure on Japan can be counterproductive by creating an anti-American reaction in Japan. This makes the attainment of U.S. objectives more difficult than would otherwise be the case by putting the Japanese government under stronger public pressure. Particularly tough and confrontational messages are more easily conveyed through the media than are moderate messages. However, in today's world, it is increasingly difficult to conveniently differentiate between messages for domestic and foreign audiences. Therefore, the mobilization of tough public opinion against foreigners can often make those foreigners equally or even more tough. Again, this may make the settlement of disputes more difficult.

American negotiators were caught in this trap when they tried to force the Japanese to commit to importing a certain number of American cars and auto parts. Mickey Kantor, the U.S. trade representative, with his aggressive media politics, kept pressing Japan with his tough attitude and tried to impress upon the American public that the Clinton administration was different from the previous administrations in its active and forceful efforts to defend American jobs. His media tactics may have been completely natural and legitimate according to what is common sense in Washington, D.C., but his aggressive approach and the American demand for a numerical commitment united the Japanese against the

U.S. demands. In particular, the cabinet of Hosokawa Morihiro, which had relied upon populist support in its defeat of the LDP regime, found it impossible to come to terms with such an agreement that obviously contradicted its proclaimed reform posture of liberalization and deregulation. The Clinton-Hosokawa summit in April 1994 ended with an explicit breakdown of the trade talks for the first time in postwar U.S.-Japan relations, which actually boosted Hosokawa's popularity at home.

Being tough with Japan on trade certainly was a popular policy in the United States, but the united objections of the Japanese to the American demands, as well as criticism at home over the approach, put Clinton's trade negotiating team in a difficult position. Because they had oversold their new aggressive, results-oriented trade policy to the public and had played up the tension by making that policy the focus of the summit meeting, they found it very awkward to back down without losing face.

After the Bubble in Japan

The heightened American media focus on Japan did not last long. While the American economy began to enjoy an extended boom from the early 1990s, the Japanese economy started to slow around the same time. The American economic revival and Japanese decline dramatically changed the public agenda in the United States. Japan ceased to be either a threat or a model. In fact, the notion of an economic threat from Japan practically evaporated. Ironically, by around 1997–1998, the same American media that had portrayed Japan as a cunning competitor was busy ridiculing and insulting the Japanese as incompetent in running their own economy. This was particularly true in the wake of the Asian financial crisis, when Japan was viewed as incapable of acting in its own interest by failing to revitalize its own economy. Stories about Japanese internal political confusion or its ailing economy became too dull and unexciting for the American news media to sell to its audience.

On the other hand, the end of the exaggerated images of Japan does not mean a simple return to the virtual neglect of the cold war era. True, with no visible and imminent challenge from abroad, be it a military threat from the Soviet Union or an economic one from Japan, foreign affairs has generally become less central to the public agenda of the American news media. Instead, sociological issues such as medical services, family values, crime, and homelessness have gained increased salience. Given that Japan is now viewed not as a marginal, exotic, oriental country, but as a super-modern society with very different historical traditions and sociological conditions from those of the United States, stories about Japanese society can now offer an interesting reference to and comparison with the new American public agenda. The limited American media attention toward Japan, therefore, has been devoted more to social and cultural aspects of the country.

One example of this can be seen in the coverage of security issues. Following the end of the cold war, there have been intensive and serious public discussions on national security in Japan, and the Japanese government has taken several significant steps such as sending mine sweepers to the Persian Gulf in 1991 despite strong objections from the progressives at home and sanctioning the participation of Japanese military personnel in the UN peacekeeping mission in Cambodia in 1992. The new Guidelines for U.S.-Japan Defense Cooperation, agreed upon by the two governments in 1997, has been a hot subject of public debate in Japan. In contrast to the extensive coverage of these issues by the Japanese press, however, the American media has paid scant attention to these discussions or to the new policies that were implemented. It certainly was not as hot and exciting a subject for media coverage as Japanese direct investment in the United States was less than a decade earlier.

Instead, "soft news" stories focusing on Japanese social issues like crime, homelessness, and the social status of women have gained salience in the American news media. For example, according to a study of *New York Times* articles on Japan, published in 1995 by a group of Japanese freelance journalists called Zipangu, many of the pieces covered Japanese social and cultural aspects and portrayed Japan, often in an insulting tone, as a strange country (Zipangu 1998). The articles were on Japanese comics for women full of rape stories, loveless Japanese marriages, superstitions, and the widespread practice of abortion in Japan. There was also a bizarre article that claimed Japanese women are forced to speak in high-pitched voices. The tone of these articles tends to play up minor but exotic and entertaining aspects of Japan for American audiences. They certainly do not demonstrate respect for the culture or customs of people with a different historical and sociological background. Even if they are not insulting, they emphasize the singularity and "otherness" of people in Japan. The recurring implicit assumption of these articles is that Japan may be super-modern on the surface but it is still full of closed, pre-modern, and undemocratic elements that are funny if not evil.

What are the possible implications of this trend for intergovernmental relationships? First, as the security alliance between the two countries began to receive shallower—although perhaps broader—support from the public, its function as the anchor of the relationship between the two countries became weaker. A relatively isolated issue now might develop into a major political issue. An illustrative example was the rape of a young girl in Okinawa by three American servicemen in 1995. Rape obviously is a serious crime and this case was all the more serious because the victim was only fourteen years old. Nevertheless, the crime was an isolated incident and the U.S. military authorities cooperated closely with the Japanese police in arresting and detaining the three servicemen. Under different circumstances, it could have been handled routinely as a regular crime without political implications. Indeed, it was not the first serious crime committed by American servicemen in Okinawa. Since Okinawa's reversion to Japan in 1972, more than 4,500 crimes, including twelve murders of Okinawans, were committed by American servicemen (Masuda and Kimura 1995). But these previous crimes did not develop into a major public issue.

The 1995 incident, however, ignited a whole range of issues concerning the American military in Okinawa and even called into question the very rationale for the American military presence in Japan, which in the end could have entailed the breakdown of the alliance itself. This evidently has much to do with the decreasing weight of the alliance as an anchor for the relationship between the two countries. Now that the cold war is over, both the American and Japanese public have difficulty in understanding the rationale for the alliance, and, accordingly, another rape incident or a crash of a U.S. military aircraft killing Japanese civilians could develop into a major challenge to maintaining the alliance.

The American media played an important role in the 1995 process as well. The rape incident was first reported on September 9 by a local Okinawan newspaper, *Ryūkyū Shimpō*, as a relatively small piece on page 29 in the society section. Although the coverage by the Okinawan press expanded as Governor Ōta Masahide took a strong stance against the rape, the major national presses were slow to react. Once this case was reported in the *Washington Post* on September 20, however, and then in a newspaper in South Korea (which also hosts American military bases), the major Japanese media outlets quickly reacted and started to pay close attention to the incident (Masuda and Kimura 1995, 108–109; *Asahi Shimbun* 22 September 1995).

Neither Tokyo nor Washington wasted any time in reacting to manage the strong reactions by Okinawans. They shared a strong concern about the possible damage to security ties and tried to alleviate the negative popular image that had been created in Japan. U.S. Ambassador to Japan Walter Mondale quickly expressed his deep regret over the crime (*Asahi Shimbun* 19 September 1995), and President Clinton also expressed his regret and his willingness to take measures to stop such a crime from recurring. In response to Clinton's remarks, Chief Cabinet Secretary Nonaka Hiromu raised the issue of reviewing the existing Status of Forces Agreement. Both governments worked hard to manage the anti-base movement in Okinawa without damaging the existing U.S.-Japan security relationship.

Meanwhile, the U.S. base authorities also made prompt and strong efforts to alleviate anti-American feelings in Okinawa. The press officer for the Marines held press conferences, repeatedly met independently with Japanese reporters, and successfully sent the message that the U.S. authorities were taking a strong stance against the crime and that the great majority of American military personnel were good neighbors to the local people.[10] The day of reflection that was set to educate all Marines in Okinawa was widely publicized. Even the base prison where the three soldiers were held was opened to the media to show that the three accused servicemen were not having a comfortable life there. When Admiral Richard Macke, commander-in-chief of the U.S. forces in the Pacific, made a comment in Washington to the effect that the three servicemen could have paid for a prostitute for what they spent to rent the car in which they committed the crime, the U.S. government did not waste any time in accepting his resignation (*Asahi Shimbun* 18 November 1995).

The second implication of the recent trend in reporting is perhaps less clear, but could be more important in the long run. As the alliance between the two countries is becoming based less on a common military threat than on a shared interest in regional order and stability, the importance of shared values and shared vision may increase as a bond in the bilateral relationship. Since the end of the cold war, the American military commitment, for example, has been increasingly influenced by media images and the public opinions behind the media. Both the involvement in and withdrawal from Somalia, the intervention in Bosnia, and the decision to launch air strikes in Kosovo were all significantly influenced by media coverage. But the media process of Japan and the United States, by focusing upon confrontation and differences of basic national values and lifestyles, might be gradually undermining the transnational ties between the two peoples. If Americans and Japanese feel that they have completely inconsistent values and worldviews, it is obviously difficult for policymakers in both countries to justify the alliance.

True, the political relations between the two nations may not be directly influenced by public images. In fact, the United States and Japan have been close allies for more than half a century despite their former status as enemies with worldviews, values, and lifestyles that were much more different in the past than today. But as the common and visible military threat disappears, what might have been regarded as minor differences in the past can now be played up by the media and become a hot issue between the two countries.

In fact, while both countries are industrial democracies sharing many basic values as well as problems, there are issues on which the two peoples sharply differ and even get emotional. A good example is the interpretation of the history of the Pacific War. The United States and Japan, while important allies for nearly a half-century, do not share any memory of fighting together against a common enemy to defend common values. Rather, their shared memory on a battlefield is not one as allies but as enemies. These awkward facts were covered up by the cold war, but now that the cold war is over, the negative side of Japan's past has gained salience in the American press.

On the American side, the Pacific War, unlike the Vietnam War, is seen as an unquestionably just war started by the unprovoked Japanese attack on Pearl Harbor. The image of "sneaky Japan"—a major element of the negative Japan image in the mind of Americans—is still connected with this collective view of American national history. The American media tend to portray Japanese attitudes toward their country's past as largely unrepentant. The comparison with Germany is repeatedly made and a sharp contrast is worked out where Germans squarely face history while the Japanese are hushing it up. Issues such as the "comfort women," the Nanking Massacre, and other war crimes committed by the Japanese military during the war are reported from time to time, which gives the American audience the impression that an unbridgeable gap exists between the two peoples.

In fact, the American view on Japanese attitudes toward history has significant support within Japan. Progressives and liberals, who were largely critical of the U.S.-Japan security alliance and who called for a more pacifist and neutralist policy, take an even more critical position than the American media does on this issue. At the same time, there are a few truly unrepentant right-wingers and conservatives who believe that the liberal views are too one-sidedly critical of Japan's past. Thus, there is a whole range of viewpoints in Japan about World War II and Japan's responsibility. The American media, however, generally fails to give a balanced image of discussions within Japan. Instead, stories are usually framed by the existing American national consensus on history that Japan was the villain in World War II.

More importantly, however, historical issues started to be more hotly debated in Japan recently, at a time when the great majority of Japanese belong to generations with no personal experience of the war. Likewise, the American media started to portray Japan from the perspective of its history more than fifty years ago, rather than focusing on the peaceful and democratic postwar Japan. While it would be an overstatement to say that this trend represents the fact that the United States and Japan have started identifying each other as former enemies rather than as present allies, there is obviously a shift in the conceptual framework away from the cold war alliance and toward a more complex one. Thorny past experiences between the two countries can no longer be easily covered over by an obvious common threat.

The American decision to drop atomic bombs on Japan, killing tens of thousands of civilians, is also a potential dynamite issue that could explode. Opinion polls show Japanese and American public opinion differ sharply on the morality of the act (see table 2) (Kondō 1997, 169). The moral judgment of the American nuclear attack is particularly troublesome because this is one of the few issues that unite both nationalist conservatives and pacifist progressives on an anti-American basis.

Table 2. Assessment of Nuclear Attack on Japan (% of respondents)

	Wrong	Not Wrong	Necessary to End the War	Not Necessary to End the War
United States	34	58	68	25
Japan	89	11	27	66

Source: CBS/NYT/TBS (August 1995), WST/Nikkei (March 1995), as quoted in Kondō (1997, 169).

The strong American sentiment that the use of the atomic bomb was justified was amply shown by the heated argument in 1994 over the planned exhibition by the Smithsonian Institution of the *Enola Gay*, the B-29 that dropped the first atomic bomb on Hiroshima. The exhibition was cancelled in the end because of strong protests from veterans associations, who viewed the exhibit as being overly sympathetic to the Japanese. The Senate supported the veterans' claim by passing a resolution which stated that the atomic bombing of Hiroshima "was momentous in helping to bring World War II to a merciful end, which resulted in saving the lives of Americans and Japanese" (Senate Resolution on the *Enola Gay* Exhibit, *Congressional Record* 22 September 1994, S11315-16). In December 1994, around the same time that the *Enola Gay* issue was being hotly debated, a plan was announced by the U.S. Postal Service to print a stamp showing a mushroom cloud with a caption saying, "the atomic bomb hastened the end of the war." The White House reacted very carefully to Tokyo's warning that this would offend the Japanese people. On the other hand, there were powerful groups like the war veterans that would be infuriated if the U.S. government accepted the view that the atomic bomb was wrong. The Clinton administration, while carefully avoiding a value judgement about the bombing, decided to change the design of the stamp in a quiet manner. Since the Americans reacted swiftly to possible Japanese public reaction, this issue was closed without causing any significant acrimonious exchanges between the two publics.

The course of events might have been very different, however, if the two governments had mishandled the issue. If either of the two governments had carelessly played up the issue, there could have been an open, emotional confrontation between the two publics across the Pacific. This was a real danger since the media in both countries tends to jump on such an open confrontation and, in the process of reporting, can fuel public tensions. One American political analyst commented that if leading conservatives like Pat Buchanan had taken up the issue, or if Rush Limbaugh had agitated Americans through his radio program, the mood might have changed overnight (Kondō 1997, 185). As noted above, many Americans believe that since the war was started by Japan, which committed many war crimes, nuclear attacks intended to accelerate the end of the war with fewer American causalities were justifiable. This view is rarely accepted in Japan, even by those who are highly critical of Japanese conduct during the war. The polarizing potential of the nuclear morality issue is perhaps a greater danger to U.S.-Japan relations than any other historical issue.

The acrimonious exchanges that could have ensued would probably have overshadowed the significant number of voices within the United States that were sympathetic to Japan's sentiment. Even among war veterans, there were those who felt that, while the dropping of the atomic bombs was justifiable, the design of the stamp was provocative and distasteful and that the message commemorating the 50th anniversary of the end of the war should be one of goodwill and peace rather than the devastation symbolized by the atomic bomb. But voices for reconciliation and moderation are less likely to be covered and amplified through the process of U.S.-Japan media coverage. On the contrary, sharp differences and open confrontation are far easier to be exacerbated unless efforts for moderation are made by the two governments and opinion leaders in both countries.

In retrospect, it is surprising how the news media both in the United States and in Japan overreacted to Japan's perceived economic rise. With the subsequent boom of the American economy and contrasting poor economic performance in Japan, economic issues have ceased to be a front-page, if not business-page, story for major American newspapers. After the end of the cold war, stories related to bilateral security issues or other political issues were not highly marketable in American journalism either. As noted above, the limited interest in Japan is now primarily devoted to social and cultural issues. The American reports on Japanese society and culture emphasize the otherness and singularities of Japanese life, rather than promoting a better understanding of a society with a vastly different history and tradition. This does not foster strong bonds between the two peoples based upon a commitment to shared values and sympathy for common problems. While the negative reports may not result in immediate tangible damage to the bilateral political relationship, the negative images built up in the minds of the two peoples may undermine close political relations between the two countries in an age when public images and shared visions, as well as geopolitics, matter more in international relations.

CONCLUSION: A CASE FOR STRONGER PUBLIC DIPLOMACY

In today's policy-making process, it is simply impossible to ignore public opinion. The media plays a critical role in shaping opinion by selecting, interpreting, and contextualizing the information the public receives. In international relations as well, politics is not conducted only by bullets and money. Particularly when it comes to relations between two allies like the United States and Japan, both with democratic political systems, foreign policy is also strongly influenced by public opinion and the media reports that reflect and shape those opinions. In this way, the media must be recognized as an important player in international relations, wielding its own power.

The American media is particularly powerful in its ability to project messages. Its reports are taken seriously not only within the United States but also around the world, including Japan. It therefore can set the international public agenda and can put governments both at home and abroad in a difficult position by projecting negative messages concerning them. But the American media, despite its international role, is still American in its perspective and conceptual framework. While this does not mean that it is necessarily pro-government, it is primarily serving an American audience, operating in an American market, and interpreting foreign affairs based upon American political, historical, and cultural assumptions and values. The international impact of the Japanese media, on the other hand, is evidently very limited. In addition, the Japanese media is extremely sensitive to American media coverage of Japan. These structural conditions have shaped the pattern of interaction among the news media and the governments in the United States and Japan.

Reflecting the changing American public agenda, the conceptual framework through which the American media views Japan has shifted over time from an ally fighting the cold war, to an economic challenger to the United States, and then to a society with a strange mixture of super- and pre-modern social practices. On the other hand, the Japanese media has constantly been devoting far keener attention to the United States, and it has always been highly sensitive to American perceptions of Japan. Reflecting the Japanese frustration with a constant dependence upon the United States for so many aspects of Japanese life, the Japanese media makes it a habit to criticize the Japanese government for being "too focused on U.S.-Japan relations" (*taibei ippentō*). But in fact, the Japanese media is even more obsessed with the United States, devoting enormous attention to that country and reacting to the public agenda set by the United States. It also tends to see U.S.-Japan relations largely from a bilateral context, forgetting that the United States, as a global power, has many other countries and many other issues to worry about besides Japan. By doing so, the Japanese media has unwittingly exaggerated American pressure on, and American attention to, Japan.

After the overreaction by the U.S. media to Japan's economic rise in the late 1980s and early 1990s, the heated verbal exchanges amplified by mutual negative reporting have subsided. But the combination of the American and Japanese media described above means any issue with strong media exposure in the United States could quickly lead to exaggerated reactions by the Japanese media, which then could attract the public attention of the two peoples. Now that Japanese domestic social practices attract more American media attention than other issues, the potential public agenda between the two countries can be enormously varied and difficult to predict. Crime, trade, and even interpretations of history, which in the past rarely became political issues, now have the potential to escalate into political crises that might even destabilize the bilateral relationship.

This may imply that the role of the leaders of both countries is becoming even more important in managing public sentiment in order to avoid an explosive public confrontation generated by the media. While a free media is an indispensable social institution in a democratic society, it is highly national in nature and tends to exaggerate the otherness between Japanese and Americans, focusing upon the negative side of events and the confrontational aspects of bilateral relations. Moreover, the media's attention is often too short-term, neglecting historical and cultural contexts as well as long-term implications of less conspicuous trends. Thus, for fostering long-lasting bonds between the Japanese and American people, the media is far from an ideal institution. There is no guarantee that constructive dialogue between the people of the two countries can take place within the context of freely competing traders of information.

The policy implication to be drawn from this analysis is that, in the aftermath of the cold war, more public diplomacy is needed to stabilize the bilateral relationship. For today's politics—and particularly in Washington, D.C.—media images are critically important and manipulating the media is obviously a part of the regular political game. When politicians and government officials try to influence public images through the news media, their efforts are still predominantly focused on the domestic audience—the voters to whom politicians are accountable—but the foreign media is quick to pick up on any comment that might cause a strong reaction among its readers. Politicians in the United States and Japan must therefore bear in mind that the foreign media today is constantly looking for provocative quotes from high-ranking officials. Those in responsible positions in the government can provoke unexpected reactions from abroad if they fail to consider the international implications of their messages.

In addition to avoiding unexpected negative reactions from abroad, positive messages should be continuously projected toward each other through the media to gain the support of the two publics for the close bilateral relationship. While tough American messages toward Japan often just unite and harden the Japanese reaction, there has been one good example of successful public diplomacy: the

Structural Impediment Initiative (SII) negotiations conducted in 1990. SII covered a wide range of issues, including Japan's land prices, savings and investment patterns, and "exclusive" business practices. The talks officially dealt with Japanese demands toward the United States as well, but the focus was obviously on Japan's domestic business practices and institutions, which are usually viewed as purely domestic matters. The American demands could have infuriated the Japanese as an infringement on Japan's sovereignty. Given Japan's frustration with an omnipresent and vocal America, the talks could have easily become a target of Japan's popular anger. However, American trade negotiators headed by Carla Hills wisely adopted a strategy that emphasized the interests of consumers in Japan rather than the regular finger-pointing at Japan's unfair trade practices. As a result, the Japanese media very warmly received these American messages. The American government was even viewed by some as Japan's only constructive opposition party, which reflected the underrepresented voices of those in Japan that are not tightly organized. The SII talks thus successfully transformed the Large Scale Retail Store Law in a way that was favorable for new participants in the market, including American chain stores such as Toys "R" Us.

Nevertheless, this episode is the exception rather than the rule. Both the American and Japanese governments have been preoccupied with the management of domestic public opinion rather than appealing to the public abroad. Despite an enormous amount of cooperative diplomatic, economic, and social exchanges going on between the two countries, if one were to only read newspapers and watch television, it would be hard to believe that the people of these two nations across the Pacific are close allies, united by shared values and a shared vision.

It is true that the news media alone does not create public opinion in either country and that successive opinion polls conducted in both the United States and Japan have shown that the people of the two countries seem to have more positive feelings toward each other than media coverage suggests. It is also true that the media of both countries report positive images as well. Nonetheless, given the structure of the media politics of the two countries as described above, there is a constant and real possibility that a relatively minor issue can be blown out of proportion and disrupt the bilateral relationship through the process of international media reporting. While a sophisticated argument on regional security or mutual economic benefits alone does not seem to be a sufficient link between the two peoples after the cold war, the sense of shared values will be increasingly important to ensure the relationship between the two countries can be managed smoothly. If the U.S.-Japan tie indeed remains "the most important bilateral relationship," the two governments and their leaders need to step up their efforts to appeal to the public not only in their own country but in the other country as well. International exchanges of perceptions and images are much too important to be left to the news media of the two countries.

NOTES

1. According to Yoel Cohen (1986, 72), leaks can take place when low-ranking officials try to attract the attention of ministers, when particular officials or ministers favor a policy that lacks the support of others, when individual ministers cannot openly disagree with a decision, or when officials, in order to gauge public reaction, want to create the impression that the government has made a decision when it in fact has not.

2. Watanabe Tsuneo, an old-time political reporter and later the president of *Yomiuri Shimbun*, proudly mentions his close relationship with Ōno Banboku (an important LDP politician in the 1960s) and his deep involvement in politics (1999, 102–108). Tase Yasuhiro, a younger-generation political journalist for the *Nikkei Shimbun*, also describes his experiences with politicians, but he sees such relations in a more critical manner (1994, 32–43).

3. In 1963, Sam Jameson, then a Tokyo correspondent for the *Chicago Tribune*, was refused admittance to a press conference at the local police office by the press club following the stabbing of Ambassador Edwin Reischauer by a Japanese boy. The local police office, however, granted him a separate briefing (Jameson 1997, 179–180).

4. See the website <www.mediainfo.com/ephome/research/researchhtm/world100.htm>.

5. According to a 1982 survey of international news reports in Japanese newspapers conducted by the Japanese Newspapers Association and the East-West Center, 44.1 percent are related to the United States. The comparable figures were 32 percent for South Korean newspapers, 28.9 percent for those in Singapore, and 34.3 percent for British papers (Fujita 1994, 35).

6. In 1965, Ambassador Reischauer, for example, complained openly that the Japanese media was biased its reporting on the Vietnam War, and that it was obviously treating Hanoi with undue favor in contrast to Saigon (see Masuda and Kimura 1995, 168–169).

7. This is based on a comment made by journalist Sam Jameson at a symposium held at the International House of Japan on March 31, 1991 (International House 1991, 39).

8. For the original Japanese remarks by Miyazawa and the misrepresentation of Japanese remarks by the American media, see the *AERA* article, "Hannichi aoru bei no waikyoku hōdō" (1992).

9. For a more detailed account of this case, see Ishizawa (1994, 199–205) and Kondō (1994, 33–38).

10. For example, an extensive interview was printed in *Asahi Shimbun* on 5 October 1995.

BIBLIOGRAPHY

Andō Hiroshi. 1991. *Nichibei jōhō masatsu* (U.S.-Japan information friction). Tokyo: Iwanami Shoten.

Buress, Charles. 1998. "American Media Coverage of Japan." In Zipangu, ed. *Warawareru*

Nihonjin (Japan Made in USA). New York: Zipangu.

Chandler, Clay. 1999. *Politics and the Media in the U.S. and Japan.* New York: Japan Society, Inc.

Cohen, Yoel. 1986. *Media Diplomacy: The Foreign Office in the Mass Communication Age.* London: Frank Cass.

Fallows, James. 1989. "Containing Japan." *Atlantic Monthly* 263(5): 40–54.

———. 1991. "Is Japan the Enemy?" *New York Review of Books* 38(10): 31–37.

———. 1996. *Breaking the News: How the Media Undermine American Democracy.* New York: Pantheon Books.

Friedman, George, and Meredith LeBard. 1991. *The Coming War with Japan.* New York: St. Martin's Press.

Fujita Hiroshi. 1994. "Nichibeikan hōdō" (U.S.-Japan media coverage). *Kokusai Mondai,* no. 413 (August): 34–46.

Fukushima, Glen S. 1992. *Nichibei keizai masatsu no seijigaku* (Politics of U.S.-Japan economic friction). Tokyo: Asahi Shimbunsha.

Hachten, William A. 1992. *The World News Prism: Changing Media of International Communication.* Third edition. Ames, Iowa: Iowa State University Press.

Hall, Ivan P. 1998. *Cartels of the Mind: Japan's Intellectual Closed Shop.* New York: W.W. Norton & Company.

"Hannichi aoru bei no waikyoku hōdō" (Distorted American reports raise anti-Japan sentiments). 1992. *AERA* 5(9): 15–17.

Hess, Stephen. 1981. *Washington Reporters.* Washington, D.C.: Brookings Institution.

———. 1996. *International News and Foreign Correspondents.* Washington, D.C.: Brookings Institution.

International House of Japan. 1991. *Nichibei komyunikeishon kaizen o mezashite* (For the improvement of U.S.-Japan communication). Tokyo: International House of Japan.

Ishizawa Yasuharu. 1994. *Nichibeikankei to masu media* (U.S.-Japan relations and mass media). Tokyo: Maruzen.

Jameson, Sam. 1997. "Kekkyoku wa taisei no kurokoyaku?" (After all they are controlled by the power?). ΑΣΤΕΙΟΝ, no. 46 (Autumn): 124–186.

Kondō Seiichi. 1994. *Beikoku hōdō ni miru Nihon* (Images of Japan in the American media). Tokyo: Simul Press.

———. 1997. *Yugamerareru Nihon imēji* (Distorted Japan image). Tokyo: Simul Press.

Maruyama Masao. 1964. "Chō-kokka-shugi no ronri to shinri" (The logic and psychology of ultranationalism in Japan). In Maruyama Masao, ed. *Gendai seiji no shisō to kōdō* (Thoughts and behavior of modern Japanese politics). Tokyo: Mirai-sha.

Masuda Hiroshi and Kimura Masato, eds. 1995. *Nihongaikōshi handobukku* (Handbook for the diplomatic history of Japan). Tokyo: Yūshindō.

Packard, George R. 1973. "Nihon rikai e no hansei" (Reflections for better understanding Japan). In Nagai Yōnosuke and Henry Rosovsky, eds. *Nichibei komyunikeishon gyappu* (Communication gap between the U.S. and Japan). Tokyo: Simul Press.

Sasaki Shin. 1992. *Howaito hausu to media* (The White House and the media). Tokyo: Chūō Kōronsha.

Seymour-Ure, Colin. 1991. *The British Press and Broadcasting since 1945.* Oxford, U.K.: Basil Blackwell.

Shimbun Hōdō Kenkyūkai. 1995. *Ima shimbun o kangaeru* (Thinking about newspapers now). Tokyo: Nihon Shimbun Kyōkai.

Tadokoro Masayuki and Kimura Masato. 1998. *Gaikokujin tokuhain* (Foreign correspondents in Tokyo). Tokyo: Nihon Hōsō Kyōkai.

Tase Yasuhiro. 1994. *Seiji jānarizumu no tsumi to batsu* (Sins and punishment in political journalism). Tokyo: Shinchōsha.

Taylor, Philip M. 1995. *Munitions of the Mind: A History of Propaganda from the Ancient World to the Present Era.* Manchester, U.K.: Manchester University Press.

Tunstall, Jeremy. 1970. *The Westminster Lobby Correspondents: A Sociological Study of National Political Journalism.* London: Routledge & Kegan Paul.

Uhm Young-suk. 1998. "Ajia keizaikiki kokufuku no tame ni nikkan wa nani o nasubeki ka" (What should Japan and South Korea do to overcome the Asian economic crisis?). *Sekai,* no. 263 (October): 103.

Watanabe Tsuneo. 1999. *Ten'un tenshoku* (Destiny and vocation). Osaka: Kōbunsha.

Wolferen, Karel van. 1990. *The Enigma of Japanese Power: People and Politics in a Stateless Nation* (paperback ed.). London: Papermac.

Zipangu, ed. 1998. *Warawareru Nihonjin* (Japan Made in USA). New York: Zipangu.

7

The Impact of Policy Ideas:
Revisionism and the Clinton Administration's Trade Policy toward Japan

Robert M. Uriu

IN SOME SIGNIFICANT WAYS, the conduct and outcome of the U.S.-Japan Framework negotiations represent a break from the past. During these negotiations, which began in 1993 and ended with the agreement on autos and auto parts in June 1995, the U.S. government deviated from its traditional focus on removing barriers to imports into the Japanese market and for the first time made the achievement of concrete *results* the centerpiece of its trade agenda with Japan. And for the first time the Japanese government said no and meant it. After three years of highly contentious interactions, including the failed summit of February 1994, one could even hear expressions of concern for the very viability of the bilateral relationship.

In this chapter, I assess the extent to which we need to incorporate new policy ideas in order to explain the U.S. decision to shift to an emphasis on results, a trade-policy approach that it applied only to a single country, Japan. I argue that rationalist accounts, based solely on material incentives and structures, are of limited usefulness in explaining this policy shift. Instead, I contend, we cannot understand what happened without recognizing the impact of new policy ideas: the fundamental reconceptualization of the Japanese economy that had become institutionalized in the U.S. government by early 1993. This rethinking of Japan drew on the body of thought known as revisionism, which held that the Japanese economic system was fundamentally different from other capitalist systems, that

I thank the other authors in this volume for their useful comments and criticisms, and especially Gerry Curtis for his trenchant and detailed suggestions. This chapter is part of a larger book project on the role of revisionist ideas in U.S.-Japan trade relations; in that book I will flesh out the arguments made here and will also analyze the way in which the Japanese government developed its policy response. In this chapter, I focus almost entirely on the U.S. policy process.

its inherently closed nature gave a significant advantage to its firms, and that these characteristics allowed Japanese firms to engage in "predatory" or "adversarial" trade practices.

Revisionist ideas influenced U.S. trade policy on two distinct levels. First, the adoption of these assumptions magnified the level of threat that the Japanese economy posed for the United States. Revisionism defined the "Japan Problem" not in terms of economics or trade but as a threat to fundamental American national interests. The revisionist logic also called for a very different trade-policy approach. Revisionists argued that efforts to remove barriers to trade or to liberalize the market *process* in the Japanese economy were doomed to fail. The revisionist strategy followed logically from these premises: The best or perhaps only way to increase market access was to focus on *outcomes*.

In the first section, I sketch two rationalist accounts of this policy shift and assess the strengths and weaknesses of each. In the second section, I discuss the need to include nonmaterial variables—new policy ideas—to explain changes in interests and policy choices. In the third section, I sketch the rise of revisionist thinking and its impact on the way key actors in the U.S. government viewed Japan. I then trace the decision-making process during the first months of the Clinton administration; it is then, I contend, that new policy ideas had a visible impact on policy choices. In the final section, I outline how the U.S. policy approach fared in bilateral negotiations with Japan—in a word, badly, since Japan was able to quash every suggestion of concrete results. By 1996, U.S. policymakers had again begun to rethink U.S. interests in the bilateral relationship, and succeeded in striking a better balance between economic and security concerns. In the conclusion, I assess the current status of revisionist assumptions and draw implications for future U.S. trade policy.

THE THEORETICAL CONTEXT: RATIONALIST APPROACHES

Rationalist explanations of international politics, whether focused on the structure of the international system or on the demands of domestic interest groups, provide powerful but incomplete explanations of U.S. trade policy during the Framework period. Although rationalist accounts differ according to which unit of analysis is chosen—the state for international relations (IR) theorists, institutions and interest groups for theorists of domestic politics, individuals for rational-choice scholars—they are similar in the sense that the analyst assumes a given set of interests for that actor and assumes that it will act to pursue those interests. In interacting with the surrounding environment, actors may be instrumentally rational, simply pursuing their interests, or strategically rational in terms of acting to change the behavior of others or the environment itself. And as the environment changes, so too does the behavior of the given actor; significantly, however, the goals and the character of the actor are assumed to remain essentially the same.

Proponents of neorealism and its variants, still the core systemic IR approach, would explain U.S. policy during the Framework period in terms of the major changes in the structure of international politics in the late 1980s. The end of the cold war in 1989, the most significant change in the structure of the international system since World War II, meant that the requirements of bipolarity and the waging of the cold war no longer dominated U.S. interests. With the military value of the U.S.-Japan security relationship diminished, the United States was no longer willing to play down its long-standing economic complaints about Japan for fear that economic frictions would damage the overall relationship. Furthermore, the end of the cold war led the United States to broaden its definition of security to encompass the importance of economic power in creating and maintaining political power; this shift also led to a greater emphasis on the economic side of the relationship (Mastanduno 1991, 1998). Finally, the United States was faced with the rising power of Japan at the precise moment that its own power seemed to be inexorably declining, leading neorealists to predict that bilateral tensions and conflicts would inevitably rise (Mastanduno 1991; Huntington 1993; Waltz 1993). Now Japan, as the second largest economy in the world and one with tremendous growth prospects, represented a mounting structural threat. The United States, enjoying its "unipolar moment," still had to worry about future shifts in power in the international system, making some degree of conflict with Japan almost inevitable (Huntington 1993; Layne 1993).

The neorealist argument makes a compelling case, at least in general terms: In the post–cold war era, some increase in tension in the U.S.-Japan relationship probably was inevitable, and in particular a growing U.S. focus on previously restrained economic problems can be understood. The Clinton administration's characterization of the relationship in 1993 as a "three-legged stool" in which the only weak leg was the economic relationship is consistent with these predictions.

I argue, however, that neorealism misses some of the most important aspects of U.S. behavior in this period. First, in its history the United States has been faced with other large or rising economic powers, has run substantial trade imbalances with many different countries, and has been economically dependent on others, but it has not always fallen into economic conflict and confrontation. It seems to me that the threat posed by the Japanese economy stemmed not merely from its size and growth rate but also from America's understanding of the *nature* of the Japanese economy—the reconceptualization of Japan as predatory and adversarial. As I argue below, the alarmism of revisionism thus magnified and redefined America's understanding of the "Japanese threat" to a degree not captured by structural realism.

Second, a structural argument does not explain the *specific content* of the choices that were made. In other words, the United States could have pursued many other policies, each of which would have furthered its national interests, ranging from using its stronger power position to coerce Japan into opening its markets to improving its own relative power resources through internal industrialization efforts. Neorealists may contend that their theories are designed to explain broad outcomes rather than the specifics of policy choices. Even granting that point, in this case the bilateral relationship (described by some as America's most important in the world) would have taken a very different turn if any of these other choices had been made. Thus, the specific content of policy choices did in reality make a huge difference. We should expect our theories to provide a fuller understanding of those choices.

Third, while changes in the international system may have predisposed the United States to greater economic conflict with Japan, they did not make that conflict inevitable. In this sense, neorealism provides us with at most a "permissive cause," albeit perhaps a necessary one: Structural changes relaxed important constraints on policy but did not in any direct way determine the policy changes that occurred. In tracing the actual policy-making process, it becomes clear that different policymakers attached different meanings to the same external realities. While some looked at Japan and thought only in terms of economic threat, others maintained a more "traditional" view of Japan, that the security tie remained the cornerstone of the relationship even after the cold war and that economic tensions therefore still needed to be managed. In other words, the exigencies of the international system, so clear and unambiguous to IR scholars, were by no means so clear and unambiguous to the policymakers who had difficult choices to make.

The policy process thus boiled down to a battle of assumptions, each based on different conceptions of the Japanese economy and its meaning for U.S. interests. While traditional views were overruled when the Clinton administration outlined its initial policy approach, this outcome was by no means inevitable. Traditional views remained strong throughout this period and in fact reasserted themselves after the Framework Talks ended. Shifts in the balance between these different assumptions at various points would have made a great deal of difference in the way the relationship evolved; at times even different personalities in certain positions would have made a difference. In other words, not much here was preordained; rather, outcomes were contingent on the shifting nature of the policy process and the strength of different policy assumptions.

A second variant of rationalism, theories that stress domestic-level determinants of foreign policy, can also explain some aspects of the shift in U.S. trade policy (Moravcsik 1997). In the case of the 1993 policy shift, domestic analysts would point to the growing discontent and anger directed at Japan that was simmering in the United States throughout the 1980s and reached boiling point in the early 1990s. With the trade numbers so out of whack and getting worse (from the American point of view), the U.S. government was under great pressure to act. At the same time, some major U.S. industries, including autos and semi-conductors, were pressing for more aggressive action to deal with competition from Japan. The Bush administration was under intense pressure to fix the "Japan Problem." This pressure was especially strong from the Democrat-con-trolled Congress, including the Super 301 provision of the 1988 Trade Act. The interest-group approach also argues that it was the election of a Democratic pres-ident in late 1992 that paved the way for a new policy approach. Indeed, at the time of Bill Clinton's election, analysts were close to unanimous in predicting a significant ratcheting up of trade pressure on Japan.

A domestic-interest explanation can account for some of the rise in U.S. trade pressure on Japan seen in the 1980s and 1990s. American politicians certainly rec-ognized the political gains to be made from capitalizing on public anger and resentment against Japan. American trade pressure on Japan has a long postwar his-tory but took a quantum leap in the last half of the 1980s, described by some as a policy of "aggressive unilateralism" (Bhagwati and Patrick, 1990; see also Janow 1994; Schoppa 1999; Destler 1995). And in its final years, the Bush administration was beginning to take a more aggressive stand on Japan trade policy. This was perhaps best symbolized by George Bush's January 1992 summit trip to Japan, in which he took along top American auto executives in a quest for "jobs, jobs, jobs."

Again, however, the interest-group approach misses key aspects of the larger picture. None of the firms or industries involved pushed for a broader redefinition of national interests or a reconceptualization of the nature of the Japanese econ-omy; rather, each group followed a narrower, more self-interested approach. In addition, the exact form and content of American demands on Japan were not entirely predictable from the nature of interest-group pressure. That is, there were a wide variety of policy options that were being pushed by different U.S. groups, all of which would have entailed a tougher line toward Japan, which would have placated public or sectoral pressures. The United States, for instance, could have pushed for a more aggressive removal of external trade barriers or fur-ther reductions in structural impediments, perhaps with an increase in sanc-tions for noncompliance, such as Super 301. And many analysts assumed that the new Clinton administration would appeal to the Democrats' traditional base, labor, by calling for straightforward trade protection. Thus, as important as domestic political interests were, it seems to me that they too are not sufficient to explain the Clinton shift to a focus on numbers. While a more aggressive U.S. pol-icy toward Japan was perhaps made inevitable by changes in domestic politics, the specific choice of a target-oriented approach was not.

Each of these orthodox explanations has considerable explanatory power—and just enough supporting evidence exists that proponents of any of these bodies of theory may not feel compelled to question their approach. But in my opinion, all fail to explain the content and timing of the shift to a numbers-oriented approach. Although they may be important permissive causes, removing previously existing constraints and opening up a "space" for new policy initiatives, I do not believe that they provide a full enough explanation for a shift to numbers. It is also necessary to incorporate an independent role for new ideas and policy beliefs.

THE THEORETICAL CONTEXT:
IDEAS AND THE DEFINITION OF INTERESTS

A growing group of IR scholars has in recent years questioned some of the essential assumptions of the rationalist approach.[1] One of the central battle-grounds has become the question of how actors come to define their interests and preferences, and how these definitions change over time. For rationalists, interests are not problematic: they can be inferred from the nature of actors or from their objective situation. Thus, for the neorealist, state interests are assumed to stem from the anarchical nature of international relations, while those who apply game-theoretic models infer interests and strategies from the nature of the situation or "game" being played. Interests can change over time, of course, but are assumed to change only as objective factors change: the shift in power relations due to the end of the cold war, a new era of budget tightness, the introduction of a new technology by a rival firm, and so forth. Again, the new set of interests corresponding to these new circumstances is inferred and asserted rather than "problematized" and made the focus of the analysis.

But are interests so straightforward? Alexander Wendt provides perhaps the clearest example of the limits of rationalist reasoning when he asks why five hundred nuclear weapons in the hands of the United Kingdom are not considered to be threatening to most, whereas the prospect of North Korea obtaining even one is considered a significant threat to regional and international stability. From a neorealist point of view, this situation makes little sense. If objective conditions, such as the balance of power capabilities, are all that matter, then it should be the United Kingdom that represents the more dangerous threat (or for that matter, the current preponderance of U.S. power). Something besides material factors is at work here (Wendt 1992).[2]

Over the past decade, IR scholars have tried to take seriously the independent impact that nonmaterial factors, such as new policy ideas, may have. These schol-ars question the assumption that interests can be taken as given or that they are completely reducible to material factors. Rather, the ideas approach argues that interests are also influenced by nonmaterial factors that help to shape how an actor *understands* his or her situation and interests. North Korea is considered a greater threat not because it has more objective capabilities but because it is perceived to be a rogue state willing to upset the status quo. Japan's security-policy commitment to nonaggression is not simply a reflection of constitutional constraints or domestic politics but has become a part of the country's national identity, even "culture" (Berger 1996). Furthermore, ideas scholars take seriously the question of how interests change—again, not simply because material factors change (although these scholars recognize that such changes may be important). Rather, actors are portrayed as also being motivated by nonmaterial factors, such as ideas and values, that can shape and reshape their definition of interests. As Judith Goldstein and Robert Keohane put it, the rationalist approach is beset by "empirical anomalies that can be resolved only when ideas are taken into account," and so "policy outcomes can be explained only when interests and power are combined with a rich understanding of human beliefs" (1993, 13). Finally, these scholars argue that ideas are not simply tools that actors use to justify or rationalize actions they desire to take for other reasons; rather, ideas have an independent effect on how actors define their situations and interests, and thus provide an actual motivation for behavior.[3]

Ideas scholars have attempted to specify the conditions under which new policy ideas are most likely to be adopted and implemented. Peter Hall, in *The Political Power of Economic Ideas: Keynesianism across Nations*, argues that successful ideas usually must first be compelling on three different policy dimensions. The first, economic viability, holds that ideas must have the "apparent capacity to resolve a relevant set of economic problems" (1989, 371). This condition is more likely to be met when "old" or "traditional" ideas are perceived to have failed, thus creating demand for some new way of thinking. New policy ideas are likely to be successful when they offer a novel approach that can explain many of the anomalies unexplained by traditional thinking and a new solution that promises to alleviate the policy crisis. The second and third conditions mentioned by Hall are that ideas must have both administrative and political viability; that is, they must be consistent with the "long-standing administrative biases of the officials responsible for approving [policy change]" and that they are "more likely to become policy if [they] also [have] some appeal in the broader political arena" (1989, 373–374).

As I discuss in the next section, by 1993 the arguments put forth by the revisionists had succeeded in meeting all of Hall's criteria. Most importantly, they presented a new and simple solution to a seemingly intractable problem and held out the promise of remedying years of "policy failure" when traditional trade remedies seemed to have had no effect. Revisionist ideas had most definitely achieved political viability in the United States by the 1980s, increased their administrative viability gradually through the 1980s, and achieved substantial administrative viability by the time Clinton was elected.

Scholars of ideas have also come to a consensus that the institutionalization of ideas is more likely when they are championed by a set of actors who have a commitment to those ideas. That is, ideas that meet all Hall's conditions may eventually be accepted, but the pace and depth of their acceptance will be quicker if pushed by motivated actors. Various scholars have referred to these sets of actors as "epistemic communities," "expert communities," and "norms entrepreneurs,"[4] but their common feature is that they have an "ideational" commitment that goes beyond narrowly defined self-interest. As Martha Finnemore and Kathryn Sikkink put it, this "ideational commitment is the main motivation when entrepreneurs promote norms or ideas because they believe in the ideals and values embodied in the norms, even though the pursuit of the norms may have no effect on their well-being" (1998, 898). In this case, the rise of the impact of revisionist ideas was also due to a relatively small group of actors, the revisionists, including not only the more noted academic and journalistic figures but also individuals from the business community and parts of the executive branch of government.

In the following section, I briefly sketch the origins of this revisionist community, the growing viability of its ideas, and their eventual impact on U.S. trade policy. I argue that this impact can be seen on two distinct levels: the reshaping of America's definition of interests, stemming from its reassessment of the threat posed by the Japanese economy, and the narrower but still significant impact on the specific policies that were chosen by the Clinton administration.

THE RISE OF REVISIONIST IDEAS

Revisionist ideas did not simply appear in 1993 but had been evolving for two decades or more. These ideas had gained gradual acceptance in the United States as a whole, and particularly within the government. One task, then, is to explain why revisionist ideas had a visible policy impact in 1993 and not earlier. In Hall's terms, the ideas pushed by the revisionists had gained gradual economic and political viability by the end of the 1980s, but remained only partially institutionalized in the Bush administration and thus had only a sporadic affect on U.S. trade policy. By the end of the Bush administration, however, revisionism was on the verge of achieving administrative viability, setting the stage for a major shift in policy under a new administration.

The concept of revisionism has taken on many forms and definitions, so any attempt to define it will be controversial. For the purposes of this chapter, I focus on revisionist ideas related to the nature of the Japanese economy: the view of

Japanese capitalism as being inherently different from other capitalist systems, the view of the economy as being inherently closed and thus offering a significant advantage to domestic firms, and the belief that these attributes made the Japanese system a predatory or adversarial one, thus making normal exchange relations detrimental to U.S. interests. In essence, then, revisionists held that the Japanese economy was different, closed, and adversarial.[5]

It is very difficult to pinpoint the exact origins of revisionist thinking, in part because it derives from a number of schools of thought and experience. Revisionist views certainly built on a long tradition of "Japanese exceptionalism," the view that Japan and its society were inherently different, even unique, and thus not understandable in terms of Western analytical categories. These views have long existed in Japan as well as the West.

Two parts of the revisionist position—that the Japanese economy was both different and closed—were widely accepted by the mid-1980s. A long line of scholars of the Japanese political economy has pointed to unique aspects of its organization and processes. A seminal academic publication was Chalmers Johnson's 1982 work on Japan's industrial policy, *MITI and the Japanese Miracle: The Growth of Industrial Policy, 1925–1975*. Here, the argument was that the Japanese government had done things differently and in many ways had done things better, a clear call for the West to learn from Japan's example of successful industrial policy. While Johnson's book certainly had a major impact on the academic debate about Japan, it is more difficult to assess its impact on the broader U.S. debate, especially in government and business circles. I suspect that impact was significant. It is my sense that many Americans already had a feeling that Japan was somehow different, but in a way that they could not quite put their finger on. Johnson's book was helpful in clarifying a lot of these thoughts. It must be stressed, however, that in this early work Johnson was not making the argument that the Japanese economy was inherently closed, and he certainly did not argue that it represented a threat to the United States or that drastic trade remedies, such as numerical targets, were required. All that would come later.

In subsequent years, Johnson and an increasing number of American academics published work focusing on unique aspects of the Japanese economy that either gave firms an advantage or worked to insulate the Japanese market: the role of the bureaucracy in guiding Japan's economy; features of Japan's industrial organization, such as the *keiretsu* industrial groups and industry associations; specific corporate structures and practices, such as cross-shareholding and labor practices; and government policy, including industrial policy, regulations, and lax antitrust enforcement. At the same time, there was a virtual explosion of "pop" publications on Japan devoted to finding the real "secret" of Japan's success.

Perceptions of the Japanese economy as different and closed also had roots among business people and government officials who had had long and direct contact with the Japanese economy. On the government side, Clyde Prestowitz discusses a number of individuals in government who through their direct dealings with Japan had developed a clear sense that the Japanese economy did not operate the way that other capitalist economies did and who thus came to see trade problems with Japan as requiring unique solutions (Prestowitz 1988). This was particularly true of the trade-related agencies, the Department of Commerce and the Office of the U.S. Trade Representative (USTR); as early as the first Reagan administration many of these officials were arguing, in vain, for a more activist policy to gain access to the Japanese market.[6] A few officials at this time began to consider the need for market-share agreements; the first concrete evidence I know of is a memo drafted by USTR in the fall of 1984 that listed numerical targets as a possible policy option.

These officials were also deeply influenced by American business people who had had direct experience (mostly bad) in the Japanese market. (Indeed, a number of the key officials mentioned by Prestowitz had brought such experience to their government positions.) They argued that their difficulties in cracking the Japanese market were not due to lack of American competitiveness or effort; rather, a growing number pointed to the inherently closed nature of the Japanese economy. Thus, even if overt barriers to imports were lowered or removed, it would still be extraordinarily difficult to penetrate the Japanese market. In their complaints to the U.S. government, they focused their criticisms on not only regulations and other policy measures but also business organization and practices that impeded access to the Japanese market.

Finally, the U.S. public and, in particular, Congress needed little convincing of the closed nature of the Japanese economy. Examples of American firms being shut out of the Japanese market abounded. The argument that Japan's economy was inherently closed was the most logical explanation for the seemingly intractable trade deficit. The public was also well aware of the economic costs of trade with Japan, since numerous industries were visibly being hurt by Japanese competition, leading to industrial dislocation and pain. In the early 1980s, Congress spent more of its time trying to protect the U.S. market from import competition than it did trying to open the Japanese market.

The view of the Japanese economy as different and closed was not uncontested, however. On the academic front, the mainstream of American neoclassical economists held to the belief that the Japanese economy was not nearly as different as the revisionists argued. That is, while Japan might have some unique aspects and institutions, so did every capitalist economy. The orthodox economist view was that these differences were marginal enough so that the system operated on essentially the same principles as capitalism did worldwide. In terms of the trade issue, economists were divided over how to define the problem and what to do about it. Many were willing to acknowledge that the Japanese market was a very difficult one to enter. But the orthodox view remained that if barriers to imports could be identified and removed, then "normal" market forces would operate and imports into Japan would increase. Another strand of orthodox thinking was that sector-specific barriers were less a problem than macroeconomic factors or exchange rates. Here, the orthodox prescription was to raise Japan's demand for imports by increasing aggregate demand, for instance through the government's fiscal or monetary policy or by manipulating the yen-dollar exchange rate. Finally, certain economists argued that the trade imbalance with Japan was not a cause for alarm. If anything, inexpensive imports were a positive thing, giving consumers greater choice, increasing competition, and lowering prices. In any case, the bilateral imbalance was not an issue, since the United States could not expect to run surpluses with all nations; what was important was America's overall economic competitiveness.

Opinion within the business community was not completely unified, either. Revisionist ideas about Japan were limited to the relatively few firms that had extensive experience in the Japanese market. Even some of them had in fact been able to succeed in that market. The consensus within the business community was that Japan's was a difficult, but not impossible, market to crack; as yet there was not full agreement that the Japanese economy was inherently closed or that drastic trade-policy remedies were required.

Most importantly, revisionists' assumptions about the closed nature of the Japanese economy had not been completely accepted within the government. Two sets of arguments, one economic, one political, made up what can be called the traditionalist view of Japan. Prestowitz describes very clearly how isolated revisionist assumptions were in the U.S. government. In fact, even within the trade agencies, Commerce and USTR, revisionist ideas were often limited to the line officials who dealt directly with Japan; the political appointees tended to take a more traditional view—what Prestowitz refers to as a "free-trade ideology." More importantly, the views of the neoclassical economists were clearly dominant in the Department of the Treasury, which was thus the biggest obstacle that revisionists in the trade agencies had to overcome. Treasury held to economic orthodoxy in all ways: that the bilateral imbalance was not the issue, that if barriers could be removed imports would increase, and that the manipulation of exchange rates or aggregate demand would lead to large changes in the trade imbalance.

Another important set of actors, organizations dealing with the political and military relationship, took a neutral position in the debate about the Japanese economy. In essence, these actors, the Departments of State and Defense and the National Security Council (NSC), could not have cared less about the U.S. trade imbalance or relative economic gains; in their view, the positive benefits of military cooperation with Japan far outweighed any economic costs. Especially in the cold-war context, these officials had no desire to raise economic issues higher on the agenda or to allow economic frictions to spill over to damage the security side of the relationship. Japan was a political ally, not an economic enemy.[7]

U.S. policy toward Japan in the early 1980s, then, was dominated by two strands of traditionalist thinking. On the political side was the view that Japan was so central to America's security interests that trade tensions should not be allowed to detract from the bilateral partnership. On the economic side the view was that gaining access to the Japanese market, although difficult, was not impossible; so long as the United States could identify specific barriers to entry, these barriers could be removed through negotiations, and market forces would then lead to an increase in imports. Since the Japanese economy was seen as operating on the same principles as other economies, the traditional view held that standard economic policies, such as manipulating exchange rates and growth rates, would lead to redressing the trade imbalance.

Attitudes in the United States, and particularly in the U.S. government, underwent a major change in the mid- and late-1980s. The view that the Japanese economy was uniquely closed became orthodoxy in most parts of the government. More importantly, the third strand of revisionist thinking—that the Japanese economy was a predatory one that thus posed a threat to U.S. interests—also became part of mainstream assumptions.

The shift in attitude was first fueled by the massive trade surpluses that Japan racked up beginning in the mid-1980s. Although orthodox economists could explain this rise as something caused by economic forces—the growing U.S. budget deficit and the still misaligned exchange rate—their explanation was not always convincing on a public or political level. By the late 1980s, it seemed clear to many that orthodox solutions were simply not working. The long record of trade negotiations with Japan seemed to have yielded many agreements but only meager results. Likewise, long-standing efforts to get the Japanese government to increase domestic demand and major efforts to manipulate the value of the yen, in particular in 1978 and again in the 1985 Plaza Accord, seemed to have had only a minor impact on the deficit. Despite a decade of efforts, all predicated on the assumption that the Japanese market operated more or less like any other, Japan's trade surplus continued to hit peak after peak.

With the orthodox policy approach facing a severe period of "policy failure," the revisionist position offered an attractive alternative that quickly grew in resonance and appeal. According to the revisionists, the problem with the traditionalist approach was its core assumption that the Japanese economy operated on the same principles as other capitalist systems. Rather, Japan's unique blend of bureaucratic dominance, close business-government relations, structural differences (such as the *keiretsu*), close collusion and cooperation among firms, and other factors made the economy impervious to imports. Orthodox prescriptions would not work because Japan was not an orthodox economy.

America was also coming to the uncomfortable realization that Japan was becoming an economic superpower at the precise moment that U.S. power was declining. By the mid-1980s, Japan had become the second largest capitalist economy and had amassed huge financial resources. Its industries had achieved dominance on all rungs of the industrial ladder. More importantly, the Japanese economy seemed to be a juggernaut that would only continue to gain momentum: If it did not already dominate future and high-technology industries, it soon would. At the same time, the U.S. economy seemed to be maturing and reaching the limits of its growth, leading to a profound crisis in confidence—what Bhagwati refers to as the "diminished giant syndrome" (1990, 11). With relative power so clearly shifting, IR analysts focused their attention on "relative gains," the notion that an increase in economic gains by a potential adversary may lead to an increase in its military power (Mastanduno 1991). The United States needed to do something to redress its deteriorating power position.

Fears about a relative loss of economic strength ran deepest in the defense community. Analysts and officials expressed concern not only about a weakening of America's industrial base but also about its growing dependence on Japan, in particular for crucial advanced technologies. The growing view was that the structure of Japan's economy and the policies followed by its government were allowing Japan to dominate world markets in high technology. These concerns were especially evident on the acquisitions side of the Defense Department, where officials supported a strong response to counter Japan's industrial targeting of critical technologies.

The Semiconductor Agreement (SCA) of 1986 was one manifestation of America's growing worries about becoming dependent on Japan in a critical industry. The concern was that if Japan were allowed to continue to increase its competitiveness it would very quickly undermine and destroy America's semiconductor base, an essential component of the military's new generation of advanced weaponry. The immediate concern was that Japan was dumping chips onto the U.S. market, a tactic it had often used successfully in the past. The semiconductor industry joined forces with the military community in pushing for an ambitious response, with the goals of putting an end to dumping and strengthening the U.S. industry by increasing U.S. government policy support and forcing open the Japanese market.

The SCA is also important for my story because it was the first to mention a numerical target for import penetration of the Japanese market. It seems to me that this inclusion of numerical targets did not represent a permanent shift in U.S. trade policy. My sense is that the call for numbers was an exception, reflecting the strategic importance of the industry and the perception that quick action was vital to America's national security. Some participants doubt that the United States would have pushed as hard as it did without the strong stance taken by Defense. It should also be remembered that the main impetus for the SCA was to end Japan's dumping of chips and that gaining access to the Japanese market was a secondary goal. Participants in the negotiations also argue that the request for numbers was driven less by the view that a numerical target was the best way to gain access to the Japanese market and more by the need to close the deal quickly; in addition, the idea of numerial targets was something the Japanese side had indicated that it would accept. Significantly, numerical targets were not considered for any other industry at the time.

The rise in bilateral economic tensions in the late 1980s can thus be attributed to a basic objective factor: the relative shift in economic power. But I believe there was more to it than that. The United States was concerned not only over the fact of Japan's rising power, but also over the *purpose* of that power.

It is here that I believe revisionist ideas had a very deep impact on how Americans understood Japan. Revisionist thought underwent a considerable coalescence in the late 1980s; indeed, it was only in 1989 that the term was first coined, in an article in *Business Week*. Important journalistic works included books by Karel van Wolferen and James Fallows, as well as the writings of Chalmers Johnson, who was soon anointed the "godfather" of this new conception of Japan. Although these publications reflected ideas that had been developing over a long period and in many parts of American society, they were important in that they solidified revisionist thought and struck a very strong chord in the United States. They cemented the view that Japan was different and closed, and also succeeded in portraying the Japanese system as one that was designed—intentionally or not—to achieve industrial dominance, and that this carried grave implications. Their deeper significance was that they sharpened the view that the Japanese economy was predatory and adversarial, and therefore a threat to U.S. interests. In essence, they helped to redefine the "Japan Problem" as less an economic or trade issue than a fundamental threat to American interests.

A further implication drawn from the revisionist position was that because Japan's purposes were so at odds with America's, Japan was therefore not a dependable or trustworthy partner. It is my sense that the revisionists themselves stopped short of actually making this charge—their focus was more on the differences that divided the two countries—but other analysts adopted this position quite clearly (see, for instance, Huntington 1993). Over time the perception grew that the problem was not simply that the United States was dependent on a foreign country but that it was dependent on *Japan*.

By the late 1980s, revisionist conceptions of Japan had clearly achieved political viability. Within Congress, as has been discussed at length by others, trade policy with Japan was a highly contentious and emotional subject. Members of Congress were increasingly frustrated by the seeming failure of traditional approaches to Japan and were thus extremely receptive to new views of Japan that were simple and that promised to fix the "Japan Problem." This political receptivity also reflected a noticeable shift in the mood of the public, which increasingly blamed Japan for the persistent trade imbalance, unemployment, and industrial dislocation.

The revisionist view of Japan as adversarial was also becoming entrenched in the business community. This was due to not only the continuing frustrations of firms that had direct dealings with Japan but also the growing number of industries that were going head to head with the Japanese in new and high-technology industries. Revisionist ideas were coming to dominate the discussions and statements of such groups as the American Chamber of Commerce in Japan, the American side of the U.S.-Japan Business Roundtable, and the Advisory Committee on Trade Policy and Negotiations (ACTPN).

The interests of firms were limited to economic and trade issues, so they stopped short of arguing for a redefinition of broader national interests. Their views did, however, lead them to begin to espouse a radically new trade policy approach—numerical targets. This approach was advocated most strongly by the ACTPN, which in 1989 approached the Bush administration calling for a radical change in policy. The "revisionist turn" in this group of firms no doubt reflected its negative experiences with Japan; in this sense one cannot ignore the importance of materially defined interests. But what I find most significant is that these firms had arrived at a new *definition* of the "Japan Problem," one that stressed the revisionist view that Japan was different, closed, and adversarial. And it was this new definition—the revisionist definition—that led them to espouse a novel approach. Their subsequent attempts to influence the policy process took the form of persuading policymakers to adopt this redefinition of Japan.[8] The ACTPN's proposals were rejected outright by the Bush administration, however. In a much publicized meeting, Carla Hills, Bush's trade representative, appeared to be receptive to its ideas at first, but very soon thereafter came back with a categorical rejection of its premises about Japan. ACTPN officials insist that this is further evidence that the top Bush administration officials were indeed still wedded to the "ideology of free trade."

Thus, in spite of the fundamental shift in American views of Japan outlined above, the Bush administration remained internally divided between "old" and "new" thinking. Revisionist ideas had been adopted within certain organizations and at certain levels; but the key decision makers, the political appointees, by and large held to traditionalist assumptions. Within the economic agencies, orthodox views were still strong at the political-appointee level. This was especially true at Treasury but also, as the ACTPN experience indicates, within the trade agencies. And in the security-related organizations, while there was growing concern over Japan's technological capabilities, traditionalist voices were also still quite strong. Within Defense, for instance, the policy side of the department, which was in charge of managing the Japan relationship, stuck to traditionalist assumptions about the value of the security tie and thus was in direct conflict with the acquisitions side, which focused on technological issues. Even with the winding down of the cold war, traditionalists argued that the U.S.-Japan relationship needed to be revised, not weakened. At the top levels of the Bush administration, the focus continued to be on the centrality of the political and security partnership.

Bush administration trade policy toward Japan also reflected this internal division. By 1992, the administration had shifted its trade policy to what might be called a two-track policy. On the one hand, the United States still sought to increase access to the Japanese market by removing impediments and structural barriers to imports or competition. In other words, efforts like the Structural Impediments Initiative (SII) were aimed at liberalizing the market *process* in Japan, based again on the assumption that imports would then increase. On the other hand, administration officials also began to stress the need for greater "results" from trade agreements, by which was meant that for trade agreements to be considered successful, there had to be some evidence of progress. This new approach was reflected in a number of trade agreements and was especially symbolized by the January 1992 "auto summit," in which the United States and Japan fought over whether and how to mention numbers in the final agreement. In my view, however, the Bush people were not arguing for results in terms of guaranteed targets but rather were reacting to criticisms that decades of trade agreements had been completely empty, yielding no benefits at all. The notion of government-guaranteed numerical targets was not a main focus of Bush's trade policy. Even in the 1992 auto agreement, administration officials were willing to accept purely private-sector statements of intent to increase purchases rather than push for a government guarantee of targets.[9]

By the 1992 election, then, the stage had been set for the adoption of new ideas and new policy directions. Orthodox assumptions were being increasingly challenged and contested, while "new thinking" about Japan was growing in acceptance at the popular and political level and had substantially permeated the bureaucracy, as well. Yet even at this point a change in policy was not inevitable. We must consider here an important counterfactual question: Had President Bush been reelected, would the United States have pursued a more concrete emphasis on numbers, including a Japanese government guarantee of market share? My evidence suggests that Bush officials were in fact ready to continue with a rules-based approach to Japan (most likely a modified version of the SII). Despite a convergence of factors, both material and ideational, in favor of a new approach to Japan, it was still not certain that the United States would take this step.

INSTITUTIONALIZING NEW POLICY IDEAS: THE CLINTON MOMENT

It was the election of Clinton that paved the way for the full institutionalization of the new ideas about Japan. The key changes came at the level of political appointees, all of whom shared the new conceptions of Japan. Among Clinton's top officials there was not a single individual who espoused a traditional view of the Japanese economy or the U.S.-Japan relationship. Many had come to these new views through direct experience with Japan in the private sector, through Congress, or through academic studies—including Robert Rubin at the National Economic Council (NEC), Lloyd Bentsen at Treasury, and Laura Tyson at the Council of Economic Advisers; even Warren Christopher at State had been involved in the "textile wrangle" negotiations, which had evidently shaped his perceptions of Japan. Others, such as Mickey Kantor at USTR and Ronald Brown at Commerce, were open and more than receptive to the new interpretation of Japan. In addition, the key deputies assigned the task of shaping Japan policy all held strong nontraditional views of Japan: Bowman Cutter at the NEC, Samuel (Sandy) Berger at the NSC, Joan Spero at State, Roger Altman at Treasury, and later Charlene Barshefsky at USTR and Jeffrey Garten at Commerce.

The adoption of new ideas also occurred at the highest level: The president himself slowly began to espouse the new conceptions of Japan. As governor of Arkansas, Clinton had taken a benign attitude toward Japan (in part due to his interest in attracting Japanese investment to his state). Even during the 1992 presidential campaign, his pronouncements on Japan were low key, reflecting a conscious decision to play down any issue that detracted from his main message of Bush's mishandling of the domestic economy. During the campaign, however, there were signs that Clinton had developed a sense that the Japanese economy was inherently different and would have to be dealt with using new and different policies. (To some extent, these views were reinforced by the steady stream of information channeled to Clinton by his top campaign advisors on Japan; in part it reflected the candidate's own experiences, perceptions, and political calculations.)

The new administration was thus relatively unified, top to bottom, around a new conception of the Japanese economy. Unlike the Bush administration, in

which revisionist-leaning career officials had had to contend with the more traditional views of top political appointees, there was now greater receptivity at the
highest levels of the government. In fact, it turned out that revisionist thinking was
even stronger at the political-appointee level, as key Clinton advisors insisted on
a new approach, including numerical targets, that went beyond even what career
officials had been advocating.

The policy assumptions held by these new officials were quickly translated
into concrete policy. With the state visit of Prime Minister Miyazawa Kiichi scheduled for April 1993, the administration put together a Deputies Committee, jointly
chaired by the NSC and the newly created NEC, to hammer out a new Japan policy.[10] Beginning in late February, this group held a series of intense meetings
and discussions that quickly laid the basis for a new policy approach. The group's
new assumptions about Japan were clear at its initial meeting. One of the first
actions taken was the rejection of a set of policy papers, drafted by State in the
final days of the Bush administration, that espoused a traditional view of the
U.S.-Japan relationship. In its place, the group decided to formulate a new policy
based on new assumptions about Japan.

The deputies found themselves united in their perception of Japan as a potential threat to U.S. economic interests. Concerns about America's dependency on
Japan and the consequences of Japan's growing economic power had reached a
peak in 1992, and alarmism permeated thinking early in the Clinton administration.[11] Although none went so far as to define Japan solely in terms of a threat, all
in the group shared the sense that the U.S.-Japan trade relationship was in a
state of crisis and that there was an urgent need for the United States to take
decisive action to meet the growing challenge from Japan. In addition, all agreed
that past U.S. policy had grossly overemphasized the political and security sides of
the relationship. The metaphor chosen was that of a three-legged stool in which
only one leg, the economic relationship, was badly in need of repair. The weight
of opinion was thus solidly in favor of redefining the trade relationship with
Japan. Even the most traditional of agencies, Defense and State, although still concerned for the military and political sides of the relationship, evidently agreed with
the need to emphasize economic problems.

There was also a remarkable degree of consensus that Japan was a unique and
inherently closed economy. This assumption led directly to the judgment that all
past negotiations with Japan had failed precisely because they had focused on trying to strengthen rules or improve the workings of market forces—a futile effort,
according to the new ideas about Japan. Not only had past negotiations failed; the
prevalent view was that further negotiations based on improving market processes
or rules would also be futile.

The Deputies Committee thus came to the conclusion that any policy toward

Japan had to be "results oriented." Although the group disagreed over tactics, it arrived at a clear consensus on an underlying focus on results, including not just a desired outcome but also the involvement of the Japanese government in guaranteeing that outcome.

Here, then, is one case in which new policy ideas had a visible and concrete effect on an important policy decision. In a very short period—from late February to April 1993—a new set of ideas about Japan was adopted and implemented, resulting in a dramatic departure in U.S. trade policy from a focus on rules, processes, and opportunities to a focus on outcomes. While many factors made this possible, it is difficult to explain the shift without incorporating the impact of new policy ideas. Furthermore, these new ideas did not stem directly from materially defined interests but rather were based on a new way of *conceptualizing* the Japanese economy—the revisionist view of the Japanese economy as different, closed, and adversarial.

THE FRAMEWORK AND ITS AFTERMATH

Once it had decided on its new policy approach, the administration turned to what it thought would be the easy part: getting the Japanese to accept this new approach to trade negotiations.[12] The United States soon learned, however, that for economic ideas to be acceptable they had to be not only domestically viable (which they were) but also *internationally* viable; that is, they had to be acceptable to foreign economic partners that would be affected by the implementation of the new ideas.

America's new policy approach, based on revisionist ideas, was definitely *not* acceptable to Japan. From the first negotiating session onward, the Japanese government embarked on a concerted and ultimately effective campaign to resist and refute the U.S. push for numerical targets.[13] It is significant that Japan's hardline stance relied less on material threats and tactics than on refutation of the *assumptions* behind America's new policy and attacks on the legitimacy of its new demands. The Japanese government mounted an impressive information campaign designed to undermine the credibility of revisionist ideas—and of the revisionists themselves. Japan also appealed to international norms at the multilateral level, in particular those that emerged from the long negotiations to create the World Trade Organization. Through these strategies Japan sought to portray American demands for indicators as evidence that the United States was pushing for a "managed trade" agenda and to delegitimize these demands as a new form of protectionism. Incredibly, Japan portrayed itself as standing for the principle of nongovernment involvement in the economy and as supporting free trade; given the role the government had played in the economy in the post–World War II period, many found these arguments highly ironic. These strategies, however, turned out to be highly effective. By the end of 1995, the United States found itself virtually isolated in its policy approach to Japan.

In the face of determined Japanese resistance, the U.S. government's initial consensus on the need for numbers began to crumble. Even as the Framework negotiations got under way in September 1993, the administration found itself divided over the question of how formal and explicit any new results-oriented agreement would have to be. What emerged was a battle between "moderate" and hard-line groups. The former, led by Cutter at the NEC, expressed a willingness to embrace a much looser approach that would include benchmarks and measures but that would also accept a less formal and explicit role for the Japanese government in terms of enforcing the achievement of results. Opposing this group, however, was a hard-line faction, led by Kantor at USTR, that continued to want the Japanese government to make an explicit commitment to results and wanted to make the new agreements enforceable and sanctionable. The U.S. position throughout the Framework Talks never coalesced around either of these distinct policy approaches. Rather, it reflected a shifting compromise between the two extremes that changed as the balance of power between the factions changed. The United States found itself with conflicting, inconsistent positions that were difficult to articulate, much less defend. As a result, when faced with criticisms from Japan and others that the U.S. sought "managed trade," Clinton administration officials were never able to convincingly deny these charges—in part because some officials did in fact prefer managed trade.

There is some evidence that the moderate faction came close to prevailing, particularly on the eve of the February 1994 summit between President Clinton and Prime Minister Hosokawa Morihiro. These efforts, however, were undermined at the last minute by the hard-line faction, culminating in the failure of the summit. By mid-1994, the more moderate approach had been discredited, and the United States pressed the Japanese government to commit itself explicitly to achieving concrete results. This approach continued through the climax of the auto talks in mid-1995.[14]

In the aftermath of the auto confrontation, the U.S. government backed away from a focus on concrete results and has since sought to strike a better balance between trade and security concerns. This shift is explainable in part—but only in part—by further changes in the policy ideas described above. First and foremost, the United States was faced with an uncomfortable objective reality: Given the Japanese government's hard-line bargaining position of automatically rejecting any demands that smacked of market shares or managed trade, the United States was left with little choice but to back away from a numbers orientation. Even if it might have been desirable, achieving anything close to numerical targets or managed trade was simply not possible. As one USTR official put it, "Those days are over."

The shift toward balance was also, however, driven by a redefinition of the threat posed by the Japanese economy. First, by the end of 1995 U.S. government officials were no longer worried about being overtaken economically by Japan. As evidence mounted that Japan's economic slump was deeper and more protracted than anyone had imagined, officials began to focus more on the problems and shortcomings inherent in the Japanese system. (In fact, U.S. policymakers began to worry more about the weakness of the Japanese economy, not its strength; the threat from Japan was now that its economy would collapse, taking the world down with it.) With fears of Japanese industrial dominance gone, there was less impetus to devise a radical Japan policy.

In addition, over time revisionist ideas became less prevalent in the upper echelons of the administration. By 1997, every political appointee involved in the original formulation of Japan policy had left the administration (the exception being Barshefsky). For the most part, their replacements held less extreme views of the Japanese economy. As a result, there is no longer the assumption that the U.S. approach to Japan must be results oriented. The debate over Japan policy has thus become more balanced and more open, and now includes the view that a rules- or process-level approach to opening the Japanese market may in fact be appropriate.

Finally, the domestic political mood began to shift after the end of the auto talks. With the economy now in full recovery, the U.S. public was visibly less concerned about any "threat" from Japan. By 1996, the bilateral trade numbers had also begun to turn around. And with no major industry raising urgent complaints about Japan—at least none that came close to matching the political importance and potential explosiveness of those from the auto industry—the political importance of Japan trade policy began to recede. As a result, the level of political pressure dissipated, and the Clinton administration felt free to declare victory and walk away from its earlier trade approach to Japan. In 1997, citing the turnaround in the sectoral and overall trade numbers—even if caused mostly by the incipient recovery in the Japanese economy and the slowdown in the United States—American officials could claim credit for the wisdom of their past trade policies.

As a result, the more traditional voices in the U.S. government, especially in Defense and State, became more vocal in reasserting the centrality of the political side of the relationship. These officials were motivated in part by changes in the regional security environment, in particular the attempt by North Korea to develop nuclear weapons and growing worries over the future role of China. They were also becoming increasingly concerned over the cost of the auto dispute on overall relations with Japan. Although they did not try to directly influence the handling of trade negotiations, they were increasingly aware that the political and security legs of the relationship were being neglected. The so-called Nye Initiative, which sought to achieve a better balance between America's economic and security interests, was one outgrowth of these fears. It was the rape of a Japanese schoolgirl by U.S. servicemen stationed in Okinawa Prefecture in September 1995, however, that provided the final incentive for the United States to strike a better balance between economic and security concerns in its Japan policy. The Washington security community was deeply concerned because the strength of the reactions to the rape in Japan made it clear that the stability of the U.S. military presence there could not be taken for granted.

At the time, many analysts expressed concern over the fragility of the relationship and predicted a further deterioration of security cooperation, especially now that there was no common threat holding the alliance together. The opposite in fact occurred: Spurred on by the mutual realization that the security relationship could no longer be taken for granted, both governments made a conscious effort to improve the security and political legs of the stool. These efforts culminated in the U.S.-Japan Joint Declaration on Security of April 1996, in which both sides reaffirmed the centrality of the alliance. More recent events in the region have deepened recognition of the need for a stable U.S.-Japan security relationship. In particular, the concern over a collapse scenario in North Korea makes the need for cooperation—in all realms—absolutely vital.

In short, changes in the security realm are fundamental and likely to be long lasting. Even without a clear common enemy, the two sides have been able to deepen and strengthen their security ties. The U.S. approach to Japan in the near future is thus unlikely to return to an overemphasis on the economic leg of the relationship.

SOME CONCLUSIONS AND IMPLICATIONS

Tracing the impact of policy ideas is always a difficult task, in particular because there is always some overlap between "objective" factors and more abstract ideas. This particular policy episode is also a "hard case" in that rationalist accounts can explain much of the dynamics of the U.S. decision-making process. Even so, I believe that a focus on the impact of revisionist ideas is important despite their relatively short period as the main driving force behind U.S. trade policy toward Japan. I find it very difficult to explain the content and timing of the Clinton administration's shift to a focus on numerical targets without analyzing this reconceptualization of Japan and the way it changed American perceptions of the Japanese economy and its meaning for the United States. On a specific policy level, the adoption of revisionist assumptions led the administration to the logical conclusion that some sort of numbers- or results-oriented trade agreement was necessary. This policy decision had deep consequences for the bilateral relationship in that it ushered in one of the most contentious trade battles the two nations have ever experienced. On a deeper level, the revisionist argument that the Japanese economy represented a fundamental threat to U.S. interests had an impact, I believe, on how the United States *defined* Japan and its interests in the bilateral relationship. Even though the rise in Japan's economic power was an objective one, the revisionist view of Japan as adversarial increased the perceived threat and spurred a stronger response than objective factors alone would have led us to predict.

Where do revisionist ideas stand now, and do they still matter? In my conversations with numerous U.S. career officials and political appointees it seems to me that the revisionist argument that the Japanese economy is different and inherently closed still prevails. This is especially true of officials in the trade agencies, the majority of whom still hold to the belief that the Japanese economy is structurally closed. The difference is that today the prevailing feeling is that it does not matter that much, at least not in the way that it did in 1993. The sense of the Japanese economy as adversarial and an economic threat to the United States has been buried by the decade-long Japanese recession.

This perception that Japan no longer presents a threat to the United States, however, may only last as long as the U.S. economy remains strong. In a pessimistic scenario of a significant slowdown in the U.S. economy and a return to rapid growth in Japan, it is highly likely that pressure for a strong response will reemerge. In my estimation, however, this new pressure will *not* take the form of a results orientation; the Japanese government has succeeded in deterring this approach as a viable policy option. The quandary for revisionist thinkers in the U.S. government is thus a significant one: Most recognize that traditionalist policy tools are no more likely to prove effective in redressing the trade imbalance today than in 1993, and yet the revisionist argument for numbers is one that simply will not be accepted by Japan. The United States is thus left with "second best" policy tools that many doubt will be effective: further encouragement of deregulation in Japan, strengthening of antitrust enforcement, and the like.

In this chapter, I have not claimed to explain every aspect of policy change in the period under review. Yet it is very difficult to understand the past decade of trade relations without reference to the rise and subsequent overshadowing of revisionist ideas within the U.S. government. In the end, this may be a case in which ideas were compelling enough to achieve domestic viability, leading the United States to make an important change in its policy, but not to achieve *international* viability.

NOTES

1. This increasingly popular "constructivist turn" has now created the main dividing line in the field of IR between "rationalist" and "constructivist" approaches (Checkel 1998; Katzenstein, Keohane, and Krasner 1998). A huge range of philosophies and approaches

has been lumped together under the term "constructivism," including at the far extreme critical theorists and postmodernists who argue that there is "no firm foundation for any knowledge" and who thus reject the very notion of a political science that is not fatally biased (Katzenstein, Keohane, and Krasner 1998, 677). Katzenstein, Keohane, and Krasner make a useful distinction between these more abstract versions of constructivism and those scholars whom they label the "conventional constructivists"—scholars who are highly critical of some rationalist assumptions but who otherwise have much in common with the rationalists. The conventional constructivists do not reject the idea of theory building, and in fact have been trying over the past decade to make their approach more "positivist." These scholars do not reject the importance of power and power relations, nor do they entirely reject the notion of rationality; that is, the assumption is that actors often, if not usually, act rationally (as utility maximizers). The difference is that the conventional constructivists focus their analysis on those crucial times when material factors fail to explain important things, in particular those "liminal" periods when actors shift their definition of interests. Thus, they are interested in "how preferences are formed and knowledge generated, prior to the exercise of instrumental rationality" (Katzenstein, Keohane, and Krasner 1998, 681), or "what happens *before* the neo-utilitarian model kicks in" (Ruggie 1998, 867; italics in original).

It also seems to me that the conventional constructivist approach should be very attractive to those engaged in "Japan studies" or "area studies" more broadly defined. After all, in the pure rationalist world logically there should not be such a thing as "area studies," since variables ideally operate in the same way regardless of the country or region involved. In that sense, the study of Japan per se becomes unnecessary or little more than an illustrative case study of rationalist theory developed elsewhere (Waltz 1979; Ramseyer and Rosenbluth 1993). Conventional constructivists, on the other hand, retain much of the methodology of the rationalists, but their focus on interest and identity formation makes them more sensitive to important internal attributes that distinguish different actors—for instance, a country's often unique historical evolution, including the path-dependent development of domestic institutions and the evolution of culture and worldviews. This approach is also willing to admit the importance of contingency and chance, including an appreciation of the importance of individuals and the impact of their actions. Methodologically, as well, the conventional-constructivist approach depends on rich empirical analysis and process tracing rather than mere correlation of independent and dependent variables (Checkel 1998). *These are precisely the types of specific knowledge that area specialists are in the best position to provide and the methodologies with which they are most familiar.* Indeed, the "constructivist turn" is currently visible in recent publications on Japan, and more is undoubtedly on the way. See Berger (1996), Gurowitz (1999), and Schoppa (1999).

2. One answer may be provided by Stephen Walt, who attempts to expand the neorealist focus on material factors to include such things as the perception of intentions, the "balance of threats" (Walt 1987). Although Walt originally intended to stick with a rationalist core, his analysis quickly takes us into the realm of ideas and conceptions rather than materially defined factors.

3. The current literature on ideas straddles the rationalist-constructivist divide. Goldstein and Keohane (1993) has taken a step beyond rationalist assumptions but has not

gone far enough for some constructivist critics. In particular, the authors have been criticized for remaining too faithful to their rationalist roots and for spending too much time analyzing the role of "principled beliefs," which specify what is considered right or wrong, and "causal beliefs," which pertain to more specific beliefs about cause-and-effect relationships. Constructivists argue that these authors need to spend more time considering the impact of "worldviews"—broader concepts such as Christianity or sovereignty, that "define the universe of possibilities for action" (Goldstein and Keohane 1993, 8); this would allow the authors to take more seriously the role that ideas can play in shaping the *identity* of actors (Blyth 1997; Ruggie 1998). Other useful reviews include Jacobsen (1995), Woods (1995), and Yee (1996).

4. These terms are from, respectively, Haas (1992); Mendelson (1998); and Finnemore and Sikkink (1998).

5. The term "revisionism" has been applied more broadly, ranging from general arguments that Japan is somehow "different" to specific arguments that Japanese political and economic institutions differ to arguments that Japan has successfully pursued a unique set of economic and industrial policies. Individuals recognized as revisionists have now parted company on some key issues, making the definition of the term even more problematic.

6. In speaking with a number of former officials, it seems to me that there were many more officials who went unmentioned in Prestowitz's book, often lower in terms of position, who held similar beliefs.

7. It should be noted that these organizations were not monolithic in their view of the Japanese economy. In State, for example, an increasing number of officials were beginning to adopt a revisionist conception of Japan. This was most evident in the Economic Bureau, which was responsible for overall economic and trade relations. And while the East Asia–Pacific Bureau and its Office of Japan Affairs continued to stress the importance of the overall relationship with Japan, revisionist ideas were gradually gaining currency there, as well.

8. In my opinion, the ACTPN was not an interest group as traditionally defined. The group was so broad and varied in interest and motivation that it is difficult to treat it as a traditional interest group. More importantly, not all members of the ACTPN stood to gain from a numerical-target approach, and not all believed this to be the best way to approach Japan.

9. The Bush administration did, however, renew the SCA in 1991, including the official mention of a 20 percent "target," understood to mean a goal rather than a commitment by the Japanese government.

10. The existence of the Deputies Committee (also referred to as the Deputies Group) and its deliberations were widely reported at the time. See, for instance, Ennis (1993), Craib (1994), and *Inside U.S. Trade* (26 February 1993, 26 March 1993, 7 May 1993, 14 May 1993, 21 May 1993). Members of the group also described the Committee's role in the policy-making process and discussed many of the group's assumptions and deliberations in later Congressional hearings. See especially testimony to the Senate Finance Committee (22 July 1993) and testimony to the House Foreign Affairs Committee (21 July 1993).

11. These concerns were voiced most strongly by Deputies Committee member Roger Altman in his Congressional testimony to the Senate Finance Committee on July 22, and reiterated by other Committee members Spero and Barshefsky. Although the Japanese economy

had slipped into recession in 1990, beginning with the crash of its stock market, the prevailing view was that this would prove to be a short-lived phenomenon and that the Japanese economy would soon recover. It was further assumed that Japanese industry would emerge from the recession "leaner and meaner," and thus more competitive, than before.

12. In my broader research project, I characterize U.S. demands as an attempt to define and implement a new international norm—a new "standard of appropriate behavior"—regarding the way the international trading community should treat Japan. In this case, the United States sought a new norm that defined Japanese capitalism as unique and adversarial, thus requiring a unique approach (Uriu 1999).

13. See Uriu (1999) for details of the debate within the Japanese government. In brief, I argue that the Japanese position was based on both material and normative interests, on the one hand the perceived benefits of deterring future U.S. trade demands but also on a deep commitment to adhering to the principles of multilateralism that were eventually embodied in the World Trade Organization (WTO). Although rational calculations formed the core of the Japanese approach, the principled position, deeply held by some bureaucrats, succeeded in hardening Japan's position even beyond what effective deterrence required. Japan's response also had an important ideational dimension: The government recognized that, given the revisionist premises underlying the U.S. demand for negotiated import targets, to agree even to discuss such targets would amount to an admission that those premises were in fact correct. Accepting import targets would only legitimize these revisionist assumptions and ultimately would spur the United States to make further, more difficult demands. This concern over the interpretation of ideas increased Japan's determination to maintain its hard line to the bitter end.

After an initial period of divisiveness, the government hammered out a consensus hard-line position. The key to this position was a cross-bureaucratic alliance in which hard-liners from the Ministry of International Trade and Industry (MITI) and the Ministry of Foreign Affairs were able to overcome "traditional" thinking in the government and thus shift Japan's position more firmly to "no." Of particular importance was a group of Foreign Ministry bureaucrats who had gained experience negotiating the WTO and who firmly agreed with MITI's position that the "era of bilateralism" had to be ended. With the election of Hosokawa Morihiro as prime minister in 1993, this faction found an important ally: Hosokawa himself came into office determined to make changes in the traditional ways of doing things, and this included a desire to make the U.S.-Japan economic relationship a more equal one.

14. Many U.S. officials now claim that the U.S. government never asked for numbers in the auto talks. This is a point that is hotly contested by Japanese participants, who insist that in private talks U.S. negotiator Garten in fact did ask point-blank for numbers. The U.S. proposal on autos was also widely reported in the U.S. trade journal *Inside U.S. Trade* and discussed in other sources (Karube 1996). Garten is the only official who refused to be interviewed for this project. It is possible that the United States in fact never *officially* presented a numbers demand on autos, but the combination of its publicly stated goals of achieving targets and the widely reported private suggestions of numbers gave the Japanese government enough evidence that the United States was at least *tacitly* insisting on numbers. Certainly this was the working assumption of virtually every Japanese policymaker with whom I have spoken.

BIBLIOGRAPHY

Berger, Thomas U. 1996. "Norms, Identity, and National Security in Germany and Japan." In Peter J. Katzenstein, ed., *The Culture of National Security: Norms and Identity in World Politics.* New York: Columbia University Press.

Bhagwati, Jagdish. 1990. "Aggressive Unilateralism: An Overview." In Jagdish Bhagwati and Hugh T. Patrick, eds. *Aggressive Unilateralism: America's 301 Trade Policy and the World Trading System.* Ann Arbor, Mich.: University of Michigan Press.

Bhagwati, Jagdish, and Hugh T. Patrick. 1990. *Aggressive Unilateralism: America's 301 Trade Policy and the World Trading System.* Ann Arbor, Mich.: University of Michigan Press.

Blyth, Mark M. 1997. "Any More Bright Ideas?: The Ideational Turn of Comparative Political Economy." *Comparative Politics* 29(2): 229–250.

Checkel, Jeffrey T. 1998. "The Constructivist Turn in International Relations Theory." *World Politics* 50(2): 324–348.

Craib, Anne B. 1994. "The Making of Japan Trade Policy in the Clinton Administration: Institutions and Individuals." *JEI Report* 39A (14 October): 1–12.

Destler, I. M. 1995. *American Trade Politics.* 3rd edition. Washington, D.C.: Institute for International Economics.

Ennis, Peter. 1993. "Trade Issues Take the Lead: Inside Clinton's Japan Team." *Tokyo Business Today* 61(7): 6–11.

Fallows, James. 1989. "Containing Japan." *Atlantic Monthly* 263(May): 40–54.

Finnemore, Martha. 1996. "Constructing Norms of Humanitarian Intervention." In Peter J. Katzenstein, ed. *The Culture of National Security: Norms and Identity in World Politics.* New York: Columbia University Press.

Finnemore, Martha, and Kathryn Sikkink. 1998. "International Norm Dynamics and Political Change." *International Organization* 52(4): 887–917.

Goldstein, Judith, and Robert O. Keohane, eds. 1993. *Ideas and Foreign Policy: Beliefs, Institutions, and Political Change.* Ithaca, N.Y.: Cornell University Press.

Gowa, Joanne S. 1994. *Allies, Adversaries, and International Trade.* Princeton, N.J.: Princeton University Press.

Gurowitz, Amy. 1999. "Mobilizing International Norms: Domestic Actors, Immigrants, and the Japanese State." *World Politics* 51(3): 413–445.

Haas, Peter M. 1992. "Introduction: Epistemic Communities and International Policy Coordination." *International Organization* 46(1): 1–35.

Hall, Peter, ed. 1989. *The Political Power of Economic Ideas: Keynesianism across Nations.* Princeton, N.J.: Princeton University Press.

Huntington, Samuel P. 1993. "Why International Primacy Matters." In Sean M. Lynn-Jones, ed. *The Cold War and After: Prospects for Peace.* Cambridge, Mass.: MIT Press.

Jacobsen, John Kurt. 1995. "Much Ado About Ideas: The Cognitive Factor in Economic Policy." *World Politics* 47(2): 283–310.

Janow, Merit E. 1994. "Trading With an Ally: Progress and Discontent in U.S.-Japan Trade Relations." In Gerald L. Curtis, ed. *The United States, Japan, and Asia: Challenges for U.S. Policy.* New York: W.W. Norton.

Johnson, Chalmers. 1982. *MITI and the Japanese Miracle: The Growth of Industrial*

Policy, 1925-1975. Polo Alto, Calif.: Stanford University Press.

Karube Kensuke. 1996. *Political Appointees: Kurinton-ryū tai Nichi senryaku no kuro-gotachi*. Tokyo: Free Press.

Katzenstein, Peter J. 1996. "Introduction: Alternative Perspectives on National Security." In Peter J. Katzenstein, ed. *The Culture of National Security: Norms and Identity in World Politics*. New York: Columbia University Press.

Katzenstein, Peter J., Robert O. Keohane, and Stephen D. Krasner. 1998. "International Organization and the Study of World Politics." *International Organization* 52(4): 645-685.

Klotz, Audie. 1995. "Norms Reconstituting Interests: Global Racial Equality and U.S. Sanctions against South Africa." *International Organization* 49(3): 451-478.

Layne, Christopher. 1993. "The Unipolar Illusion: Why New Great Powers Will Rise." *International Security* 17(4): 5-51.

Mastanduno, Michael. 1991. "Do Relative Gains Matter?: America's Response to Japanese Industrial Policy." *International Security* 16(1) 73-113.

———. 1998. "Economics and Security in Statecraft and Scholarship." *International Organization* 52(4): 825-854.

Mendelson, Sarah E. 1998. *Changing Course: Ideas, Politics, and the Soviet Withdrawal from Afghanistan*. Princeton, N.J.: Princeton University Press.

Moravcsik, Andrew. 1997. "Taking Preferences Seriously: A Liberal Theory of International Politics." *International Organization* 51(4): 513-553.

Prestowitz, Clyde V., Jr. 1988. *Trading Places: How America Allowed Japan to Take the Lead*. Rutland, Vt. and Tokyo: Charles E. Tuttle Company.

Ramseyer, J. Mark, and Frances McCall Rosenbluth. 1993. *Japan's Political Marketplace*. Cambridge, Mass.: Harvard University Press.

Ruggie, John Gerard. 1998. "What Makes the World Hang Together?: Neo-Utilitarianism and the Social Constructivist Challenge." *International Organization* 52(4): 855-885.

Schoppa, Leonard J. 1999. "The Social Context in Coercive International Bargaining." *International Organization* 53(2): 307-342.

Uriu, Robert M. 1999. "Refuting the Revisionists: Japan's Response to U.S. Trade Pressures during the Clinton Administration." Unpublished paper presented at the International Symposium on Japan and Its Neighbors in the Global Village: Current and Emergent Issues, Nagoya, Japan.

Walt, Stephen M. 1987. *The Origins of Alliances*. Ithaca, N.Y.: Cornell University Press.

Waltz, Kenneth N. 1979. *Theory of International Politics*. New York: McGraw-Hill.

———. 1993. "The Emerging Structure of International Politics." *International Security* 18(2): 44-79.

Wendt, Alexander. 1992. "Anarchy Is What States Make of It: The Social Construction of Power Politics. *International Organization* 46(2): 391-425.

Wolferen, Karel van. 1989. *The Enigma of Japanese Power: People and Politics in a Stateless Nation*. New York: Macmillan.

Woods, Ngaire. 1995. "Economic Ideas and International Relations: Beyond Rational Neglect." *International Studies Quarterly* 39: 161-180.

Yee, Albert. 1996. "The Causal Effects of Ideas on Policies." *International Organization* 50(1): 69-108.

8

The Challenges of Managing U.S.-Japan Security Relations after the Cold War

Michael Green

THE UNITED STATES AND JAPAN HAVE CLOSED the first decade of the post–cold war era by reaffirming their mutual security relationship and expanding defense cooperation in areas ranging from theater missile defense (TMD) to regional contingency planning and intelligence sharing. There is no question that the alliance continues to serve the fundamental interests of both parties. For the United States, it provides critical forward basing in East Asia and political partnership with the world's second largest economy. For Japan, it provides regional stability, a nuclear umbrella, and alignment with the world's largest economic and political power. Support for the alliance is broader than ever. There are fewer opponents to the alliance among the political elite in Tokyo and Washington than at any point since the first bilateral security treaty went into effect in 1952. Public support for the security relationship also remains high in both countries.

In spite of the reinvigoration of the alliance, however, the recent past has also seen repeated instances of tension and lingering mistrust between the two allies. Support for the alliance may be broad, but there are still questions about its depth. For example:

- U.S. bases in Okinawa Prefecture came under intense political pressure after three U.S. servicemen raped an Okinawan girl in September 1995.
- President Bill Clinton's criticism of Japanese economic policy during a June 1998 trip to China sparked charges of "Japan passing" (that is, passing Japan by) from Japanese journalists and fears of a long-term U.S. tilt toward Beijing from officials in Tokyo.
- North Korea's August 1998 launch of a Taepodong three-stage ballistic missile over Japan led to mutual recriminations by senior U.S. and Japanese officials as the two nations made divergent responses (Japan more bellicose

and the United States more subdued).

- The Japanese government's subsequent decision to develop an indigenous spy satellite caused concern in Washington about Japan's commitment to the alliance.
- The bombing of Kosovo by the North Atlantic Treaty Organization (NATO) caused unease in Tokyo about the U.S. commitment to the United Nations (U.N.) and fears of U.S. unilateralism.
- Underlying these specific points of tension and mistrust are questions in Washington about the long-term future of Japanese power after eight years of economic stagnation and questions in Tokyo about U.S. inattention to areas of political and security importance to Japan in East Asia.

Forged by former adversaries and asymmetrical in design, the U.S.-Japan alliance has never been free of headaches. But are the recent patterns of disagreement more of the same or a trend that will intensify with time? Are the sources of tension significant enough to warrant fundamental restructuring of the alliance—for example, reducing U.S. troop levels or encouraging an overseas combat role for Japanese forces (that is, making Japanese military roles more symmetrical with those of the United States)? Or are these areas of tension more of an alliance management problem that can be corrected with better coordination and communication?

This essay attempts to answer these questions by isolating five areas of alliance cooperation for further examination. These are military cooperation, U.S. military bases in Japan, policy toward China, policy toward the Korean peninsula, and multilateral security cooperation. In each area we consider the underlying sources of bilateral convergence and divergence in recent years, the advantages and disadvantages created by the current structure of the alliance, and the effectiveness of current alliance-management practices.

The chapter concludes that there is a growing realism in Japanese security thinking and fluidity in Japanese politics that will increasingly lead Japan to take independent steps to guarantee its own security when the U.S. level of commitment or attention is in doubt. At the same time, however, the United States and Japan continue to share broad strategic objectives, and for the foreseeable future neither is likely to develop a better security policy option than the alliance to safeguard its interests in the region. Moreover, in spite of a new strategic realism in Japan's security policy debate, the undertow of pacifism remains strong. Significant restructuring of the alliance faces political constraints in Japan and would be more likely to undermine regional stability than enhance security. Nevertheless, the alliance does require further attention, strengthening, and integration to remain credible. This emerges clearly in each of the areas of alliance cooperation reviewed below.

MILITARY COOPERATION

Since Thucydides, international-relations theorists have noted that small states allied with large states face a dilemma between entrapment and abandonment. If the small state aligns too closely with the large state, it risks losing control of its own interests and military assets to the large state. If, on the other hand, the small state seeks autonomy, it risks abandonment by the large state. This dilemma is particularly acute for Japan, which has codified its political/military asymmetries with the United States in the Constitution of Japan and related pacifist norms and institutions. These include cabinet decisions such as the three nonnuclear principles (*hikaku san gensoku*) and the three principles of arms exports (*buki yushutsu san gensoku*),[1] as well as broad political norms against the use of force in international relations (Berger 1993; Katzenstein 1996). The most significant of these constraints from the perspective of alliance relations is probably the Japanese government's decision not to exercise the right of collective defense (*shūdanteki jieiken*), the right to come to the defense of an ally even when Japan is not under direct attack.

If these institutional and normative constraints have increased the asymmetries vis-à-vis the United States, however, they have also served to insulate Japan against incorporation into U.S. defense planning for East Asia. Japan has no joint and combined command relationship with the United States comparable to the U.S.–South Korea or NATO command arrangements. As a result, U.S. forces have no command authority over Japanese forces or civilian authorities of any kind in any circumstances. U.S. forces in Japan have access to about three dozen bases and facilities for the defense of Japan and the security of the Far East, according to Article 6 of the 1960 U.S.-Japan Security Treaty. Seven of the largest of these bases can be automatically utilized in the event of hostilities on the Korean peninsula, according to the U.S. Status of Forces Agreement, which dates to the end of the Korean War (Giarra 1999, 125). Japan, meanwhile, maintains plausible deniability and limited liability for regional military actions by the United States even from bases in Japan.

During the cold war, this insulated strategic relationship with U.S. forces was a convenient construct for Japan, enabling it to retain a U.S. defense commitment without taking on regional security obligations that might jeopardize its own economic and political relations in East Asia or the domestic political consensus of the ruling conservatives. With time, however, the construct proved difficult to sustain. Japan moved gradually toward closer and more explicit security cooperation with the United States as the Vietnam War appeared to drain the U.S. commitment to East Asia and later as new threats emerged in the region.

In 1969, Prime Minister Satō Eisaku was pressed to agree in a joint communiqué with President Richard Nixon that Japan and the United States shared interests in stability on the Korean peninsula and in the Taiwan Strait. That explicit alignment with U.S. regional security policy was extracted from Satō in the context of the reversion of Okinawa to Japanese sovereignty and was therefore an anomaly. As one senior Defense Agency official later confessed, once Okinawa was returned, he and his colleagues spent the next two decades burying any possible commitment to regional security that might be read into Satō's statement.[2] The next test of Satō's statement came in 1976, when fears of abandonment after the end of the Vietnam War led Tokyo to negotiate the Guidelines for U.S.-Japan Defense Cooperation, the first explicit government approval for joint bilateral military planning. U.S. officials attempted to focus on contingencies in Taiwan and on the Korean peninsula, but the Japanese side limited the final 1978 agreement to the defense of Japan against direct attack. The Japanese government's steady retreat from the Satō statement of 1969 was frustrating for U.S. planners, but de facto regional defense planning became a possibility after the direct Soviet threat to East Asia increased in the late 1970s and early 1980s. By accident of geography, Japan's enhanced ability to cooperate with U.S. forces in the defense of the home islands effectively "bottled up" the Soviets' new ballistic missile submarine fleet in the Sea of Okhotsk and new Backfire bomber squadrons in the Maritime provinces. Without changing its exclusively defensive focus, the Japanese side became a player in regional U.S. military strategy. And this closer security relationship sat well with a Japanese body politic waking up to the Soviet threat around Japan.

Through the 1980s, Japanese defense budgets increased by an average of 6 percent and U.S. and Japanese forces beefed up joint training and exercises under a division of roles and missions in which U.S. forces were the "spear" and Japanese forces the "shield." But the value of Japan's exclusively defensive capabilities to global U.S. strategy was only as real as the threat of the Soviet forces in the Far East. With the end of the cold war, many in Japan expected to earn alliance partnership through international economic contributions, but the 1990–1991 Gulf War demonstrated that the United States and the world still measured security in the traditional currency of military force. The response in Japan was to push through controversial legislation allowing the Self-Defense Forces (SDF) to participate in limited peacekeeping operations under the United Nations. This empowered and internationalized the SDF, but it proved relatively ineffective as a tool when a new crisis hit in Japan's backyard in the spring of 1994. In that year, North Korean intransigence over a suspected nuclear weapons program led the United States to prepare for economic embargo, blockade, and possibly war with the North. When U.S. forces and the U.S. government approached Japan about joining this effort, the Japanese government was unable to commit any forces or participate in any significant planning at all. The new peacekeeping mission for the SDF did not apply to cases where hostilities were imminent, and the bilateral mine sweeping and sea-lane defense cooperation of the 1980s were not permissible outside the parameters of the defense of Japan. The North Korean nuclear crisis was defused without conflict, but the lessons for future bilateral defense relations were clear to the Pentagon and like-minded officials in the Defense Agency and the Ministry of Foreign Affairs. Japan had to be planned in to regional security policy (Oberdorfer 1998, 305–336).

The result was the revision of the 1978 Defense Guidelines to cover regional contingencies. The process began with the revision of the Japanese National Defense Program Outline (NDPO), which had already been under way since 1993. In the new NDPO, the Defense Agency shifted the focus of Japan's basic defense concept from defense against "small-scale limited invasion" to response to "situations in the area surrounding Japan that have a direct impact on the security of Japan." The new NDPO was approved by the cabinet in November 1995, and in the U.S.-Japan Joint Declaration on Security issued by President Clinton and Prime Minister Hashimoto Ryūtarō in April 1996 the two nations agreed to review the Defense Guidelines along the same lines. After several years of bilateral negotiations and political debate, the Japanese government approved the new guidelines in September 1997, and the National Diet approved legislation implementing them in June 1999.

This brings us back to the bilateral command arrangements and the dilemma of entrapment versus abandonment. The new Defense Guidelines outline functional areas of cooperation in the event of a regional crisis that has a direct effect on Japanese security. These functional areas include rear-area logistical support for U.S. forces, sea-lane patrol, intelligence sharing, noncombatant evacuation operations, and other missions that would not put Japanese forces into forward combat roles in third countries but would prove critical to facilitating successful resolution of conflicts (Giarra and Nagashima 1999, 96). The new guidelines have the potential to give the U.S. and Japanese governments far greater flexibility to respond to crises, but that flexibility also implies a greater integration of planning and decision making—precisely the sort of integration that the Japanese side has resisted through most of the alliance.

Recognizing this new level of integrated planning, critics of the guidelines in the Japanese Communist Party and the press have attacked the guidelines as an "automatic war machine" (jidō sansen sōchi). It is wrong, however, to assume that the guidelines will work like a vending machine, the United States dropping in a coin and receiving whatever Japanese base or hospital or destroyer is required to carry out operations. Joint defense planning is not the same as a treaty; there are no obligations under international law. The joint plan merely provides a menu or blueprint for implementing bilateral operations if the civilian authorities in Japan make a

decision to act. Nevertheless, it must be recognized that even this level of integration appears to many to threaten Japan's traditional insulation against "entrapment"
in U.S. strategy. It also places Japan in a potentially more influential role in U.S. security policy for the region. The Defense Guidelines are therefore likely to shape the
agenda for U.S.-Japan security cooperation in at least six ways.

First, the Japanese government will be under domestic political pressure to
define new checks against any direct U.S. control of Japanese military forces or
civilian assets. The Diet's passage of the implementing legislation for the guidelines was delayed for several months because the opposition Democratic Party of
Japan (DPJ) insisted on prior Diet approval before the government could implement any element of joint plans with the United States in a crisis. The ruling
Liberal Democratic Party (LDP) eventually negotiated this down to a system in
which either chamber of the Diet had the option of rejecting SDF participation in
operations prior to initiation of joint plans with the United States but the government could act first in an emergency and seek approval afterward. This
arrangement parallels the existing rules for SDF combat operations in the defense
of Japan, but it creates an uncertainty in bilateral planning that does not exist in
other U.S. alliance relationships.

Second, the United States and Japan will continue struggling to find surrogates
for the kind of joint and combined command relationship that exists in other
"real" alliances (NATO, U.S.-South Korea). In place of a joint and combined
command, the Defense Guidelines establish a "comprehensive mechanism" for
Japanese interagency participation in the planning process with the United States
and a "bilateral coordination mechanism" to "harmonize respective activities" in
a crisis. These arrangements are certainly an improvement over the ad hoc and
informal planning that U.S. and Japanese officials used to conduct in anticipation
of regional contingencies. These narrow bureaucratic conduits are essentially
expanded versions of the traditional cold war–era staffs that managed the cabinet-
level Security Consultative Committee, however. This allows the Japanese government to maintain tight control of coordination between the U.S. military and its
uniformed and civilian counterparts in Japan and avoids difficult constitutional
issues related to collective defense, but it is a far cry from the broadly integrated
joint secretariat that real military alliances maintain to allow maximum flexibility
and coordination in a crisis.

Third, effective implementation and decision making in a crisis will now require
Japan to strengthen the authority of the prime minister in times of emergency.
This controversial emergency legislation (yūji hosei) has already won broad support
within the LDP and the Liberal Party and was anticipated in Prime Minister
Hashimoto's 1998 administrative-reform proposals and in the 1999 draft interim
report of the LDP Crisis Management Project Team (Liberal Democratic Party 1999).

Legislation granting emergency powers to the prime minister will not pass easily, but through small changes, such as the creation of a streamlined emergency decision-making group in the cabinet (Kinkyū Jitai Kaishō Kaigi) and the establishment of a crisis-management center in the prime minister's official residence, the government is taking preliminary steps to allow centralized decision making in times of crisis. This centralization is being paralleled by steps among the three branches of the SDF (ground, air, and maritime) to improve jointness, including the first-ever joint exercise on Iwojima in 1998. For the United States, this in turn creates a dilemma. Greater integration and centralization of national command authority in Japan is a prerequisite for smoother bilateral planning and crisis coordination—but it also removes the impediments to independent Japanese action.

Fourth, the Japanese side is looking for a hedge against entrapment in the U.S. strategic decision-making process. Japan and the United States have enhanced intelligence sharing since 1994, and Japan's new Defense Intelligence Headquarters (established in 1996) relies on U.S. Defense Intelligence Agency analysis to enhance its own limited collection capabilities. After the tepid U.S. response to the North Korean Taepodong launch in August 1998, however, the Japanese cabinet moved to develop an indigenous satellite capability, including two optical and two radar satellites to be launched by 2002 and associated ground stations (Wanner 1999, 5).[3] By the spring of 1999, it was clear that Japanese industry did not have the capabilities to meet this goal and that the satellite system would be highly redundant and costly, given assets already available from the United States and on the commercial market ("Japan Finds" 1999). Nevertheless, the project retained broad political support in Japan, both as a measure to support the flagging Japanese aerospace industry and as a gesture of independent capacity to analyze and anticipate crises without having to rely entirely on the United States. The satellite project is a psychological and symbolic hedge rather than a substantive capability to replace the United States, but it does reveal a continuing unease in Japan with total reliance on the United States for security.

Fifth, the U.S. side is also hedging. Japanese missions under the Defense Guidelines are still redundant with planned U.S. capabilities. The U.S. military will not give up its worst-case-planning scenario, and thus the Pentagon continues planning for the possibility that Japanese forces or civilian assets may not be available in a regional crisis. The Defense Guidelines allow bilateral planning for Japanese missions that will significantly enhance the U.S. military's ability to win a victory at less cost in treasure and lives. However, Pentagon planners are not yet ready to replace U.S. rear-area support units on standby for a contingency in East Asia with Japanese units. That will require years of planning, exercises, and above all trust. The U.S. military may not have the luxury to wait much longer, however. As Operation Allied Force demonstrated in Kosovo, the logistical challenges of sustaining the "two major theater war" strategy are stretching U.S. capabilities very thin indeed. Maintaining the combat capabilities of a U.S. forward presence in the future may require turning more rear-area logistical roles over to Japan. That, in turn, will require a greater dependence on Japan and presumably a greater Japanese influence on U.S. regional security strategy.

Finally, technology is forcing the integration of bilateral decision making faster than the Japanese or U.S. governments' ability to anticipate or respond. The "revolution in military affairs" (RMA) concept suggests that the United States will pull ahead of all other states in its ability to design and deploy a "system of systems."[4] U.S. carriers, jet fighters, and ground forces will dominate the information dimension of the battlefield and will be linked through advances in information technology that no rival or ally can match. U.S.-Japan cooperation in TMD gives one example of what this will mean. The two nations agreed to cooperate on research on high-altitude navy theaterwide systems in October 1998. Assuming that these systems are jointly developed and deployed in Japan, the two nations will face a virtually integrated command and control unlike anything experienced in the previous five decades of the alliance. U.S. satellites will give warnings of enemy missile launches to U.S. and Japanese air defense commanders and cue antimissile batteries, all in a matter of minutes. There will be no time for cabinet meetings or independent confirmation through Japanese satellites. The same pattern will hold for intelligence, antisubmarine warfare, and a variety of other missions in the alliance. As the United States pulls ahead in its capabilities to integrate military systems, allies like Japan will have to either plug in to the "system of systems" or lose the advantages of interoperability. The United States, in turn, may be tempted to weaken coordination with Japan as capabilities for unilateral action increase. Technology is exacerbating Japan's dilemma between entrapment and abandonment.

Taken together, these six areas do not suggest that the United States and Japan are developing different national security interests. Instead, the two nations are confronting decisions on integration, interoperability, and jointness that most other alliances resolved decades ago. These growing pains are complicated by changing political cultures, however. The Japanese political elite is gradually embracing the trappings of a "normal" national security apparatus—one that is more centralized and capable of independent action. It is this trend that allowed the Defense Guidelines review in the first place. Some on the U.S. side remain wary of the increased internal cohesion of Japanese security institutions, a sense of mistrust that is reinforced by Japanese hedging strategies such as the independent satellite program. On the whole, however, the changes in Japan's strategic culture represent far more of an opportunity for alliance solidarity than a threat to bilateral cooperation.

The systemic problems in U.S.-Japan military cooperation could be quickly fixed by changes in Japan's Constitution either recognizing the exercise of the right of collective defense or eliminating Article 9 altogether.[5] While there is growing political momentum for reexamining the Constitution, however, these changes are unlikely to occur in the near future. The Japanese public still desires a constitutional check on the role of the SDF, and Japan's neighbors would view significant changes in the constraints on the nation's military role with alarm.[6] The "comprehensive mechanism" and "bilateral coordination mechanism" established by the Defense Guidelines are an incomplete substitute for joint and combined command, but they suffice, given the political realities. Other complementary structures are probably necessary to join the political and operational fibers of the alliance and fill in the gaps that are created by separate command structures. At the political level, the alliance would do well to establish a bilateral parliamentary organization comparable in form (if not authority) to the North Atlantic Assembly, which provides political oversight to NATO. At the operational level, the U.S. and Japanese militaries could create virtual combined commands for humanitarian relief operations or peacekeeping—areas in which Japan's ban on collective defense would not be an impediment and quick joint reaction would be useful. To deal with new technological developments, the United States and Japan would do well to establish a bilateral interagency commission on long-term defense requirements and the impact of the RMA on interoperability.

U.S. Bases in Japan

When three U.S. servicemen raped an Okinawan girl in September 1995 and protests erupted throughout Japan, officials in Washington and Tokyo, as well as governments throughout Asia, watched with deep concern. The roughly forty-seven thousand U.S. troops based in Japan are seen by many in the region as the touchstone for stability in the U.S.-Japan alliance and East Asia as a whole. As an increasingly affluent Japanese public grows uneasy with the presence of U.S. military bases established during the Allied occupation after World War II, the base issue appears ripe for bilateral friction and divergence.

The circumstantial evidence for growing tensions over the bases appears great. To defuse the crisis caused by the 1995 rape, the U.S. government agreed in April 1996 to return the Marine Corps air station at Futenma, one of the most controversial bases in Okinawa. Three years later, Futenma was still crowded with Marine Corps helicopters (though the Special Action Committee on Facilities and Areas in Okinawa [SACO] has had success with smaller base consolidations). Frustration over U.S. bases led the DPJ to float a proposal for establishing a "no-base alliance" (*kichi naki anpo*) (Democratic Party of Japan 1998a, 1998b).

Eventually the party dropped the idea, which was ill formed and futuristic, but the spectacle of Japan's largest opposition party considering a proposal that would eliminate U.S. bases was disconcerting to alliance managers, to say the least.

Frustrated with the DPJ's moderation, former Prime Minister Hosokawa Morihiro went ahead and published a proposal for eliminating all U.S. bases in two years in an article in *Foreign Affairs* in 1998, in which he cited a poll indicating that 67 percent of the Japanese public wanted fewer U.S. bases—a warning that the issue would not go away (Hosokawa 1998, 2). On closer examination, however, it is clear that support for the bases is not dissolving as quickly as suggested by Hosokawa. It is often pointed out, for example, that 89 percent of Okinawan voters supported a 1996 referendum "against" U.S. bases. But that referendum only asked, "Do you agree that the number of U.S. military bases in Okinawa should be reduced?"—something the U.S. and Japanese governments had already agreed to do. Moreover, when former Governor Ōta Masahide refused in March 1997 to extend leases on U.S. bases that were expiring, the Diet passed by 80 percent special legislation overriding the prefectural government's decision. Many of the DPJ politicians who were considering the "no-base alliance" concept voted to maintain the U.S. bases. (Ōta was later defeated in a gubernatorial election by the LDP candidate.) In the end, the polling behind Hosokawa's article, the referendum in Okinawa, and even the DPJ's short-lived "no-base alliance" proposal reflected an *expectation* that U.S. bases would gradually be consolidated, but not broad-based grass-roots opposition to the bases. The growing security problems caused by North Korea and China have seen to it that politicians are aware of the continuing need for a forward U.S. presence in Japan.

It is therefore premature for the United States and Japan to embark on dramatic restructuring of U.S. bases in Japan. Some U.S. experts have advocated cutting the number of Marines in Okinawa, but the costs in terms of capabilities and strategic signaling would more than likely outweigh any political goodwill bought in Japan (O'Hanlon 1997, 147–178). Over the long term, changes in technology—greater strategic airlift capabilities or simulated exercises, for example—will alter the shape of U.S. force structure in Japan. Changes in the strategic environment—unification on the Korean peninsula or resolution of the Taiwan Strait problem, for example—will also have an impact on the size and function of U.S. forces in Japan. For the foreseeable future, however, the costs of major restructuring will outweigh the benefits.

That having been said, the recent contretemps over U.S. bases also suggests that the status quo may not be sustainable without changes in alliance management. A U.S. presence remains as important as ever for Japanese security interests, but the modus operandi of base issues will have to change to converge with an increasingly fluid Japanese political scene and growing Japanese aspirations for control of the modalities of the alliance. Three examples illustrate this point.

First, the United States will have to consult more thoroughly with Japan on the disposition and purposes of U.S. forces in Japan. During the Okinawa crisis, some in the Japanese Foreign Ministry quietly pressed for establishment of a joint consultative mechanism on force structure. The idea was shot down by both governments because such a mechanism would have created dangerous expectations of reductions in U.S. forces, but the essence of the idea remains important.

Second, the SDF face deteriorating facilities as U.S. facilities paid for by Japanese taxpayers continue to improve (Japanese financial support for U.S. forces tops US$5 billion a year). This could easily create tensions between the two militaries. The solution is not to cut back host nation support (HNS) for U.S. forces (though some political decline is inevitable) but to demonstrate greater flexibility, as through greater integration and joint use of SDF and U.S. bases.

Third, the Okinawa crisis revealed that relations between U.S. base commanders and local communities vary widely depending on the discretion of the base commander himself. There is a clear need for systematic improvement of base-community relations, building on the successful examples that now exist around certain facilities. Other steps are also necessary, including completion of the commitments undertaken in SACO.

RELATIONS WITH CHINA

Developments in Northeast Asia since the cold war have raised the value of the U.S.-Japan alliance to both parties. Uncertainties about China's future role, coupled with new reminders about the North Korean threat to regional stability, have resulted in a common strategic context for long-term alliance cooperation even after the demise of the Soviet Union.

Both the United States and Japan want the same things in relations with China: integration into the global economy and international organizations, the establishment of consistent rule of law, peaceful resolution of the Taiwan Strait problem, and reassurance that China will not use force to resolve territorial disputes. Cooperation in achieving these common objectives has been impeded, however, by the increased fluidity in great-power relations in Northeast Asia since the end of the cold war. Japan is taking a far more realistic view of regional security threats than in the past, often responding with assertive unilateral diplomacy that defies U.S. expectations that Japanese diplomacy will continue to be passive or reactive. As a result, shared long-term objectives have sometimes been lost in the bilateral confusion over short-term priorities.

In the case of China, the United States and Japan are adjusting to a complex trilateral relationship. It would be a mistake to label this a "strategic triangle," since the U.S.-Japan leg of the triangle is closely aligned and neither Japan nor the United States is likely to shift toward China any time soon. Nevertheless, it is clear that the actions between two poles of the trilateral relationship are having more of an impact on the third pole than ever before. Few U.S. officials anticipated the negative reactions caused in China by the reaffirmation of the U.S.-Japan alliance in 1996, for example, or in Japan after the Clinton administration highlighted its "strategic partnership" with China in 1998.

During the cold war, the U.S.-Japan alliance faced a simpler equation in relations with China. With the exception of the Taiwan clause in the 1969 Satō-Nixon communiqué, the Japanese side maintained a loose "conscientious objector" status in the first decades of post–World War II Sino-U.S. confrontation. The architect of postwar Japanese diplomacy, Prime Minister Yoshida Shigeru, assumed that with time China would be weaned from the Soviet bloc. Japan withheld normalization until the United States surprised the world by opening dialogue with Beijing in 1972, but through the so-called L-T trade Japan had maintained informal economic relations with the mainland, and after the U.S. opening Japan rushed to normalize relations with Beijing. In turn, China tolerated U.S.-Japan alliance cooperation after the Sino-Soviet split because it served both to complicate Soviet planning and to contain Japanese independent rearmament. Trilateral relations also helped to stabilize U.S.-China relations after the Tiananmen Square Incident soured them in 1989, with Japan playing a bridging role between the other two nations.

The context of the trilateral relationship began changing in the mid-1990s, however. Growing Chinese economic power and assertiveness in regional diplomacy set the context. Elite ties between Beijing and Tokyo also frayed as the architects of normalization in the 1970s in both countries were replaced by a new generation of more nationalistic political leaders. When China conducted a series of nuclear tests in 1995 before joining the Comprehensive Test Ban Treaty, the Japanese Foreign Ministry's efforts to protect foreign aid to China failed as antinuclear activists on the left and anticommunists on the right forced the government to take the unprecedented step of suspending grant aid to Beijing. Beijing's March 1996 missile tests around Taiwan further deepened suspicion of China among Japan's political elite (some missiles landed within 100 kilometers of Okinawa). When the United States and Japan issued the Joint Declaration on Security and announced the review of the Defense Guidelines, the Chinese in turn attacked Japanese militarism and efforts to "contain" China.[7] Sino-Japanese relations took a further dive as the two nations confronted each other on the question of sovereignty over the disputed Senkaku/Diaoyutai Islands in 1997. Their foreign ministries attempted to stabilize relations on the twenty-fifth anniversary of the normalization of relations, declaring 1997 the "year of China" in Japanese diplomacy, but that celebration did not last beyond a disastrous summit between President Jiang Zemin and Prime Minister Obuchi Keizō in November 1998. At that summit, the Chinese insisted on a formal Japanese expression of apology (*owabi*) and remorse (*hansei*), the same formula Obuchi had given to visiting South Korean President Kim Dae Jung the month before. Unlike Kim, however, the Chinese leader was not willing to accept the apology as the final word, insisting on apologies in all future bilateral sessions, as well. As a result, the Chinese received only an expression of remorse. Tellingly, Obuchi received broad support within the Japanese political world and mainstream press. Even the Japan-China Economic Council, guardian of Japan's more than US$3 billion annual investment in China, stood by the prime minister's hard line. In the space of a few years, Japan's view of China had shifted from a faith in economic interdependence to a reluctant realism.

Sino-American relations entered a similarly turbulent era in the mid-1990s. Clinton came into office in 1993 after attacking the George Bush administration for coddling the "butchers of Beijing." The Clinton administration then spent the next eight years trying to achieve its own political equilibrium on China policy. Human rights dominated the agenda at first. Then after the administration allowed Taiwanese President Lee Teng-hui to visit Cornell University in 1995, Beijing's displeasure with U.S. policy on Taiwan caused a new round of crises, most notably the Chinese missile tests of March 1996. Two U.S. aircraft carriers (one, the U.S.S. *Independence*, homeported in Japan) were dispatched to the area of Taiwan in response, to signal U.S. concerns about the Chinese tests. The Clinton administration attempted to recast the domestic U.S. political debate over relations with China in 1997 and 1998 by arguing against a strategy of "containment" (a straw man, since no mainstream politician was calling for that anyway) and trumpeting the objective of establishing a "strategic partnership" with Beijing. The administration had the backing of the U.S. business community, and it had some success during the president's summit in China in June 1998, but the theme of "strategic partnership" obviously oversold the degree of convergent interests in Sino-American relations and dramatically understated the areas of disagreement. Predictably, the administration's China bubble burst, first with the Cox report on Chinese nuclear espionage in the spring of 1999 and then with the accidental bombing of the Chinese embassy in Belgrade during the Kosovo campaign of the same year.

U.S.-Japan alliance coordination has not always kept up as each partner has struggled to find its footing in relations with China. Neither side is eager to give credence to the Chinese charges of containment by openly coordinating China policy, nor is either bureaucracy ready to complicate its own policy-making process by further integrating approaches to Beijing behind the scenes. As a result, miscues and collisions continue to undermine each side's China policy. Following are four examples.

In 1997, the U.S. Department of State announced that it had no position on the territorial dispute between China and Japan over the Senkaku/Diaoyutai Islands. This neutrality was consistent with U.S. policy on third-country territorial disputes. In its efforts to diffuse the situation, however, the State Department went further, declaring that U.S. obligations to defend Japan under Article 5 of the U.S.-Japan Security Treaty did not apply to the Senkakus, a factual error, since technically the islands were under the administration of Japan. Rather than let this technical mistake pass (after all, China was unlikely to use force in the dispute), the Japanese government pressed for a clarification, fearing that the U.S. position would undermine Japan's test of wills with China or encourage nationalists in Japan. The State Department, uneasy about China's reaction, did not budge. Eventually the issue was resolved by a statement by Secretary of Defense William Perry that the treaty did, in fact, apply to the Senkakus.

In the summer of 1997, the Japanese Ministry of Finance proposed a separate Asian Monetary Fund to supplement the International Monetary Fund in responding to future financial crises in Asia. Confident that Asian nations would support the idea and nervous that the United States would not, the Finance Ministry chose to coordinate the proposal with members of the Association of Southeast Asian Nations (ASEAN) but not Washington. When the proposal was unveiled at a meeting of finance officials in Hong Kong in July, the U.S. Department of the Treasury predictably lobbied against the idea, but with an unexpected ally—China.[8] Subsequent Japanese diplomatic initiatives that have not been coordinated in advance with Washington have also gone down to defeat, owing to combined Chinese and U.S. opposition.[9] Japan's attempts to demonstrate independent foreign policy proposals are not always matched by a corresponding effort to win U.S. support in the conceptual phase. Washington often fails to see the consequences of playing into China's strategy of keeping Japan's diplomatic profile low.

Surprised that efforts at transparency have not fully reassured China about the nonthreatening nature of the revised Defense Guidelines, Japanese politicians have also stumbled in their efforts to reassure Beijing independently. From the beginning, the Chinese claimed that the revised guidelines must apply to Taiwan, since Taiwan is included in the traditional Japanese definition of the geographic scope of Article 6 of the Security Treaty. The U.S. and Japanese governments coordinated their response to China's complaints. The guidelines, they stated, were mission outlines, not scenario-specific agreements.[10] This explanation was accurate enough, since the United States has no clear defense commitment to Taiwan and therefore no political mandate to include Japan in formal planning for the defense of the island. The Chinese, however, saw little advantage in conceding the point. Eager to demonstrate his understanding of China and his difference from conservative rivals, LDP Secretary-General Katō Kōichi yielded to

Chinese pressure and announced in Beijing in August 1997 that the new guide-lines would not include Taiwan. This move prompted Katō's rival Chief Cabinet Secretary Kajiyama Seiroku to announce the next day in Tokyo that Taiwan could not be ruled out, since a contingency there could affect Japan's security. The Chinese government seized on that statement as evidence that the U.S.-Japan alliance was now a threat to China's Taiwan policy, significantly complicating U.S. and Japanese defense diplomacy with Beijing ("China Won't Accept" 1997). Needless to say, the Katō and Kajiyama statements strayed from the original talking points of the governments.

Chinese dissatisfaction with the U.S.-Japan alliance has also focused on TMD. Beijing argues that TMD undermines China's limited deterrent and increases the prospect that Japan will develop nuclear weapons, shielding itself with TMD to maintain parity with China (Green 1998, 116–117). More substantively, Beijing worries that TMD will lead to further integration of the U.S.-Japan alliance command structure and possibly extend missile defense cooperation to Taiwan. Beijing's resistance has complicated Japanese participation in TMD, but after the Taepodong missile launch in August 1998 Tokyo found itself ready to agree to joint research with the United States based on the immediate threat presented by North Korean missiles. Years of U.S. prodding and a growing recognition in Japan of the missile threat finally paid off. When TMD cooperation became a pawn in Sino-American nego-tiations shortly afterward, however, it put that progress at risk. Secretary of State Madeleine Albright, following a line established by lower-level officials in the administration, told the Chinese leadership in March 1999 that Japan had not yet made a final decision on TMD and that Chinese efforts to be transparent about its own missile program and to constrain North Korea might yet shape Japan's deci-sion.[11] For opponents of missile defense in the administration, this was a reasonable ploy, but it contradicted years of U.S. (and, increasingly, Japanese) arguments that TMD was a critical mission for the alliance regardless of Beijing's political intentions. Worse, it suggested that critical functions of the U.S.-Japan alliance were open for China to shape, as if there really were an equilateral "strategic triangle" linking Beijing, Tokyo, and Washington. It is difficult to imagine that U.S. officials would describe the missile defense efforts of NATO allies in the same manner.

These four examples do not suggest that U.S. and Japanese interests regarding China are divergent; nor do they suggest that restructuring of the alliance is nec-essary to manage China policy. Indeed, the delicacy of managing U.S.-Japan alliance relations vis-à-vis Beijing is one argument against restructuring the alliance. Significant reductions in U.S. force structure would signal weaker alliance resolve, with a broader impact on U.S. and Japanese diplomacy toward Beijing. Dramatically expanding Japanese offensive military missions or demanding col-lective defense could have the opposite effect of provoking Chinese efforts at bandwagoning against Japan with other concerned states in the region. As an alliance management problem, however, China policy is colossal. While U.S. and Japanese interests are not diverging on China, they are not so convergent that coordination comes naturally. The Japanese side will have to measure more carefully the effectiveness of "independent" diplomatic proposals that lead to joint Sino-American opposition. Coordination with Washington may lead to defeat for some ideas, but it will strengthen others. Ultimately, Japanese diplomacy toward China will be more effective if the United States, South Korea, and other like-minded nations are supportive from the beginning. For its part, Washington must consider carefully the consequences of discouraging Japanese diplomatic initiatives that parallel U.S. efforts to integrate China into the global economy. While fundamental U.S. and Japanese interests in China are largely congruent, containing Japanese leadership aspirations will lead in time to divergent strategies.

THE KOREAN PENINSULA

Long-term U.S. and Japanese objectives regarding the Korean peninsula also tend to converge. These objectives include stability, denuclearization, reduction of the North Korean military threat, and gradual North Korean regime transformation and reconciliation with the South. During the cold war, however, Japanese security relations with the peninsula were largely divorced from the reality of the U.S.-Japan alliance. As Victor Cha has argued, Japan and South Korea were somehow "aligned but not allied" (Cha 1998). Although U.S. bases in Japan had an obvious supporting role in the defense of South Korea, Tokyo spent the decade after the 1969 Satō-Nixon communiqué denying any role or interests in the security of the Korean peninsula. Throughout the 1970s, the Japanese government denied that there was even a North Korean threat to Japan (Murata 1997, 12). This diplomatic "free riding" on U.S.–South Korea deterrence produced deep suspicion in Seoul that Japan was pursuing a separate link with the North to impede unification. In fact, opinion polls suggest that most Japanese are not opposed to unification, and Japan's ties with the North have always been more problematic than those ties with the South.[12] Nevertheless, Japanese overtures to North Korea, such as the 1990 summit between LDP kingpin Kanemaru Shin and North Korean leader Kim Il Sung, only reinforced South Korean suspicions.

Since the mid-1990s, however, Japan's recognition of the North Korean threat and Japanese security interests on the peninsula have grown dramatically. North Korea's 1993 test launch of the Rodong missile (with a range enabling it to hit Osaka) made a strong impression in Tokyo. With the nuclear crisis of 1994, the prospect of Japan's entanglement in a peninsular conflict was reinforced. The nuclear crisis led to unprecedented trilateral diplomatic coordination among

Washington, Tokyo, and Seoul, and in 1995 Japan signaled its readiness to play a role in multilateral security on the peninsula by joining the Korean Peninsula Energy Development Organization (KEDO), which was created to provide light-water reactors (LWRs) to the North under the October 1994 U.S.-North Korea Agreed Framework. At the same time, Japan–North Korea relations soured further with revelations about North Korean abductions of Japanese citizens in the 1970s and 1980s. The August 1998 Taepodong missile launch locked North Korea in to Japanese security thinking as a major threat to peace and stability.

Over the same period, in contrast, U.S. and South Korean engagement of the North gradually expanded. In the Four-Party Talks involving the United States, the two Koreas, and China and in associated bilateral negotiations, the Clinton administration began a diplomatic process it hoped would expand with time. In 1998, newly elected South Korean President Kim Dae Jung reversed decades of confrontational policy toward the North by pushing for a broader process of engagement known as the "Sunshine Policy." Japan, the United States, and South Korea began to reverse roles. From the U.S. and South Korean perspective, it now appeared that Japan's hard line toward Pyongyang was "free riding" on U.S. and South Korean engagement with the North. Washington and Seoul pressed Tokyo to contribute food aid to the North, to maintain its commitment to KEDO, and to move forward with normalization talks with Pyongyang.[13] Japan's KEDO commitment became a particular concern after the Obuchi administration unilaterally suspended its participation in the LWR funding talks in the immediate wake of the Taepodong launch. Meanwhile, the Japanese side grew distressed at Washington's and Seoul's apparent disregard of the North Korean missile threat, particularly after the U.S. government negotiated an "acceleration" of the schedule for the LWR the week after the missile launch.[14]

The diverging U.S., Japanese, and South Korean priorities on missiles, proliferation, and engagement of the North threatened to undermine all three nations' diplomacy vis-à-vis the peninsula. It was clear to South Korean President Kim that Japan had an important security role to play on the peninsula through KEDO and could be obstructionist if not fully consulted. He took dramatic steps to improve relations with Japan, culminating in a summit meeting with Prime Minister Obuchi in October 1998 that produced a joint declaration titled "A New Japan–Republic of Korea Partnership towards the Twenty-first Century." Among other things, the declaration resolved long-standing fisheries disputes, presented a formula whereby Japan expressed and South Korea accepted its apology and remorse for the past, and proposed future mechanisms for closer security consultations (Ministry of Foreign Affairs 1998). This in turn eased the prospects for trilateral security consultations and coordination with the United States. When former Secretary of Defense William Perry was appointed by the Clinton administration to review U.S. policy toward the Korean peninsula in the fall of 1998, he used his position to schedule regular trilateral consultations with senior representatives from Japan and South Korea. When he traveled to Pyongyang in June 1999, he was able to present messages from Obuchi and Kim to the North, in addition to a comprehensive U.S. package of diplomatic proposals that reflected the integrated U.S.-Japan–South Korea approach. Perry also established an unprecedented standing trilateral committee with Japan and South Korea to facilitate an integrated strategy in future dealings with the North.[15]

The United States, Japan, and South Korea share broad objectives regarding the peninsula but differ in priorities. Japan will always be more concerned about missiles than the United States or South Korea. The United States is likely to retain the highest vigilance of the three on North Korea's potential to resume a nuclear weapons program. South Korea, at least under Kim, has embarked on a policy of engagement that moves well beyond what the political constraints in Washington and Tokyo allow. These divergent priorities mean that policy coordination will always be difficult. Nevertheless, divergent domestic political priorities in the three nations will be easier to manage if their governments are working from a common long-term strategy. The trilateral consultative processes started in 1998 are a good start. Are they enough? Given that any formal U.S-Japan–South Korea security pact or institutionalized defense arrangement would provoke a Chinese (and possibly domestic South Korean) backlash, the current arrangements are preferable to a restructuring of the trilateral security relationship. It is noteworthy, however, that the U.S. side only elevated trilateral security cooperation with Japan and South Korea after the Taepodong crisis threatened Japanese support for KEDO. Future inducements for North Korea to abandon missiles, nuclear weapons, or conventional military forces will also require Japanese funding. Tokyo, in other words, has a stake in Korean peninsula policy that Washington cannot ignore. Nevertheless, the historic North-South summit in June 2000 will add a new fluidity and complexity to U.S.-Japan coordination on Korea policy. Tokyo did not greet the summit with the same euphora as Seoul, but did move forward on normalization talks with the North. Skepticism, nevertheless, remains deep in Japan because of the issues related to missiles, kidnappings, and nuclear weapons. The North-South process of reconciliation opens up great opportunities for threat reduction on the peninsula—but also new challenges for alliance planning and diplomatic coordination.

MULTILATERAL SECURITY COOPERATION

The final area of alliance cooperation this study briefly examines is multilateral security. The April 1996 Joint Declaration on Security highlighted cooperation in regional multilateral security forums as a key theme for the United States and

Japan in the next century. In contrast, multilateral security was portrayed by editorials and news analyses in the *Asahi Shimbun* newspaper at the time as an antidote to too much reliance on the U.S.-Japan Security Treaty.[16] Which is it?

The broader answer, of course, is that multilateral security dialogue in East Asia should not conflict with the security arrangements between the United States and Japan. In fact, the revision of the Defense Guidelines led Washington and Tokyo to expand minilateral defense forums with South Korea and Russia and to provide greater transparency in the ASEAN Regional Forum (ARF) and track-two regional security forums, such as the Council for Security Cooperation in Asia Pacific.[17] Ironically, the need to explain the guidelines strengthened multilateral security dialogue. Moreover, the level of security cooperation in the ARF is still so basic that there is little likelihood it will replace any functions of the U.S.-Japan alliance. The ARF has not moved beyond the baseline of "dialogue" to establish any significant confidence- and security-building measures, let alone a collective security regime that might replace the stabilizing role played by the U.S.-Japan alliance. Both Washington and Tokyo are eager to see the dialogue function of the ARF strengthened, but neither can take the lead without causing suspicion among the ASEAN states that lie at the core of the ARF. The ARF will move at ASEAN's pace. It serves a useful function by enhancing dialogue among Asia Pacific powers. But at most it will complement rather than replace the U.S.-Japan alliance as the key security institution for Washington and Tokyo in Asia.

The United Nations provides a somewhat different case. The United States and Japan diverge in U.N. policy in the sense that Japan continues to pay its dues and aspire to a larger role, including permanent membership on the Security Council, while Congressional ambivalence about the world body has prevented the U.S. government from paying its arrears (and thus the United States faced the loss of its vote in the General Assembly in 1999). Capricious U.S. policy toward the U.N. complicates Japanese diplomacy, since the U.N. remains central to Japan's definition of its world role. Thus, Tokyo expressed "support" for U.S. force against Iraq based on a U.N. mandate in December 1998 but only "understanding" of NATO's use of force against Kosovo, which was not based on a U.N. mandate. On the whole, however, U.S.-Japan cooperation at the United Nations is strong. Even in the case of Kosovo, the Obuchi government pledged US$200 million to assist the "front line" states, indirectly supporting U.S. policy even in the absence of a U.N. mandate.

There are limits to how far allies can cooperate in multilateral security forums, particularly in Asia. For one thing, such cooperation can breed mistrust among the other states, jeopardizing the further institutionalization of such forums as the ARF. In addition, it is in the U.S. interest not to undermine Japanese diplomatic influence in the region by "bilateralizing" all Japan's new multilateral security policies. Many in Japan remain sensitive to the possibility that Washington will try to constrain or control Japan's peacekeeping role within the alliance, and for that reason the SDF have been reluctant to include peacekeeping as a major area for alliance cooperation. Peacekeeping is a legitimate and important area for independent Japanese contributions to the global community. Nevertheless, Japanese procurement of airlift and sealift for peacekeeping will be closely watched in Washington and throughout the region, and for certain peacekeeping requirements (long-range airlift, for example) there are definite advantages for the SDF in cooperating with U.S. forces.

On the whole, therefore, multilateral security regimes in Asia are still too immature either to cause bilateral divergence or to become a central component of U.S.-Japan security cooperation. Both the United States and Japan have advantages to gain from stronger regional multilateral dialogue, but the difference between Japanese idealism and American skepticism on the subject should not be mistaken for actual differences in interests.

Conclusions

This essay began by asking whether the tensions in the alliance represent repetitions of past patterns or a trend that will intensify with time and whether the alliance needs restructuring or just better management to cope with these patterns. Some historical comparison is necessary to answer the first question. It would be difficult to argue, for example, that the bilateral disagreements over Japan's indigenous satellite program in 1999 are worse than the huge 1989 confrontation over Japan's plan to develop its own jet fighter, the FSX, or that bilateral dissonance over Korean peninsula policy was any louder in 1998 (when Japan was the hawk) than in 1978 (when Japan was the dove). The source of the dissonance is different, however. The growing realism in Japanese security thinking and fluidity in Japanese politics mean that there are now greater consequences when the United States fails to address Japanese concerns about national security. With time, U.S. inattention could establish a dynamic that does harm to the alliance. On the other hand, the growth of Japanese strategic realism presents an opportunity to strengthen and integrate alliance security cooperation.

The second question also requires a mixed answer. It can be argued that the alliance is unprepared to withstand certain shocks without significant and fundamental restructuring. For example, can Japan be relied on to support the United States in a Taiwan Strait crisis without a formal commitment beforehand? Would the burgeoning U.S.-Japan–South Korea coordination prove resilient enough to weather the collapse of North Korea without a larger Japanese military role on the peninsula? Will SACO or other measures to reduce the impact of U.S. bases in Japan insulate the alliance against a major military accident in

Okinawa? The United States and Japan could restructure the alliance in anticipation of such crises. For example, the United States could push Japan to accept an explicit role in the defense of Taiwan or to apply the right of collective defense to a frontline combat role on the Korean peninsula. The United States and Japan could also cut U.S. force levels in Japan by half to buy goodwill from the Japanese population in case something went wrong at a U.S. military base.

The problem with each of these structural solutions is that the cost of the insurance policy is too high. An explicit Japanese commitment to assist the United States with the defense of Taiwan could be useful during a Taiwan crisis with China—but it could also provoke one. Similarly, Japanese acceptance of a combat role on the Korean peninsula would provide extra forces in a crisis, but in the near term it would undermine diplomatic efforts on the Korean peninsula and the progress that has been made in Japan–South Korean ties. Finally, moves to cut back U.S. force levels in Japan might or might not build goodwill in the event of future crises over bases, but it would definitely hinder the U.S. ability to respond to a crisis in the region and would be likely to undermine stability by raising questions throughout the region about U.S. staying power.

Changes in the structure of the U.S.-Japan alliance have always been incremental. The current trend toward strategic realism in Japanese security policy creates an opportunity for more changes, but the undertow of pacifism in Japan is strong, and the region's acceptance of a larger Japanese security role is only just taking root. Strategically, it is difficult to argue that regional stability or U.S. and Japanese interests would be enhanced by changing the configuration of the alliance to give Japan a military role more symmetrical with that of the United States.

At the same time, however, this essay has argued in each case study that incremental changes in the alliance continue to be necessary. Many of these changes should come in the mechanics of alliance management, including the following:

- implementation of crisis-management authority for the Japanese prime minister
- establishment of a bilateral parliamentary assembly to oversee the alliance
- establishment of combined and joint bilateral operational centers for humanitarian operations
- establishment of a bilateral requirements dialogue to assess long-term equipment needs and the impact of the RMA
- greater U.S. attention to base-community relations
- flexibility regarding the amount and use of HNS
- greater integration of U.S. and SDF bases
- better coordination and planning of each side's China and Korean peninsula policies

- further institutionalization of the U.S.–Japan–South Korea policy consultation process
- U.S. support for Japanese initiatives in multilateral security

The alliance also requires a better management philosophy. In this area, most of the burden is on the U.S. government, which has not maintained sufficient high-level coordination with the Japanese side. In the Clinton administration, Japanese security issues were managed primarily by deputy assistant secretaries in Washington, while U.S. security policy issues were managed by vice-ministers and even prime ministers in Tokyo. This particular asymmetry in the bilateral relationship is simply not sustainable. The alliance will become less than the sum of its parts unless strategic direction is consistently set at senior levels of both governments.

The U.S.-Japan alliance is based on broadly shared strategic objectives and a generally complementary division of roles and missions. But these attributes do not guarantee the continued health of bilateral security relations. Like a shark that will drown if it does not move forward, the U.S.-Japan alliance requires constant attention, strengthening, and integration.

NOTES

1. The three nonnuclear principles are not to produce, possess, or permit the introduction to Japanese territory of nuclear weapons. The three principles of arms export are not to export weapons to communist countries, countries under U.N.-mandated arms embargoes, or countries currently or likely in the near future to be embroiled in military conflicts.

2. The official was speaking on the record at "The Nixon Shocks and U.S.-Japanese Relations, 1969–1976," a symposium sponsored by the Asia Program of the Woodrow Wilson International Center for Scholars and the U.S-Japan Project of the National Security Archive, March 11, 1996, Washington, D.C.

3. Some analysts see this satellite capability as a potential source of tension in the alliance (Ennis 1999, 10).

4. For details of the RMA concept, see Office of the Secretary of Defense (1998, 16–17); Nye and Owens (1996); Binnedjiik and Clawson (1997, 3).

5. Article 9, which renounces "war as a sovereign right of the nation and the threat or use of force as a means of settling international disputes" and the maintenance of "war potential," is the basis of the government's stance that Japan cannot exercise the right of collective defense.

6. The Diet established a research commission on constitutional issues in 1999, and opinion polls as recently as 1998 show that a majority of Japanese now favor revising the Constitution. Only a minority favor eliminating Article 9, however.

7. In fact, the Joint Declaration on Security and the Defense Guidelines review had been planned for the previous fall and were announced after the Taiwan Strait crisis only because President Clinton had postponed his visit to Japan from November 1995 to April 1996.

8. For a detailed account, see "Insaido Ajia tsūka kikin" (1997).

9. These initiatives include Tokyo's June 1998 proposal of a four-way security summit

of the United States, Japan, China, and Russia and its June 1998 proposal of a meeting of the five permanent members of the U.N. Security Council plus Japan and Germany to address Indian and Pakistani nuclear tests.

10. See, for example, comments by Deputy Assistant Secretary of Defense for Asia Pacific Affairs Kurt Campbell (Green and Mochizuki 1997, 85).

11. U.S. officials denied a quid pro quo, but Albright stated clearly to Chinese officials that Chinese help to reduce missile threats in Asia would render a TMD system with Japan less necessary (Laris 1999).

12. In 1995, the thirtieth anniversary of the normalization of relations between Japan and South Korea, the *Yomiuri Shimbun* (Japan) and *Hangkuk Ilbo* (South Korea) newspapers polled Japanese about unification and found that fewer than a fifth thought it would pose a problem for Japan.

13. The Japanese government suspended funding, but some politicians wanted to go further. Some called for cutting off economic ties between Korean residents in Japan and compatriots in Pyongyang; others even called for the unilateral right to retaliate against the North for missile strikes (Chang 1998).

14. The September 5 agreement was announced in a statement by the State Department on September 11, 1998 (U.S.-DPRK Agreement, Department of State, September 10, 1998).

15. The trilateral meetings became a regular feature of U.S., Japanese, and South Korean diplomacy toward the North in 1999, though the future of the trilateral process beyond the Perry review was not institutionalized (Shin 1999).

16. A typical example is an analytical piece in the *Asahi Shimbun* on September 24, 1997, titled "Shūhenkoku no keikai maneku osore, Bei no dōmeimō ni keisha Nichi-Bei no shin bōei shishin" (Regional powers warn of U.S. alliance net and new guidelines). The analysis, by an *Asahi* editorial writer, calls for Japan to turn to multilateral approaches to security instead of relying on the U.S.-Japan alliance alone.

17. This approach is explained in Office of the Secretary of Defense (1998).

BIBLIOGRAPHY

Berger, Thomas. 1993. "From Sword to Chrysanthemum: Japan's Culture of Anti-militarism." *International Security* 17(4): 119-150.

Binnedjiik, Hans, and Patrick Clawson, eds. 1997. 1997 *Strategic Assessment: Flashpoints and Force Structure*. Washington, D.C.: Institute for National Security Studies.

Cha, Victor D. 1998. *Alignment despite Antagonism: The United States, Korea, Japan Security Triangle*. Palo Alto, Calif.: Stanford University Press.

Chang, Yvonne. 1998. "Angry Japan Sets Measures against North Korea." Reuters dispatch 1 September.

"China Won't Accept Taiwan in U.S.-Japan Alliance." 1997. Reuters dispatch 22 August.

Democratic Party of Japan. 1998a. "Our Basic Philosophy and Policies: Building a Free and Secure Society." Tokyo: Democratic Party of Japan.

———. 1998b. *Reisengo no atarashii anzen hoshō e no mosaku* (Grasping for a new national security after the cold war). Report of Project 2010. Tokyo: Democratic Party of Japan.

Ennis, Peter. 1999. "FSX x 10." *Oriental Economist* (April): 4.

Giarra, Paul S. 1999. "U.S. Bases in Japan: Historical Background and Innovative Approaches to Maintaining Strategic Presence." In Michael J. Green and Patrick M. Cronin, eds. *The U.S.-Japan Alliance: Past, Present and Future*. New York: Council on Foreign Relations.

Giarra, Paul S., and Akihisa Nagashima. 1999. "Structures and Mechanisms to Address Post–Cold War Requirements." In Michael J. Green and Patrick M. Cronin, eds. *The U.S.-Japan Alliance: Past, Present and Future*. New York: Council on Foreign Relations.

Green, Michael. 1998. "Theater Missile Defense and Strategic Relations with the People's Republic of China." In Ralph A. Cossa, ed. *Restructuring the U.S.-Japan Alliance*. Washington, D.C.: Center for Strategic and International Studies.

Green, Michael, and Mike Mochizuki. 1997. *The U.S.-Japan Security Alliance in the Twenty-first Century*. Study Group Papers. New York: Council on Foreign Relations.

Hosokawa Morihiro. 1998. "Are U.S. Troops in Japan Needed?" *Foreign Affairs* 77(4): 2–5.

"Insaido Ajia tsūka kikin" (Inside the Asian Monetary Fund). 1997. *Mainichi Shimbun* (28 September, morning edition): 2.

"Japan Finds That Creating a Spy Satellite System Is Not So Simple." 1999. *Japan Digest* (8 June): 1.

Katzenstein, Peter. 1996. *Cultural Norms and National Security: Police and Military in Postwar Japan*. Ithaca, N.Y.: Cornell University Press.

Laris, Michael. 1999. "Albright Debates Human Rights with Top Chinese Officials." *Washington Post* (2 March).

Liberal Democratic Party, Policy Affairs Research Council. 1999. *Kiki kanri purojekuto chīmu hōkoku (an)* (Draft interim report of the Crisis Management Team). 3 June.

Ministry of Foreign Affairs. 1998. "Japan–Republic of Korea Joint Declaration: A New Japan–Republic of Korea Partnership towards the Twenty-first Century." 8 October.

Murata Kōji. 1997. "The Origins and the Evolution of the U.S.-ROK Alliance from a Japanese Perspective." Conference on America's Alliances with Japan and Korea in a Changing Northeast Asia. Stanford University, Palo Alto, Calif. 21–23 August.

Nye, Joseph, and William Owens. 1996. "The Information Edge." *Foreign Affairs* 75(2): 20–36.

Oberdorfer, Don. 1998. *The Two Koreas: A Contemporary History*. New York: Basic Books.

Office of the Secretary of Defense. 1998. *United States Security Strategy for the East Asia–Pacific Region 1998*. Washington, D.C.: Department of Defense.

O'Hanlon, Michael. 1997. "Restructuring U.S. Forces and Bases in Japan." In Mike Mochizuki, ed. *Toward a True Alliance: Restructuring U.S.-Japan Security Relations*. Washington, D.C.: Brookings Institution.

Shin Jae Hoon. 1999. "Perry's Progress: U.S. Envoy Breaks the Ice in North Korea." *Far Eastern Economic Review* (10 June): 22.

Wanner, Barbara. 1999. *Japan's Push to Develop Spy Satellites Presents New Challenges to Bilateral Armaments Cooperation*. JEI Report 21A. Washington, D.C.: Japan Economic Institute.

The International Context of U.S.-Japan Relations in the 1990s

Tanaka Akihiko

THE PURPOSE OF THIS CHAPTER IS TO ANALYZE the international context of U.S.-Japan relations in the 1990s. As is often said, the end of the cold war was not as dramatic in East Asia as in Western Europe. There were no incidents comparable to the fall of the Berlin Wall or the collapse of the communist regimes in Eastern Europe. Indeed, some argue that the cold war is not quite over in East Asia even now. Hostilities and ideological differences persist in various parts of Asia, resulting in the ongoing division of countries, as in the case of the two Koreas, as well as China and Taiwan.

The end of the cold war, however, was significant even in Asia. The collapse of the Soviet Union changed the strategic landscape in the region by bringing about a radical reduction of Soviet military power in East Asia and in the western Pacific. The end of the cold war also changed the international environment for such countries as North Korea, which had depended heavily on the Soviet Union for its oil supply and other assistance. Furthermore, the end of the cold war affected the psychological landscape of major countries in the region; the disappearance of a major threat created a psychological vacuum in which people's perceptions of threats can become very unstable.

The end of the cold war was not the only significant change that affected international relations in East Asia in the 1990s, however. At least two other major trends should be recognized: democratization and globalization. Democratization was a foreign phenomenon in East Asia until the 1980s; Japan was virtually the only country that was practicing liberal democracy at that time. But the 1980s witnessed rapid democratization in the Philippines, South Korea, Taiwan, and Thailand. Although not a precise match, the end of the cold war more or less coincided with the advent of democratization in East Asia. But in contrast to the

European experience, Asian democratization was taking place not in the old communist bloc countries but in countries allied with the United States.

The second important trend in East Asia was globalization, defined in large measure by the rapid and increasing movement of capital across borders. As a result of the Group of Seven (G7) Plaza Accord of 1985 and the subsequent strengthening of the yen, a huge amount of capital flowed into East Asian countries in the form of direct investment, thus enabling many countries in the region to leapfrog in economic growth. By the beginning of the 1990s, a growing number of economists and business people were talking about the "Asian economic miracle." The late 1990s, in turn, reminded the people of Asia that globalization could not only create conditions of rapid growth but also jolt fragile political-economic systems.

In other words, the international context of U.S.-Japan relations in the 1990s was substantively different from that of previous eras, and therefore serves as an important backdrop for bilateral relations between the two countries. This chapter is not an attempt to pass judgement from any specific, widely debated theoretical perspective—be it realist, liberal, constructivist, or otherwise.[1] The purpose is more modest: The chapter tries to point out various aspects of international relations important to understanding the current conditions surrounding the U.S.-Japan relationship. To do so, I would like to turn my attention first to the problems manifested on the surface; second, to the dynamics of perceptions among major powers; and third, to the diplomatic activities that were being conducted both multilaterally and bilaterally during the 1990s. It is the assertion of this chapter that an analysis of these various dimensions in relation to the underlying structural trends should offer useful insight into the international context of the U.S.-Japan relationship.

TEN YEARS OF CRISIS IN EAST ASIA

If peace is taken to mean a condition where no wars are being waged between countries, then East Asia in the 1990s has been extremely peaceful. Since the settlement of the Cambodian conflict in 1991, no interstate wars have been fought in the region. In fact, it was 1979 when the last new war, the Sino-Vietnamese War, broke out in East Asia. This condition of peace, however, does not mean that the region is extremely stable or devoid of the possibility of future wars. On the contrary, a series of crises have served as a constant reminder to the people in the region that they live in an area where the possibility of war cannot be ruled out. Setting aside some minor conflicts, the region experienced essentially three series of crises in the 1990s: the Korean crisis, the Taiwan Strait Crisis, and the financial crisis. All three have their own historical dynamic and therefore demand a more nuanced treatment to be fully understood. For the purpose of clarifying the international context of U.S.-Japan relations, however, I would like to focus on explaining each series of events in relation to the structural trends that affected East Asia in the 1990s.

The Korean Crisis

The 1990s saw two periods of crisis on the Korean peninsula: the first in 1993–1994, and the second in 1998–1999. The former was mainly related to suspected North Korean nuclear weapons production, while the latter was concerned both with the suspected resumption of the North Korean nuclear program and the country's ballistic missile production.

North Korea signed the Nuclear Non-Proliferation Treaty (NPT) in 1985, but it did not conclude a safeguards agreement with the International Atomic Energy Agency (IAEA), thereby creating a very strong suspicion from 1989 on that Pyongyang might have extracted sufficient amounts of weapons-grade plutonium to produce a few nuclear bombs.[2] North Korea argued subsequently that it would not accept IAEA inspections as long as U.S. nuclear weapons existed in South Korea. However, the initiative of the Bush administration to withdraw all nuclear weapons from South Korea by the end of 1991 served as an impetus to improve relations between South Korea and North Korea. This paved the way for the signing of the Agreement on Reconciliation, Nonaggression and Exchanges and Cooperation between South Korea and North Korea on December 13, 1991, and the Joint Declaration on the Denuclearization of the Korean Peninsula on December 31, and North Korea's signing of the safeguards agreement with the IAEA on January 30, 1992.

The optimism created by these agreements turned out to be premature; visits by IAEA inspectors to North Korea in 1992 generated more suspicions than reassuring facts. In February 1993, the IAEA demanded a "special inspection" of suspected sites in Yongbyon, which North Korea had not declared as nuclear-related facilities. In response to this demand, North Korea announced in mid-March its intention of withdrawing from the NPT. As a result of last-minute negotiations between Americans and North Koreans in New York, North Korea agreed to postpone its withdrawal from the NPT in return for American willingness to give security assurances to North Korea and to continue official dialogue. Subsequent grueling negotiations, however, did not produce any optimistic signs, and, instead, the Korean peninsula in 1994 faced its most serious crisis since the Korean War armistice was signed in 1953.

It became clear by April 1994 that North Korean obstruction both at the negotiating table and in the field was making the IAEA inspections virtually impossible. In mid-April, North Korea announced that it would remove spent fuel rods from its five-megawatt reactor, thus heightening the sense of crisis. If all 8,000 rods were unloaded, North Korea would be able to erase the past records, thus making it impossible to verify how much plutonium had been extracted in 1989, when Pyongyang stopped the operation of the reactor for a short period of time. In addition, and more seriously, the country would be able to accumulate enough plutonium for several nuclear bombs.

International observers and decisionmakers in Washington were considering strong sanctions to stop North Korea, but the Pyongyang government warned of the possibility that Seoul would be engulfed in a "sea of fire" if measures were imposed. The United States began serious planning for a large-scale military operation on the Korean peninsula. According to a Pentagon estimate made at that time, if a war broke out, "it would cost 52,000 U.S. military casualties, killed or wounded, and 490,000 South Korean military casualties in the first ninety days, plus an enormous number of North Korean and civilian lives, at a financial outlay exceeding [US]$61 billion" (Oberdorfer 1997, 315).

What defused this crisis was a visit by former U.S. President Jimmy Carter in mid-June; Kim Il Sung agreed not to place new fuel rods in the five-megawatt reactor and not to reprocess the unloaded spent rods. Despite the death of Kim Il Sung the following month, North Korea agreed to hold negotiations with the United States on the basis of the Carter-Kim agreement, which led to the Geneva Agreement of October 21, 1994. According to a summary by Don Oberdorfer (1997, 357), the basic features of this so-called Agreed Framework between the United States and North Korea included the following:

- The United States would organize an international consortium to provide light-water reactors (LWRs), with a total generating capacity of 2,000 megawatts, by a target date of 2003. In return, North Korea would freeze all activity on its existing nuclear reactors and related facilities, and permit them to be continuously monitored by IAEA inspectors. The 8,000 fuel rods unloaded from the first reactor would be shipped out of the country.

- North Korea would come into full compliance with the IAEA—which meant accepting the "special inspections"—before the delivery of key nuclear components of the LWR project, estimated to be within five years. North Korea's existing nuclear facilities would be completely dismantled by the time the LWR project was completed, which was estimated to be in ten years.

- The United States would arrange to supply 500,000 tons of heavy fuel oil annually to make up for energy forgone by North Korea before the LWRs came into operation.

- The two states would reduce existing barriers to trade and investment and open diplomatic liaison offices in each other's capitals as initial steps toward eventual full normalization of relations. The United States would provide formal assurances against the threat or use of nuclear weapons against North Korea.

• North Korea would implement the 1991 North-South joint declaration on the demilitarization of the Korean peninsula and reengage in North-South dialogue.[3]

Based on this agreement, the Korean Peninsula Energy Development Organization (KEDO) was created in March 1995, and after further grueling negotiations over the details, it commenced operation in August 1997. It was hoped that, as a result of the Agreed Framework and the establishment of KEDO, the North Korean crisis would finally be over. Subsequent developments, however, proved that this hope was again premature.

As a result of floods in the summers of both 1995 and 1996, North Korea experienced terrible famines from 1995 to 1997. South Korea, Japan, the United States, and other countries concerned about the North Korean military threat were now confronted with a country that was asking for international emergency aid while at the same time displaying erratic and menacing behavior in a number of instances—North Korean soldiers intruded into the Demilitarized Zone (DMZ) in April 1995, for example, and a North Korean submarine was discovered in South Korean coastal waters in September 1996. Furthermore, in the summer of 1998, serious suspicions of a North Korean violation of the Agreed Framework emerged when U.S. reconnaissance discovered a huge underground facility that could be used for nuclear development in Kumchang-ni, 40 kilometers northwest of Yongbyon. A few weeks after the revelation of that suspicious site, on August 31, North Korea launched a Taepodong 1 missile over Japan. The Japanese media and public were shocked by the revelation that North Korea had developed the capability to attack the entire territory of Japan. Although North Korea had previously demonstrated that at least the western part of Japan was within its range by launching a Nodong missile in 1993, the degree of shock elicited among the Japanese public by the launch of the Taepodong missile was incomparable.

The next year closely resembled the crisis diplomacy pattern of 1994: The United States demanded an inspection of Kumchang-ni while North Korea demanded financial compensation in return for such an inspection. After North Korea allowed a May 1999 "visit" of U.S. specialists to Kumchang-ni, where they found only huge, empty holes, North Korea made preparations to launch another Taepodong missile. However, through a series of negotiations conducted in Berlin, North Korea agreed not to proceed with the missile launch as long as it was engaged in negotiations with the United States.

The end of 1999 saw some signs of greater openness and flexibility on Pyonyang's part. This can probably be attributed to three factors: the review of U.S.

policy toward North Korea that was conducted by former Secretary of Defense William Perry; Kim Dae Jung's policy of "engagement" (known as the "Sunshine Policy"); and successful coordination among the United States, South Korea, and Japan. Nonetheless, given the underlying problems in North Korean society, it would hardly be surprising if another crisis should arise in the near future.

It is impossible in this chapter to fully explain the causes of this North Korean crisis; many complex factors have come into play. But among those various factors, I would argue that the end of the cold war has been the most important underlying structural cause. The end of the cold war in East Asia has not brought about the termination of hostilities on the Korean peninsula, but it has clearly affected North Korea's political and economic conditions. Nuclear development and ballistic missile development programs were conceived of in North Korea before the end of the cold war. But the need for a strategic counterweight against the United States has been amplified with the disappearance of the Soviet security support. Furthermore, the collapse of the Soviet Union and the subsequent termination of economic assistance have created a disastrous economic plight for a country without hard currency or energy resources. Ballistic missile development has undoubtedly also become attractive as a means to gain hard currency. The economic disaster that was triggered by the end of the cold war in turn has heightened the basic instability of the North Korean government. While it may not lead to the collapse of the regime, the economic crisis might tempt them to conduct erratic international actions that could destabilize security conditions in East Asia. In other words, as long as the basic tenets of the North Korean political-economic system created during the cold war— i.e., a highly authoritarian (and feudalistic) political economy that can function only by depending on outside support—do not change, the crisis surrounding North Korea will persist. In East Asia, clearly the legacy of the cold war and the impact of the end of the cold war are nowhere more conspicuous than in North Korea.

The Taiwan Strait Crisis

The Taiwan Strait has been a constant source of international concern since 1949, when the Kuomingtang (KMT) forces under Chiang Kai-shek fled from mainland China after their defeat by the Communist forces there. Following the outbreak of the Korean War, President Harry Truman ordered the Seventh Fleet to the Taiwan Strait to prevent military activity there. In order to dissuade Chiang from taking advantage of the Korean hostilities to reopen the Chinese civil war, and to deter a Communist invasion of Taiwan, the United States declared a policy of "neutralization" of the Strait. This policy effectively succeeded in preventing the Communists and the KMT from launching major attacks on each other.

In December 1954, however, the United States abandoned that policy when it concluded the U.S.–Republic of China Mutual Defense Treaty. By then, it had become clear that the KMT did not have the capability of launching a major attack on the mainland, and thus there was no longer a need for a "neutralization" policy. Instead, the U.S. guarantee of Taiwan's security has prevented any major war over the Taiwan Strait since then.

While military attacks have been avoided, however, the People's Republic of China and Taiwan continued to compete for the position of the sole and legitimate government of China for the more than four decades from 1949 until the early 1990s. Up until 1971, the year of the so-called Nixon shock and the admittance of the People's Republic to the United Nations, Japan had recognized Taiwan as the legitimate government of China, but from 1972 it switched to the People's Republic.[4] The United States made a similar shift in 1979.[5] Although the loss of recognition from Japan and the United States represented a tremendous blow to the Taiwan government, it did not give up its claim of representing all of China. It was in fact this consensus between Taiwan and the People's Republic on the existence of a single China—despite their differing opinions on where the legitimate government of that one China resides—that led the United States to declare in the 1972 Shanghai communiqué that it "acknowledges that all Chinese on either side of the Taiwan Strait maintain there is but one China and that Taiwan is a part of China" (Kajima Heiwa Kenkyūjo 1985, 534).

Significant changes have taken place in Taiwan since the 1970s.[6] Chiang Ching-kuo, son of Chiang Kai-shek, started a process of gradual democratization in the mid-1980s. The first legalized opposition party, the Democratic Progressive Party (DPP), whose members argued for the independence of Taiwan, was formed in 1986. In 1987, martial law, which had been the legal basis of the authoritarian rule of the KMT, was lifted. After the death of Chiang Ching-kuo in January 1988, Lee Teng-hui, a native Taiwanese (*benshengren*), succeeded him as the chairman of the KMT and the president of Taiwan. The first election of the Legislative Yuan after the lifting of martial law was held in December 1989, at which time the DPP candidates and others who argued for independence won a considerable number of seats. In 1991, the National Assembly undertook an extensive revision of the Constitution to democratize the political system. The revision included the abolishment of clauses that applied specifically to the period of the "civil war," thus formally ending the previous stance that regarded the People's Republic as Taiwan's enemy.

It seems ironic that this change of attitude, which the leaders of the mainland welcomed, turned out to be the beginning of future tensions. As President Lee began diplomatic efforts to cultivate relations with many countries around the world, he applied a new line of reasoning: Taiwan, since it was no longer engaged in a "civil war," should hold a more normal status in international society. This line of argument eventually led to his description in 1999 of the cross-strait relationship as a "special state-to-state relationship."[7] In fact, since 1991, the opposition DPP started campaigns to rejoin the United Nations, and included in the party charter a platform demanding the independence of Taiwan. President Lee never explicitly mentioned independence as a necessary course of action. But in a democratic society where the Taiwanese people had begun to increasingly demand that their views be heard, he needed to devise policies that would satisfy the people and that would help get him reelected when the first legitimate democratic presidential elections were held in March 1996.

President Lee's attendance in June 1995 at the commencement ceremony of his alma mater, Cornell University, triggered a spiral of tensions between the mainland on the one hand and Taiwan and the United States on the other. As a result of Lee's visit, the Chinese became suspicious both of Lee and the United States. Although the Clinton administration had previously implied to Beijing that it would not grant a visa to Lee, it acquiesced in the end to the demands of the U.S. Congress, both houses of which passed nearly unanimous (non-binding) resolutions to allow Lee's visit. Should it become a precedent, worried Beijing, Lee would be able to travel to any country, including those having no diplomatic relations with Taiwan.

What was even more worrying to Beijing, however, was the potential outcome of the March 1996 presidential election, since a victory by a DPP candidate who argued for a more independent course would be a nightmare. Thus, Beijing launched experimental missiles near Taiwan in July 1995, conducted naval exercises in December when the elections for the Legislative Yuan were held, and conducted major military exercises and missile launches immediately before the presidential election the following March. Alarmed by this significant rise in tensions, the United States sent two aircraft carrier task forces to the vicinity of Taiwan to cope with unexpected contingencies. Thus was created the first serious military escalation over the Taiwan Strait since 1958.

The crisis was primarily a psychological game. Militarily, the Chinese did not have the capability to launch an outright invasion of Taiwan, nor did Beijing have the intention of actually engaging in military combat. The effect of the intimidation, however, was diminished by the presence of the American aircraft carrier task forces. The result of the election was mixed for Beijing; the defeat of the DPP candidate was positive but, as a result, Lee achieved an easy victory. Because the candidate from another opposition party (the New Party) who explicitly opposed independence never really had a chance of victory, Beijing's intimidation in fact helped Lee. It persuaded those voters who might have been uneasy about the radical policy of the DPP to support the seemingly more moderate Lee, who did not explicitly mention independence. Since his election, however, Lee has turned out to be the prime mover of all sorts of changes that have served to solidify the separation of Taiwan from the mainland.

Sino-American relations, as well as Sino-Japanese relations, became strained immediately after this Taiwan Strait Crisis, partly because both the United States and Japan were very critical of China's military intimidation and partly because President Bill Clinton and Prime Minister Hashimoto Ryūtarō issued the U.S.-Japan Joint Declaration on Security. Although the Joint Declaration was not a reaction to the Taiwan Strait Crisis (it was originally planned to be issued in November 1995, but was postponed when President Clinton cancelled his visit to Japan because of a budget stalemate in the United States), the Chinese became suspicious of the wording in the declaration that specified the possibility of U.S.-Japan cooperation in a contingency in the "areas surrounding Japan." The Chinese constantly asked if the "areas surrounding Japan" included Taiwan. Although there have been some vacillations among Japanese politicians, the position of the governments of both Japan and the United States has been that the phrase was intended as a concept that pays attention to the nature of the situation rather than to any strict geographical delimitation.

Sino-American relations and Sino-Japanese relations have improved in subsequent years. In the process, Beijing insisted that Washington and Tokyo should oppose Taiwan's attempt to expand its diplomatic scope. The major achievement was the "Three No's"—a verbal declaration that President Clinton made during his nine-day visit to China in 1997. While in Shanghai, Clinton stated in a discussion with a group of local intellectuals that the United States would not support the "two Chinas" or "one China, one Taiwan" concept, would not support Taiwanese independence, and would not support Taiwan's participation in an international organization composed of sovereign states. The Japanese government has never made these Three No's explicit, but Prime Minister Hashimoto, when he visited China in September 1997, did state that he did not support the "two Chinas" or "one China, one Taiwan" formula and that he did not support Taiwanese independence.

The Taiwan situation became tense again as the next presidential election drew near. In July 1999, President Lee, in an interview for German television, declared that the relationship between Beijing and Taipei was not one between a central government and a "renegade province" but rather "a special state-to-state relationship."[8] According to Lee, Taiwan has consistently been a "sovereign state," coequal with the People's Republic.[9] Chinese reaction to this statement was severe and quite personal, denouncing Lee as a "troublemaker."[10] Informal contacts between Beijing and Taipei, which had resumed in 1998 through exchanges between the chairmen of the two semiofficial groups assigned to handle contacts between Taipei and Beijing (Taiwan's Strait Exchange Foundation Chairman Koo Chen-fu and his Chinese counterpart at the Association for Relations Across the Taiwan Strait, Wang Daohan), were virtually suspended. But Beijing this time has not conducted any large-scale military activities.

The degree to which President Lee's statement represented a new stance is a matter of contention. While some in Taiwan have said that the statement was a departure from the government's previous position, others, including Lee himself, argue that the new statement was nothing but an articulation of the position implied by the constitutional revision of 1991.

In any case, tensions over the Taiwan Strait continue to be a source of significant concern for international relations in East Asia, and thus for U.S.-Japan relations. But as the above discussion demonstrates, the overall structural background of such tensions has little to do with the end of the cold war; it has more to do with democratization in Taiwan. To the extent that Taiwanese (*benshengren*), as well as some who fled from the mainland after 1945, develop their own identity as "Taiwanese" rather than "Chinese" and desire to manage their own affairs democratically, the Chinese leaders in Beijing worry that the "unity of China" is at risk. If the prudent management of military balance was sufficient to preserve the status quo over the Taiwan Strait during the cold war, it is no longer sufficient as democratization proceeds in Taiwan. Unless a clever attempt at accommodation can be made between the two sides of the Strait, these tensions will continue to be around for the foreseeable future.

The Financial Crisis

The financial crisis that started in July 1997 was a shock to many Asians. It reminded them not only of the shallowness of their "economic miracle" but also of the political and social fragility of at least some countries in the region. Three countries that suffered the most serious economic damage, Thailand, South Korea, and Indonesia, seem to offer contrasting lessons. The democratic polities, Thailand and South Korea, managed their respective financial crises without major impact on their basic political frameworks, although they were very much resentful of the policy recommendations made and imposed by the International Monetary Fund (IMF). Prime Minister Chuan Leekpai and President Kim Dae Jung, both democratically elected leaders, implemented austerity measures and demanded sacrifice on the part of the people to overcome the crisis. By 1999, their policies of retrenchment bore fruit and the two countries registered a strong recovery by most economic measures.

Indonesia, in contrast, had to undergo a major change in its political system, which had potential implications for its national integration since the assertiveness of separatist movements in various parts of Indonesia—such as those in Aceh, Irian Jaya, and Moluccas—increased as the political grip of the central government in Jakarta weakened.[11] It was unfortunate for Indonesia that the financial crisis hit the nation precisely at a time when people were tiring of the long and corrupt reign of the Suharto government; the combination of political and economic crises undoubtedly exacerbated the degree of disorder that the country experienced. Anti-Suharto pressures from inside and from abroad took advantage of the financial crisis to make a radical change in the basic polity of Indonesia. Measures recommended by the IMF were supported not only by economic reasoning, at least part of which was later criticized as flawed, but also by the political motivation of ending the Suharto regime. It seems wrong, however, to argue that the Suharto regime was toppled by some outside plan or conspiracy. After the terrible economic shock that occurred when the value of the rupiah tumbled from 2,000 to 15,000 rupiah per U.S. dollar, a mixture of mismanagement and structural problems plunged the Indonesian society into a state of near chaos. It was bad enough that Suharto's illness effectively immobilized the government at a critical period in December 1997, but his appointment of a new cabinet in March 1998 proved disastrous as he surrounded himself with his relatives and those deeply connected with the structural corruption of the regime. The riots of May 1998, which rang the death knell for the thirty-two-year-long Suharto regime, might have been averted if the government had postponed price hikes for gasoline and electricity. But some similar disorder seemed unavoidable in any case.

Indonesia after Suharto proves to be both reassuring and worrisome. It is reassuring because it successfully changed constitutions and conducted the first democratic election of the National Assembly, which helped establish a democratic government led by President Abdurrahman Wahid and Vice President Megawati Sukarnoputri. But the prospects for Indonesia are still worrisome, as the accumulated government debts are staggering and prospects of attracting foreign capital are not very bright (Shiraishi 1999). Furthermore, the independence of East Timor could possibly accelerate separatist tendencies in other areas of Indonesia such as Aceh and Irian Jaya.[12]

In any case, the 1990s have demonstrated that the process of globalization is not at all static; its dynamic character made rapid growth possible, but it also produced a spiraling decline and ensuing social chaos. The recent episodes seem to suggest that authoritarian regimes without transparency, accountability, and a functioning system of the rule of law are extremely susceptible to the wild fluctuations of economic dynamics inherent in the process of globalization. In this respect, Indonesia's crisis of 1998–1999 may not be the last episode of globalization-induced disruptions in East Asia.

UNSTABLE PERCEPTIONS IN MAJOR POWER RELATIONS

Along with the crisis-ridden state of international affairs in East Asia, the end of the cold war created a dangerous fluctuation of perceptions among the major powers of the region—China, Japan, and the United States. The disappearance of the Soviet threat compelled some segments of the influential circles within the respective capitals to search for other "threats."[13] The first major appearance of such a threat that might replace the Soviet threat was a "threat" from Japan. This perception became most apparent in the United States during the late 1980s, even before the collapse of the Soviet Union.[14] Although the cold war was not quite over, most adherents of this school of thought had come to view economic power as more important than military power as a measure of national power and hence of "threats" to the national interest. By the end of the 1980s, articles and books with titles like *Containing Japan* or *The Coming War with Japan* had become popular in the United States (Fallows 1989; Friedman and Lebard 1991). A similar perception of Japan was emerging in some quarters in China, too. In the view of these Chinese, now that Japan had attained a position of economic power, it would next be contemplating ways to become a political power, and then a military power.

In the United States, the basis for such a perceived threat from Japan was the so-called revisionist view, which considered the political-economic system of Japan to be intrinsically different from those of the United States and other Western countries. According to this understanding, in order to resolve economic issues with Japan, simply resorting to policies based upon the functioning of market mechanisms would not work and some kind of coercive diplomacy to impose "numerical targets" was therefore needed. The Clinton administration's negotiations with Japan in the Framework Talks (1993–1995) were largely informed by this type of thinking. An ironical fact is that when the Clinton administration started its negotiations, the bubble had already burst and the foundation of the "threat from Japan" had been largely lost. By the time the Framework Talks ended in 1995, with Hashimoto Ryūtarō, then minister of international trade and industry, saying "no" to U.S. Trade Representative Mickey Kantor, few in the United States worried about the rise of Japan. On the contrary, some were beginning to worry about inept Japanese economic management.

As the perception of the threat from Japan receded in the United States, the "threat from China" began to attract the attention of the media and of decision-making circles in Washington, Tokyo, and elsewhere. The turning point in the development of this perception was sometime around 1992, when China reemerged as an economic dynamo after its virtual isolation following the Tiananmen Square Incident of 1989. After Deng Xiaoping's call for a reactivation of the open-door policy in 1992, China resumed its double-digit economic growth. The World Bank and the IMF's 1993 estimates of the gross domestic product of the countries of the world in terms of purchasing power parity (PPP) had a significant impact on people's perceptions: The World Bank report predicted that the combined economic power of China, Hong Kong, and Taiwan would reach US$9.8 trillion in terms of PPP by 2002, thus surpassing the U.S. economy (World Bank 1993, 66–67; see also *Economist* 28 November 1992, (survey) 3–6).

The growth of China's defense budget also appeared less reassuring; its annual growth rate was nearly 15 percent—higher than that of the gross domestic product. The purchase of military equipment, mainly from the former Soviet Union, became a source of concern among neighboring countries, and a rumor that China might be buying a full-fledged aircraft carrier, comparable to those of the United States, persisted for several years. Furthermore, Chinese naval activities in the South China Sea fueled the concerns; in 1995, China constructed permanent facilities on the Mischief Reef, over which the Philippines also claimed sovereignty. Certain statements by People's Liberation Army (PLA) admirals and Chinese publications around this time were similarly worrisome, as they emphasized Chinese maritime interests and the new role of the PLA navy as the protector of such interests.[15] Chinese military exercises in the Taiwan Strait in March 1996 further aggravated these concerns.

As a result, lively debates arose in Washington, Tokyo, and various capitals of Asia. A book entitled *The Coming Conflict with China* was published in the United States in 1996, and such leading journals as *Foreign Affairs* and *Foreign Policy* featured articles outlining the pros and cons of the China threat thesis (Bernstein and Munro 1997; Ross 1996 and 1997; Freeman 1996; Mastel 1996). A debate between "engagement" and "containment" advocates was waged in Washington, especially after the 1996 Taiwan Strait Crisis. In Japan, too, various articles were written emphasizing the potential power of China.

The rise of the "China threat" thesis in surrounding countries prompted a strong reaction in China. Chinese officials quickly pointed out that many of the arguments of this thesis were exaggerated. In addition, unofficial and often quite emotional anti-foreign publications appeared in China, including a book entitled *China Can Say No* (Song, Zhang, and Qiao 1996).

While the perception of China as being threatening has not disappeared, the degree to which that perception pertains has fluctuated, particularly in the United States. When President Clinton visited China in the summer of 1997, for example, the sense of a China threat receded, while 1999 saw a resurgence when the so-called Cox report revealed that China has been conducting extensive espionage activities to "steal" American nuclear weapons technology.[16]

Although the Chinese did not propagate their views in terms of an "America threat" thesis, they have long expressed the view that the United States is the main source of international problems. The Chinese media and official publications are full of books and articles pointing out the "hegemonism" (*baquan zhuyi*) and "power politics" (*qiangquan zhengzhi*) of the United States. There have been two waves in China of increased perceptions of a threat from the United States: The first was the period in the immediate aftermath of the Tiananmen Square Incident and the Gulf War, and the second was in 1998, triggered particularly by the Kosovo crisis and the bombing of the Chinese Embassy in Belgrade by the North Atlantic Treaty Organization (NATO). The basic perception common to these two periods is the current dominance of American power in the post-cold war period. While Chinese leaders often emphasize that the basic trend since the 1990s has been one of "multipolarization" (*duojihua*), which they view as desirable, they also note that the United States is the only superpower (*zhaoji daguo*). Sometimes, Chinese analysts describe this combination as a system composed of one superpower and many strong powers (*yizhao duoqiang*).

This dominant superpower is perceived in China to be threatening in at least two ways: first, in its perceived intentions, and second, in its military capability. The Chinese concerns about the U.S. intentions were most acute in the first few years following the Tiananmen Square Incident. In the eyes of the Chinese, the United States was plotting a conspiracy of "peaceful evolution" (*hepin yanpian*)—a conspiracy to topple communist governments by nonmilitary means, just as it was perceived to have done in the case of communist countries in Eastern Europe. In the late 1990s, the Chinese were no longer concerned about the U.S. intention to topple communist governments, but rather with its intention to interfere in the internal affairs of China—most notably with regard to the Taiwan issue and Tibet.

The U.S. military might was demonstrated to the Chinese first, and most vividly, by the Gulf War and then by the NATO bombings in Kosovo in the late 1990s. The Chinese did not oppose the Gulf War per se, since they were also critical of Saddam Hussein. What worried Beijing, however, was the sheer military might that was displayed on CNN. The Kosovo intervention, on the other hand, was doubly threatening. It indicated the U.S. intention to interfere in the internal affairs of other countries, as well as its capability to conduct highly sophisticated warfare with pinpoint bombing of military targets. The somewhat paranoid reaction to the U.S. bombing of the Chinese Embassy in Belgrade was understandable from this standpoint: It fit very nicely with the perception of U.S. hegemonism threatening China.[17]

All three major powers in East Asia—China, Japan, and the United States—have been perceived by each other as sources of "threats," albeit to varying degrees and with some ups and downs. This is not the emergence of a simple cold-war type of confrontation among the three major powers. The perceived threats posed by China, Japan, and the United States have been partial. Even at the height of the "Japan threat" thesis, Japan and the United States were the other's most important trade partner. Similarly, during this period, more and more McDonald's restaurants (and Starbucks coffee shops in the late 1990s) opened in China. And, just a few weeks after massive demonstrations protesting the bombing of the Chinese Embassy had surrounded the American Embassy in Beijing, one could see long lines forming in the same spot of people waiting to obtain visas for travel to the United States. It is worrisome, however, that the three powers have not been able to establish more stable mutual perceptions, especially given the various crises outlined above.

The international context of U.S.-Japan relations in the 1990s might seem rather grim if we were to pay attention only to these crises and uncertain mutual perceptions. However, without discounting the seriousness of the problems facing the international environment in East Asia, I would like to argue that the picture is incomplete if we fail to grasp other—in many ways more positive—developments in East Asian international affairs in the 1990s: namely, the rise of multilateralism and the revival of major power diplomacy.

THE RISE OF MULTILATERALISM

One prominent diplomatic trend that Asia Pacific saw in the 1990s was the rise of multilateralism. It is quite possible that the multilateral networks now proliferating at various levels and on various subjects could introduce a change to international politics in Asia Pacific as significant as the change brought about by the end of the cold war. It should be remembered that Asia Pacific had essentially been a region of bilateralism virtually until the end of the 1980s. Almost all military alliances were bilateral alliances; no significant multilateral economic frameworks existed. There were exceptions, to be sure. The Association of Southeast Asian Nations (ASEAN), formed in 1967, was a subregional success story (Yamakage 1991, 1997). Some nongovernmental, multilateral economic dialogue mechanisms also existed, such as the Pacific Economic Cooperation Council (PECC) and the Pacific Basin Economic Council (PBEC), but they were the exceptions that proved the rule. The creation of the Asia Pacific Economic Cooperation (APEC) forum in 1989 was a watershed in the history of Asia Pacific regional integration. The subsequent decade saw the emergence of increasingly dense and overlapping networks. As will be shown below, by the end of the 1990s, these multilateral frameworks had begun to show their limitations and to cause disappointment. It is nevertheless the case that they provide a new and different environment in which international relations are now conducted in East Asia.

APEC

APEC has been the flagship of Asia Pacific networking activities since it was created. It was the first governmental, multilateral meeting with nearly comprehensive membership in the Asia Pacific region.[18] The original members were Australia, Canada, Japan, South Korea, New Zealand, the United States, and six ASEAN countries (Brunei, Indonesia, Malaysia, Singapore, Thailand, and the Philippines). China, Hong Kong, and Taiwan joined APEC at the Third Ministerial Meeting, held in Seoul in 1991; Mexico and Papua New Guinea became members as of the Seattle meeting in 1993; and Chile became a member at Jakarta in 1994. It was decided in 1997 that Russia, Vietnam, and Peru would join APEC as of 1998.

The creators of APEC conceived of it as a deterrence against a "Fortress Europe," which had become a concern of Asians as well as Americans as they saw Europe moving toward a single market. It was also a hedge against the possible rise of protectionism in Europe and North America.[19] To prevent a self-fulfilling prophecy, APEC itself did not try to create any measures that might be viewed as discriminatory, and hence it adopted the catchphrase of "open regionalism." As the Uruguay Round came to a successful conclusion, and as the "Fortress Europe" specter faded from view, APEC took on more substantive goals. In 1994, APEC members set for themselves the goal of "free trade," which was to be actualized by the year 2010 for developed countries and 2020 for developing countries. An "action agenda" to realize that goal was agreed upon in 1995, and a more concrete "action plan" was adopted the following year.

In terms of the impact on international politics, the evolution of APEC-related institutions seems at least as important as its economic goals. The first significant innovation was the informal Leaders Meeting, created at the initiative of President Clinton in 1993. The Seattle meeting of the APEC leaders that year was in fact the first summit meeting of the heads of government of Asia Pacific nations in history. Second, within the context of the Ministerial Meeting (which is the original body of APEC, participated in by foreign ministers and trade ministers), various specialized meetings, committees, and working groups have been created. As a result, APEC-related meetings have increased tremendously, with fifty to eighty such meetings now held regularly each year.

When APEC was created, it was agreed to avoid too much institutionalization. Thus, it was only in 1992 that the secretariat was created. Obviously, the level of institutionalization of APEC is still far more limited than such full-fledged organizations as the EU Commission; such a path was ruled out from the beginning. But the proliferation of regular committees and working groups is nonetheless an unprecedented phenomenon in Asia Pacific, where the daily contact among working-level officials used to be very limited. In the 1950s and 1960s, a number of scholars who subscribed to the theory of "functionalism" were arguing about the possible "spillover" effects in Europe as they saw the beginning of European integration (Mitrany 1943; Haas 1964). This school of thought holds that the habits of cooperation formed in such functional areas as technology or trade will "spill over" into more general foreign policy interaction, thereby encouraging peace. Now, Asia Pacific may be witnessing the emergence of conditions that lend themselves to the theory of "functionalism," making the possibility of "spillover" increasingly real. In this sense, although APEC is a forum to discuss economic issues, it also has begun to have at least an indirect effect on the security conditions of Asia Pacific.

The ASEAN Regional Forum

Just as APEC marked a fundamental change in the economic relations of the Asia Pacific region, the creation of the ASEAN Regional Forum (ARF) was a watershed event in the region's security relations.[20] The main initiative came from the ASEAN countries, who felt the necessity to create a security framework in which they could wield power against the major powers in the region. It was a response by the ASEAN countries to various calls for a multilateral security framework, including an Australian idea for a Conference on Security Cooperation in Asia (CSCA) and a Canadian proposal for a North Pacific security forum. The establishment of ARF was agreed upon in July 1993, at the ASEAN Post Ministerial meeting, and the first ARF meeting took place in July 1994. The original members included the six ASEAN countries, as well as Australia, Canada, China, Japan, Laos, New Zealand, Papua New Guinea, Russia, South Korea, the United States, Vietnam, and a representative of the EU. ARF's membership expanded to include Cambodia in 1995, India and Myanmar in 1996, and Mongolia in 1998.

As was the case with APEC, ARF started without any grand design; the purpose was stated vaguely. The first meeting was ridiculed by some as being a mere "talk shop." It was only in the second meeting in 1995 that the medium-term goals were set and the members agreed to gradually proceed with three stages of action: first, confidence-building; second, preventive diplomacy; and third, conflict resolution. In order to promote confidence-building, they agreed to strengthen political-security dialogues, to increase transparency by publishing the member countries' documents on defense policy, to promote further exchanges among the military forces of member countries, and to encourage the members to participate in the UN Register of Conventional Arms.

The initial organizational apparatus of ARF was also minimal, consisting of Ministerial Meetings and Senior Officials Meetings (SOMs). But as was the case with APEC, the number and variety of meetings increased, gradually at the outset and quite rapidly in subsequent years. In accordance with the medium-term goals described above, at the 1995 meeting ARF's members decided to create various additional "inter-sessional meetings" (ISMs), including the Inter-Sessional Support Group on Confidence-Building Measures, the Inter-Sessional Meeting on Search and Rescue Coordination and Cooperation, and the Inter-Sessional Meeting on Peacekeeping Operations. In 1996, the Ministerial Meeting decided to create another ISM: the Inter-Sessional Meeting on Disaster Relief. In 1997, the Ministerial Meeting also confirmed that the examination of preventive diplomacy should be started at the governmental level.

Obviously, there are many limitations to the activities of ARF. The initial criticism of ARF as being a mere "talk shop" continues to retain some validity. It cannot make any decisions that are opposed by a member state. In terms of being a talk shop, however, its quality has improved. The discussion on the Cambodian situation at the 1997 Ministerial Meeting and the discussion at the 1998 Ministerial Meeting on nuclear tests conducted by India and Pakistan were at least quite frank and active. In terms of institutionalization, the issue of establishing a secretariat remains to be resolved. In contrast to APEC, which as noted above established its secretariat in 1992, ARF still has no secretariat; it is managed by the chair country, which rotates annually among the ASEAN countries. As the issues and meetings multiply, the current management style has begun to show some strains, and not all ASEAN countries may be able to fulfill the roles of chair and host as well as secretariat. On the other hand, some countries such as China are resisting the creation of a permanent secretariat.

Nonetheless, immediate conflict resolution and rapid institutionalization have never been the goals of ARF. Its effect should be judged by its long-term impact on socializing the governing elites in the region who are in control of security affairs. As was discussed in the section on APEC, the multiplication of meetings is in itself important. A significant development in this respect was the participation of defense personnel in Ministerial Meetings and SOMs as support staff from 1997 on. Another positive development has been the increasing willingness and readiness of China to engage in the ARF processes. One of the original goals of ARF was to encourage Chinese participation in multilateral dialogues, and this goal has been more or less achieved, although China's active participation has not yet necessarily led to agreements with other countries.

ASEM and ASEAN+3

In contrast to APEC and ARF, which generally have been welcomed by most countries in Asia Pacific, Malaysian Prime Minister Mahathir bin Mohamed's idea of an East Asian Economic Caucus (EAEC), first proposed in 1991, has been controversial. The U.S. reaction (particularly from Secretary of State James Baker) was almost hostile, Japan was very cautious, and other ASEAN countries' support was lukewarm. The proposal was seen as an attempt to drive a wedge between Caucasian Asia Pacific and non-Caucasian (or Asian) Asia Pacific. Furthermore, it was interpreted as a movement toward a more "closed" regionalism. As a result, this idea was regarded as more or less dead until, by a certain accident of events, it returned through a backdoor called ASEM (the Asia-Europe Meeting), which was first held at the initiative of Singapore in 1996. The main motivation for creating ASEM was to promote the relatively weaker link between Asia and Europe (as opposed to the Europe–North America or Asia–North America links) in the economic, political, and cultural areas. ASEM itself was not intended as a way of promoting Mahathir's EAEC idea, but when the Asian members of ASEM were selected, it just so happened that those countries regarded as somehow the "natural" choices to represent Asia included China, Japan, South Korea, and the ASEAN members as of 1996. These were in fact the countries that Mahathir had proposed as the members of the EAEC. As it turned out, in the ASEM scheme, it was agreed that the Asian side and the European side would meet separately before all twenty-six members got together. In this way, through the ASEM process, the leaders that Mahathir had wanted to participate in his EAEC met for the first time in history. But the ASEM process in and of itself did not produce a full-blown East Asian framework; it simply introduced an East Asian meeting through the backdoor. The front-door entrance of a new framework had to wait until the following year, when the "ASEAN+3" summit was created through a somewhat unintended initiative.

In January 1997, Prime Minister Hashimoto was on a visit to ASEAN countries when he declared that he wanted to have regular summit meetings between Japan and the ASEAN leaders. The initial response from the ASEAN countries to Hashimoto's idea was rather cautious. If Japan alone were to have a regular summit with ASEAN, what would be the Chinese reaction? This was a real concern for the ASEAN countries. But in due course, ASEAN decided to invite not only the leader of Japan but also the leaders of China and South Korea to the ASEAN summit held in December 1997. Japan's idea of an "ASEAN+" summit was transformed into an "ASEAN+3" summit (which in fact took place as scheduled, despite the absence of President Kim Young Sam, who could not attend because of the South Korean presidential election and the economic turmoil that was occurring; a representative attended on his behalf).

The substance of this ASEAN+3 summit meeting in December was not significant. Even as talk shops go, the meeting may well be regarded as a failure. But the significance of this summit lay not in substance but in form. In contrast to ASEM, where East Asian leaders got together as part of a larger Asia-Europe framework, the ASEAN+3 summit offered an independent occasion for East Asian leaders to sit around a single table for the first time in history. In December 1998, the second ASEAN+3 summit took place in Hanoi, attended by the ASEAN leaders as well as by Japanese Prime Minister Obuchi Keizō, South Korean President Kim Dae Jung, and China's Vice President Hu Jintao. As it is now expected that this summit will take place regularly, it creates another layer of interaction among the countries involved, in addition to APEC and ARF. Institutionally, this is clearly the most rudimentary—nothing exists other than the summit meeting. But in contrast to APEC and ARF, whose scopes are limited to economics and security respectively, the ASEAN+3 does not specify any subject for discussions, thereby permitting its scope to become most comprehensive.

The ASEAN+3 came perhaps at the right moment. Despite having exactly the same membership as Mahathir's EAEC, the ASEAN+3 was able to avoid the pitfalls of the EAEC as conceived in the early 1990s. As originally proposed, the EAEC was potentially dangerous because it could have become a competing regional scheme with APEC. But by the end of the decade, APEC had established its position as an increasingly solid scheme of cooperation. In addition, ARF has been around for some years with more inclusive membership than the ASEAN+3. There is no possibility that this new grouping will endanger the former two. On the contrary, it could now be argued that, if only to promote the respective cooperative activities of APEC, ARF, and ASEM more constructively, the countries of ASEAN+3 should coordinate their views more fully beforehand.

The Potential for Multilateral Frameworks in Northeast Asia

Northeast Asia is conspicuous for its absence of multilateral frameworks. Although ARF can theoretically cover Northeast Asia, it is still a Southeast Asia-centered scheme. The density of overlapping institutions in Southeast Asia—with ASEAN, the ASEAN Post Ministerial Conferences, ARF, APEC, and more—is much higher than that in Northeast Asia. In fact, the only multilateral governmental framework in Northeast Asia is the Four-Party Talks, which were proposed by President Kim Young Sam and President Clinton in 1996 (Oberdorfer 1997). The main purpose of these talks was to explore a permanent peace agreement on the Korean peninsula to replace the armistice agreement of the Korean War. Official meetings were finally started in December 1997, but the future is still quite uncertain. Some, including Prime Minister Obuchi, have advanced the desirability of expanding the talks to a 2+2+2 format, with the added participation of Japan and Russia. But this still remains just an idea. Although not an intergovernmental organization for the general purpose of either economic or security policy, KEDO may function as a confidence-building mechanism involving North Korea. Ultimately, however, while the desirability of a multilateral dialogue mechanism in Northeast Asia is clear, as long as North Korea retains its current internal and external policies, the realization of such a dialogue remains difficult, to say the least.

A REVIVAL OF MAJOR POWER DIPLOMACY

Potentially the most significant development in international politics in Asia Pacific in the late 1990s was the resumption of major power diplomacy. The four major countries—China, Japan, Russia, and the United States—began to increase meetings of high-ranking officials and politicians from sometime around 1996. As discussed above, the relations among the four were strained until that time. To be more exact, for some time Russia's relations with others were not so much "strained" as they were nonexistent. Relations among the other three were strained not only because of the uncertain dynamics of mutual perceptions, as discussed previously, but also by a number of incidents and developments. For example, Japan's relations with the United States in 1995 were already complicated enough because of the automobile and auto parts talks, but the rape of a Japanese schoolgirl by U.S. servicemen in Okinawa in September placed the U.S.-Japan alliance in a serious crisis. At the same time, Japan and China were arguing with each other over various issues including China's nuclear tests, Japan's history, territorial issues, and Taiwan. And as discussed above, China and the United States resorted to brinkmanship over Taiwan in 1996.

Fortunately, it seems that all four major countries, after these unhappy experiences, have come to realize that the strained relations among them are simply counterproductive for their respective national goals. The first diplomatic attempt to restore stability to bilateral relations was made by Japan and the United States by "redefining" their security relationship. Partly because of the effect of the "Japan threat" debate, partly as a result of truly acrimonious trade talks, and partly because of the delayed articulation of post–cold war security strategy by both Japan and the United States, the alliance was depicted as being "adrift" (Funabashi 1997). This drifting alliance was shaken by the Okinawa rape incident of September 1995. At one point shortly afterward, a Japanese public opinion poll indicated that the level of support for the alliance had dropped to almost the same level as those opposing it—the first such dramatic decline since 1973 (*Nihon Keizai Shimbun* 17 October 1995).[21]

The alliance was saved from this crisis by various factors. The U.S. response to the rape incident, including an immediate apology by President Clinton, was prompt and appropriate. In addition, uncertain developments on the Korean peninsula, increasing concerns about the future of China (including, but not necessarily limited to, the "China threat" thesis), and a recognition of the limitations of multilateral security frameworks such as ARF brought the security debates in Tokyo back from an emotional reaction to the incident to a more coolheaded strategic calculation. To assuage the people of Okinawa, who are resentful of the disproportionate allocation of U.S. bases to Okinawa (in terms of area, 70 percent of the U.S. bases in Japan are located on Okinawa), Prime Minister Hashimoto personally took the initiative to persuade the Clinton administration to relocate the Futenma Air Base, which was located in a congested urban area of Ginowan City. The U.S. agreement to the return of Futenma in April 1996 ushered in a successful Clinton visit to Tokyo and the general acceptance by the Japanese public of the U.S.-Japan Joint Declaration on Security. The subsequent negotiations between Washington and Tokyo to revise the Guidelines for U.S.-Japan Defense Cooperation solidified security relations between the two. Thus, when Asia was struck by a financial crisis in the summer of 1997, and Japan became the focus of international criticism for its economic management, the basic framework of the security relationship was more or less intact (although there were strains over certain other issues, including the possibility of an Asian Monetary Fund, a Japanese idea that failed to materialize due to the strong opposition of the United States).

Despite the existence of serious issues and mutual threat perceptions, Washington and Beijing also made diplomatic efforts to keep their relations more or less "normal." After the Taiwan Strait Crisis of March 1996, President Clinton and President Jiang Zemin met on the occasion of the APEC Leaders Meeting held in Manila in November 1996 and agreed to mutual state visits in the following years. Vice President Al Gore visited China in March 1997, and President Jiang made a state visit to the United States in late October 1997, which was then reciprocated by President Clinton's state visit to China in June–July 1998. Sino-American relations became strained again after the Clinton visit, however, first by the revelation of the alleged Chinese espionage activities related to nuclear weapons technology, and then by the U.S. bombing of the Chinese Embassy in Belgrade. But diplomatic negotiations such as those over China's accession to the World Trade Organization (WTO) have been facilitated by such occasions as Premier Zhu Rongji's visit to Washington in April 1999. On the occasion of the APEC Leaders Meeting at Auckland, New Zealand, President Clinton and President Jiang had a separate meeting to mend their relations, as well as to agree to accelerate their negotiations on China's WTO accession, on which agreement was reached between the two countries two months later, in November 1999.

Japan's relations with China in the 1990s have experienced ups and downs. After the Tiananmen Square Incident, Japan also imposed sanctions against China, including a freeze on the implementation of official development assistance

(ODA) for fiscal year 1990 to fiscal year 1995, which had already been agreed to in principle. But among the G7 countries, Japan was quickest to resume a normal relationship with China, and it resumed its ODA planning within a year. In the Japanese thinking, a destabilized China was not in their best interest. The official visit by the Japanese emperor to China in 1992 represented a high mark in Sino-Japanese relations. Subsequently, however, relations between Tokyo and Beijing took a turn for the worse. Between 1993 and 1995, several cabinet members in the series of coalition governments in Japan made controversial statements concerning the history of Sino-Japanese wars and Japanese colonization, thus attracting criticism from China and other countries. Conversely, Chinese nuclear tests in 1995 and 1996 elicited critical reactions from Japan, where the public and particularly some members of the Diet viewed the Chinese (and French) nuclear tests as being contrary to the spirit, if not the letter, of the indefinite extension of the Nuclear Non-Proliferation Treaty that was ratified by an overwhelming number of countries in May 1995. As a result, the Japanese government decided to freeze its grant aid program to China, which in turn angered the Chinese. In addition, the construction of a small lighthouse on one of the Senkaku Islands by a rightwing Japanese organization appeared provocative to the Chinese (and to the people of Taiwan and Hong Kong), who believe that the islands belong to China. The U.S.-Japan Joint Declaration on Security also appeared to the Chinese to be an effort to "contain" China. Thus, the summer of 1996 witnessed the low point of the decade in Japan-China relations.

However, strained relations between the two were not perceived in either capital as being productive. In fact, economic relations between Japan and China in 1995–1996 were quite positive. A huge number of direct investment projects were undertaken in China by Japanese firms. Diplomatically, a turn for the better was signaled by a meeting between Jiang and Hashimoto during the Manila APEC Leaders Meeting in November 1996, at which time they agreed to exchange visits. In the fall of 1997, Hashimoto visited China and Prime Minister Li Peng visited Tokyo shortly thereafter. Unfortunately, President Jiang's state visit to Japan in November 1998 was a disappointment to both the Japanese and the Chinese. From the Chinese perspective, the fact that Japan would not agree to insert an explicit "apology" in the joint statement was unsatisfactory, while to the Japanese, Jiang's insistence on repeatedly raising the history issue at almost all occasions while he was in Japan appeared excessive.[22] Nonetheless, relations between Tokyo and Beijing did not deteriorate too much, since Prime Minister Obuchi's visit to Beijing in July 1999 was largely successful.

Russia, nearly absent from the Asian scene in the early 1990s, started to reenter later in the decade, first by increasing contacts with China. President Boris

Yeltsin and President Jiang agreed in April 1996 to call their relationship a "strategic partnership." The year 1997 saw a rapid improvement of relations between Japan and Russia as well. After a short encounter at Denver, Prime Minister Hashimoto and President Yeltsin agreed to mend the almost frozen relations between the two countries, and when they met in November, they agreed to make efforts to realize a peace treaty by 2000. President Yeltsin visited Japan in April 1998 and Prime Minister Obuchi went to Moscow in November 1998. President Vladimir Putin, who won the presidential election in March 2000 after the sudden resignation of Yeltsin, visited Japan in September 2000. It is doubtful, however, that the two countries will reach a mutually agreeable compromise over the territorial issues by the end of the year. Nonetheless, the general atmosphere does not seem to be as chilly as it was in previous years.

It is hard to summarize the full implications of these diplomatic activities of the major powers. But, taken together with the advent of increasingly overlapping multilateral networks, the revitalization of major power diplomacy could dampen the effect of unstable mutual threat perceptions among the major powers. It could also offer possibilities for mutual cooperation in resolving, or at least managing, crises that might be produced by the combined effects of the end of the cold war, democratization, globalization, and various local circumstances.

The experiences of the last ten years seem to indicate that multilateral frameworks alone have not been very effective in coping with the types of serious problems that this chapter has termed "crises." ARF did not play a role in dealing with either the Korean peninsula or the Taiwan Strait. APEC was not particularly impressive in coping with the financial crisis or the Indonesian political turmoil that followed. The roles of major powers are essential in coping with these hard issues that require substantive and quick reactions. The revival of major power diplomacy around 1996 was, in this sense, necessary and understandable.

However, major power diplomacy is not a panacea. Given the essential instability of mutual threat perceptions, major power diplomacy may tumble into a major power confrontation. The development of multilateral frameworks in Asia Pacific, though not very impressive in managing crises, has played a certain role in preserving major power diplomacy. As the previous discussion indicates, the annual APEC Leaders Meetings often provide occasions to resume diplomatic dialogues after some strains in various bilateral relations. The Manila Meeting in November 1996 offered opportunities for both the Sino-American and Sino-Japanese relationships to move back to more normal diplomatic dialogues. The Auckland Meeting in September 1999 did likewise with respect to Sino-American relations. A similar tendency can be attributed to the annual ARF and ASEAN PMC meetings in terms of facilitating dialogues at the level of foreign ministers.

CONCLUDING REMARKS

All in all, East Asia in the 1990s has offered a difficult international context for the U.S.-Japan relationship. The Korean peninsula, the Taiwan Strait, and the financial crisis challenged both Washington and Tokyo. The game of major power relations among China, Japan, and the United States has been bewildering, and threat perceptions seem to be constantly in flux. But the overall tendencies seem to force the two allies to cooperate more rather than to tread divergent courses. It is in the interest of both Americans and Japanese to have a nuclear-free and missile-free Korean peninsula. It is in the interest of both peoples to have peace over the Taiwan Strait. And the smooth and safe transition of the political-economies of East Asian countries to systems that can cope with globalization is certainly welcome to both Japanese and Americans, who are increasingly dependent on the prospect of a prosperous and peaceful Asia Pacific.

It was in this sense inevitable and wise for Japan and the United States to reconfirm the importance of their alliance in 1996. That reconfirmed alliance system seems to have worked as glue when the two countries were confronted with the challenge of the financial crisis. Certainly there were strains (for example over the AMF issue, as noted), but the belief that the two countries share more or less identical security interests has prevented the fissures in the economic realm from damaging the overall relationship.

The reaffirmed alliance has a positive function in the overall international relations of East Asia by removing one important element of uncertainty from the game of threat perception. At least from 1995 on, the United States and Japan have no longer suffered from mutual threat perceptions. Put differently, no countries need to contemplate a circumstance where Japan and the United States are fundamentally at odds with each other, and no countries can try to play Japan and the United States off against each other. This significantly increases the level of predictability in East Asia—a virtue for a region so full of uncertainty.

There is, however, one possible disadvantage that could stem from a solidified U.S.-Japan relationship in terms of the overall international relations in East Asia: If China believes that the U.S.-Japan alliance is anti-China in nature, the solidification of the alliance might push East Asia into an arena of confrontation. A series of Chinese expressions of concern over the last several years has indicated that such a possibility does exist. Declarations by Japan and the United States that their alliance is not directed at any single country are important. But, along with such expressions, it seems extremely important for both Japan and the United States to help develop multilateral frameworks in Asia Pacific. The experiences of the APEC Leaders Meetings have proven that such gatherings can serve a very positive function by increasing the venues for communication at the highest level. Under the current circumstances in East Asia, the more the leaders have an opportunity to see each other, the better. And one important virtue of regular meetings set up by multilateral frameworks is that it is hard to cancel them simply because of a slight downturn in a bilateral relationship.

A bilateral relationship between highly sophisticated countries such as the United States and Japan is molded and affected by various complex factors. Domestic factors are in many ways critical, as is elucidated in the other chapters of this book. But from the perspective of the international context, there is a solid and continuing basis for further cooperation. This is the major conclusion of this chapter. In addition, this examination of the international context also indicates that the two countries need to have much broader perspectives in dealing with international affairs, extending beyond the management of the alliance. If only to preserve the alliance as a positive factor in international politics in East Asia, the two countries need to cultivate healthy multilateral frameworks that can embrace China and other countries.

NOTES

1. Some of the theoretically informed treatments of post–cold war international politics in East Asia include Betts (1994), Friedberg (1994), Buzan and Segal (1994), and Tanaka (1994). Tanaka (1996) adopts somewhat novel theoretical categories to describe East Asian international politics.

2. The best account of North Korea's nuclear weapons development program and the subsequent crisis is Oberdorfer (1997).

3. The full text of the Geneva Agreement can be found at <http://csf.colorado.edu/dfax/npn/npn18.htm>.

4. Japan's position with respect to Taiwan was based on the commitment it made in the San Francisco Peace Treaty, in which it declared that "Japan renounces all right, title and claim to Formosa and the Pescadores" (Kajima Heiwa Kenkyūjo 1983, 420). When it normalized relations with China in 1972, Japan's position was expressed in a rather circuitous way in a joint communiqué. Paragraph 2 of that communiqué stipulates: "The Government of Japan recognizes the Government of the People's Republic of China as the sole legal Government of China," and paragraph 3 states, "The Government of the People's Republic of China reiterates that Taiwan is an inalienable part of the territory of the People's Republic of China. The Government of Japan fully understands and respects this stand of the Government of the People's Republic of China, and it firmly maintains its stand under Article 8 of the Potsdam Proclamation" (Kajima Heiwa Kenkyūjo 1985, 593). Article 8 of the Potsdam Proclamation stipulates that "the terms of the Cairo Declaration shall be carried out" (Kajima Heiwa Kenkyūjo 1983, 74). And the Cairo Declaration stipulates that "all the territories Japan has stolen from China," which included Taiwan, "shall be restored to" China (Kajima Heiwa Kenkyūjo 1983, 55–56). Simply put, this indicates that, having given up Taiwan under the San Francisco Peace Treaty, Japan is not in a position to say anything about the current disposition of the island beyond that it "understands and respects" the

Chinese position and that, in accordance with the Cairo Declaration and the Potsdam Proclamation (the acceptance of which was the basis of the settlement of World War II for Japan), it does not oppose the restoration of Taiwan to China. For background on Sino-Japanese relations, see Tanaka (1991).

5. The U.S. position with respect to Taiwan is expressed in the Joint Communiqué on the Establishment of Diplomatic Relations between the United States of America and the People's Republic of China (January 1, 1979), which stipulates: "The United States of America recognizes the Government of the People's Republic of China as the sole legal Government of China. Within this context, the people of the United States will maintain cultural, commercial, and other unofficial relations with the people of Taiwan." The joint communiqué also stipulates: "The United States of America acknowledges the Chinese position that there is but one China and Taiwan is part of China" (Kajima Heiwa Kenkyūjo 1985, 1023–1024). For background on U.S. relations with Taiwan and China, see Harding (1992), Mann (1999), and Tucker (1994).

6. The best short history of Taiwan's transition from authoritarian rule to democracy is Wakabayashi (1997). For a general account in English, see Copper (1996).

7. For a concise review of the relations between China and Taiwan, see Nakagawa (1998).

8. See <http://taiwansecurity.org/TS/SS-990709-Deutsche-Welle-Interview.htm>.

9. A 1999 *Foreign Affairs* article by Lee provides his full justification for this statement.

10. See <http://taiwansecurity.org/AFP/AFP-TaiwanPressidentSaysHeNoTroublemaker.htm>.

11. For a detailed description of political change in Indonesia, see Research Institute for Peace and Security (1999, 16–25).

12. East Timor, a former Portuguese colony, was annexed by Indonesia by force in 1975, when Portugal withdrew. Neither the United Nations nor any country except Australia recognized Indonesia's annexation, because they believed that Indonesia, a country composed of former Dutch colonies, did not have a legitimate claim over the former Portuguese colony. The independence movement in East Timor, which has existed since that time, became very vocal as the Suharto regime went through political turmoil. President B. J. Habibi, who replaced Suharto, allowed a referendum in August 1999 in East Timor to decide its future. That vote clearly showed the desire of the overwhelming majority of citizens for independence. The Indonesian military, which had a strong interest in East Timor, carried out a campaign of harassment and massacre there in the aftermath of the referendum. But as multilateral peacekeeping forces were dispatched to East Timor in late 1999 to restore order, the Indonesian military withdrew and the Indonesian Parliament agreed to the independence of East Timor.

13. Samuel Huntington (1997) once wrote that the United States needs an outside threat to maintain its national identity.

14. The precursor was an article in the *New York Times* by Theodore White (1985).

15. Admiral Zhang Lianzhong said in an interview with the Chinese weekly magazine *Liaowang* in April 1992 that "the Chinese Navy is becoming a 'convoy' of China's reforms and opening," adding that "the wish of the Chinese sailors is to realize a prosperous country and a strong military" (Huang 1992).

16. The Cox report, or the "Final Report of the Select Committee on U.S. National

Security and Military/Commercial Concerns with the People's Republic of China," was issued on January 3, 1999. It was named for Rep. Christopher Cox, who chaired the bipartisan committee.

17. See, for example, various articles in *Pekin Shūhō* (the Japanese edition of *Beijing Review*) 1 and 8 June 1999.

18. Kikuchi (1995) provides a general review of the formation of APEC.

19. For a vivid journalistic account of the formation and development of APEC, see Funabashi (1995).

20. The most detailed chronicle of the formation of ARF is Leifer (1996). See also Yamakage (1997, chap. 9).

21. The poll showed that 40.2 percent were for the abrogation of the security alliance, as compared to 43.5 percent who supported its maintenance. This is in sharp contrast to a poll taken just months earlier, in August 1995, in which only 28.7 percent supported the abrogation of the alliance and 59.8 percent supported its maintenance.

22. The following is the statement issued in the Joint Declaration agreed upon between Jiang and Obuchi: "The Japanese side is keenly conscious of the responsibility for the serious distress and damage that Japan caused to the Chinese people through its aggression against China during a certain period in the past and expressed deep remorse for this." (The text of the statement is available at <http://www.mofa.go.jp/region/asia-paci/china/visit98/joint.html>.) Under other circumstances, these words could generally be taken as a statement of apology.

However, the Joint Declaration between Japan and South Korea, which was issued the previous month stated: "Looking back on the relations between Japan and the Republic of Korea during this century, Prime Minister Obuchi regarded in a spirit of humility the fact of history that Japan caused, during a certain period in the past, tremendous damage and suffering to the people of the Republic of Korea through its colonial rule, and expressed his deep remorse and heartfelt apology for this fact" (<http://mofa.go.jp/region/asia-paci/korea/joint9810.html>). Reading this, the Chinese believed that their document should include the same word, "apology." Therefore, when Obuchi did not agree to use the same word, Jiang felt that he was being unfairly treated by the Japanese. It is reported that Kim Dae Jung insisted that if Japan agreed to include the word "apology," he would agree to put the history issue completely behind the two countries. The Chinese negotiators did not offer such a commitment, and thus the Japanese responded that they would rather use indirect words than an explicit apology. It was unfortunate in any case that these exchanges seem to have degenerated into a political game of symbolic words. As a result, the perception emerged that Japan did not apologize at all. Very few people bothered to read the actual statement.

BIBLIOGRAPHY

Bernstein, Richard, and Ross Munro. 1997. "The Coming Conflict with America." *Foreign Affairs* 76(2): 18-32.

Betts, Richard K. 1994. "Wealth, Power, and Instability: East Asia and the United States after the Cold War." *International Security* 18(3): 34-77.

Buzan, Barry, and Gerald Segal. 1994. "Rethinking East Asian Security." *Survival* 36(2): 3-21.

Copper, John F. 1996. *Taiwan: Nation-State or Province?* 2nd ed. Boulder, Colo.: Westview Press.

Fallows, James. 1989. "Containing Japan." *Atlantic* (May): 40–54.

Freeman, Charles. W., Jr. 1996. "Sino-American Relations: Back to Basics." *Foreign Policy*, no. 104: 3–17.

Friedberg, Aaron L. 1994. "Ripe for Rivalry: Prospects for Peace in a Multipolar Asia." *International Security* 18(3): 5–33.

Friedman, George, and Meredith Lebard. 1991. *The Coming War with Japan*. New York: St. Martin's Press.

Funabashi Yōichi. 1995. *Ajia Taiheiyō fyūjon: APEC to Nippon* (Asia Pacific fusion: Japan's role in APEC). Tokyo: Chūō Kōronsha.

———. 1997. *Dōmei hyōryū* (Alliance adrift). Tokyo: Iwanami Shoten.

Haas, Ernst. 1964. *Beyond the Nation State: Functionalism and International Organization*. Stanford: Stanford University Press.

Harding, Harry. 1992. *A Fragile Relationship: The United States and China since 1972*. Washington, D.C.: The Brookings Institution.

Huang Caihong. 1992. "Zhongguo haijun wei gaige kaifeng 'baojiahuhang'—fangwen silingyuan Zhang Lianzhong shogjiang" (The Chinese Navy becomes a convoy of China's reforms and opening). *Liaowang* (overseas edition) 20 April.

Huntington, Samuel P. 1997. "The Erosion of American National Interests." *Foreign Affairs* 76(5): 28–49.

Kajima Heiwa Kenkyūjo. 1983. *Nihon gaikō shuyō bunsho/nenpyō, dai-ikkan* (Basic documents on Japanese foreign relations, vol. 1). Tokyo: Hara Shobō.

———. 1985. *Nihon gaikō shuyō bunsho/nenpyō, dai-sankan* (Basic documents on Japanese foreign relations, vol. 3). Tokyo: Hara Shobō.

Kikuchi Tsutomu. 1995. *APEC: Ajia Taiheiyō chitsujo no mosaku* (APEC: Exploration of an Asia Pacific order). Tokyo: Nihon Kokusai Mondai Kenkyūjo.

Lee Teng-hui. 1999. "Understanding Taiwan." *Foreign Affairs* 78(6): 9–14.

Leifer, Michael. 1996. *The ASEAN Regional Forum*. Adelphi Paper No. 302. Oxford, England: Oxford University Press.

Mann, James. 1999. *About Face: A History of America's Curious Relationship With China, From Nixon to Clinton*. New York: Alfred A. Knopf.

Mastel, Greg. 1996. "Beijing at Bay." *Foreign Policy*, no. 104: 27–34.

Mitrany, David. 1943. *A Working Peace System*. London: Royal Institute of International Affairs.

Nakagawa Yoshio. 1998. *Chūgoku to Taiwan* (China and Taiwan). Tokyo: Chūō Kōronsha.

Oberdorfer, Don. 1997. *The Two Koreas: A Contemporary History*. Reading, Mass.: Addison-Wesley.

Research Institute for Peace and Security. 1999. *Asian Security 1998–1999*. Tokyo: Research Institute for Peace and Security.

Ross, Robert. 1996. "Enter the Dragon." *Foreign Policy*, no. 104: 18–25.

———. 1997. "Beijing as a Conservative Power." *Foreign Affairs* 76(2): 33–44.

Shiraishi Takashi. 1999. "Indoneshia wa dō naru?" (What will happen to Indonesia?). *Chūō Kōron*, no. 1385: 60–67.

Song Qiang, Zhang Zangzang, and Qiao Bian. 1996. *Zhongguo keyi shuo bu* (China can say no). Beijing: Zhonghua Gongshang Lanhe Zhubanshe.

Tanaka Akihiko. 1991. *Nicchū kankei 1945–1990* (Sino-Japanese relations: 1945–1990). Tokyo: University of Tokyo Press.

———. 1994. "Two Faces of East Asian Security and Japan's Policy." In *Korean Peninsula Trends and U.S.-Japan-South Korea Relations.* Washington, D.C.: The Center for Strategic and International Studies.

———. 1996. *Atarashii chūsei: 21-seiki no sekai shisutemu* (New middle ages: The world system in the 21st century). Tokyo: Nihon Keizai Shimbunsha.

———. 1997. *Anzen hoshō* (National security). Tokyo: Yomiuri Shimbunsha.

Tucker, Nancy Bernkopf. 1994. *Taiwan, Hong Kong, and the United States, 1945–1992.* New York: Twayne Publishers.

Wakabayashi Masahiro. 1997. *Shō Keikoku to Ri Tōki* (Chiang Ching-kuo and Lee Teng-hui). Tokyo: Iwanami Shoten.

White, Theodore. 1985. "The Danger from Japan." *New York Times Magazine* (28 July).

World Bank. 1993. *Global Economic Prospects and the Developing Countries 1993.* Washington, D.C.: World Bank.

Yamakage Susumu. 1991. *ASEAN: Shimboru kara shisutemu he* (ASEAN: From symbol to system). Tokyo: University of Tokyo Press.

———. 1997. *ASEAN pawā: Ājia Taiheiyō no chūkaku he* (ASEAN power: Toward the core of Asia Pacific). Tokyo: University of Tokyo Press.

About the Contributors

GERALD L. CURTIS is Burgess Professor of Political Science and former Director of the East Asian Institute at Columbia University. Professor Curtis is the author of numerous books and articles in English and Japanese on Japanese society and politics, foreign policy, and the United States' relations with Japan and policy in East Asia. His most recent book, *The Logic of Japanese Politics*, draws on his intimate knowledge of the personalities that have dominated Japan's political landscape for the past thirty years. His earlier study of political change in postwar Japan, *The Japanese Way of Politics*, was awarded the Masayoshi Ohira Memorial Prize for 1989. Professor Curtis is advisor and monthly columnist for the *Chunichi/Tokyo Shimbun* and Special Advisor to *Newsweek* for Newsweek Japan and Newsweek Korea. He is a member of the Board of Directors of the U.S.-Japan Foundation and the Advisory Council of the Center for Global Partnership of the Japan Foundation.

ROBERT W. BULLOCK is Assistant Professor of Government at Cornell University. He earned a Ph.D. in Political Science from the University of California, Berkley in 1997. Professor Bullock has published articles on rice liberalization, the Japan Agricultural Co-operatives (formerly known as Nōkyō), and the postwar conservative coalition in Japan. He is presently completing a book manuscript entitled *Politicizing the Developmental State: Agriculture and the Conservative Coalition in Postwar Japan*.

JENNIFER HOLT DWYER is Assistant Professor of Political Science at Hunter College of the City University of New York. She teaches international political economy and Japanese politics and specializes in financial market regulation and reform. She has written several book chapters on financial market reform in

Japan and is currently working on a book manuscript on financial and administrative reform.

MICHAEL GREEN is Senior Fellow for Asian Security Studies at the Council on Foreign Relations. He is also a lecturer in East Asian Studies at the Paul H. Nitze School of Advanced International Studies (SAIS) of Johns Hopkins University and a consultant to the Office of the Secretary of Defense. Dr. Green received his M.A. from SAIS in 1987 and his Ph.D. in 1994. Dr. Green's most recent books and monographs include *State of the Field Report: Research on Japanese Security Policy* (1998); *The U.S.-Japan Alliance: Past, Present, and Future* (co-edited, 1999); and *Reluctant Realism: Japanese Foreign Policy in an Era of Uncertain Power* (2000).

KATŌ JUNKO is Associate Professor of Political Science at the University of Tokyo. She earned her Ph.D. in Political Science from Yale University in 1992 and her M.A. and M.Phil. in Political Science from the same university in 1989. Dr. Katō also received an M.A. in Political Science from the University of Tokyo in 1986. Dr. Katō is the author of numerous articles and books in Japanese and English, among the most recent being "When the Party Breaks Up: Exit and Voice among Japanese Legislators," in *American Political Science Review* (December 1998), and *The Problem of Bureaucratic Rationality: Tax Politics in Japan* (1994).

KOJŌ YOSHIKO is Professor of International Relations, Department of Advanced Social and International Relations, at the University of Tokyo. She obtained her B.A. and M.A. in International Relations from the University of Tokyo in 1980 and 1982, respectively. Dr. Kojō also earned an M.A. and a Ph.D. in Political Science from Princeton University in 1986 and 1993, respectively. Her major publications include *Keizaiteki sōgoizon to kokka* (Economic interdependence and state: Political economy of international payments adjustment in the postwar period, 1996) and "Kokusai seijikeizaigaku no dōkō: 'Keizai no gurōbaru ka' to kokka, kokkakan kyōchō no bunseki shikaku" (The trends in international political economy: 'Economic globalization,' state, and international cooperation), in *Kokusai Mondai* (1998).

TADOKORO MASAYUKI is Professor of International Relations at the National Defense Academy, Yokosuka. He earned an LL.B. from Kyoto University in 1979, and an LL.M. in 1981. Dr. Tadokoro's recent publications include *Gaikokujin tokuhain: Kōshite Nihon imēji wa keisei sareru* (Foreign correspondents: How Japan's image is created, co-authored, 1998); "Breton Uzzu kōshō no bunseki" (Anglo-American negotiation over the establishment of the Bretton Woods

System), in *Kokusai kōshō gaku* (International negotiations, 1998); and "Keizai taikoku no gaikō no genkei: 1960 nendai no Nihon gaikō" (The prototype of diplomacy of an economic power: Japan's diplomacy in the 1960s), in *Sengo Nihon gaikōshi* (Diplomatic history of postwar Japan, 1999).

TANAKA AKIHIKO is Professor of International Politics at the Institute of Oriental Culture, University of Tokyo. He obtained his Ph.D. in Political Science from the Massachusetts Institute of Technology in 1981. His recent books include *Atarashii "chūsei": 21 seiki no sekai shisutemu* (New Middle Ages: The world system in the 21st century, 1996) and *Anzen hoshō: Sengo 50 nen no mosaku* (National security: 50 years' exploration in postwar Japan).

ROBERT M. URIU is Assistant Professor of Political Science at the University of California, Irvine, where he specializes in international economy and the international relations of East Asia. He received his Ph.D. from Columbia University in 1993; he has also received masters degrees from Columbia and a B.A. from the University of California, Davis. Dr. Uriu is the author of *Troubled Industries: Confronting Change in Japan* (1996). In 1996–1997 he served as Director of Asian Affairs at the National Security Council.

Index

The Japan Center for International Exchange

Founded in 1970, the Japan Center for International Exchange (JCIE) is an independent, nonprofit, and nonpartisan organization dedicated to strengthening Japan's role in international affairs. JCIE believes that Japan faces a major challenge in augmenting its positive contributions to the international community, in keeping with its position as one of the world's largest industrial democracies. Operating in a country where policy making has traditionally been dominated by the government bureaucracy, JCIE has played an important role in broadening debate on Japan's international responsibilities by conducting international and cross-sectional programs of exchange, research, and discussion.

JCIE creates opportunities for informed policy discussions; it does not take policy positions. JCIE programs are carried out with the collaboration and cosponsorship of many organizations. The contacts developed through these working relationships are crucial to JCIE's efforts to increase the number of Japanese from the private sector engaged in meaningful policy research and dialogue with overseas counterparts.

JCIE receives no government subsidies; rather, funding comes from private foundation grants, corporate contributions, and contracts.

Other JCIE Books

Japan

How Electoral Reform Boomeranged: Continuity in Japanese Campaigning Style, edited by Ōtake Hideo

The Japan-U.S. Alliance: New Challenges for the 21st Century, edited by Nishihara Masashi

Old Issues, New Responses: Japan's Foreign & Security Policy Options, edited by Nishihara Masashi

Power Shuffles and Policy Processes: Coalition Government in Japan in the 1990s, edited by Ōtake Hideo

Asia Pacific

Asia Pacific Security Outlook 2000, edited by Richard W. Baker and Charles E. Morrison

Challenges for China-Japan-U.S. Cooperation, edited by Kokubun Ryōsei

China-Japan-U.S.: Managing the Trilateral Relationship, by Morton I. Abramowitz, Yōichi Funabashi, and Wang Jisi

China-Japan-U.S. Relations: Meeting New Challenges, by Morton I. Abramowitz, Funabashi Yōichi, and Wang Jisi

East Asian Crisis and Recovery: Issues of Governance and Sustainable Development, edited by Chia Siow Yue

Engaging Russia in Asia Pacific, edited by Watanabe Kōji

Major Power Relations in Northeast Asia: Win-Win or Zero-Sum Game, edited by David M. Lampton

New Dimensions of China-Japan-U.S. Relations, edited by Japan Center for International Exchange

Rethinking Energy Security in East Asia, edited by Paul B. Stares

Road to ASEAN-10: Japanese Perspectives on Economic Integration, edited by Sekiguchi Sueo and Noda Makito

Globalization, Governance, and Civil Society

Changing Values in Asia: Their Impact on Governance and Development, edited by Han Sung-Joo

Corporate-NGO Partnership in Asia Pacific, edited by Tadashi Yamamoto and Kim Gould Ashizawa

Deciding the Public Good: Governance and Civil Society in Japan, edited by Yamamoto Tadashi

Domestic Adjustments to Globalization, edited by Charles E. Morrison and Hadi Soesastro

Governance in a Global Age: The Impact of Civil Society from a Comparative Perspective, edited by Yamamoto Tadashi

Guidance for Governance: Comparing Alternative Sources of Public Policy Advice, edited by Kent Weaver and Paul B. Stares

States and Nonstate Actors: Creating a New Model for International Affairs, edited by Yakushiji Taizō

The Third Force: The Rise of Transnational Society, edited by Ann M. Florini

Human Security

The Asian Crisis and Human Security

The New Security Agenda: A Global Survey, edited by Paul B. Stares

Sustainable Development and Human Security

Japan Center for International Exchange

Fax: 81-3-3443-7580 • E-mail: books@jcie.or.jp

URL: http://www.jcie.or.jp